MARX'S ECOLOGY

MARX'S ECOLOGY

Materialism and Nature

JOHN BELLAMY FOSTER

Monthly Review Press
New York

Library of Congress Cataloging-in-Publication Data
Foster, John Bellamy.
    Marx's ecology : materialism and nature / John Bellamy Foster.
        p. cm.
    Includes bibliographical references and index.
    ISBN 1–58367–011–4 (cloth). — ISBN 1–58367–012–2 (pbk.)
    1. Communism and ecology. 2. Marx, Karl, 1818–1883. I. Title.
HX550.E25F67   2000
577—dc21   99–38837
                                                                          CIP

ISBN 1–58367–012–2 (paper)
ISBN 1–58367–011–4 (cloth)

Monthly Review Press
122 West 27th Street
New York, NY 10001

Manufactured in Canada
10 9 8 7 6 5 4 3 2 1

CONTENTS

PREFACE

The original title for this book, at its inception, was *Marx and Ecology*. At some point along the way the title changed to *Marx's Ecology*. This change in title stands for a dramatic change in my thinking about Marx (and about ecology) over the last few years, a change in which numerous individuals played a part.

Marx has often been characterized as an anti-ecological thinker. But I was always too well acquainted with his writing ever to take such criticisms seriously. He had, as I knew, exhibited deep ecological awareness at numerous points in his work. But at the time that I wrote *The Vulnerable Planet: A Short Economic History of the Environment* (1994), I still believed that Marx's ecological insights were somewhat secondary within his thought; that they contributed nothing new or essential to our present-day knowledge of ecology as such; and that the importance of his ideas for the development of ecology lay in the fact that he provided the historical-materialist analysis that ecology, with its generally ahistorical and Malthusian notions, desperately needed.

That it was possible to interpret Marx in a different way, one that conceived ecology as central to his thinking, was something that I was certainly aware of, since it was raised day after day in the 1980s by my friend Ira Shapiro, New York–expatriate, farmer, carpenter, working-class philosopher, and at that time a student in my classes. Going against all the conventions in the interpretation of Marx, Ira would say to me "look at this," pointing to passages in which Marx dealt with the problems of agriculture and the circulation of soil nutrients. I listened attentively, but did not yet appreciate the full import of what I was being told (in this I was no doubt held back, in contrast to Ira, by the fact that I had no real experience in working the land). In these same years, my friend Charles Hunt, radical activist, sociologist, part-time professor, and professional beekeeper, told me that I should become better acquainted with Engels's

vi

Dialectics of Nature, because of its science and its naturalism. Again I listened, but had my hesitations. Wasn't the "dialectic of nature" flawed from the outset?

My path to ecological materialism was blocked by the Marxism that I had learned over the years. My philosophical grounding had been in Hegel and the Hegelian Marxist revolt against positivist Marxism, which began in the 1920s in the work of Lukács, Korsch, and Gramsci, and which had carried over into the Frankfurt School and the New Left (part of the much greater revolt against positivism that dominated European intellectual life from 1890 to 1930 and beyond). The emphasis here was on Marx's practical materialism, rooted in his concept of praxis; which in my own thinking came to be combined with the political economy of the *Monthly Review* tradition in the United States, and the historical-cultural theories of E.P. Thompson and Raymond Williams in Britain. There seemed little room in such a synthesis, however, for a Marxist approach to issues of nature and natural-physical science.

It is true that thinkers like Thompson and Williams in Britain, and Sweezy, Baran, Magdoff, and Braverman associated with the *Monthly Review* in the U.S., all insisted on the importance of connecting Marxism to the wider natural-physical realm, and each contributed in his way to ecological thinking. But the theoretical legacy of Lukács and Gramsci, which I had internalized, denied the possibility of the application of dialectical modes of thinking to nature, essentially ceding that entire domain to positivism. At the time, I was scarcely aware of an alternative, more dialectical tradition within the contemporary life sciences, associated in our time with the work of such important thinkers as Richard Lewontin, Richard Levins, and Stephen Jay Gould. (When this awareness finally did dawn on me, it was a result of *Monthly Review*, which has long sought to link Marxism in general back up with the natural and physical sciences.) Nor was I yet acquainted with the critical realism of Roy Bhaskar.

To make matters worse, like most Marxists (outside of the biological sciences, where some of this history was retained), I had no knowledge of the real history of materialism. My materialism was entirely of the practical, political-economic kind, philosophically informed by Hegelian idealism and by Feuerbach's materialist revolt against Hegel, but ignorant of the larger history of materialism within philosophy and science. In this respect the Marxist tradition itself, as it had been passed down, was of relatively little help, since the basis on which Marx had broken with mechanistic materialism, while remaining a materialist, had never been adequately understood.

It is impossible to explain the stages (except perhaps by pointing to the argument that follows) of how I finally came to the conclusion that Marx's world-view was deeply, and indeed systematically, ecological (in all positive senses in which that term is used today), and that this ecological perspective derived from his materialism. If there was a single turning point in my thinking, it began shortly after *The Vulnerable Planet* was published when my friend John Mage, radical lawyer, classical scholar, and *Monthly Review* colleague, said that I had made an error in my book and in a subsequent article in tentatively adopting the Romantic Green view that capitalism's anti-ecological tendencies could be traced in considerable part to the scientific revolution of the seventeenth century, and in particular to the work of Francis Bacon. John raised the question of the relation of Marx to Bacon, and the historical meaning of the idea of "the domination of nature" that emerged in the seventeenth century. Gradually, I realized that the whole issue of science and ecology had to be reconsidered from the beginning. Among the questions that concerned me: Why was Bacon commonly presented as *the* enemy within Green theory? Why was Darwin so often ignored in discussions of nineteenth-century ecology (beyond the mere attribution of social Darwinist and Malthusian conceptions to him)? What was the relation of Marx to all of this?

I concluded early on in this process that attempts by "ecosocialists" to graft Green theory on to Marx, or Marx on to Green theory, could never generate the organic synthesis now necessary. In this respect I was struck by Bacon's famous adage that, "We can look in vain for advancement in scientific knowledge from the superinducing and grafting of new things on old. A fresh start (*instauratio*) must be made, beginning from the very foundations, unless we want to go round for ever in a circle, making trifling, almost contemptible progress" (*Novum Organum*). The problem then became one of going back to the foundations of materialism, where the answers increasingly seemed to lie, reexamining our social theory and its relation to ecology from the beginning, that is, dialectically, in terms of its *emergence*.

What I discovered, much to my astonishment, was a story that had something of the character of a literary detective story, in which various disparate clues led inexorably to a single, surprising, source. In this case, the materialism of Bacon and Marx, and even that of Darwin (although less directly), could be traced back to a common point of origin: the ancient materialist philosophy of Epicurus. Epicurus' role as the great Enlightener of antiquity—a view of his work that was shared by thinkers as distinct as Bacon, Kant, Hegel, and Marx—provided me for the first time with a coherent picture of the emergence of materialist ecology, in the context of a dialectical struggle over the definition of the world.

In a closely related line of research, I discovered that Marx's systematic investigation into the work of the great German agricultural chemist Justus von Liebig, which grew out of his critique of Malthusianism, was what led him to his central concept of the "metabolic rift" in the human relation to nature—his mature analysis of the alienation of nature. To understand this fully, however, it became necessary to reconstruct the historical debate over the degradation of the soil that had emerged in the mid-nineteenth century in the context of the "second agricultural revolution," and that extends down to our time. Herein lay Marx's most direct contribution to the ecological discussion (see Chapter Five). I am extremely grateful to Liz Allsopp and her colleagues at IACR-Rothamsted in Hertfordshire for making Lady Gilbert's translation of Liebig's "Einleitung," which lies in the Rothamsted archives, available to me. In conducting this research, I benefited from close collaboration with Fred Magdoff and Fred Buttel in the context of coediting a special July–August 1998 issue of *Monthly Review*, entitled *Hungry for Profit*—now expanded into book form. I also gained from the support of my coeditor for the journal *Organization & Environment*, John Jermier. Some of this work appeared in earlier, less developed forms in the September 1997 issue of *Organization & Environment* and the September 1999 issue of the *American Journal of Sociology*.

Given the complex intellectual history that this book attempts to unravel, its excursions into areas as seemingly removed from each other as ancient and modern philosophy, I was obviously in need of an interlocutor of extraordinary talents. That role was played throughout by John Mage, whose *classical* approach to knowledge, and immense historical and theoretical understanding, is coupled with a lawyer's proficiency at dialectic. There is not a line in this book that has not been the subject of John's searching queries. Much that is best here I owe to him, while whatever faults remain in this work are necessarily, even stubbornly, my own.

Paul Burkett's magisterial work *Marx and Nature: A Red and Green Perspective* (1999) constitutes not only part of the background against which this work was written, but also an essential complement to the analysis provided here. If I have sometimes neglected to develop fully the political-economic aspects of Marx's ecology, it is because the existence of this work makes this unnecessary and redundant. Years of stimulating dialogue with Paul have done much to sharpen the analysis that follows.

To Paul Sweezy, Harry Magdoff, and Ellen Meiksins Wood, the three editors of *Monthly Review*, I am indebted for their encouragement and the force of their example. Paul's commitment to environmental analysis was a major factor thrusting me in this direction. Christopher Phelps, who, as Editorial Director of Monthly Review Press, was involved with this book from its inception, has aided me in numerous, important ways.

It goes without saying that love and friendship are essential to all that is truly creative. Here I would like to thank Laura Tamkin, with whom I share my dreams, and Saul and Ida Foster; and also Bill Foster and Bob McChesney. To Saul and Ida, and their entire young generation, I dedicate this book.

INTRODUCTION

It is not the *unity* of living and active humanity with the natural, inorganic conditions of their metabolic exchange with nature, and hence their appropriation of nature, which requires explanation or is the result of a historic process, but rather the *separation* between these inorganic conditions of human existence and this active existence, a separation which is completely posited only in the relation of wage labour and capital.

Karl Marx, *Grundrisse*[1]

The argument of this book is based on a very simple premise: that in order to understand the origins of ecology, it is necessary to comprehend the new views of nature that arose with the development of materialism and science from the seventeenth through nineteenth centuries. Moreover, rather than simply picturing materialism and science as the enemies of earlier and supposedly preferable conceptions of nature, as is common in contemporary Green theory, the emphasis here is on how the development of both materialism and science promoted—indeed made possible—ecological ways of thinking.

The overall discussion is structured around the work of Darwin and Marx—the two greatest materialists of the nineteenth century. But it is the latter who constitutes the principal focus of this work, since the goal is to understand and develop a revolutionary ecological view of great importance to us today; one that links social transformation with the transformation of the human relation with nature in ways that we now consider ecological. The key to Marx's thinking in this respect, it is contended, lies in the way that he developed and transformed an existing Epicurean tradition with respect to materialism and freedom, which was integral to the rise of much of modern scientific and ecological thought.[2]

In this Introduction, I will attempt to clarify these issues by separating at the outset the questions of materialism and ecology—although the whole point of this study is their necessary connection—and by commenting briefly on the problem at which this critical analysis is ultimately aimed: the crisis of contemporary socio-ecology.

Materialism

Materialism as a theory of the nature of things arose at the beginning of Greek philosophy. "It has persisted down to our own time," Bertrand Russell was to observe early in this century, "in spite of the fact that very few eminent philosophers have advocated it. It has been associated with many scientific advances, and has seemed, in certain epochs, almost synonymous with a scientific outlook."[3]

In its most general sense materialism claims that that the origins and development of whatever exists is dependent on nature and "matter," that is, a level of physical reality that is independent of and prior to thought. Following British philosopher of science Roy Bhaskar we can say that a rational *philosophical materialism* as a complex world-view comprises:

(1) *ontological materialism*, asserting the unilateral dependence of social upon biological (and more generally physical) being and the emergence of the former from the latter;

(2) *epistemological materialism*, asserting the independent existence and transfactual [that is, causal and lawlike] activity of at least some of the objects of scientific thought;

(3) *practical materialism*, asserting the constitutive role of human transformative agency in the reproduction and transformation of social forms.[4]

Marx's materialist conception of history focused principally on "practical materialism." "The relations of man to nature" were "practical from the outset, that is, relations established by action."[5] But in his more general materialist conception of nature and science he embraced both "onto-logical materialism" and "epistemological materialism." Such a materialist conception of nature was, in Marx's view, essential in the pursuit of science.

It is important to understand that the materialist conception of nature as Marx understood it—and as it was frequently understood in his day— did not necessarily imply a rigid, mechanical determinism, as in mechanism (that is, mechanistic materialism). Marx's own approach to materialism was inspired to a considerable extent by the work of the ancient Greek philosopher Epicurus, the subject of his doctoral thesis. "Epicurus," in Russell's words, "was a materialist, but not a determinist."[6] His philosophy was devoted to showing how a materialist view of the nature of things provided the essential basis for a conception of human freedom.

Marx's interest in Epicurus had grown out of his early studies of religion and the philosophy of the Enlightenment, in which he was influenced by Bacon and Kant—each of whom had pointed to Epicurus as fundamental to the development of his philosophy. It was given further impetus in his encounter with Hegel, who saw Epicurus as "the inventor of empiric Natural Science" and the embodiment of the "so-called enlightenment" spirit within antiquity.[7] And it was further accentuated by the renewed interest in materialist doctrines that had emerged, beginning with Feuerbach already in the early 1830s, among many of the Young Hegelians. As Engels was to explain in *Ludwig Feuerbach and the Outcome of Classical German Philosophy* (1888), "the main body of the most determined young Hegelians" had "by the practical necessities of its fight against positive religion" been "driven back to Anglo-French materialism"—that is, to thinkers such as Bacon, Hobbes, Locke, and Hume in England and Scotland, and to La Mettrie, Diderot, and Holbach in France. The common basis for the materialism of these thinkers, as Marx was well aware, was the philosophy of Epicurus. Above all, Epicureanism stood for an anti-teleological viewpoint: the rejection of all natural explanations based on final causes, on divine intention. It is here that materialism and science were to coincide.

To understand the significance of all of this it is crucial to recognize that one question was at the forefront of all philosophical discussions in the early nineteenth century. Namely, as Engels put it:

> "Did god create the world or has the world been in existence eternally?" The answers which the philosophers gave to this question split them into two great camps. Those who asserted the primacy of spirit to nature and, therefore, in the last instance, assumed world creation in some form or other—(and among philosophers, Hegel, for example, this creation often becomes still more intricate and impossible than in Christianity)—comprised the camp of idealism. The others, who regarded nature as primary, belong to the various schools of materialism. These two expressions, idealism and materialism, primarily signify nothing more than this; and here also they are not used in any other sense.[8]

Such materialism was commonly associated with both sensationalism and empiricism within theories of human cognition, due to its opposition to teleological explanations. Hence, materialism and sensationalism were often counterposed to idealism and spiritualism. As the great German poet (and prose writer) Heinrich Heine observed in the early 1830s, "spiritualism," in its purely philosophical sense, could be defined as "that iniquitous presumption of the spirit which, seeking to glorify itself alone, tries to crush matter or at least to defame it." "Sensualism," in contrast, could be defined as "the energetic opposition which aims to rehabilitate matter and vindicate the rights of the senses." Another name for the first was "idealism," for the second, "materialism."[9]

Both materialism and idealism, however, were confronted with the skepticism that was common to both David Hume's empiricism and the transcendental idealist philosophy of Immanuel Kant. True, Kant admitted, there exists a reality beyond our senses, but one which can be perceived only through our senses and not directly. For Kant, this reality was the realm of the "noumena" or the "thing-in-itself"—and was unknowable and transcendent. Hence, the need for certainty required for Kant that we rely not simply on *a posteriori* knowledge (based on experience) of which we can never be sure, but also on *a priori* certain knowledge (rooted in categories of our understanding, such as space and time) that as a matter of logic must be relied upon in order for our experience to be possible. The Kantian criticism of any view that relied on the causal powers of "things-in-themselves" seemed to undermine all attempts to construct a consistent materialist philosophy. The real structure and powers of matter not present to the senses (such as the "atoms" of the ancient materialists and all other attempts to characterize the non-actual but real components and powers of matter) fell prey to Kantian rationalism—as did all attempts by absolute idealists to postulate the identity of thinking and being. In his brief "History of Pure Reason" at the end of his *Critique of Pure Reason* Kant had written that "Epicurus can be called the foremost philosopher of sensibility, and Plato that of the intellectual," while Kant's own critical philosophy was an attempt to transcend both at once.[10]

The significance of Georg Wilhelm Friedrich Hegel's dialectical philosophy, from the standpoint of Marx (and Engels), was that he showed a way out of the Kantian dilemma of the thing-in-itself, insofar as this was possible from an idealist standpoint. He did so by arguing that the objectification and alienation that separated human beings from the external world, and thus set up problems of cognition, is in the process of being overcome through the development of the spirit in history.[11] The correctness of our views of the world, the confirmation of our reason, is established as we transform the world and ourselves with it. It is this process of contradiction and transcendence, and the stripping away of alienation, which constitutes the essence of the dialectic. Yet, for Hegel, all of this occurred in the realm of the development of thought alone, and tended to reinforce in the end an idealist (indeed religious) point of view. "The proposition that the finite is ideal," that it has no existence in and of itself but exists only through thought, Hegel wrote in his *Logic*, constitutes idealism. The idealism of philosophy consists in nothing else than recognizing that the finite has no veritable being. Every philosophy is essentially an idealism or at least has idealism for its principle.... This is as true of philosophy as of religion; for religion equally does not recognize finitude as a veritable being, as something ultimate or absolute or as something underived, uncreated, eternal.[12]

Yet, for Marx, this attempt to subsume material reality/existence under thought, which characterized Hegel's idealist philosophy, led precisely to a religious world-view, and to the denial of humanism along with materialism. Hence, to be truly meaningful, the dialectical conception of a totality in the process of becoming, associated with Hegel, had to be placed in a practical, materialist context, transcending Hegel's whole project of dialectically restoring seventeenth-century metaphysics at the expense of Enlightenment materialism.[13] According to Marx, we transform our relation to the world and transcend our alienation from it—creating our own distinctly *human–natural* relations—by acting, that is, through our material praxis.

If, for Kant, the materialist and idealist wings of philosophy had as their foremost representatives Epicurus and Plato, for Marx, they were represented by Epicurus and Hegel. The ancient materialist Epicurus had played a crucial role in the formation of a dialectical conception of reality, in Marx's view, because he "was the first to grasp appearance as appearance, that is, as alienation of the essence," and to "acknowledge human self-consciousness as the highest divinity." "Philosophy, as long as a drop of blood shall pulse in its world-subduing and absolutely free heart," Marx declared, "will never grow tired of answering its adversaries with the cry of Epicurus: 'Not the man who denies the gods worshipped by the multitude, but he who affirms of the gods what the multitude believes about them, is truly impious.'"[14] Impiety here consists in the denial both of *human* self-determination and freedom, and of the *mortal*, material basis of life.

Epicurean materialism emphasized the mortality of the world; the transitory character for all of life and existence. Its most fundamental principles were that nothing comes from nothing and nothing being destroyed can be reduced to nothing. All of material existence was interdependent, arising from (and passing away again into) atoms—organized in unending patterns to produce new realities. The depth of Epicurus' materialism, for Marx, was revealed by the fact that within this philosophy—and in the concept of the atom itself—"the death of nature has ... become its immortal substance; and Lucretius correctly exclaims: 'When death the immortal has taken his mortal life.'"[15] Hence, in Epicurus' philosophy there was no need for Aristotelian final causes; rather the emphasis was on the constantly changing arrangements within nature itself, conceived as mortal and transitory (*mors immortalis*).

The Young Hegelian Ludwig Feuerbach's materialist critique of Hegel, which emerged most forcefully in his *Preliminary Theses on the Reform of Philosophy* (1842), overlapped with the critique that Marx was already developing through his doctoral thesis on Epicurus, completed only the year before. In his earlier *History of Modern Philosophy from Bacon to Spinoza* (1833), which Marx referred to in his thesis on Epicurus, Feuerbach had been struggling to develop a materialist stance, although rejecting the abstract, mechanical, or "pure materialism" of Hobbes and Descartes (in his physics). Feuerbach's determination to develop an alternative to mechanical materialism, with which to counterpose to Hegel's idealism, led him eventually to an emphasis on sensationalism in his *Preliminary Theses*, in which he counterposed a human essence to the abstract essence of the spirit, as the key to dialectical development (and the transcendence of the thing-in-itself). Nevertheless, like all earlier forms of materialism, most notably that of Epicurus, as Marx was to argue in his *Theses on Feuerbach*, Feuerbach's materialism fell prey to a purely contemplative materialism (more abstractly contemplative in fact than Epicurus because completely lacking in any positive ethical content). What was needed, according to Marx, was to shift materialism in the direction of practice, into an active principle.[16]

What is important to understand, though, is that in making materialism *practical*, Marx never abandoned his general commitment to a materialist conception of nature, that is, to materialism as both an *ontological* and an *epistemological* category. Materialism both in the sense of "a unilateral dependence of social on biological (and more generally physical) being and the emergence of the former from the latter," and in the sense of "the independent existence and transfactual activity of at least some of the objects of scientific thought" (referring to Bhaskar's first two components of materialism), remained essential to Marx's analysis. Behind this lay a radical materialist critique of all teleological forms of thinking.

In this regard Marx took what would now be considered a "realist" ontological stance, emphasizing the existence of the external, physical world, independent of thought. Here it should be noted that the first two components of rational materialism, as designated by Bhaskar, actually constitute the ontological and epistemological starting points for Bhaskar's own "critical realism." From an avowedly materialist perspective,

Marx thus adopted an approach that was both realist and relational (that is, dialectical). Hegel, as we have seen, had sought by means of the dialectic to overcome the antinomies represented by the Kantian thing-in-itself. Yet, in Hegel's philosophy, according to Bhaskar, this involved

> precisely the denial of the *autonomous* existence of matter; that is, of its existence except as one moment in the development of Geist [spirit], the self-realization of the absolute idea. For Marx, in contrast, "neither thought nor language ... form a realm of their own, they are only *manifestations* of actual life" ... so that "consciousness can never be anything else than conscious existence."[17]

The importance of this approach in relation to the subsequent development of philosophy and social science cannot be exaggerated. As a form of realism, it insisted on a perpetual and close connection between natural science and social science, between a conception of the material/natural world and the world of society. For this reason, Marx continually defined his materialism as one that belonged to the "process of natural history."[18] At the same time, he emphasized the dialectical-relational character of social history and the embeddedness of human society in social praxis. Any attempt to divorce materialism from the realm of nature and natural-physical science was therefore rejected from the outset. At the same time, his materialism took on a unique, practical character in the social realm, which reflected the freedom (and alienation) that existed within human history.

All of this may seem incontrovertible, but its supreme importance lies in the fact that it establishes what Bhaskar has called "the possibility of naturalism," that is, "the thesis that there is (or can be) an essential unity of method between the natural and the social sciences"—however much these realms may differ. This is important because it leads away from the dualistic division of social science into a "hyper-naturalistic positivism," on the one hand, and an "anti-naturalistic hermeneutics," on the other.[19] Western, critical Marxism (along with much of contemporary philosophy and social science) was defined by its rejection of crude nineteenth-century positivism, which attempted to transfer a mechanistic and reductionist world-view (which was credited with some notable successes in the development of science) to the realm of social existence. However, in rejecting mechanism, including mechanistic biologism of the social Darwinist variety, thinkers in the human sciences, including Marxists, increasingly rejected realism and materialism, adopting the view that the social world was constructed in the entirety of its relations by human practice—including, notably, those aspects of nature that impinged on the social world—thereby simply denying intransitive objects of knowledge (objects of knowledge which are natural and exist independently of human beings and social constructions).

Within Marxism this represented a turn in an idealist direction. In particular, it was commonly argued, in opposition to Engels—as if he alone, and not Marx, was responsible for the existence of a materialist conception of nature within Marxism—that the dialectic related only to praxis, and thus to the social-human world.[20] For this reason, Marxist social scientists became increasingly disengaged from science—although a Marxist tradition within science continued to exist quite separately. And in this way Marx's own ideal, clearly expressed in *Capital* itself, of an analysis that combined a materialist conception of history with a materialist conception of nature with all the force of natural history was declared a violation of reason.

The tragic result for Marxism was that the concept of materialism became increasingly abstract and indeed meaningless, a mere "verbal category," as Raymond Williams noted, reduced to some priority in the last instance of the production of life, and of economic existence, over "superstructural" elements, such as ideas.[21] It thus became inseparable from a reified conception of the famous base–superstructure metaphor, which Marxist theorists sought in vain to dispense with.

Ironically, given the opposition of critical, Western Marxism generally (at least outside of the structuralist tradition) to the base–superstructure metaphor, the lack of a deeper and more thoroughgoing materialism made the dependence on this metaphor unavoidable—if any sense of materialism was to be maintained. Such a deeper materialist view is only possible by connecting materialism as it relates to productive existence to the natural/ physical conditions of reality—including the realm of the senses—and indeed to the larger natural world. Only in this way can such fundamental issues as life and death, reproduction, dependence on the biosphere, and so on, be truly addressed.

"For a generation now," Raymond Williams wrote in 1978, "there has been an unusual uneasiness between Marxism and the natural sciences," regrettable "not only because there are then gaps in knowledge and fail-ures in its [Marxism's] development, but because through the gaps, and from both sides, pour the enemies of materialism."[22] Within science the renewal of biologism, or extreme social Darwinism, is a concern that can only be combated effectively through a non-mechanistic, non-reductionist, critical materialism that retains a connection to a materialist conception of history—as such great natural scientists as Richard Lewontin and Stephen

Jay Gould have thoroughly demonstrated.[23] Likewise in the social sciences, the only real defense against idealist views that reduce reality to the realm of innate ideas and abstracted culturalist notions (as distinguished from cultural materialism of the kind associated with Raymond Williams) is the development of a *strong historical materialism* that does not impoverish its materialism by denying the natural-physical aspects of material existence.

Marx's standpoint thus demanded of science that it be materialist, if it were to be scientific at all. In this view, no study of changing historical developments and possibilities could be free from the study of natural-physical science. Hence, Marx labored relentlessly, throughout his life, to keep abreast of developments within science. The common misconception that this was an obsession of Engels's, of which Marx was not a part, is contradicted by an enormous mass of evidence—a fact much more obvious to us today, after additional scientific notebooks by Marx have been published, than was true even a decade ago.

Ecology

Although there is a long history of denouncing Marx for a lack of ecological concern, it is now abundantly clear, after decades of debate, that this view does not at all fit with the evidence. On the contrary, as the Italian geographer Massimo Quaini has observed, "Marx ... denounced the spoliation of nature before a modern bourgeois ecological conscience was born."[24] From the start, Marx's notion of the alienation of human labor was connected to an understanding of the alienation of human beings from nature. It was this twofold alienation which, above all, needed to be explained *historically*.

Hence, even many of Marx's most virulent critics have been forced to admit of late that his work contains numerous, remarkable ecological insights. Rather than simply condemning him out of hand in this respect, six closely connected arguments are now commonly employed by critics. First, Marx's ecological statements are dismissed as "illuminating asides" that have no systematic relation to the main body of his work.[25] Second, these ecological insights are said to arise disproportionately from his early critique of alienation, and are much less evident in his later work. Third, Marx, we are told, ultimately failed to address the exploitation of nature (neglecting to incorporate it into his value theory), and adopted instead a "Promethean" (pro-technological, anti-ecological) view.[26] Fourth, as a corollary to the "Promethean" argument, it is contended that, in Marx's view, capitalist technology and economic development had solved all problems of ecological limits, and that the future society of associated producers would exist under conditions of abundance. It would not be necessary therefore, as economist Alec Nove writes, supposedly conveying Marx's logic, "to take seriously the problem of the allocation of scarce resources" or to develop an "ecologically conscious" socialism.[27] Fifth, Marx is said to have taken little interest in issues of science or in the effects of technology on the environment and hence had no real scientific basis for the analysis of ecological issues. According to prominent British sociologists Michael Redclift and Graham Woodgate, Marx suggested that human interactions with the natural environment, while social, were also "ubiquitous and unchanging, common to each phase of social existence.... Such a perspective does not fully acknowledge the role of technology and its effects on the environment."[28] Sixth, Marx is said to have been "speciesist," radically disconnecting human beings from animals, and taking sides with the former over the latter.[29]

All of these criticisms are flatly contradicted by the analysis that follows in this book, which attempts a systematic reconstruction of Marx's ecological thought. Many of these criticisms confuse Marx with other socialist theorists whom Marx himself criticized, following a long-established tradition in Marx criticism whereby, to quote Jean-Paul Sartre, "an 'anti-Marxist' argument is only the apparent rejuvenation of a pre-Marxist idea."[30] Hence, Marx is attacked for his supposed technological "Prometheanism," even though the strongest attack ever written against such "Promethean" views was leveled by Marx himself, in his critique of Proudhon's *System of Economical Contradictions*. Similarly, Marx is condemned for failing to recognize nature's contribution to wealth, even though he sharply criticized the German socialist Ferdinand Lasalle for adopting the "supernatural" view that labor was the sole source of wealth, and for thus ignoring nature's contribution.

More fundamentally, however, what is being questioned in most of these criticisms is Marx's materialism. Here Marx's materialism is said to have led him to emphasize a kind of "Baconian" domination of nature and economic development, rather than asserting ecological *values*. Thus Marx becomes a kind of radical Whig opposed to the nature-worshipping Tories, a representative of utilitarian anthropocentrism as opposed to Romantic ecocentrism. The problem with this criticism, like so much of contemporary socioeconomic thought, is that it fails to recognize the fundamental nature of the *interaction* between human beings and their environment. The ecological question is reduced first and foremost to one of *values*, while the much more difficult issue of understanding the *evolving material interrelations* (what Marx called "metabolic relations") between human beings and nature is thereby missed altogether. From a consistent materialist standpoint, the question is not one of anthropocentrism vs. ecocentrism—indeed such dualisms do little to help us understand the real, continuously changing material conditions of human existence within the biosphere—but rather one of *coevolution.* Approaches that focus simply on ecological *values*, like philosophical idealism and spiritualism more generally, are of little help in understanding these complex relations. In contrast to all such views, which "descend from heaven to earth," it is necessary to "ascend from earth to heaven."[31] That is, we must understand how spiritual conceptions, including our spiritual connections to the earth, are related to our material, earthly conditions.

More is in question here than simply Marx of course. What is really at issue is the whole history of materialist approaches to nature and human existence. Within contemporary Green thought a strong tendency has developed to attribute the entire course of ecological degradation to the emergence of the scientific revolution in the seventeenth century, represented above all by the contributions of Francis Bacon. Bacon is depicted as the principal proponent of the "domination of nature"—a point that is usually developed by quoting certain aphorisms, without any systematic consideration of his thought. Hence, the idea of the "domination of nature" is treated as a simple, straightforward anthropocentric perspective, characteristic of mechanism, to which a Romantic, organicist, vitalistic, postmodern view can be opposed.[32]

Yet, by focusing on the conflict between mechanism and vitalism or idealism (and losing sight of the more fundamental issue of materialism), one falls into a dualistic conception that fails to recognize that these categories are dialectically connected in their one-sidedness, and must be transcended together, since they represent the alienation of capitalist society. As noted in the 1930s by Christopher Caudwell (1907–1937), unquestionably the greatest Marxist thinker of his generation in Britain, the mechanist is "driven by reflection upon experience to the opposite pole, which is merely the other aspect of the same illusion—to teleology, vitalism, idealism, creative evolution, or whatever one likes to call it, but what is certainly the fashionable ideology of decaying capitalism."[33]

The perpetuation of this dualistic perspective is intrinsic to much of contemporary Green theory, and has led that tradition to a crude rejection, at times, of nearly all of modern science, together with the Enlightenment and most revolutionary movements—a tendency that has fed into the antirationalism of much of contemporary postmodern thought. From the seventeenth century to the twentieth almost all thinkers, with the exception of a few poets, artists and cultural critics, stand condemned in this view for adherence to anti-ecological values and the deification of progress.[34]

In this strange, idealist context, in which only values matter, real historical-material issues disappear, and great historical and intellectual struggles are reduced to mere phrases. It is obvious, or ought to be, that the notion of the human "domination of nature," while tending toward anthropocentrism, does not necessarily imply extreme disregard of nature or its laws. Bacon himself argued that the mastery of nature was rooted in understanding and following her laws. Although Marx was to condemn this mainly as a "ruse" for making nature conform to the needs of bourgeois development, the formulation nonetheless expressed a true contradiction of the human condition.[35]

Thus, starting out from the concept of the "mastery of nature," Caudwell was to write in *Illusion and Reality* (1937) that

> Men, in their struggle with Nature (i.e. in their struggle for freedom) enter into certain relations with each other to win that freedom…. But men cannot change Nature without changing themselves. The full understanding of this mutual interpenetration of reflexive movement of men and Nature, mediated by the necessary and developing relations known as society, is the *recognition* of necessity, not only in Nature but in ourselves and therefore society. Viewed objectively this active subject–object relation is science, viewed subjectively it is art; but as consciousness emerging in active union with practice it is simply concrete living—the whole process of working, feeling, thinking and behaving like a human individual in one world of individuals and Nature.[36]

In such a dialectical conception, emphasizing "reflexivity," the so-called "mastery of nature" turns into an unending process of dialectical interaction. Hence, it come as no surprise that in his work *Heredity and Development*, drafted shortly after *Illusion and Reality* but not published until a half-century later in 1986, Caudwell was to make a strong case for a coevolutionary approach to human–nature relations, rooted in both Darwin and Marx.

Once we recognize, in accordance with the above argument, that there is no necessary fundamental contradiction between the mere idea of the "mastery of nature" and the concept of sustainability, it will come as no surprise that the notions of "mastery" and "sustainability" arose together in the very same Baconian tradition. It is no accidental occurrence that Baconian "improvers" also included the first advocates of sustainable development, as in John Evelyn's great defense of forests in his *Sylva* (1664), and his attack on air pollution—the greatest materialist critique of air pollution ever written—in his *Fumifugium* (1661). As not only a Baconian improver but also a translator of part of Lucretius' *De rerum natura* (*On the Nature of Things*), the poetic masterpiece of ancient Epicurean materialism (which was to be a starting point for Marx's own materialism), Evelyn stands for the very complex set of questions involved here.[37]

In fact, the greatest developments in the evolution of ecological thought up through the nineteenth century were results of the rise to prominence of materialist conceptions of nature, interacting with changing historical conditions. In medieval times, and indeed up through the nineteenth century, the dominant world-view was the teleological one of the Great Chain of Being (later modified by natural theology), which explained everything in the universe in terms of divine providence, and secondarily in terms of the creation of the earth by God for "man." All species were separately created. The earth was the center of the universe and time and space were limited. The great enemy of this viewpoint, from the start, was ancient materialism, particularly Epicurean materialism, which was to be resurrected within Renaissance and Enlightenment science.

Questioning the scholastic-Aristotelian viewpoint, materialism also questioned the anthropocentrism that was central to this teleology: the earth was displaced from the center of the universe; time and space were discovered to be infinite (and even the history of the earth was found to be tied into the "deep abyss" of time); and, finally, human beings were shown to share a common ancestry with the apes, having branched off the same evolutionary tree. At each point in this growth of science, which came to be equated with the growth of materialism, God was dislodged from the material universe—from the solar system, from the evolution of the earth, eventually from the evolution of life itself; so that God in the view of modern science, like the gods of Epicurus, increasingly dwelt in effect in the *intermundia*, in the pores between the worlds, having no relation to the material universe. Equally important, the great discovery was made—essential to ecological analysis—of the interdependence of human beings with the earth over the entire course of material evolution. No longer could it be assumed that human beings were simply dominant, or supreme, occupying their own fixed position in the Great Chain of Being half-way between the lowest organisms and the highest angels (or God). Instead, what mattered was the nature of the interaction between human beings and the material world of which they were a part. The human relation to nature was, as Bacon had emphasized, a phenomenon of *natural history*, or, as Darwin stressed, of a long course of natural selection.[38]

Darwin's own evolutionary account of nature derived from his fundamental, uncompromising (with respect to the natural world) materialism.
It represented at one and the same time the "death of teleology" (as
Marx stressed) and the growth of an anti-anthropocentric viewpoint. It
was on the basis of Darwin's biohistorical work, complemented by the
biophysical discoveries of other scientists, like the great German agricultural chemist Justus von Liebig, with his emphasis on the circulation
of soil nutrients and its relation to animal metabolism, that modern
ecology can be said to have emerged in the mid-nineteenth century.
Although Darwinism was often converted into just another mechanistic
outlook, "Darwininism as found in Darwin's writings," Caudwell wrote,

> is still fresh from contact with the multitude of new biological facts then being
> discovered. It does not as yet pose organism aridly against environment, but the
> web of life is still seen fluidly interpenetrating with the rest of reality.... The
> extraordinary richness of the pageant of change, history and conflict in life,
> which Darwin unfolds, gives an insurgent revolutionary power to his writings
> and those of such immediate followers as Huxley.[39]

The importance of Darwin's analysis for us today was emphasized above
all by Rachel Carson, who wrote: "Today, it would be hard to find any
person of education who would deny the facts of evolution. Yet so many
of us deny the obvious corollary: that man is affected by the same environmental influences that control the lives of all the many thousands of other
species to which he is related by evolutionary ties."[40]

The wider implications of this and the overall significance of materialism to the development of ecological thought can be understood more
clearly from a contemporary ecological perspective by looking at Barry
Commoner's well-known four "informal laws" of ecology. These are: (1)
everything is connected to everything else, (2) everything must go some-
where, (3) nature knows best, and (4) nothing comes from nothing.[41]

The first two of these "informal laws" and the last were leading
principles of Epicurean physics, emphasized in Book I of Lucretius' De
rerum natura, which was an attempt to present Epicurean philosophy in
poetic form.[42] The third "informal law" seems, at first glance, to imply a
naturalistic, teleological determinism, but in the context of Commoner's
argument is better understood as "evolution knows best." That is, over
the course of evolution—which is properly understood not as a rigidly
determined or teleological process, but as one containing enormous levels
of contingency at every stage—species, including human beings, have
become adapted to their environments through the means of a process of
natural selection of innate variations, operating on a time scale of millions

of years. According to this perspective, then, we should proceed with caution in making fundamental ecological changes, recognizing that if we introduce into the environment new, synthetic chemicals, not the product of long evolution, we are playing with fire.

Ultimately, human beings of course are not determined in their entirety by natural conditions (beyond death, which, in Epicurus' words, is "nothing to us"). There is, in fact, an element of human freedom, an ability to "swerve," but always on the basis of material conditions that exist as antecedents and that carry with them some limitations. Hence, human beings, as Epicurus emphasized, exist in a world governed by the extinction of those species that are unable to adapt (not to be confused with a fully developed theory of natural selection in the Darwinian sense), and characterized by development in the human relation to subsistence. All of this is subject to contingency, and in the human case to ethical choice: including the formation of social compacts. (All of this is to be found in Book V of Lucretius' great poem.)

It is this fundamental materialist philosophy that Marx struggled with, at least to some extent, from his earliest days. Even as a student in the gymnasium, long before he had any acquaintance with Hegel, Marx was grappling with the Epicurean critique of the religious conception of the world. Later Epicureanism became the topic of his doctoral thesis, allowing him to focus, at one and the same time, on the earliest materialist theories; their conceptions of human freedom; the sources of the Enlightenment; the problem of the Hegelian philosophy of nature; the critique of religion; and the development of science.

For Marx, the main limitation of Epicurus' philosophy was the fact that its materialism was merely "contemplative," a problem that later reappeared in Feuerbach. Taking over the activist element in the Hegelian philosophy and dialectic, Marx developed a practical materialism rooted in the concept of praxis. But this was never divorced at any point in his work from a deeper materialist conception of nature that remained implicit in his thinking. This gave Marx's work great theoretical power, beyond what is usually attributed to it. It is this which accounts for the fact that Marx was so quick to ascertain the significance of the work of both Liebig and Darwin. Moreover, it helps us to understand how Marx, as we shall see, was able to build an understanding of sustainable development based on the work of the former and of coevolution based on the latter.

A thoroughgoing ecological analysis requires a standpoint that is both materialist and dialectical. As opposed to a spiritualistic, vitalistic view of the natural world which tends to see it as conforming to some teleological purpose, a materialist sees evolution as an open-ended process of natural history, governed by contingency, but open to rational explanation. A materialist viewpoint that is also dialectical in nature (that is, a non-mechanistic materialism) sees this as a process of transmutation of forms in a context of interrelatedness that excludes all absolute distinctions. Life (organisms) and the physical world, as Rachel Carson was wont to emphasize, do not exist in "isolated compartments." Rather there is an "extra-ordinary unity between organisms and the environment."[43] A dialectical approach forces us to recognize that organisms in general do not simply adapt to their environment; they also affect that environment in various ways, and by affecting it change it. The relationship is therefore a reciprocal one. For example, "the soil undergoes great and lasting evolutionary changes as a direct consequence of the activity of the plants growing in it, and these changes in turn feed back on the organism's conditions of existence."[44]

An ecological community and its environment must therefore be seen as a dialectical whole; one in which different levels of existence are ontologically significant—and in which there is no overall purpose guiding these communities. Even supposedly universal human purposes are open to question for their limited character. Human beings, Marx noted, attribute universal, "useful" characteristics to the "goods" they produce, "although it would scarcely appear to a sheep as one of its 'useful' properties that it is edible by man."[45] This kind of dialectical complexity in the understanding of ecological relations was aimed at the transcendence of all one-sided, reductionist standpoints.

As Richard Levins and Richard Lewontin explain in *The Dialectical Biologist*,

> Both the internal theoretical needs of ecology and the social demands that inform our planned interactions with nature require making the understanding of complexity the central problem. Ecology must cope with interdependence and relative autonomy, with similarity and difference, with the general and the particular, with chance and necessity, with equilibrium and change, with continuity and discontinuity, with contradictory processes. It must become increasingly self-conscious of its own philosophy, and that philosophy will be effective to the extent that it becomes not only materialist but dialectical.[46]

The Crisis of Socio-Ecology

Most contemporary social-scientific analyses of environmental problems have centered on what is now widely believed to be a global crisis in the human relation to the earth, and can be understood as a response to that crisis. At a theoretical level, however, social-scientific treatments have tended to be ill-equipped to deal with the enormity of the problems involved. Until recently, most general theoretical analyses have centered on two issues that have been predominant within Green thinking in general: namely, the idea of natural limits to human expansion and the question of anthropocentric vs. ecocentric viewpoints. Classical social thought (that is, social thought inherited mainly from the nineteenth century) has been traditionally condemned by environmental sociologists as a form of "radical constructionism" that denies the ontological priority of the natural world, perceiving nature as the product of human development. This is seen as reflecting a deep-seated anthropocentrism, an instrumentalist approach to nature, and the failure to take into account natural limits (including limits to growth).[47]

The virtues of this critique derive from its implicit realism; that is, its insistence on the ontological (and material) priority of the natural world; its recognition of the ultimate human dependence on the earth; and its understanding of the existence of irrevocable change (the arrow of time). Ultimately, this suggests that we are at a turning point in the human relationship to the earth. Still, social theory, it is emphasized, has been built without any strong material foundations, since it lacks any meaningful theory of the dependence of human beings on the environment.

Yet, despite the salience of this critique, environmental social theory has not thus far been sufficiently materialist, historical, or dialectical in orientation to reconstruct social theory along more ecologically conscious, realist lines. The typical environmental sociologist takes on a centaur-like existence: with the head of one creature and the body of another.[48] As sociologists, they adhere to the great classical traditions stemming from Marx, Durkheim, and Weber, as these have passed down to us. As environmentalists, they reject that tradition as one that was developed "as if nature didn't matter."[49] The complex task, meanwhile, of going back historically to the roots of social theory, and discovering what was missed and needs to be recovered, as well as what needs to be dialectically transcended, is ruled out, for many of these thinkers, by the lack of an intellectual heritage of critique. Hence, the debate within environmental sociology remains mired in the split between constructionist (mainly culturalist) and anti-constructionist (deep ecological) perspectives, while the attempt to transcend this dualism has merely produced the notion of a "cautious constructionism"—an important result but lacking any substantive content or clear theoretical orientation.[50]

As a result, there is a tendency to turn endlessly in circles, so that the analysis stops where it started, no more equipped at the end than at the outset to deal with the real problems of environment and society. Numerous studies have been written on anthropocentrism vs. ecocentrism, arguing that this or that thinker, culture, or civilization was more or less anthropocentric.[51] Although this has frequently opened our eyes to issues that have too often been downplayed, the dualistic perspective perpetuated here tends to block any genuine development of knowledge or meaningful practice. Indeed, the dichotomization embodied in such views tends to perpetuate the "humanity vs. nature" conceptions which are, in many ways, the source of the problem. Thus, while it is undeniable that the concept of "the domination of nature" has been a constant theme of modern Western thought, there has never been (as we have seen) anything simple about the concept of "the domination of nature" itself, which has often been conceived, even by those who have adopted this terminology, in complex, dialectical ways—concerned with the nature of the interaction. But if this is true, then such distinctions as anthropocentric and ecocentric are revealed as empty abstractions—mere restatements of old dualisms such as the human conquest of nature vs. nature worship.

Nor can we understand the issue of natural limits or "limits to growth" as these have entered Western culture without analyzing the way in which these issues have emerged historically over centuries in the great political-economic debates, and in the problems of agriculture and the soil as these were understood in the nineteenth century. The reasons for going back to nineteenth- (or eighteenth- or seventeenth-) century theory go beyond the need to understand the inception of a logical train of reasoning. Rather the importance of classical theory for social scientists derives from the inherently historical nature of social theory itself. The classical theories were written in a context of the transition from feudalism to capitalism, and from medieval scholasticism to modern science. Because of this the theoretical insights into the changing human relation to nature characteristic of classical social theory were tied up with an understanding of the transition taking place from one historical social system to another.

If we, in our time, have persistently failed to understand this, it is partly due to the subsequent narrowing of fields of knowledge, and partly due to the fact that in the reconstruction of social thought following the Second World War there was a tendency in whole fields, such as sociology, to develop purely constructionist arguments, downgrading connections to the natural-physical environment (or simply adopting a triumphalist view of this in which nature is progressively replaced by "man"), and hence severing any genuine links between social theory and reflection on the human relation to nature. Human beings became "Homo faber," not in a revolutionary Promethean sense, but in what was redefined as a techno-logical Prometheanism (prefigured by Proudhon in the nineteenth century). The mythological struggle over "fire" ceased to stand for a revolutionary struggle over the human relation to nature and the consti-tution of power (as in Aeschylus, Shelley, and Marx) and became instead simply a symbol of unending technological triumph.

Marxism has an enormous potential advantage in dealing with all of these issues precisely because it rests on a theory of society which is materialist not only in the sense of emphasizing the antecedent material-productive conditions of society, and how they served to delimit human possibilities and freedom, but also because, in Marx and in Engels at least, it never lost sight of the necessary relation of these material conditions to natural history, that is, to a materialist conception of nature. It thus points to the necessity of an ecological materialism, or a dialectical conception of natural history. Although this overlaps with what was later to be called (following Engels) "dialectical materialism," it would be a mistake to interpret Marx's own analysis from the standpoint of this later, still largely undifferentiated category. Rather a full examination of the development of Marx's thinking in this area will provide a basis for a renewed critical scrutiny of the debate over the "dialectics of nature"—recognizing all along that it is here that the principal lacunae in the development of Marxist thought are to be found.[52] Since this work is framed around Marx's life and work (and that of Darwin) and essentially ends with the death of the nineteenth century's two greatest materialists in 1882–1883, a full engagement with the later concept of the dialectics of nature goes beyond the range of the present analysis. But some reflections on the later development of Marxist theory in this area, and the tragic fate of the classic phase of historical-materialist ecology, are presented in the Epilogue to this work.

No doubt this analysis, since it emphasizes the ecological elements of Marx's thought, will be criticized by some for merely reading contemporary views on ecology ahistorically back into his work. But such a criticism would completely miss the point, since the intention here is not to "Green Marx" in order to make him "ecologically correct." Rather the aim is to highlight the weaknesses of contemporary Green theory itself, as a result of its failure to come to terms with materialist and dialectical forms of thinking that, in a period of the revolutionary rise of capitalist society, led to the discovery of ecology (and more importantly socio-ecology) in the first place. Put differently, the goal is to transcend the idealism, spiritualism, and dualism of much of contemporary Green thought, by recovering the

deeper critique of the alienation of humanity from nature that was central
to Marx's work (and, it will be argued, to Darwin's).

Marx's often brilliant ecological insights were not mere flashes of genius. Rather his insights in this area derived from a systematic engagement
with the seventeenth-century scientific revolution and the nineteenth-
century environment via a deep philosophical understanding of the materialist conception of nature. Thus, Marx, from his earliest years (for
example, the *Economic and Philosophical Manuscripts* of 1844) analyzed the
human alienation from nature in a sophisticated and ecologically sensitive
form. This tendency was reinforced by his concerns regarding human
subsistence and the relationship to the soil, and the whole problem of
capitalist agriculture. Central to this thinking was a concern regarding the
antagonistic division between town and country. These themes in Marx's
thought do not diminish in his later work, but take on new importance
as he attempted to address problems of prehistory and archaic communal
forms in the ethnological writings of his final decade.

The present investigation derives much of its significance, with respect
to the reinterpretation of Marx, from the light that it throws on various
anomalies, hitherto unexplained, in Marx's intellectual development: Why
did Marx write his doctoral thesis on the ancient atomists? What were the
roots of his materialist critique of Hegel (given the superficial nature of
Feuerbachian materialism and the philosophical inadequacies of political
economy)? What was Marx's relationship to the Enlightenment? How does
one explain the fact that in *The Holy Family* Marx expressed great esteem
for the work of Bacon, Hobbes, and Locke? Why did Marx engage in the
systematic study of natural and physical science throughout his life? What
lay behind Marx's complex, continuing critique of Malthusian theory?
How do we explain the sudden shift, from friend to foe, in Marx's attitude
toward Proudhon? Why did Marx declare that Liebig was more important
than all of the political economists put together for an understanding of
the development of capitalist agriculture? What explanation are we to give
for Marx's statement that Darwin's theory of natural selection provided
"the basis in natural history for our view"?[53] Why did Marx devote his last
years principally to ethnological studies, rather than completing *Capital*?
Answers to these and other vexing questions that have long puzzled analysts of Marx's vast corpus are provided here, and strongly reinforce the
view that Marx's work cannot be fully comprehended without an understanding of his materialist conception of nature, and its relation to the
materialist conception of history. Marx's social thought, in other words, is
inextricably bound to an ecological world-view.

CHAPTER I

THE MATERIALIST
CONCEPTION OF NATURE

In 1837 a young Charles Darwin, recently back from his five-year voyage of discovery in the HMS *Beagle*, opened the first of a series of notebooks on the "transmutation of species," beginning a systematic study into that elusive subject. It was when he was reading Thomas Malthus's *Essay on Population* a little more than a year later in the fall of 1838 that Darwin had his great revelation that species transmutation occurred by means of natural selection brought on by the struggle for existence. Inspired by Malthus's description of the exponential growth of populations when unchecked, and hence the need for natural checks on population growth in order to maintain an equilibrium between population and the means of subsistence, Darwin observed in his notebook that checks on the growth of population among species operated as "a force like a hundred thousand wedges" thrusting "every kind of adapted structure into the gaps in the oeconomy of Nature"—a form of expression he was later to repeat more than two decades later in his great work *On the Origin of Species by Means of Natural Selection*.[1] As Darwin recalled this great moment many years later in his *Autobiography*:

In October 1838, that is, fifteen months after I had begun my systematic enquiry, I happened to read for amusement Malthus on *Population*, and being well prepared to appreciate the struggle for existence which everywhere goes on from long-continued observation of the habits of animals and plants, it at once struck me that under these circumstances favourable variations would tend to be preserved, and unfavourable ones to be destroyed. The result of this would be the formation of new species. Here, then, I had at last got a theory by which to work; but I was so anxious to avoid prejudice, that I determined not for some time to write even the briefest sketch of it. In June 1842 I first allowed myself the satisfaction of writing a very brief abstract of my theory in 35 pages; and this was enlarged during the summer of 1844 into one of 230 pages, which I had fairly copied out and still possess.[2]

Since Darwin did not actually present his discovery until 1858, first in a joint presentation with Alfred Russell Wallace, and then in the following year through the publication of *On the Origin of Species by Means of Natural Selection*, one of the great puzzles in the annals of science has been the reason for this long delay. Why did he wait two whole decades before making his ideas public, only doing so when a younger rival, Wallace, threatened to scoop him?[3]

Of course it has long been supposed that a major factor in Darwin's delay in going public with his ideas had to do with the blasphemy against established views that his theory of natural selection represented. But material evidence as to the extent of the blasphemy in which he was caught up, and the inner intellectual turmoil that it represented, came to light only gradually. Soon after the death of his wife Emma in 1896 a collection of notebooks was found in a cupboard under the staircase at the Darwin home in Kent. This included the two manuscripts mentioned in the *Autobiography*, in which Darwin had developed early versions of his theory—one dated 1842 and one (much longer) dated 1844. Also discovered, however—but only published during the last few decades—were a series of notebooks that Darwin had written between 1836 and 1844, in which he had abstracted notes from various works and gradually worked out his ideas, leading up to the 1844 version of his theory. Among these were included not only a series of notebooks on the "transmutation of species" but also, more surprisingly, notebooks in the area of "metaphysical enquiries" (known as the *M and N Notebooks*).

It is in his *M and N Notebooks* that Darwin reveals himself as a dedicated materialist—an idea that was extremely heretical in his time, especially if extended to human development, and the development of the mind. As biologist Stephen Jay Gould has written,

> The notebooks prove that Darwin was interested in philosophy and aware of its implications. He knew that the primary feature distinguishing his theory from all other evolutionary doctrines was its uncompromising philosophical materialism. Other evolutionists spoke of vital forces, directed history, organic striving, and the essential irreducibility of mind—a panoply of concepts that traditional Christianity could accept in compromise, for they permitted a Christian God to work by evolution instead of creation. Darwin spoke only of random variation and natural selection.[4]

The dominant perspective on the natural world in Darwin's day, though of declining influence among scientists and philosophers, was one that was teleological in conception, rooted in a notion of divine providence. The traditional concept was that of the "Scale of Nature" or "Chain of

Being," which assumed not only that there was a fine scale or gradation of nature, leading up to human beings, but also the immutability of species—all of whom had originally been created separately by God. This scale was essentially static. A common assumption was that human beings, although not much lower than the lowest angels, were actually in the middle of the scale, and that the higher angels were as far above humans as human beings were above the lower organisms. As Sir William Petty, the founder of political economy, had written in 1677 in a philosophical essay on "The Scale of Creatures," "The principall use of considering these scales of Creatures is to lett man see that beneath God there may be millions of creatures superior unto man. Whereas Hee generally taketh himself to be the chiefe and next to God."[5]

Attempts were made in the eighteenth and early nineteenth centuries, as evolutionary ideas assumed greater prominence, to "temporalize" the "Scale of Nature." Nevertheless, most scientists and literary figures assumed, following Carolus Linnaeus, the great eighteenth-century taxonomist of species, that while some "improvement" of species was possible (say through artificial selection within agriculture), this was in general quite limited.[6]

It was only near the end of the eighteenth century that the French anatomist Georges Cuvier and others made the discoveries pointing definitively to the extinction of species, and the science of paleontology was born, seriously undermining the centuries-long belief in the scale of nature. And it was only in the early nineteenth century, particularly with the publication of Charles Lyell's *Principles of Geology* (1830–1833), that the idea that the earth was only a few thousand years old was definitively surpassed and the notion of geological time firmly established—making the idea of a process of slow evolution conceivable.

Still the religious view interfered with most attempts to conceive the reality of natural evolution. In geology much of the thought of the period took the form of catastrophism, a compromise between the biblical account of creation and growing scientific knowledge of geological formations, whereby it was assumed that the history of the earth was characterized by successive catastrophic upheavals forming distinct geological epochs, in which life was destroyed and successive creations occurred. Closely related to catastrophism in geology was progressionism within biology, which temporalized the scale of nature, arguing that life had emerged from simple to more complex forms through successive eras of creation, leading to "man." Rather than "descent with modification," as in evolutionary theory, this view did not include the notion of phylogenetic descent, but rather relied on divine creation at every stage—successive creations that were linked only through the mind of God.[7]

With the development of science the traditional view of the Scale of Nature and the Christian religious view rooted in biblical scripture receded somewhat, and there emerged the tradition of natural theology, which was used "to both attack and defend Christianity."[8] Thus the leading figures in the English scientific revolution, such as Robert Boyle, Isaac Newton, and John Ray, incorporated natural theology into their views. According to this perspective, the reality of God and a teleological understanding of the world were to be derived not from scripture but by ascertaining the divine laws of providence that governed nature, often involving direct acts of creation by God (particularly in the biological realm). It was the fact that it grew up alongside of science, while also opposing materialism, that gave natural theology its resilience.

It was in this complex context, in which the life sciences were still governed by teleological concepts drawn from religion, that Darwin sought to develop his theory. He was aided in this struggle by the previous growth of materialist ideas in astronomy, physics, chemistry, and psychology and in the Enlightenment in general. In Britain, materialism, as far back as Thomas Hobbes (1588–1679), was seen as compatible with religion (particularly deist accounts of religion). Nevertheless, the growth of materialism, both in science and in society at large, was viewed as threatening by the established church.

The heresy of materialism, by the eighteenth century, was often associated with the revolutionary pantheistic naturalism or materialism that had characterized radical popular movements during the English revolution (the Levellers, Diggers, Muggletonians, and so on), and that was later evident in the radical Enlightenment in France (in the work of the Baron d'Holbach and others). Although the mechanical philosophy of the "Newtonian synthesis" that dominated the Anglican Whig oligarchy in England in the eighteenth century had broken to some extent with previous religious views (the scholastic or Aristotelian view of the universe), it also resisted the more radical materialist and pantheistic views of the English revolution. In the Newtonian world-view nature was seen as governed by external mechanical laws determined by divine providence. Outright materialists, in contrast, were those who saw no need for explanations outside of nature itself. Moreover, the more moderate Enlightenment thinkers tended to preserve the distinction between mind (as spirit) and body. Hence, any attempt to reduce mind to purely mechanical and material explanations was generally seen as evidence of heretical materialist and atheistic views.[9]

A somewhat circumscribed, but nonetheless threatening, materialism played a prominent part in the physiological psychology of David Hartley (1705–1757), who adopted what was generally a materialist approach to knowledge (though insisting on "the immateriality of the soul") in his *Observations on Man* (1749). Joseph Priestley (1733–1804), the great chemist and physicist, who was influenced by Hartley, took a more decided materialist stance, which he presented in such works as *A Free Discussion of the Doctrine of Materialism* (1778). Priestley's outlook was generally in accord with John Locke's tentative suggestion in his *Essay Concerning Human Understanding* (1690) that thought might simply be a property that God chose to "superadd to matter"—rather than being a pure, immaterial manifestation of the soul.[10] Psychology, for Priestley, was essentially a physiology of the nervous system. Although Priestley's view of human beings was generally mechanistic and deterministic, he defended this vision as a tribute to God's creativity and criticized more thoroughgoing French materialists like Holbach who attacked religion. In this respect he represented the tradition of natural theology which dominated much of English science and theology from the seventeenth to the early nineteenth century, whereby divine providence was to be found in the laws of nature, as revealed by utilitarian arguments. Hence, it was possible to move considerably in the direction of the recognition of a material universe operating according to its own laws, while still finding in this the "proof" of God's existence.[11]

Erasmus Darwin (1731–1802), Charles Darwin's grandfather, also adopted materialistic views, and was likewise inspired by Hartley. An early evolutionary theorist, he advanced the notion that all of life descended from one filament of life that God had created.[12]

In France materialism took an even more radical form with the work of Julian Offray de la Mettrie (1709–1751), Paul Henri Thiery, Baron d'Holbach (1723–1789), and Denis Diderot (1713–1784). La Mettrie, who advanced a mechanistic materialism in which everything could be traced to matter and motion, believed that mind was only a function of the brain and did not differ in this respect from the other functions of the body. Human beings were essentially machines, as were other animals and even plants.

Holbach is principally known for his work *The System of Nature* (1770). Applying the idea that nature was simply matter and motion and that movement was conditioned by such forces as resistance, attraction, and repulsion, Holbach insisted that the soul was in actuality nothing more than the brain. His materialistic philosophy took on a more politically significant form, however, through his attack on all attempts to see nature in religious terms. To see God in nature was for Holbach an unnecessary duplication, since nature could be explained in its own terms. The doctrine of the immortality of the soul, he argued, distracted humanity from its present conditions and the need to make the world over according to its own freedom and necessity. "Morals and politics would be equally enabled," Holbach wrote, "to draw from *materialism*, advantages from which the dogma of spirituality can never supply, of which it even precludes the idea. Man will ever remain a mystery, to those who shall obstinately persist in viewing him with eyes predisposed to metaphysics."[13] For Holbach, theology had split nature into two: into a *power of nature* prior to nature, which it called God; and into inert nature that was devoid of power.

Diderot, the editor of the *Encyclopédie*, adopted a materialism similar to that of Holbach, who influenced him, but drew also on the history of materialism in philosophy extending back to the ancient Greek philosophers Democritus and Epicurus. For Diderot, the ultimate reals were atoms endowed with both motion and sensibility. Soul is manifested only in certain combinations of atoms. Nature is complete within itself—requiring no teleological principles of a religious nature. Individual objects come into being in the form of particular combinations of atoms and then pass away, in ceaseless cycles.[14]

Materialism in the eighteenth and the early nineteenth century can thus be seen as taking two related forms. One was an emphasis on materialism in more mechanical terms (and more easily integrated with notions of a divine spirit above and beyond nature and thus a moderate deism), and the other was an approach that focused more on organic interactions (and sense experience), sometimes leading to a universal vitalism, and often of a pantheistic character. The latter came to be thought of as naturalism, vitalism, or pantheism and was frequently separated from materialism, which came to be interpreted as mere mechanism. But the broad designation of materialist for these theories owed much to their common repudiation (to greater or lesser degrees) of divine principles in nature. A classic example of the more pantheistic version of materialism was to be found in the great French biologist Georges Louis Leclerc, Comte de Buffon (1707–1788), who saw all of nature as composed of "organic molecules." Nature as a whole became not a giant machine, but a vast organism, which could be explained in its own terms without recourse to a transcendental God.[15]

What all of these thinkers shared—despite their differences—was a radical tendency to look at reality and even the human mind as dependent on nature understood in physical terms; and to steer away from recourse to ideas of divine guidance or teleological principles in understanding the world about them—though sometimes what this amounted to was simply a displacement of divinity to nature or to external laws established by divine providence. In general both the mechanical philosophy associated with Newton and a more thoroughgoing materialism raised the issue of where to perceive the divine influence. The complex nature of the relation between religion and science paralleled in some ways the ancient Epicurean philosophy, since Epicurus, despite his materialist philosophy of a universe governed by the arrangement of atoms, had chosen ultimately to give the gods a place—if only in the spaces between the worlds.

Paradoxically, the intellectual culture of Britain in the seventeenth, eighteenth, and early nineteenth centuries was dominated not only by the growth of science, materialism, and utilitarianism, but also by a shift within theology toward natural theology in which divine providence was discovered in the natural laws and utilitarian principles that were presumed to govern the material universe. Hence, there was an attempt, represented at its zenith by Archdeacon William Paley (1743–1805), whose *Natural Theology* (1802) and other works were to form an important part of Darwin's own course of study at Cambridge, to construct a scientific or utilitarian theology which uncovered teleological principles (and thus the proof of God's existence) in nature and "expediency." For Paley, "The marks of *design* are too strong to be got over. Design must have had a designer. That designer must have been a person. That person is God."[16] Nevertheless, all of this meant that the theological view was on the defensive, since it now sought to prove God's existence primarily through his works (as revealed by nature and science), rather than divine revelation. The Supreme Deity was more and more in the background— the ultimate designer of the world, but one who constructed a nature so contrived, in Paley's view, that it was in a sense self-organizing. As science and materialism progressed, there were attempts, at each stage, to synthesize this with a theological understanding of the world. But the realm attributable directly to divine providence, as opposed to the realm of science and nature, kept on receding, creating a perpetual crisis for Christian theology, and for the system of privilege with which it was associated.

Hence, despite the elasticity that theological doctrines displayed throughout this period, there can be no doubt that the growth of thoroughgoing materialism was perceived as a threat by the established order—one that was resisted every step of the way. Giordano Bruno

(1548–1600), the Italian materialist who helped develop Copernicus's teaching on the universe, was burned at the stake by the Catholic church—not so much for following Copernicus as for his adherence to Epicurean philosophy with its anti-theological implications. Although Bruno was accused of numerous heresies, his most serious heresy had been to adopt the Epicurean argument (via Lucretius) on the boundless nature of the universe. "Bruno's principal contribution" to science, according to historian of science Thomas Kuhn, was his recognition and elaboration of "the affinity" between Copernicanism and Epicurean atomism. "Once the affinity was recognized, atomism proved the most effective and far-reaching of the several intellectual currents which, during the seventeenth century, transformed the finite Copernican cosmos into an infinite and multipopulated universe." Thus while the question has frequently been raised as to whether Bruno, who was condemned for various "theological heresies," deserves to be considered a "martyr to science," the fact that included among these heresies was his adherence to the Epicurean notion of an infinite universe would seem to leave little room for doubt. The fate of Bruno was one that Darwin knew well.[17]

The close relations between state and church in most countries in Europe even into the nineteenth century meant that charges of materialism and atheism constituted very serious attacks—directed against the individual scientific investigator. In 1819 William Lawrence, a lecturer in the Royal College of Surgeons, published his *Lectures on Physiology, Zoology, and the Natural History of Man* in which he presented materialist ideas. The book resulted in such a storm of public outrage that Lawrence had the book withdrawn. And when three years later a publisher brought out a pirate edition, Lawrence sued the publisher. The court ruled that Lawrence's book was so seditious and immoral that the author had no property rights in it; which meant—according to an odd English law dating back to the seventeenth century—that a publisher was legally entitled to issue a pirate edition without paying the author.

Lawrence, who was a sophisticated biological thinker for his day, had argued that living organisms conformed to higher natural laws than those that could be attributed to inanimate nature. Yet he denied any "vital principle" beyond that of the organization of matter and bodily organs, and thus denied the existence of any mental property independent of the brain. For the British establishment this was simply too much. The Tory *Quarterly Review* castigated "the doctrine of materialism, an open avowal of which has been made in the metropolis of the British Empire in the lectures delivered under public authority by Mr. Lawrence," demanding that the offending passages be struck from the book. Lawrence was thus forced to withdraw the book and to resign from his post as lecturer.[18]

Charles Darwin, struggling internally with his own materialist views when writing his notebooks on transmutation, was well aware of what had happened to Lawrence. He owned a copy of Lawrence's book which he had marked up with marginal strokes, and he referred to Lawrence's work in his notebooks on transmutation and later in *The Descent of Man*. Only a few years after the persecution of Lawrence, moreover, a young Charles Darwin had personally witnessed a similar case of the suppression of materialist ideas. In 1827 Darwin attended a meeting of the Plinian Society—a club formed by undergraduates at Edinburgh University for the formal reading of papers on natural history—in which a fellow student, William Browne, presented a paper that proposed that life was merely a product of the way the body was organized and that "mind, as far as one individual's senses and consciousness are concerned, is material." This created such a controversy that Browne's remarks were struck from the minutes of the society, and Browne afterwards curtailed his inquiries to non-philosophical subjects.[19]

The idea that the brain was the organ from which all mental faculties derived received strong support in the late eighteenth century in the work of Franz Joseph Gall (1758–1828). Although Gall is today associated with the long-discredited "science" of phrenology, it was not this, but rather Gall's pathbreaking insistence on a materialistic interpretation of the body–mind relationship which led to his lectures in Vienna being proscribed as dangerous to religion in 1802. In 1807 Gall emigrated to Paris, where his books were placed on the Index Librorum Prohibitorum; on his death he was denied a religious burial.[20]

In his metaphysical notebooks Darwin took a position that was unequivocally materialist in nature. As the editors of his *Notebooks* observed: "He embraced materialism enthusiastically and argued, using associationist language, that thought originated in sensation." "What is intellect," he asked himself at one point in his *Notebooks*, "but organization, with mysterious consciousness superadded?" Or as he stated in his *Notebook C*: "Thought (or desires more properly) being heredetary—it is difficult to imagine it anything but structure of brain heredetary.... oh you Materialist!"[21]

These developing materialist views lay at the heart of Darwin's emerging theory of the transmutation of species. "Plato," he wrote, "says in *Phaedo* that our 'necessary ideas' arise from the preexistence of soul, are not derivable from experience.—read monkeys for preexistence."[22] He agreed with Francis Bacon's claim in *Of the Dignity and Advancement of*

Learning that any argument with respect to nature rooted in final causes was "barren, and like a virgin consecrated to God produces nothing." Observing that Malthus had argued from final causes in his recourse to divine providence, Darwin noted in his *Notebooks* that his own materialism prevented him from following Malthus in this respect. "Is it an anomaly in me to talk of Final causes: consider this!—consider these barren Virgins."[23]

Darwin was acutely, painfully aware of the heretical nature of his views and struggled over whether materialism necessarily led to atheism—he contended it did not.[24] Materialism in Darwin's day was commonly associated in the public mind not only with atheism but also with the ideology of revolutionary France. There were laws on blasphemy and sedition acts aimed at radical freethinkers. Between 1837 and 1842 the newspapers were full of the notorious activities of Chartists, Owenites, and others who espoused materialism in the cause of social reform. There were also radical materialists, particularly in medical circles, centered in London who were embracing evolutionary ideas, but whose views were anathema to Darwin because of their extreme anti-church and anti-state character.[25] Desiring that his own ideas not be proscribed within respectable circles, Darwin strategized on ways to get around the explicit avowal of his materialism. "To avoid stating how far, I believe, in Materialism," he wrote, "say only that emotions, instincts, degrees of talent which are heredetary are so because brain of child resemble, parent stock."[26]

Darwin realized that the blasphemy in which he was caught up was all the more heretical because it dethroned not only religious teleology but also anthropocentric views—in the sense that God in the Scale of Nature view was purported to have created the world for "man," and mind was thought to be sharply separated from matter. Darwin's views, on the one hand, tended to reduce the stature of the human species by attributing their origin to descent from other, "lower" species. Monkeys and apes— hitherto viewed as only slightly lower in the scale of nature but immeasurably divided off from "man" by separate creation—could now be seen as sharing a common, if extremely distant, ancestry. On the other hand, Darwin's views tended to elevate the stature of other species in relation to human beings, since in his eyes animals too expressed intelligence in limited ways.

Under no illusions about the reaction of Victorian sensibilities to such materialist heresies, Darwin again and again pondered on this problem in his *Notebooks*, reiterating at least a half-dozen times somewhat enigmatically, though clearly in defiance of the traditional Scale of Nature conception: "If all men were dead, then monkeys make men—Men make angels"[27] This statement has to be viewed in two parts (and is in fact built around a twofold criticism of the traditional Scale of Nature idea). If human beings were to die out, Darwin was suggesting in his *Note-books*, other species—say "monkeys"—would evolve to fill the ecological niche left behind by the disappearance of an intelligent hominid—though Darwin made it clear that the resulting species would not be "man," as we know it. But it was also true that human beings were evolving and could evolve into another species. Playing on the traditional Scale of Nature conception in which human beings were seen as halfway up the scale of creation, Darwin wrote: "Men make angels"—thereby suggesting that human beings might evolve into something higher (not literally "angels" of course in Darwin's generally non-religious view). In this way he struggled with the implications of his own ideas and the probable reaction of Victorian society: that human beings were a product of chance evolution; that other hominids could evolve to fill the human space in nature if it were once vacated; and that human beings, like all species, were not fixed species, but continued to be subject to the evolutionary process.

In his later published writings on the transmutation of species Darwin was to stave off much of the criticism by dividing the question up and leaving the more dangerous issues until later. Thus the question of the evolution of human beings was almost entirely excluded from *The Origin of Species* when it was published in 1859 and was not treated until later—when some of the controversy was dying down—in *The Descent of Man* (1871); while the issue of the continuity in the minds and emotions of human beings and animals was dealt with—materialistically—in his *Expression of the Emotions in Man and Animals* (1872). The latter work was in some ways Darwin's most radical, since it literally annihilated the traditional anthropocentric interpretation of "brute creation," which was thought to be inseparably divided from human beings by lack of intelligence—as well as by the supposed fact that the earth and all of its creatures had been created by God for "man." In Darwin's view, in contrast, all of animate life was united by a common set of material relations and evolutionary laws. In the words of the noted Darwinian scholar John Durant, "Darwin elaborated his views on nature and human nature within a larger vision of a world continuously active in the generation of new forms of life and mind. This was materialism, and Darwin knew it; but it was a naturalism that humanized nature every bit as much as it naturalized man."[28]

Materialism and the Very Early Marx

In the period 1839–1844, while Darwin in England was struggling with his views on evolution and materialism, a young German scholar, nine years Darwin's junior—whose reputation as a nineteenth-century thinker was eventually to rival Darwin's own—was struggling in a quite different way with his own emerging materialist outlook, attempting to wrench himself free from the essentially theological outlook of German idealist philosophy. As a student in Berlin, Karl Marx had come partly, reluctantly, under the spell of the idealist philosophical system of Georg Wilhelm Friedrich Hegel (1770–1831) which then dominated German philosophy, and which purported to explain the development of spirit (or mind) in history. Yet Marx's very first complete work, his doctoral thesis on the *Difference Between the Democritean and the Epicurean Philosophy of Nature* (written in 1840–1841), although starting with an essentially left-Hegelian view, was already beginning to transcend that by raising the issue of the conflict between speculative philosophy (or idealism) and materialism.[29]

Most discussions of Marx's doctoral thesis have argued that Marx and the Young Hegelians in general were drawn to the ancient Hellenistic philosophies (Stoicism, Epicureanism, and Scepticism) simply because these philosophies had followed in the wake of the total philosophy of Aristotle, which seemed to prefigure the position of the Young Hegelians in the wake of the total philosophy of Hegel. Hence, Marx, we are led to believe, was not attracted so much to the content of Epicurus' philosophy as to the fact that it reflected a sort of parallel "spirit" of the times. Closely associated with this is the assumption that in writing his doctoral thesis Marx remained entirely enclosed within the Hegelian world-view. Thus while Marx's thesis is seen as an attempt to delineate (in Hegelian terms) an Epicurean dialectic of self-consciousness, the whole relation of Epicureanism to the Enlightenment and to British and French materialism in particular is ignored, as if it had no bearing on the subject—or was completely beyond his consciousness.[30]

Such an omission is all the more startling in that Marx had strongly emphasized in his doctoral thesis itself that Epicurus was the Enlightenment figure of antiquity—a point also made by Hegel, but in a less positive fashion. Further, Marx was to go on to insist in his subsequent writings that Epicurus was central for all those thinkers who developed materialist views in the seventeenth and eighteenth centuries. Thus the conventional interpretation of Marx's doctoral thesis becomes less and less credible when one looks at the larger intellectual atmosphere in which the thesis was written—extending beyond mere Hegelianism.[31] Here it is important to remember that Marx's relation to the Hegelian system was ambivalent from the start; indeed his initial inclination appears to have been to see it as a threat to the Enlightenment views that had inspired him thus far. He referred to falling into the "arms of the enemy"; to making "an idol of a view that I hated"; and to his repeated attempts to escape its "grotesque craggy melody."[32]

In opposition to the standard interpretation, it will be argued below that Marx's doctoral thesis is not merely an anomaly left over from his Hegelian period, but constituted an effort to come to terms with the implications of the materialist dialectic of the ancient Greek philosopher Epicurus, both from the standpoint of Hegelian philosophical system, and to some extent going beyond the latter. More than that, it was an indirect attempt to come to grips with the problem that the materialist tradition of the English and French Enlightenments—which drew heavily upon Epicurus for their inspiration—raised for Hegelian philosophy. Given its importance for British and French materialism, "atomistic philosophy," as James White has observed, "...had strong political overtones, and these were well known to Marx when he embarked on his dissertation ... in 1840."[33] Marx studied Bacon in 1837 (in the same year that he became acquainted with Hegel's philosophy) and was well aware of the influence of Epicurus on Bacon, as well as on Enlightenment thinkers generally. Marx's interest in the relation of Epicureanism to the Enlightenment, and to British and French materialism in particular, is evident not only in the doctoral thesis itself but also in the seven *Notebooks on Epicurean Philosophy* which he compiled in 1839 when working on his thesis, as well as in subsequent works that he wrote together with Friedrich Engels—*The Holy Family* (1845) and *The German Ideology* (1846).

As Maximilian Rubel and Margaret Manale have remarked, Marx's decision to do his doctoral thesis on Epicurus was

> a most un-Hegelian turn.... Marx's attention is drawn to Epicurus by his naturalness, his manifestation of intellectual and sensual freedom, a freedom from gods and from doctrines which concede to chance an equally great, if not greater, role in human life as to necessity. Individual will is asserted; an understanding of contingency becomes central to the wisdom of life. Man frees himself here from superstition and fear and becomes capable of forging his own happiness.[34]

Epicurus

Epicurus was an Athenian citizen who was born on the island of Samos in 341 B.C., six years after Plato's death in 347 and six years before Aristotle opened up his school in the Lyceum. In 306 he opened up the "Garden," the home of his school of philosophy, which by the time of his death in 271 B.C. had gained influence throughout the Greek world. Epicurus lived through the tragic aftermath of the Macedonian hegemony during which Alexander's successors battled over his empire; a time in which political activity seemed particularly ineffective. Hence, he preached a kind of contemplative materialism to his followers—yet one in which more radical, practical implications could be perceived. Epicurus' philosophy had a large impact on ancient thinking up through Roman times, but his work had been almost entirely lost during the Middle Ages when he and his followers were declared among the leading heretics opposed to Christianity. Hence his work was known in modern times principally through secondary sources, the most important of these being the Roman poet Lucretius' great work *De rerum natura* (literally *On the Nature of Things*), in which Lucretius (c. 99–55 B.C.) faithfully reproduced, as modern scholarship has demonstrated, the main ideas and even phraseology of the master.[35] (Lucretius too lived through a period of severe political crisis, the fall of the Roman Republic.)

Epicurus was inspired by the work of the Greek atomists Leucippus (fl. c. 430 B.C.) and Democritus (fl. c. 420 B.C.), who saw all of reality as consisting of an infinite number of unchanging atoms too tiny to be seen, but of different shapes and sizes, which existed in a void. These atoms had the quality of motion and combined and separated in various ways to form the objects of the senses. In Democritus, atoms had two primary qualities: size and shape. Many interpretations of Democritus (since the ancient sources conflict) also claim that he assigned the quality of weight to the atom, so that motion occurred in a downward direction and in straight lines (though these properties of atoms are more closely associated with the work of Epicurus). Where Epicurus most clearly deviated from Democritus was in his addition of the proposition that atoms did not move according to patterns that were entirely determinant; rather some atoms "swerved," creating the element of chance and indeterminancy (and thus leaving room for free will).[36] "It is in the theory of atoms," Hegel wrote, "that science first feels released from the sense of having no foundation for the world."[37]

Epicurus' philosophy was an extremely tight logical system, and, once a few initial assumptions were granted, most of the rest seemed to follow mainly by deduction. Among the most important deductions were the notions of boundless space (including infinite numbers of worlds) and infinite time. Epicurus also referred to the extinction of species and human development from feral origins. His materialist philosophy seemed to anticipate to a remarkable degree the discoveries of science, and indeed was extremely influential among many of the leading scientists of the seventeenth-century scientific revolution and the Enlightenment. The initial propositions of Epicurean natural philosophy were that "Nothing is ever created by divine power out of nothing" and "nature ... never reduces anything to nothing." Together these two propositions constituted what is now known as "the principle of conservation."[38] Epicurus' materialism meant the expulsion of divine power—all teleological principles—from nature. The gods, though they continued to exist, were confined to the spaces in between the worlds. Further, Epicurus opposed all teleology and all absolute determinism in the treatment of nature: "It were better to follow the myths about the gods," he wrote, "than to become a slave to the destiny of the natural philosophers: for the former suggests a hope of placating the gods by worship, whereas the latter involves a necessity which knows no placation."[39]

No determinism or essentialism—that is, developments based on the mere property of things—could explain "events" that were "done," according to Epicurus, because such events belonged to the realm of accident (contingency):

> So you may see that events never at all
> Exist by themselves as matter does, nor can
> Be said to exist in the same way as void.
> But rightly you may call them accidents
> Of matter and place in which things happen.[40]

Epicurus' rejection of any form of reductionism, which has commonly been attributed to materialist viewpoints, was evident in the development of a sophisticated epistemology in his work *The Canon* (which formed the introduction to his overall system), which relied not simply on sensations, but also on his famous concept of "anticipation" (sometimes referred to as "preconception")—a concept which he originated.[41] According to Cicero, Epicurus' notion of "anticipation" (*prolēpsis*) was that of a thing "preconceived by the mind, without which understanding, inquiry and discussion are impossible." Hence, "the materialist Epicurus," Farrington has observed, "must be credited with a clear understanding of the activity of the subject at every stage in the acquisition of knowledge."[42] This suggested that human beings were physically endowed with characteristics that included the ability to reason. While sensation itself has no mental content, it gives rise to the mental process of sorting out sensations in terms of general categories built up on the basis of repeated sensations, but that once acquired exist in the mind somewhat independently and become the basis for organizing data into ready-made categories. It is in this sense that Epicurus refers to them as "anticipations." As Farrington notes, "'anticipations' do not precede all experience; but they do precede all systematic observation and scientific discussion, and all rational practical activity. Again they denote the activity of the subject in the acquisition of knowledge."[43] Given all of this, it should come as no surprise that in the section of his *Critique of Pure Reason* devoted to "Anticipations of Perception," Kant wrote, "One can call all cognition through which I can cognize and determine *a priori* what belongs to empirical observation an anticipation, and without doubt this is the significance with which Epicurus used his expression."[44]

Epicurean ethics derived from Epicurus' materialist perspective, his emphasis on mortality and freedom. "For the Epicureans," as Marx observed, "the principle of the concept of nature is the *mors immortalis* [immortal death], as Lucretius says."[45] The essential starting point for a materialist ethics was overcoming the fear of death promoted by established religion and superstition. "Death," Epicurus wrote in his *Principal Doctrines*, "is nothing to us; for that which is dissolved is without sensation; and that which lacks sensation is nothing to us." Freedom of the individual began only when it was possible to ascertain by means of "natural science" the mortality of the world and the individuals within it.[46]

Epicurus advanced a mainly contemplative materialism that could be sharply distinguished from Plato's more idealist love of contemplation. What mattered for Epicurus, as George Panichas has written, "was the contemplation of what could materialize in human existence and not in an eternal beyond." Epicurean ethics, which advocated the satisfaction of one's needs in this world, were based on the expedient pursuit of pleasure and the avoidance of pain. But Epicurus saw this not in short-sighted, crudely hedonist terms, but rather in terms of the whole of existence, which recognized that some immediate egoistic pleasures only created greater pains. He therefore argued for a simple life, abandoning the pursuit of wealth. "The wealth demanded by nature," he wrote, "is both limited and easily procured; that demanded by idle imaginings stretches on to infinity."[47]

The most important requirement of a good life for Epicurus was friendship, which became for him the principle through which life and society should be ordered. "Of all the things which wisdom acquires to produce the blessedness of the complete life, far the greatest is the possession of friendship." This was not just an ethical principle related mainly to relations between individuals, but carried larger political implications. "Friendship, in its Graeco-Roman usage," A.A. Long and David Sedley point out, "has a political resonance absent from the modern concepts ... *philia* in Greek (*amicitia* in Latin) was regularly conceived as the foundation of social cohesion." In the garden of Epicurus women were welcome and respected members of the community and philosophical discussions. Among Epicurus' most important contributions was his concept of justice (which heavily influenced Marx). "Justice," he wrote, "never is anything in itself, but in the dealings of men with one another in any place whatever and at any time it is a kind of compact not to harm or to be harmed." If the law "does not turn out to lead to advantage in men's dealings with each other," if it ceases to be in accord with its general concept, and if it no longer conforms to material circumstances, "then it no longer has the essential nature of justice." In Epicurus was thus to be found a materialist, as opposed to idealist, conception of law that denied that law had a transcendent aspect apart from the needs of human social intercourse. As Marx was later to point out, it was Epicurus who first originated the notion of the social contract.[48]

The Epicurean philosophy of nature had as its starting point the "principle of conservation," and hence tended toward an ecological world-view. This is particularly evident in Lucretius' work, which, in the words of noted historian of ancient ecological thought J. Donald Hughes, "asked some questions that are now regarded as ecological." Lucretius alluded to air pollution due to mining, to the lessening of harvests through the degradation of the soil, and to the disappearance of forests; as well as arguing that human beings were not radically distinct from animals.[49]

"Having totally dispensed with teleology in his cosmology," Long and Sedley write, "Epicurus opted for an evolutionist or experimental account of the origin and development of human institutions."[50] Thus Epicurus' materialism led to a conception of human progress. "We must suppose," he wrote in his "Letter to Heredotus," "that human nature ... was taught and constrained to do many things of every kind merely by circumstances; and that later on reasoning elaborated what had been suggested by nature and made further inventions, in some matters quickly, in others slowly, at some epochs and times making great advances, and lesser again at others."[51] Human nature is itself transformed with the evolution of human society; friendship and sociability are a product of social compacts that emerge in the process of the satisfaction of the material means of subsistence.[52]

It was also in Epicurus, as seen through Lucretius, that the most explicit statement of evolutionary views, involving questions of species adaptation and survival, was to be found, in the writings of antiquity. The idea had originally been raised by Empedocles (*fl. c.* 445 B.C.) and Anaxagoras (*c.* 500–428 B.C.), and had been attacked by Aristotle in his *Physics*. Summarizing Empedocles, Aristotle had written,

> Why then should it not be the same with the parts in nature, e.g., that our teeth should come up *of necessity*—the front teeth sharp, fitted for tearing, the molars broad and useful for grinding down the food—since they did not arise for this end, but it was merely a coincident result; and so with all other parts in which we suppose that there is purpose? Wherever then all the parts came about just what they would have been if they had come to be for an end, such things survived, being organized spontaneously in a fitting way; whereas those which grew otherwise perished and continue to perish, as Empedocles says his "man-faced ox-progeny" did.[53]

Aristotle responded to this by reasserting the importance of final causes: "It is plain," he wrote, "that nature is a cause, a cause that operates for a purpose."[54] Epicurus, although deriding Empedocles' "ox-children, man-faced" as a bizarre collection of random combinations contrary to nature, nonetheless defended materialist-evolutionary views against Aristotle. Those species that survived, and were able to perpetuate "the chain of offspring," Lucretius explained, were those that had developed special attributes that protected them from their environment in the struggle for existence, "but those who were gifted with none of these natural assets ... were free game and an easy prey for others, till nature brought their race to extinction." Hence, it is through Empedocles, Epicurus, and Lucretius that an important element of evolutionary analysis, later to appear in Darwinian theory, is thought to have originated.[55]

Central to Epicurus' view, as represented by Lucretius, was that life was born from the earth, rather than descending from the skies (or the result of creation by the gods). "The animals," Lucretius wrote, "cannot have fallen from the sky, and those that live on land cannot have emerged from the briny gulfs. We are left with the conclusion that the name of mother has rightly been bestowed on the earth, since out of the earth everything is born." This, as W.K.C. Guthrie, an authority on the proto-evolutionary thought of antiquity, remarked, "was perhaps, in the absence of modern biological knowledge and a soundly-based theory of evolution, the only reasonable alternative": namely, that the earth itself deserved "the name of mother."[56]

In his *Ideas of Life and Matter: Studies in the History of General Physiology*

600 B.C. to 1900 A.D., Thomas Hall has argued that Epicurus was the principal ancient source of the view (anticipated by Empedocles and Democritus) that life was an "emergence consequence" of the organization of matter. "In antiquity," Hall writes, "Epicurus used life, explicitly, as an example of emergence, insisting that it was absent from the body's atoms considered singly." Hence, for Epicurus, "life is, in the strict sense, emergent." Material existence, in Epicurus, was thus only evident through change, that is, evolution.[57]

The same evolutionary perspective was also evident in Epicurus' treatment of human society. In the 1860s and 1870s, following "the revolution in ethnological time" associated with Darwin's *The Origin of Species* and with the first widely accepted scientific discoveries of human fossils, it became common for important Darwinian thinkers, such as John Lubbock and Henry Morgan, to refer back to Lucretius' discussion on ethnological development, which had taken account of the evolution from an age of stone and wood, to that of bronze, and then of iron—also incorporating discussions of the development of speech, of mutual assistance, the revolution in the use of fire, and so on.[58]

Ultimately, Epicurus' view was that an understanding of nature and its laws, that is, the progress of science, would disperse terror inflicted by religion. As Lucretius wrote:

> Therefore this terror and darkness of the mind
> Not by the sun's ray's, nor the bright shafts of day,
> Must be dispersed, as is most necessary,
> But by the face of nature and her laws.

It is therefore not surprising, as evolutionary biologist Michael Rose has noted, that "Lucretius is regarded by some scholars as the greatest classical forerunner to modern science."[59]

Epicurus and the Revolution of Science and Reason

Epicurus' philosophy was to play an extraordinary role in the development of the materialism of the English and French Enlightenments, which took the form of a struggle against the essentially Aristotelian philosophy of nature promoted under Christianity.[60] According to the version of Christianized Aristotelianism or scholasticism still taught in English universities in the seventeenth century, matter consisted of four elements: air, earth, fire, and water. Elaborate scholastic taxonomies were combined with a view of nature that was essentially static and tautological. Nevertheless, such views could not easily stand up given the changing material context of English society in the seventeenth century in which medieval institutions were rapidly disappearing and a dynamic capitalist order was emerging in agriculture and industry. As a result the leading scientists turned to Greek atomism, and particularly to the ideas of Epicurus. "The slightest acquaintance with post-Renaissance physiology (from Descartes to the present)," Thomas Hall has written, "will make Epicurus seem closer than any other ancient scientist to the emergentism and mechanistic materialism of the modern era."[61] The same was true of science in general. Thomas Hariot, Francis Bacon, Thomas Hobbes, Robert Boyle, and Isaac Newton were all deeply affected by Greek atomism, and from Bacon on by the philosophy of Epicurus in particular.[62] Matter came to be understood as consisting of atoms, and hence, following Epicurus, in terms of particles of matter which could be explained simply in terms of size, shape, and motion—a view easily translated into essentially mechanical terms.

Thomas Hariot (1560–1621), one of the most brilliant figures of the English scientific revolution, had been exposed to Epicurean atomism by Bruno. In a letter to Johannes Kepler explaining the workings of physical optics, Hariot wrote: "I have now led you to the doors of nature's house, wherein lie its mysteries. If you cannot enter because the doors are too narrow, then abstract and contract yourself into an atom, and you will enter easily. And when you later come out again, tell me what wonders you saw."[63] Hariot was denounced in 1591 as an Epicurean atheist, and later arrested and imprisoned in 1605 (following the Guy Fawkes plot to blow up parliament) on baseless suspicions of heresy, in which his connection to ancient atheistic materialists like Lucretius and Epicurus was raised.[64]

Francis Bacon (1561–1626) too was strongly influenced by Democritus and Epicurus (including Lucretius) and tried to justify Greek atomism—from which he borrowed profusely in the development of his ideas—in religious terms, arguing that Epicurus' philosophy of nature was infinitely superior in this respect to that of Aristotle, "For it is a thousand times more credible, that four mutable elements, and one immutable fifth essence, duly and eternally placed, need no God, than that an army of infinite small portions or seeds unplaced, should have produced this order and beauty without a divine marshal."[65] More important, he argued in his *Of the Dignity and Advancement of Learning* (1623) that the natural philosophy of the ancient materialists like Democritus and Epicurus (including also Lucretius) who removed God and Mind from the structure of things, and attributed the form thereof to infinite essays and proofs of nature … and assigned the causes of particular things to the necessity of matter, without any intermixture of final causes, seems to me (as far as I can judge from the fragments and relics of their philosophy) to have been, as regards physical causes, much more solid and to have penetrated further into nature than that of Aristotle and Plato; for this single reason, that the former never wasted time on final causes, while the latter were ever inculcating them.[66]

In his essay on Prometheus in *The Wisdom of the Ancients* Bacon described Prometheus as representing within Greek mythology two kinds of providence: that of the gods and that of human beings. Bacon went on in his essay to displace Prometheus with the figure of Democritus, who, along with Epicurus, represented the true heroic quality of Prometheanism in its materialist guise. For Bacon, Epicurus was an inferior figure to Democritus because he subordinated "his natural to his moral philosophy," refusing to accept anything counter to freedom. Yet, Bacon was to see Epicurus' attack on superstition as the essence of enlightenment. Here he quoted Epicurus' statement in his "Letter to Menoeceus" that, "Not the man who denies the gods worshipped by the multitude, but he who affirms of the gods what the multitude believes about them is truly impious."[67]

Bacon was also to follow up on Epicurean notions of evolution, pointing to the reality of "transmutation of species." As he wrote in his *Sylva Sylvarum; or a Naturall History in Ten Centuries*, "the transmutation of species is, in the vulgar Philosophy, pronounced impossible; … but seeing there appear some manifest instances of it, the opinion of impossibility is to be rejected, and the means thereof to be found out."[68]

Lucretius' manuscript, which had been copied but lost sight of in medieval times, was rediscovered in 1417. It was printed in 1473 and went through some thirty editions between then and the beginning of the seventeenth century. However, it wasn't until the early to mid-seventeenth century that Epicureanism was to make major inroads into European thought. In 1647–1649 Pierre Gassendi (1592–1655), a French cleric, theologian, philosopher, and mathematician and one of the leading proponents along with his contemporaries Hobbes and Descartes of the mechanical philosophy, produced a grand Epicurean–Christian synthesis. Gassendi's explicitly stated purpose was to overthrow the old Aristotelian conception of nature.[69] For Gassendi, as Marx was to note, it was astounding that Epicurus by means of reason had "anticipated the experimentally demonstrated fact that all bodies, although very different in weight and mass, have the same velocity when they fall from above to below."[70]

As the restorer of Epicurus, Gassendi, as Marx observed, became the principal opponent of René Descartes's metaphysics embodied in his *Discourse on Method* (1637) and his *Meditations* (1641). In his *Doubts*, written in 1644, Gassendi attacked Cartesian metaphysics, which had as its starting point innate ideas: "I think therefore I am." In his critique Gassendi generally took a materialist stance against the idealist position embodied in Descartes's concept of mind (Decartes's metaphysics differed widely from his physics, which were mechanistic in nature). Emphasizing the priority of the material world and the senses, Gassendi insisted that to think without knowing anything prior and with your senses blocked would only result in an endless "I, I, I," since "you would not be able to attribute anything to yourself in your thought for you would never know any attribute, and you would not know the force of the verb 'am,' since you would not know what being is or the difference between being and not-being."[71]

In England, Walter Charleton (1619–1707), physician to Charles I and Charles II, who was introduced to Gassendi's work by his friend Thomas Hobbes, transmitted the results of Gassendi's research to British scientific circles, developing his own version of a "purified" Epicureanism compatible with Christianity.[72] Charleton's *Physiologia Epicuro-Gassendo-Charltonia* (1654) was the first systematic effort in England to merge Epicurus with the mechanical philosophy. Charleton's work was soon followed by John Evelyn's translation of Book I of Lucretius' *De rerum natura* into English in 1656. In his *History of Philosophy, Containing the Lives, Opinions, Actions and Discourses of the Philosophers of Every Sect* (1660) Thomas Stanley devoted the largest part of the whole work to Epicurus, who took up more pages than Plato and Aristotle combined.[73]

John Evelyn (1620–1706) was not only an admirer of Epicurus but also one of the figures behind the formation of the Royal Society, and the greatest proponent of conservation in England of the seventeenth century. In his *Sylva, Or a Discourse of Forest-Trees and the Propagation of Timber in His Majesties Dominions* (1664), the first official publication of the Royal Society (a work that went through four editions in Evelyn's lifetime), he complained of the "prodigious havoc" wreaked on English forests by the demands of shipping, glassworks, iron furnaces, and the like. "This devaluation," he observed, "is now become so *Epidemical*, that unless some favourable *expedient* offer it self, and a way be seriously, and speedily resolv'd upon, for the future repair of this important *defect*, one of the most glorious, and considerable *Bulwarks* of this *Nation*, will, within a short time be totally wanting to it." Evelyn recommended that Elizabethan

Acts prohibiting the cutting of any tree "one foot square" or more within twenty-two miles of London be enforced, and that seedlings be planted on the large estates.

Even more important, Evelyn authored the great work *Fumifugium: Or, the Inconvenience of the Aer and Smoake of London Dissipated* (1661), which he presented to Charles II. Here Evelyn's enthusiasm not only for Baconianism but also for Epicurean materialism was evident. In Book VI of his great poem Lucretius had written, "How easily the drowsy fume and scent of charcoal passes into the brain," which Evelyn quoted on the title page of his work. Decrying the general pollution in London, Evelyn went on to consider the issue of air pollution, which he attributed not to the culinary fires of the population, but to

> Issues belonging only to *Brewers, Diers, Lime-burners, Salt,* and *Sope-boylers,* and some other private Trades.... Whilst these are belching it forth their sooty jaws, the City of *London,* resembles the fact rather of *Mount Ætna, the Court of Vulcan, Stromboli,* or the *Suburbs of Hell....* It is this [horrid smoake] which scatters and strews about those black and smutty Atomes upon all things where it comes.

"The consequences ... of all of this," he wrote, were to be seen in the fact that "one half of them who perish in *London,* dye of *Phthisical* and *Pulmonic distempers;* That the *Inhabitants* are never free from *Coughs.*" In all of this Eveyln was clearly influenced by the materialist epidemiology to be found in Book VI of Lucretius' poem, with its emphasis on the existence of certain atoms of substances that were "a cause of disease and death."[74]

The fact that Epicureanism was being revived during the age of Cromwell and the restoration that followed meant that its radical, anti-religious implications were always threatening to break free. Thus the famous poet and friend of Hobbes, Edmund Waller, wrote a poem to Evelyn in which he expounded the atheistic world-view of Lucretius,

> Lucretius with a stork-like fate
> Born and translated in a State
> Comes to proclaim in English verse
> No Monarch rules the Universe.
> But chance and *Atomes* makes *this All*
> In order Democratical
> Without design, or Fate, or Force.[75]

The dominant tradition within the scientific community, although adopting a mechanical materialism and Epicurean atomism (purified of its more atheistic elements), repudiated the radical materialism often identified

with the English revolution. Chemist Robert Boyle (1627–1697), the leading British scientist of his time prior to Newton, and a Baconian, adopted
a moderate, Christianized mechanistic philosophy that relied on atomism
for its ultimate conception of matter. He first learned of Gassendi's work
on Epicurus in 1648, the year before it was published, from Samuel
Hartlib, a leading promoter of the Baconian tradition.[76] Boyle's moderate
mechanistic philosophy was explicitly developed in opposition to the pantheistic materialism associated with the more radical elements of the
English revolution. After 1660 Boyle and his associates attached themselves to the restored monarchy. In 1662 the Royal Society was established, which was to become the formal mechanism for institutionalizing
the new science, adopting an Anglican ideology centered on the compat-
ibility of science and religion.[77] This compromise was symbolized by
Boyle's rejection of the anti-theological implications of Greek atomism:

> I am far from supposing, with the *Epicureans*, that atoms, accidentally meeting
> in an infinite vacuum, were able, of themselves, to produce a world, and all its
> phenomena: nor do I suppose, when God had put into the whole mass of
> matter, an invariable quantity of motion, he needed do no more to make the
> universe; the material parts being able, by their own unguided motions, to
> throw themselves into a regular system. The philosophy I plead for, reaches but
> to things purely corporeal; and distinguishing between the first origin of things
> and the subsequent course of nature, teaches, that God, indeed, gave motion to
> matter, but that, in the beginning, he so guided the various motions of the
> parts of it, as to contrive them into the world he design'd they should compose;
> and established those rules of motion, and that order amongst things corporeal,
> which we call the laws of nature. Thus, the universe being once form'd by God,
> and the laws of motion settled, and all upheld by his perpetual concourse, the
> general providence; the same philosophy teaches, that the phenomena of the
> world, are physically produced by the mechanical properties of the parts of
> matter; and, that they operate upon one another according to mechanical laws.[78]

Thus Boyle managed to combine a mechanical view of the laws of nature
rooted in an atomistic concept of matter with a theological position that
attributed both the origin of matter and the laws of motion of nature to
the design of an omniscient God.

Indeed, Boyle wrote as much on theology as science and can be regarded as one of the principal proponents of natural theology. His *Disquisition About the Final Causes of Natural Things* (1688) represented an early
articulation of the argument from design for the existence of God,
developed also by Boyle's contemporary John Ray, that foreshadowed the
ideas of William Paley a century later. For Boyle "Epicurus and most of
his followers ... banish the consideration of the ends of things [final

causes] because the world being, according to them, made by chance, no ends of anything can be supposed to be intended."[79] Chance in this sense meant not pure chance such as results from the casting of dice, but rather an argument based on the contingent nature of the universe, and thus of natural and social history—a view directly opposed to the argument from design. Hence, while Boyle adopted certain hypotheses from Epicurean atomism, essential to the construction of his own mechanistic views, he rejected thoroughgoing materialism and atheism. Instead, as Stephen Jay Gould has written, he "neatly married mechanism and religion into a coherent system that granted higher status to both sides."[80]

Isaac Newton (1642–1727), who revolutionized science with the publication of his *Philosophiae Naturalis Principia Mathematica* (*Mathematical Principles of Natural Philosophy*) in 1687, adopted a view almost identical to that of Boyle.[81] Newton relied heavily on Epicurean atomism in his early work, but was later to suppress some of these early reflections on atomism, no doubt because of the anti-religious implications of classical Epicureanism. Newton's *Principia*, while offering a particulate, or atomic, view of matter, did so only after this was widely accepted within science, which had been inoculated against the worst heresies of the Epicureans by means of the previous development of the mechanical philosophy in the work of Gassendi, Charleton, and Boyle.

Newton's own philosophy of nature and its relation to natural theology stands out most clearly in four letters that he wrote in 1692–1693 to Richard Bentley, who, in devising the final two of eight sermons in natural theology (the Boyle Lectures), which were targeted at the threat posed by Epicurean materialism and atheism, called on Newton for help in providing a scientific rationale. Newton, as these and other letters reveal, was not above abandoning his commitment to the mechanical philosophy at points when he thought it necessary in order to combat materialism and to defend his religious beliefs. Thus he hypothesized in a letter to Thomas Burnett that the earth's rotation had originally occurred very slowly, producing days of virtually any length, in order to square the biblical story of the creation of the world in seven days with geological evidence on the earth's antiquity.[82]

Still none of the attempts to restrict the influence of Epicurean materialism, with its challenge to traditional religious views, went so far as to erase the underlying influence of ancient atomism on Newton and the scientists of the early Royal Society. As historian of science Robert Kargon has noted, "Much of the *Principia* can be, and was, viewed as presenting the mechanics of atomic motion"—as Newton's contemporary Edmund

Halley actually interpreted it at the time—"although the work" itself, Kargon adds, "referred primarily to visible bodies." Halley's ode to Newton prefixed to the *Principia* used language drawn from Lucretius, "purified" along Christian lines, to introduce readers to Newton's work.[83] As Alan Cook has indicated in his magnificent new biography of Halley, Halley and to a large extent Newton, like "Galileo and Gassendi ... traced their metaphysics to Epicurus rather than Aristotle."[84] Likewise Peter Gay, the author of several authoritative historical studies of Enlightenment thought, has written: "It is clear that Gassendi's corpuscular physics impressed Boyle, and through Boyle, Newton.... [W]hile the Epicurean model of a world of atoms whirling in the void was crude and arbitrary, it was a useful corrective to the scientific world picture that had dominated Christian civilization for many centuries."[85]

All of this was captured by a piece of doggerel that appeared soon after the incorporation of the Royal Society by Charles II in 1662 and went as follows: "These Collegiats do assure us,/ Aristotle' an ass to Epicuras."[86]

The declining influence of Aristotelian philosophy in the seventeenth century did not therefore take the form, as is commonly supposed, of a straightforward conflict between the ancients and the moderns. Rather "the history of early modern thought," as Margaret Osler and Letizia Panizza have noted, "can perhaps be understood at least in part as the interplay of one set of ancient models with another."[87] Still, the challenge that Epicurean materialism raised for religion resulted in an odd compromise in the work of many of the leading scientists, such as Boyle and Newton, who developed a mechanistic view of the material world which nonetheless left God intact in the background as the prime mover within nature.

It was not just the atomism of Epicurus and Lucretius that created a storm of controversy in the seventeenth and eighteenth centuries, but also the notions of "deep time" associated with the ancient materialists (though in Lucretius the earth, as opposed to the universe, was explicitly referred to as "newly made"), which threatened the Christian world-view, and yet which seemed to be receiving increasing support with the development of science. Such major natural-theological works as Edward Stillingfleet's *Origines sacrae* (1662), John Woodward's *Essay Towards a Natural History of the Earth* (1695), and Samuel Shuckford's *Sacred and Profane History* (1728) all had Epicurus and Lucretius, and after them Hobbes, as their principal adversaries. The religious struggle against what is now called "geological time" thus had, as its classical adversaries, the Epicurean materialists.[88]

The heretical nature of Epicureanism meant that the influence of Epicurus on the great Italian philosopher Giambattista Vico (1668–1744), including his *magnum opus, Scienza nuova* (*The New Science*), remained to a considerable extent hidden. Vico derived many of his ideas from Lucretius, particularly in relation to the developmental notions of human culture to be found in Lucretius' great poem. Nevertheless this had to remain hidden, since the Inquisition in Naples had led to the imprisonment of some of Vico's friends on charges which included the mere mention of Epicurus or Lucretius. The religious view that had consigned Epicurus and his followers to the sixth circle of Hell in Dante's *Inferno*, where they were to be found in countless half-opened burning tombs, still prevailed. Vico himself was attacked for having adopted Lucretian ideas on the feral origins of human beings. As a result, Vico—as modern scholarship has conclusively demonstrated—adopted a posture of the "feigned repudiation of Lucretius," while building on and refashioning Lucretian ideas.[89]

In the eighteenth century, Epicureanism continued to play a major part in the development of materialist ideas both in England and on the Continent. The development of science only seemed to offer confirmation of Epicurean materialism.[90] In his *Enquiry Concerning Human Understanding* (1748) the great Scottish philosopher David Hume (1711–1776) devoted a section of his work to an imaginary speech of defiance by Epicurus, who in this fictional account was supposed to have been put on trial in Athens for denying "divine existence" and undermining morality. Through the arguments of the ancient materialist Epicurus, Hume thus presented some of his own self-justification in response to those who had leveled similar charges against him.[91] In his last months Hume cheered himself in the face of his approaching death by rereading Lucretius and Lucian. In France Voltaire considered Lucretius' *De rerum natura* so important that he kept six different editions and translations on his shelves.[92] "Lucretius," he wrote, "is admirable in his exordiums, in his descriptions, in his ethics, in everything he says against superstition." The impact of Lucretius on Voltaire can be better understood when one recognizes that the very idea of "Enlightenment," as it was understood in the eighteenth century, as Gay has argued, was to a large extent inspired by Lucretius. For "when Lucretius spoke of dispelling night, lifting shadows, or clarifying ideas, he meant the conquest of religion by science."[93] Voltaire, however, was too much of a deist and a Newtonian to accept thoroughgoing materialism, given its atheistic implications, and hence, beginning in the 1740s (when he first came under the influence of Newton), he issued a series of sharp attacks against materialists such as Buffon and Holbach.[94]

The work of French materialists such as La Mettrie, Helvétius, Holbach, and Diderot was seen as emanating to a considerable extent from Epicurean materialism. Epicurean atomism, ethics, discussions of animate nature, criticisms of religion, and treatments of mortality were evident throughout their work. At the end of his life, La Mettrie authored a series of materialist musings on Lucretius entitled *The System of Epicurus* (1750). Holbach's *System of Nature* (1770) was written in a Lucretian vein, and was condemned by parliamentary decree to be burned in the very year of its publication. The indictment spelled out the Epicurean origin of his theories.[95]

In his great contribution to scientific cosmology, *Universal Natural History and the Theory of the Heavens* (1755), the young Immanuel Kant (1724–1804) not only advanced the revolutionary view that the earth and the entire solar system had come into being in time, but developed an argument for deep time to accompany a vision of boundless space. What interested Kant was essentially an evolutionary account of the universe. Such views were widely associated with Epicurean materialism, causing Kant to declare that

> I will ... not deny that the theory of Lucretius, or his predecessors, Epicurus, Leucippus and Democritus, has much resemblance with mine. I assume, like these philosophers, that the first state of nature consisted in a universal diffusion of the primitive matter of all the bodies in space, or of the atoms of matter, as these philosophers called them. Epicurus asserted a gravity or weight which forced these elementary particles to sink or fall; and this does not seem to differ much from Newton's Attraction, which I accept. He also gave them a certain deviation from the straight line in the falling movement, although he had absurd fancies regarding the causes and consequences of it. This deviation agrees in some degree with the alteration from the falling in a straight line, which we deduce from the repulsion of particles.[96]

Nevertheless, Kant opposed the Epicurean attribution of all of this to mere "chance"; rather he pointed to certain "necessary laws" producing a "well-ordered whole." As in Newtonian mechanical philosophy, with its counterpart in the form of natural theology, Kant attributed the existence of such laws to a "universal Supreme intelligence."[97] In his *Critique of Judgement*, and in particular his critique of teleological judgement, the mature Kant, author of critical philosophy, was to argue against a purely teleological view of nature, in which purposiveness or final causes were attributed to nature as an ontological reality. He thereby agreed in part with the materialist tradition stemming from Epicurus, with its strong anti-teleological orientation. Yet Kant was to argue that such teleological judgements were necessary as a *heuristic* (that is, interpretive) device since science requires the *a priori* assumption of an intelligible, law-given, and purposeful universe. Hence, while the material world did not offer proof of God, it was necessary to examine the material world *as if* there were intelligence behind it. Kant thus tried to square a materialist method-ology with a notion of teleological judgement as a regulative principle of knowledge. For Kant, Epicurean philosophy belonged to a group of theo-ries in which purposiveness or intelligibility existed but was undesigned.[98] Although critical of Epicureanism for its "hyperphysical" orientation, Kant nonetheless grounds his analysis of the physical world in a mechanistic viewpoint, rejecting natural theology (which he calls "physicotheology"). "That Kant ... leaves the door open for a mechanistic explanation," states Daniel Dahlstrom, "is not surprising given the primacy he repeatedly accords to such an explanation. Only on the basis of nature's mechanism, he maintains, are we able to have any insight into the nature of things at all and without that mechanism there can be no natural science."[99]

The importance of Epicurus, for Kant, was equally apparent in his first and second critiques, the *Critique of Pure Reason* and the *Critique of Practical Reason*. In the *Critique of Pure Reason* Kant stressed that it was Epicurus who was the dialectical counterpart to Plato within epistemology. "Epicurus," he wrote, "can be called the foremost philosopher of sensibil-ity, and Plato that of the intellectual." As a philosopher of sensibility, Epicurus, Kant argued, was "more consistent in accord with his sensual system (for in his inferences he never exceeded the bounds of experience) than Aristotle and Locke." In the *Critique of Practical Reason* Kant empha-sized this again, referring to Plato and Epicurus as representing the funda-mental division within epistemology (between materialism and idealism, the sensible and the intellectual) which Kant's *Critique of Pure Reason* had sought to transcend by means of analysis of *a priori* knowledge—thus allowing for a more complete development, under the rule of practical reason, of theology and morals.[100]

In his *Logic*, published in 1800, four years before his death, Kant referred to the Epicureans as "the *best philosophers of nature* among Greek thinkers." For Kant, philosophy owed "its improvement in recent times partly to the intensified study of nature.... The first and greatest student of nature in modern times was Bacon of Verulam."[101] The implicit con-nection drawn here between Epicurus and Bacon was no doubt intended.

In contrast to the great, critical admiration for Epicurus displayed by Kant, Friedrich Schelling (1775–1854), in his Romantic, pantheistic philosophy, depicted Epicurean materialism as a philosophy of lifeless mechanism; one into which the philosophy of nature needed to instill a mystical spirit. Schelling's spiritualistic response to materialism is most evident in his poem "The Epicurean Confession of Faith of Hans Brittleback," in which his fictional protagonist, Brittleback, an irreligious, Epicurean materialist, turns abruptly, in the midst of a long confession, into a German idealist discovering behind the senses a "giant spirit," which, struggling "against a cruel environment," eventually triumphs through the emergence of human beings: the "outcome and crown of the spirit's plan."[102]

In the much more formidable philosophy of Georg Wilhelm Friedrich Hegel (1770–1831), and to an even greater degree in the philosophy of the radical Young Hegelians with whom Marx was associated in the late 1830s and early 1840s (most notably Bruno Bauer and Karl Friedrich Köppen), Epicureanism, along with Stoicism and Scepticism, were seen as representing the development of "self-consciousness" in ancient Greek and Roman society.[103] Self-consciousness, in Hegelian terms, meant the principle of abstract subjective freedom seeking self-awareness and self-satisfaction, and coming to recognize all outside of itself as thought separate from itself. Philosophical criticism thus meant the laying bare of all of those forces that stood opposed to the free development of human self-consciousness, recognizing them for what they were—the alienation of thought or mind. The highest form of such self-consciousness was the Enlightenment itself.

In Hegel's *History of Philosophy* Epicureanism was depicted as representing the development of abstract individuality; Stoicism, abstract universality; and Scepticism as the school that nullified the other two. Epicurus' physics, in the view of Hegel, was "nothing else but the principle of modern physics." "Epicurus," Hegel observed, "is the inventor of empiric Natural Science, of empiric Psychology.... [T]he physics of Epicurus were ... famous for the reason that they introduced more enlightened views in regard to what is physical, and banished fear of the gods." Here was to be found in ancient clothing the abstract individualism of "the so-called enlightenment." Yet, Epicurus, although representing the viewpoint of modern science for Hegel, also represented the philosophical poverty of science. Thus he wrote (not entirely consistently with all that he had said before): "We can have no respect for the philosophic thoughts of Epicurus, or rather he has no thoughts for us to respect."[104] This same view of Epicureanism was later carried forward by the Young Hegelians, who contended that Epicureanism, in particular, had prefigured the European Enlightenment of the seventeenth, eighteenth, and nineteenth centuries, which they also saw as constituting a period of growing self-consciousness, abstract individuality, and rejection of divine power in relation to nature.[105]

For Hegel and the Young Hegelians, Frederick the Great (1712–1786), King of Prussia from 1740 to 1786 and the patron of Voltaire and La Mettrie, was known as "materialism wearing a crown," that is, a modern adherent of Epicureanism, in the words of Heinrich Heine. In 1840 Marx's friend Köppen (who was ten years Marx's senior) published a book entitled *Frederick the Great and His Opponents*. In contrast to German Romantics like Friedrich Schlegel who had attacked "the crude materialism of Epicurus," and who had deplored the fact that in modern times "the teaching of Epicurus, augmented and supplemented by modern discoveries in the Natural sciences," had grown "to be the dominant philosophy of the latter half of the eighteenth century especially in France," Köppen—who later indicated that all of his thinking in this period derived from Marx—saw the connection between Greek atomism and the Enlightenment as a virtue: "All the figures of the Enlightenment are indeed related to the Epicureans in many respects, just as from the opposite point of view the Epicureans have shown themselves chiefly to be the Enlightenment figures of antiquity." Significantly, Köppen dedicated his book to his friend Karl Marx.[106]

Marx and Epicurus

In the preface to his doctoral thesis, which was submitted in 1841 (and accepted shortly after), Marx referred favorably to Köppen's *Frederick the Great*. But Marx chose in his thesis to look back at Epicurus' philosophy itself—in order to throw light on the way in which Epicurean philosophy had prefigured the rise of the materialism, humanism, and abstract individualism of the European Enlightenment of the seventeenth and eighteenth centuries. For Marx, Epicurus was "the greatest representative of the Greek Enlightenment, and he deserves the praise of Lucretius."[107] (Lucretius in his eulogy to Epicurus, in *De rerum natura*, had referred to him as the bringer of reason or enlightenment, understood as an inner mental light, more able than sunbeams themselves to dispel the shadows of superstition.[108]) Not only did the Epicureans, Stoics, and Sceptics offer the clue to the whole development of Greek philosophy, but also Epicureanism in particular, his argument implied, was the key to the European present.[109] Marx, who had studied Bacon's *Of the Dignity and Advancement of Learning* (1623) even before he turned to the systematic study of Hegel, was well aware of Bacon's criticism of Epicurus for "accommodating and subjecting his natural to his moral philosophy," but Marx was to turn this disposition on Epicurus' part into a strength (when compared to Democritus' philosophy).[110] Moreover, Marx was undoubtedly influenced by Bacon's attack on reasoning by final causes in the manner of natural theology, and by Bacon's argument that the natural philosophy of the ancient materialists Democritus, Epicurus, and Lucretius was superior to that of Plato and Aristotle, precisely because of their refusal to argue from final causes and their removal of "God and Mind from the structure of things."[111] Like Bacon in *The Wisdom of the Ancients*, Marx coupled the image of Prometheus in his dissertation with the Greek atomists, though in Marx's case it was Epicurus rather than Democritus who was to be Prometheus' ancient counterpart.

At the time that Marx was studying Bacon he was also spending "a good deal of time" on the work of the German natural theologian (later deist) Hermann Samuel Reimarus (1694–1768), especially the latter's *Considerations on the Art Instincts of Animals* (1760). Reimarus, most famous for his posthumous *Fragments* (1774–1777), also wrote an influential critique of Epicurean materialism, from the standpoint of natural theology, entitled *The Principal Truths of Natural Religion Defended* (1754), which passed through six German editions, as well as being translated into Dutch, English, and French, by 1791. A subtitle added in the English translation of this work read: *Wherein the Objections of Lucretius, Buffon, Maupertuis, Rousseau, La Mettrie, and other Ancient and Modern Followers of Epicurus are Considered, and their Doctrines Refuted.* In both the *Considerations on the Art Instincts of Animals* and *The Principal Truths of Natural Religion* Reimarus sought to demonstrate the argument from design for the existence of God, and was hence the German counterpart of Paley in the late eighteenth century. It was to such issues as well, associated with materialism and its conflict with natural theology, that Marx was to turn—if somewhat indirectly—in choosing the topic of his doctoral thesis.[112]

The argument of the doctoral thesis itself pivoted on the differences in the physics of the atom, to be found in Democritus and Epicurus— differences that pointed beyond physics to epistemology. As the great Epicurean scholar Cyril Bailey, who translated Epicurus into English, was to exclaim in 1928: "Looking back on his [Marx's] work now it is almost astonishing to see how far he got considering the materials then available.... Almost as a pioneer he rejects the ancient tradition, represented glibly in the histories of his time, that Epicurus adopted the Atomism of Democritus wholesale, changing it here and there for the worse." Marx, according to Bailey, was "probably the first to perceive" the true distinction between the Democritean and Epicurean systems, by focusing on the meaning to be attached to the Epicurean swerve. "He sees rightly ... that the real difference between the two thinkers lies in their underlying 'theory of knowledge.'" Democritus had simply accepted the paradox that while truth was to be found in appearance, the truth of the atom was beyond human senses and thus ultimately remote and unknowable. Epicurus' own atomism, in contrast, allowed him to delve into the nature of human sensation and existence.[113] As Benjamin Farrington noted in his book *The Faith of Epicurus*:

> Oddly enough it was Karl Marx in his doctoral thesis ... who first took the measure of the problem and provided the solution.... Marx reversed their roles making Epicurus appear as the deeper of the two [in comparison to Democritus] inasmuch as he had labored to find room in his system both for animate and inanimate being, both for nature and society, both for the phenomena of the external world and the demands of the moral consciousness.

Writing elsewhere, Farrington observed "While Plato warred against the scientific materialists, Epicurus [as Marx was to show] based his philosophy upon them, rejecting only the theory of mechanical determinism."[114]

Indeed, Marx was the first to discover what modern scholarship has confirmed, that, as Farrington observed in *Science and Politics in the Ancient World* (1939), Epicureanism was "not a purely mechanical system; it was the specific originality of Epicurus in the domain of physics to have defended freedom of the will in man as a product of evolution." In his "Letter to Heredotus" Epicurus made clear that human nature was originally constrained by natural circumstances, and that "later on reasoning elaborated what had been suggested by nature and made further inventions ... at some epochs and times making great advances, and less again at others." Out of these changes in practical circumstances, Epicurus argued, language itself had evolved. The analysis thus pointed to human cultural evolution as representing a kind of freedom for rational organization of historical life, building on constraints first established by the material world. "Thus Purpose," Farrington writes, "makes its appearance in the course of history. It is not a metaphysical, but an historically acquired, character of man."[115] This point was made forcefully by A.H. Armstrong in an essay in the *Classical Quarterly* in 1938, where he states:

> We see that what Epicurus has done, and he seems to have been original in doing it, is to split the traditional conception of Chance–Necessity so that, while remaining strictly within the bounds of his system and involving no principle of explanation which is immaterial or possessed of reason [that is, teleological], he provides himself with a framework or background of regularity

and order while leaving room for an erratic, capricious principle in the world.... It is tempting to recognize in this distinction a conscious attempt to provide an adequate substitute for the Platonic cosmology, on a materialistic basis.[116]

Marx himself started off, in the preface to his doctoral thesis, by observing that "Hegel has on the whole correctly defined the general aspects" of the Epicurean, Stoic, and Sceptic philosophies, which he had viewed in terms of the development of self-consciousness, but had fallen short of a full explanation of these systems.[117] In contrast to the dominant interpretation of Epicurus within German Romantic philosophy which saw him as a poor imitator of Democritus, who only introduced "arbitrary vagaries" into the system of the former, Marx argued that the philosophical system of Epicurus broke with that of the more skeptical Democritus, by positing the empirical world as the "objective appearance" of the world of the atom (rather than a mere "subjective semblance" as in Democritus).[118] Implicit in Epicurus' philosophy was the notion that knowledge both of the world of the atom (imperceptible to the senses) and of sensuous reality arose from the inner necessity of human reason embodied in abstract individuality and freedom (self-determination). In Epicurus, Marx contended, the one-sided determinism of Democritus is transcended. For Democritus, necessity is everything, but Epicurus also recognizes chance, contingency, and the possibility of freedom.[119]

Marx's general argument commences with the swerve or the declination of the atom from the straight line which separated Democritus' philosophy from that of Epicurus. It was "an old and entrenched prejudice," Marx observed, "to identify Epicurus' modifications" of Democritus in this area "as only arbitrary vagaries." Rather Epicurus' swerve—a swerve that was a slight deviation—created the realm of chance (in the sense of contingency) and hence possibility free from determinism. It made the world itself possible, as Lucretius had written, since otherwise there would be no collision of atoms and "the world would never have been created." Those who objected, as in the case of Cicero, that there was no *cause* given for such a swerve and hence demanded absolute determinism from atomism, Marx argued, were not thereby more logical since the atom itself had no *cause*. Further, to argue, as some did, that one needed merely to add some degree of spirituality to the argument—referring to the "soul of the atom"—gained nothing from this but the addition of a word and the introduction of non-material principles.[120]

What fascinated Marx was the fact that Epicurean philosophy "swerves away" from all restrictive modes of being, just as the gods in Epicurean philosophy swerve away from the world—a world of freedom and self-determination over which they hold no sway. In Epicurus "the law of the atom" is "repulsion," the collision of elements; it no longer needs fixation in any form. Indeed, Epicurus, Marx contended (following Kant in this respect), was "the first to grasp the essence of the repulsion." Hence, "Lucretius is ... correct," Marx observes, "when he maintains that the declination [the swerve] breaks the *fati foedera* [the bonds of fate]."[121]

Fundamental to Epicurus' whole philosophy, according to Marx, was that sensuousness was a temporal process. "Human sensuousness is ... embodied time, the existing reflection of the sensuous world in itself." Mere perception through the senses is only possible because it expresses an active relation to nature—and indeed of nature to itself. "In hearing nature hears itself, in smelling it smells itself, in seeing it sees itself." But this is necessarily experienced as a "passing away" of things at the same time as they become available to senses—since according to Epicurus the senses are activated by external stimuli that are themselves transitory. Hence, "the pure form of the world of appearance is time." It was on this basis that Marx was to argue that "Epicurus was the first to grasp appearance as appearance, that is, as alienation of the essence, activating itself in its reality as such an alienation."[122]

Ancient materialism is often portrayed as a view that reduces thought to "passive sensations," which are themselves "merely a product of forces acting from without, to Democritus' view that nothing exists but 'atoms and the void'"—as the young Sidney Hook wrote. Idealism, in contrast, is usually credited with having provided the "active" side to the "dialectic of perception." Yet, Marx clearly saw this active side as already present in Epicurus' materialism, with its conception of sensation as related to change and "passing away." Already there is an understanding of the existence of alienated self-consciousness, and of knowledge as involving both sensation and intellectual abstraction (a complex relation that Marx was to refer to in his notes on Epicurus as "the dialectic of sensuous certitude").[123] Moreover, in Epicurus is found even the view that our consciousness of the world (for example, our language) develops in relation to the evolution of the material conditions governing subsistence.

Hence, "in Epicurus," Marx contended, "...*atomistics* with all its contradictions has been carried through and completed as *the natural science of self-consciousness*." In perceiving the reality of the world of appearance as "the alienation of the essence," Epicurus recognized the estrangement of human beings from the human world. Human beings cease to be mere products of nature or of supernatural forces—Marx observed, basing himself on Epicurus—when they relate themselves not to some "different existence" but to other individual human beings.[124] Rather than reflecting an "ordinary logic," as depicted by Hegel, Epicurus, for Marx, already provided a dialectic of self-consciousness—if still largely in contemplative form.[125]

Epicurus' philosophy derived much of its distinctive character, Marx stressed, from the fact that it was opposed both to the determinism of Democritus' physics and to the teleological principles of religion. Thus Epicurus wrote that "It would be better to follow the myth about the Gods than to be a slave to the destiny of the physicists. For the former leaves hope for mercy if we do honour to the gods, while the latter is inexorable necessity. But it is *chance*, which must be accepted, *not God*, as the multitude believe."[126] "To serve philosophy," according to Epicurus, is to seek "true freedom." Central to Epicurus' philosophy, in Marx's view, was his emphasis on freedom that knows no final constraints. This was evident in his statement, quoted by Seneca in his *Epistles*, that "'It is wrong to live under constraint; but no man is constrained to live under constraint.' Of course not. On all sides lie many short and simple paths to freedom; and let us thank God that no man can be kept in life. We may spurn the very constraints that hold us. 'Epicurus,' you reply, 'uttered these words.'"[127] As Marx explained almost two decades later to Ferdinand Lassalle, Epicurus was for "ever turning the argument [of Democritus] inside out"— a fact that eluded not only Cicero and Plutarch but even Hegel.

In recent years the recovery of portions of Epicurus' great work *On Nature* from the charcoal remains of the papyri found in Philodemus' library in Herculaneum has provided powerful direct confirmation of Marx's interpretation, much of which had been based on conjecture and dialectical reasoning. Thus in Book XXV of *On Nature* Epicurus provided a critique of the mechanistic determinism of Empedocles and Democritus. "The first men to give an adequate account of causes—men generally excelling not only their predecessors but also, many times over, their successors, although in many matters they alleviated great problems," he wrote, "turned a blind eye to themselves in order to blame everything on necessity and accident" (*events* that were *done* by human beings were, Epicurus insisted, the result of human freedom, not *mere necessity*, nor *mere accident*). Epicurus of course never sought to deny necessity altogether (which would mean, as he said, that everything could come from anything), but simply emphasized the *possibility* of freedom, breaking the bounds of such necessity. Thus, defending materialism, he nonetheless opposed any kind of strict determinism, since if the determinist were to take this view seriously, life itself would become meaningless.[128] "From the very outset," Epicurus wrote in *On Nature*, "we always have seeds directing us some towards these, some towards those, some towards these *and* those, actions and thoughts and characters, in greater and smaller numbers. Consequently that which we develop—characteristics of this or that kind—is at first absolutely up to us."[129]

Indeed, Epicurus, though a materialist, erred if at all, according to Marx, mainly on the side of abstract possibility, which exaggerated chance and free volition, as opposed to real possibility, which also recognizes necessity, and hence is bounded. In insisting that no judgement should contradict the senses, he preferred to retain a clear conception of the *possible*, while remaining open and non-determinant (even at the risk of making this possibility an abstract one). Epicurus' resolutely non-deterministic mode of thinking was indicated by his stance that, in Marx's words, "it is rash to judge apodictically about that which can only be deduced from conjectures."[130] Epicurus was thus sometimes contemptuous of the one-sided claims of positive science and scorned simple empiricism.[131]

Appended to Marx's doctoral thesis was "A Critique of Plutarch's Polemic against the Theology of Epicurus," of which only a fragment has survived. But we still have Marx's extensive *Notebooks on Epicurean Philosophy*, large parts of which are devoted to the critique of Plutarch and the defense of Epicurus from the attacks of the former—which are closely related to the fragment of the Appendix that still exists. It is here that Marx, partly under the influence of Epicurus and Lucretius, provided his first great critique of religion, calling for the removal of all supernatural, teleological principles from nature. Plutarch had attacked Epicurus for removing all pleasure from the world, by removing God from the world. He also criticized Epicurus for seeking by means of natural science to remove the fear of mortality that lay behind the belief in the immortality of the soul. For Plutarch himself, such fear was an important element of faith in God.[132] Marx, in the notes to the Appendix to his dissertation (which are more extensive than this fragmentary section of the text itself), countered with a quote from Holbach's *System of Nature* in which Holbach, in a Lucretian vein, argues that the idea of divine powers that rule the world "has always been associated with that of terror.... Nothing therefore could be more dangerous than to persuade man that a being superior to nature exists, a being before whom reason must be silent and to whom man must sacrifice all to receive happiness."[133] In "fear, and specifically in an inner fear that cannot be extinguished," Marx wrote, following Epicurus, "man is determined as an animal," shorn of all self-determination.[134] This, for Marx, is the greatest sin of religion. It is no accident that Epicurean philosophy, which revealed all of this, was so hated by the founders of Christianity. "Lucretius," Marx and Engels observed in *The German Ideology*, "praised Epicurus as the hero who was the first to overthrow the gods and trample religion underfoot; for this reason among all church fathers, from Plutarch to Luther," they went on to observe, "Epicurus has always had the reputation of being the atheist philosopher *par excellence*, and was always called a swine; for that reason too. Clement of Alexandria says that when Paul takes up arms against philosophy he has in mind Epicurean philosophy alone."[135]

Marx saw the essence of Epicurean materialism as lying in its conception of the mortality of both human beings and the universe. Lucretius had written that "One who no longer is cannot suffer, or differ in any way from one who has never been born, when once this mortal life has been usurped by death the immortal." For Marx, this was the key to Epicurean materialism itself: "*It can be said that in the Epicurean philosophy it is death that is the immortal.* The atom, the void, accident, arbitrariness and composition are themselves death." The Epicurean emphasis on material "conditions" was a recognition of immortal death—of the role of accident and of antecedent conditions—which was the context in which human self-consciousness and freedom must necessarily develop.[136]

In his critique of Plutarch, Marx also indicates his opposition to none other than the German idealist philosopher Friedrich Schelling, whose earlier criticisms of an "objective god" Marx counterposed to Schelling's current reactionary position in defending religious principles, which became the basis for the later Schelling's equally reactionary philosophy of nature. Significantly, it was the appointment of Schelling as Rector at the University of Berlin that symbolized the closing off of the German universities to the Young Hegelians, and that had clearly sealed the academic fate of the young Marx.[137] It is no wonder, then, that Marx's doctoral thesis (if only in its Appendix) sided with Epicurus and Holbach, representing the "ancient Enlightenment" and the modern Enlightenment, against Plutarch and Schelling. Plutarch, Marx argued, represented "the theologizing intellect to philosophy."[138] Epicurus, in contrast, had vanished God from the world. Indeed, for Epicurus, in Marx's words, "no good for man lies outside himself."[139]

In the preface that Marx wrote for what was intended to be the published version of his doctoral thesis he lauds Epicurus for expelling the gods from the natural world, and rejecting all superstition. "Philosophy, as long as a drop of blood shall pulse in its world-subduing and absolutely free heart, will never grow tired of answering its adversaries with the cry of Epicurus: 'Not the man who denies the gods worshipped by the multitude, but he who affirms of the gods what the multitude believes about them, is truly impious.'" Here Marx deliberately echoed Bacon, who (as we have seen) had also praised the very same passage in Epicurus.[140]

From "the cry of Epicurus" against those who would reduce nature to teleology, Marx turns to Prometheus' defiance of the gods in Aeschylus' *Prometheus Bound*, where Promethus, chained to the rocks by Zeus, replies to Hermes, the messenger of the gods:

> Be sure of this, I would not change my state
> Of evil fortune for your servitude.
> Better be the servant of this rock
> Than to be faithful boy to Father Zeus.[141]

For Marx, Epicurus represented the bringing of light or enlightenment, which was a rejection of the religious view of nature—a materialism which was also a form of naturalism and humanism. Epicurus' philosophy emphasized the sensational and empirical world, and yet recognized the role of reason in interpreting that world, and thus had no need in its interpretation of the world for the gods, who dwelt simply in the spaces between the worlds.

Nevertheless, Marx adopted Hegel's framework to the extent of arguing that "Epicurus has … carried atomistics to its final conclusion, which is its dissolution and conscious opposition to the universal."[142] Epicurus' materialism, to the extent that it rested on mere atomism, and thus mechanism, was itself a one-sided distortion, which set it in opposition to the universal and marked its own dissolution. The greatest shortcoming of Epicurus' natural philosophy was that Epicurus "knows no other nature but the mechanical." It is true that Epicurus—Marx writes with reference to Lucretius' great poem—celebrates sensation, but herein lies the strange character of Epicurus' natural philosophy, in that it "proceeds from the sphere of the sensuous" and yet posits "as principle such an abstraction … as the atom."[143] This tension is never fully resolved, though Epicurus, as Marx himself emphasized in his doctoral thesis, rose beyond mechanistic materialism to a considerable extent. As Farrington notes,

> It was not the intention of Epicurus, if he could rescue the Greek world from the influence of the Academy [Plato and Aristotle], to restore the physical system of Democritus without change. The atomic system, as constituted by Leucippus and Democritus, suffered, in his eyes, from a fundamental defect; it established a doctrine of universal determinism, including man in the same chain of mechanical causation as inanimate matter. The doctrine of mechanical determinism was, in the eyes of Epicurus, a worse incubus on the human race than a belief in the myths.[144]

Marx's occasional reservations about the mechanism that Epicurus to some extent carried over from Democritus did not, however, erase the real contribution of Epicurus, which pointed toward the transcendence of such a mechanism; nor that of Lucretius, whom he described as "fresh, keen, poetic master of the world."[145] It was not Epicurean (or Democritean) physics, but rather Enlightenment materialism-humanism prefigured by Epicurus' ancient philosophical revolution, that was of the most lasting influence.

Marx's doctoral thesis was a transitional work. It was to a considerable extent Hegelian in spirit (though much less so in substance) at a time when Marx, along with other Young Hegelians such as Bruno Bauer, thought that Hegelianism was a revolutionary philosophy. The true spirit of Hegel, they believed, was to be found in its anti-religious (if not atheist) implications, and in the fact that it united the radical Enlightenment with reason to be embodied in the ideal state. Because of the transcendent nature of the Hegelian doctrine, which conceived all of previous philosophy as a partial development of its own total philosophy, it was possible for Marx to identify to a considerable extent with the revolutionary self-consciousness of Epicurus and the British and French materialists, while still seeing this as one-sided, not yet unified with the principle of reason in its ideal form. Yet, in reality, the antinomy between materialism and speculative philosophy was not so easily resolved, and Marx had already moved decisively in a materialist direction, so decisively that although his ideas were speculative (or idealist) in their outer form, they were increasingly materialist in essence. Marx's critique of religion at this point took the form (perhaps in response to the Romantic reaction represented by the later Schelling) of a repudiation of the philosophy of nature of German idealism.[146] At the same time he enthusiastically embraced the broadly materialist/naturalist views (in the sense of opposition to Aristotelianism) of such thinkers as Epicurus, Lucretius, Bacon, Hume, and Holbach.[147]

Marx clearly recognized that his interpretation of Epicurus was heavily dependent on the accounts of others. Much of his detailed knowledge of Epicurus (particularly in relation to Epicurus' concept of freedom) was culled from mere fragments in the works of other writers, such as Seneca and Sextus Empiricus. (Nowadays, however, with considerably more of Epicurus' work available to us, Marx's interpretation has been shown to be substantially correct.) Thus Marx was later to acknowledge in a letter to Ferdinand Lassalle, May 31, 1858, that in writing his doctoral thesis he was fully aware that the complete system of thought associated with abstract individuality that he had attributed to Epicurus was no more than "implicit" in the fragments left behind by that great thinker, but that he was convinced that it was correct nonetheless. Marx thus could not "prove" his interpretation to his satisfaction; nor could he easily express to others what he had gained from Epicurus, since it was based on a deep knowledge of numerous Greek and Latin texts and differed considerably from existing philosophic interpretations. Hence, he seems to have internalized Epicurean materialism (like much else—for example, Hegel's dialectic) within his own thinking, while *explicitly* referring back to it only on occasion.

In some ways Marx's insights into the origins of materialism were easily subsumed within his later analysis, since the origin of modern science in the materialist philosophies of Epicurus and Bacon was a widely accepted proposition in his time. In fact a closely related attempt to transcend Hegel's idealism and to reconcile philosophy with naturalism/materialism is to be found in the Russian populist Alexander Herzen's *Letters on the Study of Nature*, written in 1845–1846. Herzen too turned to the great materialists—Epicurus, Lucretius, Bacon, Hume, Holbach, and eventually Feuerbach—in his attempt to reconcile science and philosophy, materialism and idealism, adopting an approach that, though lacking in depth (and dialectical insight) when compared with Marx, made up for this in part through the lucidity and sweep of his analysis. "Epicureanism," Herzen observed, "dealt the death-blow to paganism" (that is, to ancient religion). Epicurus had thus foreshadowed Bacon and modern science. Nor was Epicureanism devoid of dialectics. "Lucretius begins *à la* Hegel from being and non-being as active first principles which interacted and coexisted." He portrayed not only "a certain fraternal affectionate attitude for all things living," but also "conjectured the existence of fossils." Herein, Herzen argued, lay the strengths of materialism—particularly in its more dialectical, ancient form. In contrast, for the modern idealist, "nature is an absurdity and ... the transient does not deserve his attention."[148]

Marx's own contributions in this area did not cease with his doctoral thesis. Rather the broader historical significance of Epicurus' philosophy was later taken up by Marx and Engels in *The Holy Family*, where they explained that in the dualistic philosophy of Descartes materialism in physics was accompanied by a metaphysics of the mind. This seventeenth-century view, arising out of Cartesian metaphysics, had as its natural opponent Epicurean materialism, as restored by Gassendi. "French and English materialism," Marx and Engels noted, "was always closely related to Democritus and Epicurus." Gassendi, the restorer of Epicureanism, together with Hobbes, thus represented the greatest enemies of Cartesian metaphysics.[149] Epicureanism had played a central role in this struggle, Marx and Engels observed in *The German Ideology*, simply because "Epicurus was the true radical Enlightener of antiquity," whose influence had carried over into the Enlightenment itself. The Epicureans argued that "the world must be *disillusioned*, and especially freed from fear of gods, for the world is my *friend*." Indeed, the very "idea that the state rests on mutual agreement of people, on a *contract social*," they pointed out, "...is found for the first time in Epicurus."[150] Lucretius depicted the creation of a social contract among free individuals as the process that followed the slaying of the kings:

> Therefore the kings were killed, and in the dust
> The ancient majesty of thrones and sceptres proud
> Lay overthrown. The sovereign head's great crown
> Bloodstained beneath the rabble's trampling feet,
> All honor lost, bewailed its high estate.[151]

The incendiary implications of Epicurean materialism, despite Epicurus' own request that his followers remove themselves from Hellenistic public life, were thus fairly obvious in the European climate of the seventeenth and eighteenth centuries, as they had been to ancient commentators. Plutarch had complained that the Epicureans wished to "abolish laws and governments."[152] In fact it was precisely because Epicurean materialism was more than mere atomism—more even than the rejection of the gods as forces in the material world—but also represented, from a more positive standpoint, the self-conscious development of genuine humanism and naturalism in the life of antiquity, that its impact on the Enlightenment was so great.

The materialism of the Enlightenment was not confined simply to France, as Marx and Engels stressed in *The Holy Family*, but was in fact "the *natural-born* son of *Great Britain*" in the years leading up to and immediately following the English revolution. The "real progenitor of *English materialism* and all *modern experimental* science," they wrote, "is Bacon." Nevertheless, in Bacon, its "first creator," materialism "pullulates with inconsistencies imported from theology." It was Hobbes who "systematises Baconian materialism." But it was Locke in his *Essay Concerning Human Understanding* who supplied the "proof for Bacon's fundamental principle, the origin of all human knowledge and ideas from the world of sensation." And scientists like Hartley and Priestley attacked the "theological bars that still hemmed in Locke's sensationalism." The significance of Locke, for Marx and Engels in 1845, was that he "founded the philosophy of ... common sense; i.e., he said indirectly that there cannot be any philosophy at variance with the healthy human senses and reason based on them."[153]

It was left to thinkers like Helvétius and Holbach in France, however, to carry materialism into the social realm. And this eventually led, by means of historical struggle, to the rise of the more radical materialism of communism and socialism.

> If man draws all his knowledge, perception, etc., from the world of the senses and the experiences gained in it, then what has to be done is to arrange the empirical world in such a way that man experiences and becomes accustomed to what is truly human in it.... If correctly understood interest is the principle of all morality, man's private interest must be made to coincide with the interest of humanity.[154]

By the time Marx finished his doctoral thesis he had arrived at a position that was materialist in orientation, though distinguished from that of the French materialists of the eighteenth century by its non-mechanist, non-determinist character (based as it was on a different interpretation of Epicurus). Nevertheless, his viewpoint was still "tinged," as he was to recall afterwards, by the philosophy of German idealism.[155] His encounter with Epicurus and the British and French materialists had brought him face to face with what Engels was later to call "the materialist conception of nature." Yet, Marx was wary of any tendency toward vulgar or mechanical materialism that ignored the practical role of rationality.[156] Inspired by Epicurus and Bacon, he had embraced an anti-teleological view as the core of materialism. Just as Darwin had in the 1840s, Marx focused his whole critical attention on Bacon's "barren virgins" remark. "Bacon of Verulam," he wrote in 1842, "said that theological physics was a virgin dedicated to God and barren, he emancipated physics from theology and it became fertile."[157]

We can understand Marx's philosophical development better by recognizing that it was in some ways analogous to (and seems indeed to have been influenced by) that of Kant, who, as we have seen, presented "Epicurus as the foremost philosopher of sensibility, and Plato that of the intellectual"—an antinomy that was the starting point for Kant's own critical, transcendental philosophy. (Kant also, as we have noted, depicted Bacon as the foremost modern student of nature.) For Marx, Epicurus remained the foremost philosopher of sensibility, who had discovered the alienation of human beings from the world, and the necessity of science

(Enlightenment), based on a materialist conception of nature, to counter this. Hegel replaced Plato in Marx's conception, however, as the greatest philosopher of the intellect, who, as we shall see in Marx's critique of Hegel below, discovered the alienation of labor in history—although abstractly, in the form of *intellectual* labor. It was through a critical transcendence of these views that Marx's own practical materialism, which nevertheless retained a realist ontology (that is, a materialist conception of nature) as its foundation, emerged as a dialectical transcendence in the Hegelian sense. Feuerbach, as explained in the next chapter, was to carry out a similar critique of Hegel (inspired by Bacon and Gassendi rather than Epicurus directly) and did so in the form of an explicitly humanist and materialist standpoint. But like Epicurus, Feuerbach's materialism was mainly of the contemplative variety. For Marx the goal was to make it *practical*.

More than a half a century after Marx authored his doctoral thesis, in 1893, Alexei Mikhailovich Voden (1870–1939), a Russian man of letters who took part in Social Democratic Party activities in the 1890s, visited London and had a series of conversations with Engels. In the last of these conversations, Voden recalled,

> Engels asked me whether I was interested in the history of Greek philosophy and then offered to expound for me Marx's first philosophical work. He gave me an account of Marx's doctor's thesis, with many details but, without the help of the manuscript, quoting by heart not only Lucretius and Cicero but a great number of Greek texts (from Diogenes Laertius, Sextus Empiricus, and Clement).

Engels went on to explain that the criticism of Epicurus, leveled by Cicero and others, that his theory denied any attempt to account for causality was in fact wrong, and that Epicurus' work represented a dialectically self-conscious "call to investigate the causal connections from various sides, provided that they were not in contradiction to the basic thesis."[158] As Voden further recalled,

> When I asked whether Marx was ever a Hegelian in the strict sense of the word, Engels answered that the very thesis on the differences between Democritus and Epicurus allows us to state that at the very beginning of his literary career, Marx, who had completely mastered Hegel's dialectical method and had not yet been obliged by the course of his studies to replace it by the materialist dialectical method, showed perfect independence of Hegel in the application of Hegel's own dialectics, and that in the very sphere in which Hegel was strongest—the history of thought. Hegel gives not a reconstruction of the immanent dialectics of the Epicurean system, but a series of scornful opinions of that

system. Marx, on the other hand, gave a reconstruction of the immanent dialectics of Epicureanism, not idealizing it, but bringing out the poverty of its content compared with Aristotle.... He mentioned that Marx had intended to continue the study of the history of Greek philosophy and had even subsequently spoken to him on the matter. In doing so he had not displayed any one-sided preference for the materialist systems, but had dwelt particularly on the dialectics in Plato and Aristotle.[159]

Voden's reminiscences of his conversations with Engels did not appear until 1927 (when they were first published in Russian) and seem to have been overlooked by all of those who have commented on Marx's doctoral thesis. At the time Engels had asked Voden to inquire and report back to him on whether any interpretation of Epicurus resembling Marx's existed in the current literature on the subject, though there is no record that Voden complied with this request. (Voden burned Engels's letters to him in haste in 1893 in Paris when he was warned of an impending search for documents showing revolutionary connections only minutes before the actual arrival of the police.[160]) The fact that Marx's interpretation was eventually to be recognized by twentieth-century Epicurean scholars like Cyril Bailey as the first true understanding of Epicurus' system would doubtless have interested Engels greatly. All of this suggests that Engels himself had a very different view from what has become the standard interpretation of Marx's development. Not only did Marx demonstrate an independence from Hegel in his very first literary work; he did so on the basis of an encounter with ancient materialism, which was to have a lasting influence on his thinking. Finally, Engels's remarks suggest that Marx's dissertation was neither Hegelian nor fully materialist, but a transitional work, in which Marx was already considering the issue of materialist dialectics, but had not yet replaced Hegel's dialectical method with a "materialist dialectical method."

In 1842, not long after Marx completed his doctoral thesis, Darwin in England finished struggling over his metaphysical notebooks (the *M and N Notebooks*) and ventured to draft in pencil the first, short version of his theory of transmutation of species. It was in this very same year that Marx, having finished his thesis on Epicurus, began his systematic encounter with the philosophy of Ludwig Feuerbach, English political economy, and French socialism. The political-economic realities of Germany, France, and England, which were increasingly forced on his attention, were in the next few years to push Marx much more decidedly in the materialist direction, and to generate the more profound synthesis of historical materialism.

CHAPTER 2

THE REALLY
EARTHLY QUESTION

Marx's doctoral thesis was accepted in April 1841 but his hopes of pursuing an academic career were soon disappointed when the Prussian authorities began to crack down on the radical Young Hegelians. In March 1842 Marx's close associate Bruno Bauer was deprived of his teaching post for spreading unorthodox doctrines. Forced to give up on an academic career, Marx turned to journalism and in October 1842 assumed the position of editor of a major Rhineland paper, the *Rheinische Zeitung*, which represented the rising middle class of Cologne, but which was then dominated editorially by the Young Hegelians. His article "Debates on the Law on Thefts of Wood," written after becoming editor, marked an intellectual turning point in his life. This, he insisted, was "the really earthly question in all its life-size."[1] For the very first time Marx took up the cause of the poor, and he did so with all the fervor that was to characterize his subsequent work. He was later to recall this as the moment when he first realized his "embarrassing" lack of knowledge of political economy and the need to direct his studies at economic matters.[2]

In taking up the issue of the theft of wood Marx was not addressing a minor issue. Five-sixths of all prosecutions in Prussia during this period had to do with wood, and in the Rhineland the proportion was even higher.[3] What was at issue was the dissolution of the final rights of the peasants in relation to what had been the common land—rights that had existed from time immemorial but which were being eliminated by the growth of industrialization and the system of private property. Traditionally the people had had the right to collect dead wood (wood from dead trees or that had fallen in the forest), which enabled them to heat their homes and cook their food. Landowners, however, increasingly denied the ordinary people the right to dead wood along with everything else in the forest. Theft of wood, along with poaching and trespassing, were treated with the utmost severity.

Marx addressed this subject through a searching examination of the debates taking place in the Rhenish Diet (the provincial assembly of the Rhineland) on the theft of wood. These were primarily about whether the large landed proprietors deserved the same protections for their forests already available to the small landed proprietors. The latter were able to guard their forests against trespassing, poaching, the cutting of live wood, and the gathering of dead wood by virtue of the fact that their holdings were small and that they themselves lived on the land. The large landed proprietors, in contrast, were dependent on the forest wardens to protect their land, but this was only possible if these actions by the poor, including the gathering of dead wood, were made into penal offenses. Nowhere were the rights of the poor themselves considered in this parliamentary debate—the task that Marx took up in his article.[4]

Marx observed that the taking of dead wood was now included under the category of theft and prosecuted as severely as the cutting down and stealing of living timber. In this way the forest owner managed to turn into a "value" (a source of private wealth) that which had not previously been sold and had no market value. Even the gathering of cranberries from the forest was now being treated as theft, despite the fact that this had been a traditional activity of the children of the poor. All customary relations of the poor to the land (including what was defined as "trespassing") were prohibited and seen as transgressions against the monopoly of the forest owners over the land. "Wood thieves," whose only fault was to pursue the customary rights of the poor in order to maintain their families, were turned over to the forest owner under these barbaric forest regulations and obligated to do forced labor for the owner, thereby providing profits for the forest proprietor. Marx relentlessly hammered at the contradictory role of the wardens of these private forests, who, although ostensibly guardians of the forests, that is, foresters, were reduced to mere "valuers"—and whose valuations under oath might just as well be left to the forest owners themselves since these were the interests served. The state, by supporting such an irrational law, Marx argued, was turning the ordinary citizen, pursuing customary rights (which were in reality the "anticipations" of rational law), into a criminal, an "enemy of wood." The poor were thus denied any relation to nature—even for their survival—unmediated by the institutions of private property. From this point on, throughout his life, Marx was to oppose the parcelization out of portions of the globe to the owners of private property.[5]

All of his arguments on rational law and customary rights, however, Marx was eventually to conclude, had failed to uncover the reasons for this inexorable process of expropriation on behalf of the forest owners. The answers lay rather in political economy, the study of which he was to take up with unrivaled fervor when, as a result of growing government repression and lack of support from the shareholders, he decided there was no other recourse but to resign as editor of the *Rheinische Zeitung* in March 1843, after five stormy months as editor.

Feuerbach

Before Marx took up the study of political economy in earnest, however, a more decisive philosophical break with the Hegelian system, which had treated the development of history as a reflection of the development of mind, was necessary. For Marx, this took place largely through his response to the critique of the Hegelian system introduced by Ludwig Feuerbach (1804–1872). A central figure among the Young Hegelians, Feuerbach had turned back as early as 1833 in his *History of Modern Philosophy from Bacon to Spinoza* to a consideration of materialism as a means of combating positive religion. In this work he exhibited a critical affinity for the philosophy of Bacon, whom he was to describe as "the true father of science," and to whom he attributed a qualitative (as opposed to quantitative or mechanistic) materialism. Bacon, Feuerbach wrote, "was the first to recognize the originality of nature: to recognize that nature cannot be conceived in derivation from mathematical or logical or theological presuppositions, or anticipations, but can and ought to be conceived and explained only out of itself." In this respect, Bacon's philosophy of nature (and science), Feuerbach argued, was far superior to that of Descartes. "Bacon takes nature as it is, defines it positively, whereas Descartes defines it only negatively, as the counterpart of spirit; Bacon's object is actual nature; Descartes', only an abstract, mathematical, artificial nature."[6]

Feuerbach gained increasing fame as a result of the publication in 1841 of *The Essence of Christianity*, in which he argued that the idea of God was simply an inversion of real, genuine human sensibility; that humanity had created God in its own image. Although the chief impact of Feuerbach on Marx has usually been attributed to this work (an interpretation that Engels himself advanced), there is no actual evidence that this was the case. For Marx, Feuerbach's argument in *The Essence of Christianity* was anything but startling, since it had already been anticipated by others among the Young Hegelians, most notably David Strauss in *The Life of Jesus* (1835). Already in his doctoral thesis Marx had criticized Hegel for "turning all ... theological demonstrations [of the existence of God] upside-down, that is, he has rejected them in order to justify them."[7] Much more important for Marx—indeed it came as a major revelation— was Feuerbach's *Preliminary Theses on the Reform of Philosophy* (1842).[8]

The *Preliminary Theses* broke with Hegel at the weakest point in his system—the philosophy of nature. In Hegel's philosophy, nature was not something that contained within itself the means of its own self-determination, its own meaningful action; rather it was merely the estrangement that thought was compelled to undergo in abstract-general form before it could return to itself fully as spirit. Nature, which had no active principle within itself, was therefore reduced in his system to a mere mechanical entity, or taxonomic realm.

Feuerbach broke decisively with this conception by insisting that the material world was its own reality, a reality that included human beings and their sensuous perception of the world. For Feuerbach, Hegel had separated essence from existence and therefore

> essence in Hegel's *Logic* is the essence of nature and man, but *without essence, without* nature, and *without* man.... *Life and truth* are ... only to be found where essence is united with existence, thought with sense-perception, activity with passivity, and the *scholastic ponderousness of German metaphysics with the anti-scholastic, sanguine principle of French sensualism and materialism.*[9]

For the Young Hegelians up to this point, Hegel's speculative philosophy was anti-theological in its implications; in fact the critique of religion constituted its true purpose. This interpretation was held to despite the Lutheranism that Hegel had explicitly adopted in developing his system, and the fact that in his own time his work had been viewed as a bulwark for the faith. In the *Preliminary Theses* (and later in his *Principles of the Philosophy of the Future*) Feuerbach, however, took the position that speculative philosophy, rather than constituting a critique of theology, was in fact the "last rational mainstay" of the latter: "Just as once the Catholic theologians became *de facto* Aristotelians in order to combat Protestantism, so now the Protestant theologians must *de jure* become Hegelians in order to combat 'atheism.'" The abstraction of the human mind and the conception of humanity from nature which Descartes had initiated constituted for Feuerbach the origin of modern speculative philosophy. It had created a dualistic world in which essence (mind) was separated from existence, and in which the subsumption of all of existence under the development of mind was the philosophical end-result.[10]

For Feuerbach, the Hegelian system amounted to a denial of the world of sensuous existence; one that merely replicated, in the name of secular philosophy, rather than religious theology, the estrangement of human beings from nature that was the principal obstacle to the development of freedom. Speculative philosophy, like theology before it, had thus developed in inverted form, "from the ideal to the real.... [O]nly the perception of things and beings in their objective reality can make man free and devoid of all prejudices. The transition from the 'ideal' to the real has its place only in practical philosophy." The self-consciousness that the Hegelian philosophy had gloried in was for Feuerbach merely an alienated self-consciousness (for all of its pretenses of abstract Enlightenment), since abstracted from humanity, that is, from real sensuous existence. It was "an abstraction without reality." In reality, "man *is* self-consciousness" and nature is the ground of man.[11]

For Feuerbach, "there is no other essence which man can think, dream of, imagine, feel, believe in, wish for, love and adore as the *absolute*, than the essence of human nature itself." Here he embraced also "external nature; for as man belongs to the essence of Nature, in opposition to common materialism; so Nature belongs to the essence of man—in opposition to subjective idealism; which is also the secret of our 'absolute' philosophy, at least in relation to Nature. Only by uniting man with Nature can we conquer the supranaturalistic egoism of Christianity."[12]

Feuerbach's critique was decisive, from Marx's standpoint, since it made Hegel's speculative philosophy into a rational justification for what still amounted to an essentially theological world-view, in which human self-consciousness and material existence, and the possibilities of freedom contained therein, were sacrificed on the altar of the abstract spirit. The mode of speculative philosophy must therefore be abandoned for more materialist forms of analysis. As Marx declared in 1842,

> I advise you, speculative theologians and philosophers: free yourselves from the concepts and prepossessions of existing speculative philosophy, if you want to get at things differently, as they are, that is to say, if you want to arrive at the *truth*. There is no other road for you to *truth* and *freedom*, except that leading *through* the stream of fire [the *Feuer-bach*]. Feuerbach is the *purgatory* of the present times.[13]

This concern with Feuerbachian naturalism in turn reinforced Marx's growing concern with political economy, which he realized, following his article on the theft of wood, held the key to the human-material appropriation of nature.

Moreover, it was not simply Feuerbach's rejection of Hegel's speculative philosophy that was important to Marx, but also the sensuous character of Feuerbach's materialism, its emphasis on naturalism. Feuerbach, in rejecting Hegel, also provided as an alternative the rough outlines of a materialistic view that bridged the gap between philosophical criticism and natural science. "All science," Feuerbach wrote, "must be grounded in *nature*. A doctrine remains a *hypothesis* as long as it has not found its *natural basis*. This is true particularly of the *doctrine of freedom*. Only the new philosophy will succeed in *naturalizing freedom* which was hitherto an *anti-hypothesis*, a supernatural *hypothesis*." This natural basis, for Feuerbach, was to be found in matter itself. "Matter," he declared, "is an essential object for reason. If there were no matter, reason would have no *stimulus* and no *material* for thought, and, hence, no content. One cannot give up matter without giving up reason; one cannot acknowledge matter without acknowledging reason. Materialists are rationalists."[14] For Feuerbach, the real world, the finite, did not dissolve itself in the universal spirit, but rather the finite (in true Epicurean form) became the infinite.

Marx responded enthusiastically to this construction of a humanist materialism, rooted in a sensationalist epistemology. A distinctive characteristic of Epicurean materialism had been its emphasis on the truth of sensations. This aspect of Epicurus had been heavily emphasized in the French Renaissance humanist Michel de Montaigne's *Apology for Raymond Sebond* (1580) and was given new life by Lockean sensationalism.[15] Hence, Feuerbach's materialism, which emphasized sensationalism in these terms, appeared to be anything but mechanical. It was related, rather, to what Marx himself in *The Holy Family* was later to call the branch of materialism arising out of sense experience, which began within modern philosophy in Locke, and could be traced back within ancient philosophy to Epicurus. Although Feuerbach's materialism was essentially an anthropological materialism, this emphasis on human sensibility did not negate the rest of nature. "The new philosophy," he wrote in *Principles of the Philosophy of the Future*, "makes *man, together with nature*, as the basis of man, the *exclusive, universal*, and *highest* object of philosophy; it makes *anthropology, together with physiology*, the *universal science*."[16]

Marx wrote to the Young Hegelian Arnold Ruge in 1843 that "Feuerbach's aphorisms [*Preliminary Theses on the Reform of Philosophy*] seem to me incorrect in only one respect, that he refers too much to nature and too little to politics.... But things will probably go as they did in the sixteenth century, when the nature enthusiasts were accompanied by a corresponding number of state enthusiasts."[17] Marx's first major work after resigning as editor of the *Rheinische Zeitung* was an extensive textual *Critique of Hegel's Philosophy of Right*, in which he tried to apply Feuerbach's transformative method to the political domain.

The Alienation of Nature and Humanity

Marx's critique of Hegel's philosophy of the state was, however, to remain unfinished. In the Fall of 1843 Marx, recently married to Jenny von Westphalen, moved to Paris with the object of starting up a new publication, the *Deutsch–Französische Jahrbücher* (the Franco-German Yearbooks), to be published in Paris, free from the Prussian censor, and then sent back to Germany. The new publication was to be short-lived. Only one double-issue was to appear in 1844. The journal was immediately banned in Prussia and copies seized on entry into the country. Warrants were issued for the arrest of Marx and the other principal editors. At the same time the journal received little attention in France.

It was in the more radical political climate of Paris, however, that Marx, by then engaged in a serious study of English political economy and French socialist politics, was to write his *Economic and Philosophical Manuscripts of 1844*—the first truly comprehensive outcome of his wide-ranging critical studies. This work is best known for the development of the concept of the alienation of labor. But this estrangement of the worker from (1) the object of his/her labor, (2) the labor process, (3) human species-being (that is, the transformative, creative activity that defined human beings as a given species), and (4) each other—which together constituted Marx's concept of the alienation of labor—was inseparable from the alienation of human beings from nature, from both their own internal nature and external nature.

"The universality of man," Marx wrote,

> manifests itself in practice in that universality which makes the whole of nature as his *inorganic* body, (1) as a direct means of life and (2) as the matter, the object and the tool of his activity. Nature is man's *inorganic* body, that is to say, nature in so far as it is not the human body. Man *lives* from nature, i.e. nature is his *body*, and he must maintain a continuing dialogue with it if he is not to die. To say that man's physical and mental life is linked to nature simply means that nature is linked to itself, for man is a part of nature.[18]

From the *Economic and Philosophical Manuscripts* on, for the rest of his life, Marx always treated nature, insofar as it entered directly into human history through production, as an extension of the human body (that is, "the inorganic body" of humanity). The human relation to nature, according to this conception, was mediated not only through production but also, more directly, by means of the tools—themselves a product of the human transformation of nature through production—that allowed humanity to transform nature in universal ways. For Marx, the relationship was clearly an organic one but one that physically transcended, while at the same time practically extending, the actual bodily organs of human beings—hence the reference to nature as the "inorganic body of man."

Human beings, according to this conception, produce their own historical relation to nature in large part by producing their means of subsistence. Nature thus takes on practical meaning for humanity as a result of life-activity, the production of the means of life. "Man," Marx wrote, "reproduces the whole of nature." But the practical activity through which human beings accomplish this is not merely production in the narrow economic sense; "hence man also produces in accordance with the laws of beauty."

It follows that alienation is at one and the same time the estrangement of humanity from its own laboring activity and from its active role in the transformation of nature. Such alienation, according to Marx, "estranges man from his own body, from nature as it exists outside him, from his spiritual essence, his *human* essence." Moreover, this is always a social estrangement: "every self-estrangement of man from himself and nature is manifested in the relationship he sets up between other men and himself and nature."[19]

For Marx, it was Hegel who had first advanced the notion of the alienation of human labor. But he had done so in an idealist context, in which such alienation was conceived simply as the alienation of intellectual labor. Hence, Hegel was unable to perceive the self-alienation of human practical activity as the basis of people's estrangement not only from themselves but also from their real, sensuous existence: their relation to nature.[20]

Marx's notion of the alienation of nature, which he saw arising out of human practical life, was no more abstract at its core than his notion of the alienation of labor. Both were grounded in his understanding of the political-economic thrust of capitalist society. The alienation of labor was a reflection of the fact that labor (power) had become reduced virtually to the status of a commodity, governed by the laws of supply and demand. This proletarianization of labor, though, was dependent, as the classical political economists Smith, Malthus, Ricardo, and James Mill had insisted, on the transformation of the human relation to the land. "It is only through labour, through agriculture, that the land exists for man," Marx wrote. But the relationship to the land was being rapidly transformed through what Adam Smith had called "primitive accumulation," which included the enclosure of common lands, the rise of great estates, and the displacement of the peasantry.

The domination of the earth itself, for Marx, took on a complex, dialectical meaning derived from his concept of alienation. It meant both the domination of the earth *by* those who monopolized land and hence the elemental powers of nature, and also the domination of the earth and of dead matter (representing the power of landlord and capitalist) *over* the vast majority of human beings. Thus the alienation of the earth, and hence its domination *over* the greater part of humanity (by being alienated in favor of a very few), was an essential element of private property and had existed in feudal landed property—which was "the root of private property"—prior to the rise of capitalism. "In feudal landownership," he observed, "we already find the domination of the earth as an alien power over man." Already the land "appears as the inorganic body of its lord," who is its master and who uses it to dominate the peasantry. But it is bourgeois society which brings this domination of the earth (and through the domination of the earth the domination of humanity) to perfection, and while apparently opposing the system of landed property comes to depend upon it at a key phase in its development. Thus "large-scale landed property, as in England, drives the overwhelming majority of the population into the arms of industry and reduces its own workers to total misery."[21]

The role of large-scale landed property in monopolizing the land—and thereby alienating the earth—was analogous, according to Marx, to the domination of capital over money, understood as "dead matter." The expression "money knows no master" was simply an "expression of the complete domination of dead matter over men." It was the fullest expression of the fact "that land, like man," had sunk to "the level of a venal object."[22]

"The view of nature which has grown up under the regime of private property and of money," Marx wrote in 1843 in "On the Jewish Question," "is an actual contempt for and practical degradation of nature…. In this sense Thomas Müntzer declares it intolerable that 'all creatures have been made into property, the fish in the water, the birds in the air, the plants on the earth—all living things must also become free.'" Here Marx took his inspiration from the revolutionary leader of the great Peasant War in Germany at the beginning of the sixteenth century, who saw the transformation of species into so many forms of property as an attack on both humanity and nature. As Müntzer had further exclaimed, "Open your eyes! What is the evil brew from which all usury, theft and robbery springs but the assumption of our lords and princes that all creatures are their property?"[23]

For Marx, this alienation from nature, depicted by Müntzer, was expressed through the fetishism of money, which becomes the "alienated essence": "Money is the universal and self-constituted *value* of all things. It has therefore deprived the entire world—both the world of man and of nature—of its specific value."[24]

It was not just in relation to agriculture and the large estates, however, that the system of private property was antagonistic to nature. Ecological degradation could also be seen in what Marx referred to in his *Economic and Philosophical Manuscripts* as "the universal pollution to be found in large towns."[25] In such large towns, he explained,

> Even the need for fresh air ceases to be a need for the worker. Man reverts once more to living in a cave, but the cave is now polluted by the mephitic and pestilential breath of civilization. Moreover, the worker has no more than a precarious right to live in it, for it is for him an alien power that can be daily withdrawn and from which, should he fail to pay, he can be evicted at any time. He actually has to *pay* for this mortuary. A dwelling in the *light*, which Prometheus describes in Aeschylus as one of the great gifts through which he transformed savages into men, ceases to exist for the worker. Light, air, etc.— the simples *animal* cleanliness—ceases to be a need for man. *Dirt*—this pollution and putrefaction of man, the *sewage* (this word is to be understood in its literal sense) of civilization—becomes an *element of life* for him. Universal *unnatural neglect*, putrefied nature, becomes an *element of life* for him.[26]

The alienation of the workers in the large towns had thus reached the point where light, air, cleanliness, were no longer part of their existence, but rather darkness, polluted air, and raw, untreated sewage constituted their material environment. Not only creative work but the essential elements of life itself were forfeited as a result of this alienation of humanity and nature.

If Feuerbach's naturalistic materialism helped bring nature and its alienation alive for Marx, this point of view only highlighted the weaknesses of Hegel's system by contrast, where nature, viewed apart from the spirit, degenerates into the "crassest materialism." "The purpose of nature," Hegel had written in his *Philosophy of Nature*, "is to extinguish itself, and to break through its rind of immediate and sensuous being, to consume itself like a Phoenix in order to emerge from this externality rejuvenated as spirit." Hence, in Hegel's system, according to Marx, nature (and more specifically matter) "is shorn of its reality in favour of human will" or spirit, which alone gives it meaning.[27] At the same time, human beings were viewed by Hegel as non-objective spiritual beings.

Alienation for Hegel, then, becomes an estrangement of spiritless matter from non-material spiritual beings—all of which reflects the alienation of spirit from itself. In the end Hegel transcends this alienated dualism by sublating the objective world (realism), that is, matter or existence apart from the spirit's consciousness of its own self-mediation. Hegel's *Philosophy of Nature* is little more than a Great Chain of Being, a view of nature as stratified in conformity with principles of logic—and which, minus the self-conscious spirit, lacks any real life or development of its own. The issue of ontology, of being, is thus entirely subordinated to epistemology, that is, human knowledge and self-consciousness.

This is most evident in Hegel's treatment of evolution within his *Philosophy of Nature*. For Hegel, nature is "a system of stages," but these stages are demarcated by the development of the idea. "*Metamorphosis* pertains only to the Notion as such, since only *its* alteration is development." Hegel was thus driven by his idealist dialectic to deny the material evolution of nature, its emergence independent of human cognition. "A thinking consideration," he wrote, "must reject such nebulous, at bottom, sensuous ideas, as in particular the so-called *origination*, for example, of plants and animals from water, and then the *origination* of the more highly developed animal organisms from the lower, and so on."[28]

This idealist attempt to subsume the real world under the absolute idea created manifest absurdities—of a classical teleological variety. As Auguste Cornu has explained in his *Origins of Marxian Thought*, while "it might be relatively easy to establish a rational concatenation and dialectical order among concepts; it is already harder to do so in history, where the contingent and the accidental play a greater part; and by the time we come to the realm of nature, this assimilation of the real to the rational can be carried out only by extremely arbitrary procedures." Hence, the weakness of Hegel's *Philosophy of Nature* stemmed directly from his attempt to reduce natural phenomena to the dialectic of concepts. Hegel sought to account for nature's failure to realize the absolute idea by arguing that nature was the externalization or alienation of the idea in a form outside itself, that it was, in a sense, the negation of the idea. Alienated from reason, nature is subject to blind chance and blind necessity, reflecting change that is mechanical (minerals), unconscious (plants), and instinctive (animals), and which, unlike human activity, does not proceed from conscious, purposive will. Still, nature as part of a real that was rational, according to Hegel, conformed to the essential form of reason, and displayed a rational order, a kind of inner purposiveness, requiring only the spirit to make it whole.

But it was here that Feuerbach's critique was most devastating since it served to highlight this outlandish philosophy of nature, leaving the emperor without any clothes. It was precisely in his inability to develop a genuine naturalism, and the makeshift fashion in which he tried to subsume external nature (conceived mechanically) under the absolute idea, that Hegel's speculative philosophy—his dialectic—failed most spectacularly.[29]

In Marx's view, following Feuerbach, it is essential to posit the existence of an objective world and human beings as objective beings, that is, genuine realism and naturalism.

> To say that man is a *corporeal*, living, real, sensuous, objective being with natural powers means that he has *real, sensuous objects* as the objects of his being and of his vital expression, or that he can only *express* his life in real, sensuous objects…. *Hunger* is a natural *need*; it therefore requires a *nature* and an *object* outside itself in order to satisfy and still itself…. A being which does not have its nature outside itself is not a natural being and plays no part in the system of nature.[30]

For Marx, who by this time was trying to lay out a consistent naturalism, humanism, and materialism, "Man is directly a *natural being* … equipped with *natural powers*…. On the other hand, as a natural, corporeal, sensuous, objective being he is a *suffering*, conditioned and limited being, like animals and plants. That is to say, the *objects* of his drives exist outside him as *objects* independent of him." Nevertheless, human beings are to be distinguished from other living species in that these objects of their drive, that is, human needs, are transformed in the process of their realization in a distinctively human way in human history, which is the "true natural history" of humanity. Indeed, "only naturalism," Marx contends, "is capable of comprehending the process of world history."[31] Drawing, in the context of his critique of Hegel, on Epicurus' materialist-humanist argument, in which Epicurus had contended that "death is nothing to us," Marx argued that "*Nature* … taken abstractly, for itself, and fixed in its separation from man, is *nothing* for man." Our ideas about nature consist merely of "*abstractions* from *natural forms*."[32]

Marx's naturalistic materialism was evident in his contention that "*Sense perception* (see Feuerbach) must be the basis of all science. Only when science starts out from sense perception in the dual form of *sensuous* consciousness and *sensuous* need—i.e. only when science starts out from nature—is it *real* science." Not only that but history was for Marx a "real part of *natural* history…. Natural science will in time subsume the science of man just as the science of man will subsume natural science: there will be *one* science." Marx's critical realism was to be found in his recognition of the objectivity of humanity and the world (that is, its ontological basis), and his recognition of natural history and human history as interconnected. "The idea of *one* basis for life and another for *science* is from the very outset a lie." Natural science, he argued, has served to transform the human relation to nature in a practical way by altering industry itself, and thus has "prepared the conditions for human emancipation, however much its immediate effect was to complete the process of dehumanization."[33]

Feuerbach, Marx contended, was to be commended for breaking with the Hegelian system in three ways: first, for showing that Hegelian speculative philosophy, rather than superseding spiritualism, that is, theology, in the name of philosophy, had merely restored it in the end; second, for founding "*true materialism* and *real science* by making the social relation of 'man to man' the basic principle of his theory"; and, finally, for opposing Hegel's negation of the negation, which had represented the linking of "uncritical positivism and equally uncritical idealism" through what Hegel himself had called "revelation"—"the creation of nature as the mind's being."[34]

Having freed himself completely in this way, via Feuerbach, from Hegel's idealism—which despite his own early fascination with materialism and his consistent opposition to theological conceptions had nonetheless exerted its influence on him—Marx proceeded to reject all purely philosophical solutions to estrangement. Moreover, in Marx's perspective it was no longer possible to pretend to transcend the division between the objective and the non-objective—an issue that only arose when the relation to the world was posed theoretically rather than sensuously, and in terms of practice. Human beings were themselves objectively delimited, suffering beings, insofar as they found their objects outside of themselves and were finite. Nature could not therefore be seen anthropocentrically (or spiritually) "as mind's being." But human beings were not simply circumscribed by nature: as Epicurus had pointed out, they were capable of changing their relation to it through their inventions. The solution to the alienation of human beings from nature, Marx insisted, was to be discovered only in the realm of practice, in human history. The self-alienation of human beings both from human species-being and from nature, which constituted so much of human history, also found its necessary resolution, in that same human history, through the struggle to transcend this human self-alienation.

Association versus Political Economy

It is in the *Economic and Philosophical Manuscripts* that Marx first introduced his notion of "association" or the "associated producers," an idea that he derived from his critique of landed property, and that was to play a defining role in his conception of communism for the rest of his life. The abolition of the monopoly of private property in land, Marx argued, would be realized through "association," which, "when applied to the land,"

> retains the benefits of large landed property from an economic point of view and realizes for the first time the tendency inherent in the division of land, namely equality. At the same time association restores man's intimate links to the land in a rational way, no longer mediated by serfdom, lordship and an imbecile mystique of property. This is because the earth ceases to be an object of barter, and through free labor and free enjoyment once again becomes an authentic, personal property for man.[35]

The benefits of large-scale agriculture, Marx argued, had always been associated in the apologetics of the landed interests, with large landed property itself—"as if these advantages would not on the one hand attain their fullest degree of development and on the other hand become socially useful for the first time once property was abolished."[36]

Communism for Marx was nothing other than the positive abolition of private property, by means of association. Such positive communism "as fully developed naturalism, equals humanism, and as fully developed humanism, equals naturalism; it is the *genuine* resolution of the conflict between man and nature, and between man and man, the true resolution of the conflict between existence and being, between freedom and necessity, between individual and species." This human essence of nature and natural essence of humanity exists only for associated (fully social) beings. Society under communism, no longer alienated by the institution of private property and the accumulation of wealth as the driving force of industry, "is therefore the perfected unity in essence of man with nature, the true resurrection of nature, the realized naturalism of man and the realized humanism of nature." It is contrasted by Marx to a world of the "universal prostitution of the worker" and the "universal pollution" of the large cities—a world where "dead matter" in the form of money has come to dominate over human needs and self-development. The revolutionary knowledge of a world beyond capitalism, a world of "the realized naturalism of man and the realized humanism of nature"—constituting the essence of the historical process—is not to be had directly, according to Marx, but finds "both its empirical and its theoretical basis in the [alienated] movement of *private property* or, to be more exact, of the economy." Marx's naturalistic, humanistic vision is thus at the same time one of historical transcendence—the overcoming of an alienated world.[37]

Late in his life, Feuerbach, perhaps unbeknown to Marx, was to be a great admirer of the latter's *Capital*, which Feuerbach referred to in 1868 as Marx's "great critique of political economy." He was particularly impressed by what Marx's *Capital* had to say about the alienation of nature. To quote Feuerbach himself:

> Where people are crowded together, as, e.g., in the English factories and workers' housing, when one may just as well call such houses pigsties, where there isn't even enough oxygen in the air to go around,—one may refer here to the incontestable facts in the most interesting at the same time horrifying and rich work of K. Marx: "*Das Kapital*"—then there ... is no room left for morality ... and virtue is at best a monopoly of the factory owners, the capitalists.[38]

Since Feuerbach never saw Marx's *Economic and Philosophical Manuscripts*, he was not aware, in writing this, of the extent to which Marx had already developed his critique of the "universal pollution" of the large towns in the 1840s, as an outgrowth of his early encounter with Feuerbach's naturalistic materialism.

Although Marx in his later works was to repudiate the contemplative, ahistorical aspects of Feuerbach's philosophy, Feuerbach's naturalistic materialism continued to resonate within Marx's mature historical materialism. Further, in Feuerbach, as in Epicurus, Marx had found a critique of religion which was to become an integral part of his own developing materialist world-view.

CHAPTER 3

PARSON NATURALISTS

Near the end of his life, in his *Autobiography*, Charles Darwin made a startling acknowledgement—namely that the work of William Paley, the arch-natural theologian of the eighteenth and nineteenth centuries, had been one of the most important intellectual influences governing his early thinking. At Cambridge Darwin had been required for his BA examinations to read Paley's *Evidences of Christianity* (along with his *Principles of Moral and Political Philosophy*), which he learned practically by heart. The logical structure of the *Evidences* and Paley's later *Natural Theology*, he recalled, "gave me as much delight as did Euclid.... I did not at the time trouble myself about Paley's premises; and taking these on trust I was charmed and convinced by the long line of argumentation."[1]

What makes Darwin's statement here so important is that it was Paley's natural theology which was, at the time he was developing his own theory, the most influential argument from design for the existence of God. Darwin's own intellectual development, his materialism, and the formation of his evolutionary perspective, can therefore be seen to a considerable extent as a struggle against Paley. Indeed, this is how it was presented by Darwin himself, who wrote, from his mature perspective, that "the old argument of design in nature, as given by Paley, which formerly seemed to me so conclusive, fails, now that the law of natural selection has been discovered." But if it is true, as Darwin here acknowledges, that Paley's view had once seemed "conclusive" to him, then his own work can readily be seen as a more or less conscious struggle against an idealist, theological world-view. Indeed, Darwin scholars have frequently characterized Darwin's intellectual revolution as an attempt to transcend Paley—or at least to turn him on his head.[2]

All of this takes on a more concrete meaning within Darwin's own biography. Here it is important to recognize that Darwin, at the urging of his father, had originally perceived himself—once a career in medicine was ruled out—as destined for the clergy.[3] This did not necessarily conflict with his naturalistic studies since at the time it was an accepted practice for the clergy to engage in such studies, as part of the tradition of natural theology (commonly pursued by "parson naturalists"). It was in precisely this area that Paley's *Natural Theology: Or Evidences of the Existence and Attributes of the Deity, Collected from the Appearances of Nature* (1802) was preeminent.

Natural theology's reach at this time, it should be emphasized, extended far beyond issues of nature and theology, also encompassing the wider moral universe of the state and economy. Thus Thomas Malthus, a Protestant cleric and one of the early classical political economists—most famous for his *Essay on Population*, which was to play an important role in inspiring Darwin's theory of natural selection—was part of this same tradition of parsonic naturalism, adopting an outlook in theological matters that was essentially Paleyian (while Paley in turn adopted Malthus's population theory in his own *Natural Theology*). For Malthus, the Supreme Deity had through "the gracious designs of Providence ... ordained" that population should tend always to press on the means of subsistence.[4] In 1834 Malthus's follower the Reverend Thomas Chalmers was to attempt to merge Paley's natural theology with Malthusian political economy in the first of the *Bridgewater Treatises*—a series of eight treatises funded by a bequest from Francis Henry Egerton, the eighth Earl of Bridgewater, who died in 1829, and which constituted the greatest systematic attempt in the nineteenth century to create a natural theology that would dominate over all areas of intellectual endeavor.

Hence, Darwin's great intellectual breakthrough can be viewed against the background of the natural theology that preceded it. But not only the work of Darwin. Karl Marx too was to emerge as a strong critic of the parsonic naturalism of Thomas Malthus and Thomas Chalmers, and of the entire attempt to insert teleological principles into nature—and was to celebrate Darwin principally for his triumph over the teleological view of nature.

Natural Theology

If the Enlightenment, and more specifically the scientific revolution of the seventeenth and eighteenth centuries, had broken down the old scholastic world-view, with its teleological perspective, rooted in the scriptures and ancient Aristotelian philosophy, it cannot be said that the Enlightenment was unambiguously anti-religious or materialist. There were at the same time powerful attempts to reestablish religion within a general Enlightenment perspective—which, by reconnecting the worlds of nature, science, religion, the state, and the economy within a single teleology, also had the effect of reinforcing the established system of property and power. Thinkers like Boyle and Newton had sought to merge their atomism with a theological world-view. In Boyle's case this led to the development of a natural theology manifest in his *Disquisition About the Final Causes of Natural Things* (1688). Indeed, it was the tradition of natural theology, which rose to prominence in this period in the work of John Ray and Boyle, that was to go the furthest in reconnecting nature, science, religion, the state, and the economy, so as to resurrect a teleological view compatible with—if not a feudal universe—at least the system of landed property and industry that constituted early agrarian capitalism.

Natural theology was first developed by theologians in the late sixteenth and seventeenth centuries in order to establish God's existence through the study of nature (although the argument from design itself could be traced back to the Stoics in their reply to the Epicurean critique of religion—as depicted by Cicero in *The Nature of the Gods*). Bacon's definition of the subject in his *Advancement of Learning* was as follows: "Divine philosophy or Natural Theology ... is that knowledge or rudiment of knowledge concerning God which may be obtained by the contemplation of his creatures; which knowledge may be truly termed divine in respect of the object, and natural in respect of the light," that is, the source of enlightenment. Bacon gave little room in his philosophy for natural theology, however. Rather he warned against all arguments based on final causes, or teleology, and lauded the ancient materialists who had "removed God and Mind from the structure of things."[5]

Nevertheless, hundreds of treatises in natural theology were written in the seventeenth, eighteenth, and nineteenth centuries that relied on the very teleological arguments that Bacon had warned against. One of the leading naturalists in England in the seventeenth century, and one of the earliest of the parson naturalists, was Reverend John Ray (1627–1705), the author of *The Wisdom of God Manifested in the Works of Creation* (1691) and one of the founders along with Boyle of the Royal Society of London, which Newton soon joined. Ordained in 1660, Ray was never able to take up his chosen calling, as a result of his refusal to sign the anti-Puritan affidavit required of the clergy under Charles II. Instead he pursued naturalistic studies, albeit always with the object of displaying "god's wisdom as revealed by creation." In his attempt to describe what he called the "natural system," Ray was a forerunner of Linnaeus, Paley, and even Darwin.[6]

But Ray's *Wisdom of God* not only advanced naturalism; it was also the single most influential treatise in natural theology prior to Paley. Ray's treatise starts out with a critique of atheistic and materialist views, focusing in particular on what he called the "Atheistik Hypothesis of Epicurus and Democritus." He argued vehemently against Epicurus' theory of the declination of the atom (as presented by Lucretius), and insisted instead that the turbulent course of atoms was incapable of composing the ordered structure of the natural world as we know it. (Ray, who, along with his scientific colleagues, Robert Boyle and Isaac Newton, had been converted to a kind of atomism, did not reject the existence of atoms altogether, but rather any thoroughgoing materialism that might be thought of as arising from that.) "A wonder then it must needs be," Ray wrote, "that there should be any Man found so stupid and forsaken of Reason, as to persuade himself, that this most beautiful and adorn'd World was or could be produced by the fortuitous concourse of Atoms." Nor was Ray inclined to accept the views of Descartes, who, influenced by the ancient materialists, advanced the notion of matter and motion apart from ends—leaving to God only the act of original creation, and the establishment of a few governing laws.[7]

For Ray, the design of nature was a sign of the providence of God. In the "multitude of species" (he estimated the total number of species in the world to be "perchance more than 20,000"), as well as in the organic variety of what he was to call "plastik Nature or the Vital Principle," one could discover the complexity of God's design. If God introduced subordinate principles such as a plastic nature or vegetative soul to guide the development of the natural world, this vitalism (animated spirit) was itself a sign of the active role played by divine spirituality. "If the Works of *Nature* are better, more exact and perfect than the Works of *Art*, and *Art* effects nothing without Reason; neither can the Works of *Nature* be thought to be effected without Reason." For Ray, this was the reason of the divine Architect. In developing this argument, Ray resorted to teleology, argument from final causes, explanations as to the contrived character of nature at every point: the air was there to allow animals to breathe; vegetables and plants were endowed with "a Vegetative Soul"; the erect posture of human beings was expressly designed to support the head. For Ray, the fact that nature had been designed could be seen by drawing on the analogue of a clock. Just as the clock gave evidence of its designer, so did nature of its own supreme designer. The whole image of nature Ray provided was one of immutable being based on the blueprint of God.[8]

As John Greene has written in *The Death of Adam*, "The concept of Nature set forth in Ray's pages was to dominate the stuff of natural history for nearly two hundred years to come. Profoundly nonrevolutionary in character, it was to constitute the chief obstacle to the rise of evolutionary views."[9] Archdeacon Paley's *Natural Theology*, which appeared a little more than a century after Ray's *The Wisdom of God*, was closely related in its arguments to the latter, but was written in a way that reflected the somewhat different atmosphere of the late eighteenth and early nineteenth centuries. Hence, Paley's work read like a geometrical proof, and derived much of its significance from a merging of eighteenth-century utilitarianism with natural theology.

Nevertheless, the arguments were similar to those of Ray. The same emphasis is to be found on the argument from design, through which God was manifested in the works of his creation. Where Ray had pointed to a clock, Paley made the analogue of a watch and the notion of a watchmaker God the foundation of his natural theology. For Paley, it was obvious to anyone who looked that nothing so artfully contrived as a watch could possibly exist without a maker, yet nature was far more wonderful and intricate in its mechanism—so was this not true of nature as well? So far did he take the watch analogy in the opening chapter of his *Natural Theology* that he developed the fanciful image of a watch that begets other watches—a notion that is supposed to lead to nothing more than "admiration of the contrivance" and "the consummate skill of the contriver."[10]

Paley didn't stop with the watch metaphor but discussed in great detail some of the particular "contrivances" of nature and providence, in which he argued that design was evident. Thus he laid great emphasis on the marvels of the human eye and the geometric perfection of a beehive. Darwin, who was enormously impressed by this part of Paley's argument, found it necessary to discuss these same natural-historical manifestations in order to counter the teleological view of natural theology.

Perhaps the best example of the extraordinary lengths to which Paley took his argument for design is to be found in a statement that he made on the instinctive behavior behind a maternal bird's sitting on her eggs. "I never see a bird in that situation," he wrote, "but I recognise an invisible hand, detaining the contented prisoner from her fields and groves." Here Paley invoked Adam Smith's "invisible hand"—but this hand was the hand of God.[11]

Despite his detailed knowledge of biological conditions, Paley's natural-theological view was a static, mechanical one, divorced from all notions of time, of natural *history*. Paley's watch analogue referred only to the watch as a machine that constituted the centerpiece in a teleological argument on the benevolence of God; it was quite immaterial that such a watch ticked—reflecting ongoing and frequently irreversible changes in nature itself. There is no conception in his analysis of the arrow of time. It was precisely for this reason that Darwin's *The Origin of Species* was eventually to spell the defeat of Paley's watchmaker God vision of the universe.[12]

Natural Theology and Political Economy

Paley's eighteenth-century mixture of utilitarianism and natural theology, as developed in his *Principles of Moral and Political Philosophy* (1785), defended existing property relations even where they seemed unnatural, arbitrary, and unfair. Such property rights, he contended, even if conferred not by natural right but by civil authority, should be treated as inviolate, not open to seizure, since they should be viewed as if arising from "the appointment of heaven." "The world," Paley argued, "abounds with contrivances; and all contrivances which we are acquainted with are directed to beneficial purposes"—proving both "design" and "divine benevolence." Writing at a time, four years before the French Revolution, in which the relations of property seemed relatively stable and expediency always seemed on the side of the propertied, Paley confidently insisted that "Whatever is expedient is right."[13]

In Paley's *Principles of Moral and Political Philosophy* there are signs of a patriarchal view of society—of responsibility to the poor—which was later to disappear from his natural theology. The general happiness of society, he argued at this time, was increased along with an increase in population. Although population was ultimately limited by food supply and the fertility of the earth, there was at present abundant fertile land to accommodate increases in population. "The decay of population," he wrote, "is the greatest evil that a state can suffer; and the improvement of it the object which ought, in all countries, to be aimed at, in preference to every other political purpose whatsoever." Moreover, in these years prior to the French Revolution Paley still believed that some degree of public charity was natural. All things were once held in common among the "primitive Christians," he argued, but there were reasons for the division of property among mankind—necessary for the development of a large and mixed community—which were "ratified" by God. Yet the "Supreme Proprietor" had only consented to such separation of property on the basis that each person would be left with sufficient provision on which to live. It was here, Paley insisted, that the natural-theological grounds for public charity were to be found: the need of paupers to be free from absolute suffering—from indigence and distress—conformed to the will of God.[14]

Yet Paley's views in this regard were to change dramatically by the time he had authored his *Natural Theology*. In the late eighteenth and early nineteenth centuries the question of population became the peculiar province of parsonic naturalism, which in this way penetrated the discourse of classical political economy. In 1798 an anonymous work was published in England entitled *An Essay on the Principle of Population as it Effects the Future Improvement of Society; with Remarks on the Speculations of Mr. Godwin, M. Condorcet and Other Writers*. It consisted of a loosely printed, small octavo volume of 396 pages, containing around fifty thousand words. This anonymous work, as its title indicated, was principally aimed at countering the ideas of such influential thinkers as William Godwin in England and the Marquis de Condorcet in France, both of whom had argued in the general spirit of the Enlightenment, and in response to the French Revolution, that unending human progress was possible. In contrast, the author of the anonymous essay advanced the dismal view that the most fundamental principle guiding human society, governing the prospects for its future improvement, was the "principle of population," whereby human population, if unchecked, tended to increase at a geometrical rate (1, 2, 4, 8, 16, and so on), while food supply tended to increase only at an arithmetical rate (1, 2, 3, 4, 5, and so on). Since population growth could never for long exceed the growth of food, certain natural checks to the growth of population were necessary in order to maintain an equilibrium between population and the means of subsistence. But all of these natural checks, it was emphasized, were reducible to misery or vice, and thus constituted an insurmountable barrier to the indefinite improvement of society, and to all happy schemes promulgated by Enlightenment optimists.

Impressed by this treatise, Paley was to conclude his *Natural Theology* with warnings that "Mankind will in every country" always "*breed up* to a certain point of distress," which was part of the design imposed by the Deity. Hence, "population naturally treads upon the heels of improvement." Yet, such limits, if they can be spoken of at all, apply," he insisted, "only to provisions for animal wants," while moral needs are capable of unlimited fulfillment.[15]

The anonymous author of the *Essay on Population*, who had such an impact on Paley, was none other than Thomas Robert Malthus (1766–

1834). At the time that he wrote the first version of his *Essay* Malthus was a thirty-two-year-old English curate. He was later to emerge as one of the leading classical political economists. Malthus had come from a well-to-do family and was educated at Cambridge University. His father, David Malthus, was both a friend of David Hume and a friend and follower of Jean-Jacques Rousseau. It was as a result of a fireside dispute with his father over the work of the English Enlightenment utopian William Godwin that Malthus had first developed the idea for his essay on population.

After a few years as a country curate Malthus was appointed in 1805 to the faculty of the East India Company's college at Haileybury, where he occupied the first British professorship in political economy—a post that he filled until his death in 1834. He was known in his lifetime not only for his *Essay on the Principle of Population*, which was to go through six editions, but also for his *Principles of Political Economy*, published in 1820.

Malthus's *Essay on Population*, although a work of political economy, was equally a product of Malthus's parsonic naturalism. Adopting the standpoint of natural theology, Malthus insisted that "we should reason from nature up to nature's God and not presume to reason from God to nature." The Supreme Being, through the "gracious designs of Providence ... ordained that population should increase faster than food"—a general law that he argued produced "partial evil" but an "overbalance of good" in that it compelled further exertion in the form of human labor to obtain the means of obtaining subsistence. Even human inequality and distress could be justified on the grounds that "a uniform course of prosperity" was thought "rather to degrade than exalt the character." Thus hardship awakened "Christian virtues." Indeed, there was every reason, Malthus believed, to adapt to, rather than interfere with, "the high purpose of creation" as shown by the population principle. The impoverished head of household who has chosen to marry without the means of supporting a family, he insisted, "should be taught to know that the laws of nature, which are the laws of God, had doomed him and his family to starve for disobeying their repeated admonitions; that he had no claim of right on society for the smallest portion of food, beyond that which his labour would fairly purchase."[16]

Malthus frequently backed up such harsh admonitions with references to God. Nevertheless, he sought at all times—in conformity with natural theology—to demonstrate first that such principles as he had pointed to were laws of nature, which should only then be interpreted, once one had shown the natural expediency that lay behind them, as reflecting the "express commands of God"—the benign intent of the Creator to promote the general happiness. Malthus took his ethical philosophy at all times from the Paleyian view of utilitarianism, which argued that virtue lay in deriving from the materials of nature provided by the Creator the greatest happiness of the greatest number.[17]

From the first, Malthus's *Essay* thus had a very polemical intent derived from natural theology. The nature of his argument—its precise polemical purpose—shifted, however, in later editions of his work. The *Essay on Population* went through six editions in Malthus's lifetime (1798, 1803, 1806, 1807, 1817, and 1826). The 1803 edition was almost four times as large as the first edition while excluding large sections of the former. It also had a new title and represented a shift in argument. It was therefore in reality a new book. In the subsequent editions, after 1803, the changes in the text were relatively minor. Hence, the 1798 edition of his treatise is commonly known as the *First Essay* on population, and the 1803 edition (together with the editions of 1806, 1807, 1817, and 1826) is known as the *Second Essay*. In order to understand Malthus's overall argument, it is necessary to see how his position changed from the *First Essay* to the *Second Essay*.

The *First Essay*

The full title of the *First Essay*, as we have seen, was *An Essay on the Principle of Population as it Effects the Future Improvement of Society; with Remarks on the Speculations of Mr. Godwin, M. Condorcet and Other Writers.* As the title indicates, it was an attempt to intervene in a debate on the question of the future improvement of society. The specific controversy in question can be traced back to the publication in 1761 of a work entitled *Various Prospects of Mankind, Nature and Providence* by Robert Wallace, an Edinburgh minister. In his earlier writings Wallace had demonstrated that human population, if unchecked, tended to increase exponentially, doubling every few decades. In *Various Prospects* he went on to argue that while the creation of a "perfect government," organized on an egalitarian basis, was possible, it would be at best temporary, since under these circumstances "mankind would encrease so prodigiously, that the earth would at last be overstocked, and become unable to support its numerous inhabitants." Eventually, there would come a time "when our globe, by the most diligent culture, could not produce what was sufficient to nourish its numerous inhabitants." Wallace concluded that it would be preferable if the human vices, by reducing population pressures, should prevent the emergence of a government not compatible with the "circumstances of Mankind upon the Earth."[18]

The leading opponent of Wallace's argument was the English radical William Godwin (1756–1836), who enunciated an Enlightenment utopian argument for a more egalitarian society in his *Enquiry Concerning Political Justice and its Influence on Morals and Happiness*. First published in 1793, it was followed by a second edition in 1796 and a third edition in 1798. In answer to Wallace, who had claimed that excessive population would result eventually from any perfect government, Godwin contended that human population always tended toward equilibrium with its means of subsistence, so that population "will perhaps never be found, in the ordinary course of affairs, greatly to increase, beyond the facility of subsistence." For Godwin population tended to be regulated in human society in accordance with conditions of wealth and wages. "It is impossible where the price of labour is greatly reduced, and an added population threatens a still further reduction, that men should not be considerably under the influence of fear, respecting an early marriage, and a numerous family." He went on to observe that there were "various methods, by the practice of which population may be checked; by the exposing of children, as among the ancients, and, at this day, in China; by the art of procuring abortion, as it is said to subsist in the island of Ceylon ... or, lastly, by a systematical abstinence such as must be supposed, in some degree, to prevail in monasteries of either sex." But even without such extreme practices and institutions, "the encouragement or discouragement that arises from the general state of a community," Godwin insisted, "will probably be found to be all-powerful in its operation."[19]

If, however, it were not the case, as Godwin firmly believed, that population growth tends to be regulated by, and always remains in equilibrium with, the means of subsistence, the problems raised by Wallace only existed at "a great distance" since "three fourths of the habitable globe, are now uncultivated." Moreover, "the improvements to be made in cultivation, and the augmentations the earth is capable of receiving in the article of productiveness, cannot, as yet, be reduced to any limits of calculation.... The very globe that we inhabit, and the solar system, may, for any thing we know, be subject to decay." For Godwin, it was most rational under these circumstances to do what was possible to improve the conditions of human society and to promote equality and justice, with the hope that remedies (some of which could not even be conceived of at present) would be available in time for their practical application—

to meet such distant eventualities as the overstocking of the earth with human inhabitants or any other imaginable apocalyptic prospects, such as the decay of the globe.[20]

A similar position was taken by the Marquis de Condorcet (1743–1794) in his great work, first published in 1794, entitled *Sketch for a Historical Picture of the Progress of the Human Mind*. "Might there not ... come a moment," Condorcet asked in his contemplation of the future of humankind,

> when the number of people in the world finally exceeding the means of subsistence, there will in consequence ensue a continual diminution of happiness and population, a true retrogression, or at best an oscillation between good and bad? In societies that have reached this stage will not this oscillation be a perennial source of more or less periodic disaster? Will it not show that a point has been attained beyond which all further improvement is impossible?[21]

Condorcet's answer to this question was that "It is impossible to pronounce about the likelihood of an event that will occur only when the human species will have necessarily acquired a degree of knowledge of which we can have no inkling." "The progress of reason will have kept pace," it was to be hoped, "with that of the sciences," and hence if "the limit" to the means of subsistence of the earth should "one day arrive, nothing follows from it that is in the least alarming as far as either the happiness of the human race or its indefinite perfectibility is concerned." As human beings come to know that they "have a duty towards those who are not yet born," they will regulate human population accordingly "rather than foolishly to encumber the world with useless and wretched beings."[22]

Malthus's 1798 essay was devoted to countering these arguments advanced by Godwin and Condorcet, and to demonstrating that the population principle stood in the way of the very realization of a more egalitarian society. In doing so he took a much more extreme stance than the one earlier made famous by Wallace. Although the former had merely argued that population growth must eventually be checked by the limits of the earth as a whole, Malthus insisted that checks to population were *always* necessary, taking the form of "a strong and constantly operating check," since the population principle was about not the ultimate limits of the earth, but the more immediate limits of subsistence (food).[23] Like Godwin, Malthus argued that there was a tendency toward equilibrium between population and the means of subsistence. Nevertheless, he argued that population tended naturally, when unchecked, to increase at a geometrical rate, while food supply increased at best at an arithmetical rate.

Under these circumstances attention needed to be given to the actual checks that ensured that population stayed in equilibrium (apart from minor fluctuations) with the limited means of subsistence. These checks, Malthus argued, were all associated with vice and misery, taking such forms as promiscuity before marriage, which limited fecundity (a common assumption in Malthus's time), sickness, plagues—and ultimately, if all other checks fell short, the dreaded scourge of famine. Since such vice and misery were necessary at all times to keep population in line with subsistence, any future improvement of society, as envisioned by thinkers like Godwin and Condorcet, he contended, was impossible. "The principal argument of this *Essay,*" Malthus wrote—in a passage that was later to be underscored by Marx in his excerpts from Malthus's work—"only goes to prove the necessity of a class of proprietors, and a class of labourers."[24]

Malthus himself did not use the term "overpopulation" in advancing his argument—though it was used from the outset by his critics.[25] Natural checks on population were so effective, in Malthus's late-eighteenth-century perspective, that overpopulation in the sense of the eventual over-stocking of the globe with human inhabitants was not the thing to be feared. The problem of an "overcharged population" existed not at "a great distance" (as Godwin had said) but rather was *always* operative even at a time when most of the earth was uncultivated.[26] In response to Condorcet, Malthus wrote:

> M. Condorcet thinks that it [the arrival of a period when the world's popula-
> tion has reached the limits of subsistence] cannot possibly be applicable but at
> an era extremely distant. If the proportion between the natural increase of
> population and food which I have given be in any degree near the truth, it will
> appear, on the contrary, that the period when the number of men surpass their
> means of subsistence [in later editions this was changed to "easy means of subsist-
> ence"] has long since arrived, and that this necessary oscillation, this constantly
> subsisting cause of periodical misery, has existed ever since we have had any
> histories of mankind, does exist at present, and will for ever continue to exist,
> unless some decided change take place in the physical constitution of our nature.[27]

In the 1803 edition of his work on population he added: "Other persons besides Mr. Godwin have imagined that I looked to certain periods in the future when population would exceed the means of subsistence in a much greater degree than at present, and that the evils arising from the principle of population were rather in contemplation than in existence; but this is a total misconception of the argument."[28]

Rather than basing his argument on the notion that population growth and production would overwhelm the carrying capacity of the earth,

Malthus actually insisted that "No limits whatever are placed to the productions of the earth; they may increase for ever and be greater than any assignable quantity."[29] In his analysis, it was not the problem of carrying capacity as such that was the issue (as later interpretations of his doctrine mistakenly contended) but merely the natural rate of growth of population relative to the natural rate of growth of subsistence. And since the latter was ultimately forced to conform to the latter, despite its "overcharged" character, this could only point to the lawful necessity of the various natural checks on human population associated with misery and vice.

Relatively low or stagnant population growth was taken by Malthus as a sign of population pressing on the means of subsistence; while high population growth was a sign that a country was underpopulated. "In examining the principal states of modern Europe," he wrote, "we shall find that though they have increased very considerably in population since they were nations of shepherds, yet that at present their progress is but slow, and instead of doubling their numbers every twenty-five years they require three or four hundred years, or more, for that purpose."[30] Nothing else, in Malthus's terms, so clearly demonstrated the reality of a population that had reached the limits of subsistence.

Malthus agreed with the prevailing view, voiced by Godwin, Condorcet, and others, that population had always remained basically in equilibrium with the means of subsistence. Yet, what these previous thinkers had failed to recognize, he argued, was: (1) the *disproportion* that constantly existed between an "overcharged population" which naturally increased, if unchecked, at a geometrical rate, doubling as frequently as every twenty-five years, and the more limited growth in the means of subsistence, which increased only at an arithmetical rate, at best; and (2) the *mechanism* by which an equilibrium between population growth and the growth of the means of subsistence must be achieved under these circumstances—the existence of vice and misery as necessary checks on the rate of population growth.

But it was precisely with respect to the logical coherence of these two points, on which Malthus's distinct contribution rested, that he ran into trouble. There never was any question about the possibility of human population increasing at a geometrical rate. That point had been empirically established before Malthus wrote his essay. Malthus's original contribution with regard to the rates with which population and food could be expected to increase was thus entirely confined to his contention that the supply of food could only increase at an arithmetical rate. But the basis for this contention was extremely flimsy from the start. Malthus simply argued that population in North America had doubled in twenty-five years and that food supply could not be expected to increase at anything like this rate. But it was a fallacy to deduce from this, as he appeared to do, the notion that food could not increase at more than an arithmetical rate. As Edwin Cannan pointed out, even if the increase in food supply were such that it doubled only once in every fifty thousand years, it could still be said to be increasing by geometric progression. By saying that the means of subsistence could only increase at an arithmetical rate, Malthus was in fact saying that the periodic additions to average annual agricultural product could never possibly be increased.[31]

In effect, Malthus's argument involved a sleight of hand. After introducing his axiom on the means of subsistence by assuming for the sake of argument that food could only increase by a fixed amount—a proposition that appeared more reasonable since he set the maximum level of this fixed amount as equal to the entire amount of food currently produced—he then treated this as a settled conclusion without any further evidence. It thus became the basis for an insurmountable contradiction between an exponential rate of population increase (if unchecked) and a food supply which could never be expected to increase at an exponential rate. Needless to say, Malthus's own empirical data did not support this axiom. Thus in analyzing the rapid growth of population in North America, which had increased geometrically, he was forced to point to numbers that indicated that food supply had increased geometrically too. Faced with this obvious contradiction, he could merely contend (utilizing the metaphor of a reservoir) that the inhabitants were drawing down a fixed resource and that eventually these reserves would be exhausted and population increase would have to conform to the actual increase in food supply. But to admit this was to take a position that was closer to that of Wallace and Godwin (who had argued that the limits would not be fully in effect until the entire earth was under cultivation) rather than the position that Malthus himself had set out to establish.[32]

In short, Malthus had no evidence to support what Marx was to call his one original idea in his theory of population: the arithmetical ratio. He merely espoused it on the authoritative basis that it conformed to what, he claimed, any knowledgeable observer of the state of agriculture would be forced to admit (a view that was immediately criticized by the Scottish political economist, agronomist, and practicing farmer James Anderson, one of the leading authorities on agriculture of the age). Indeed, if there was a basis at all for Malthus's arithmetical ratio it could be found in his pre-Darwinian understanding of the natural world (as represented in his time by the work of thinkers like Carolus Linnaeus and William Paley), which assumed that there was only limited room for "improvement" in plant and animal species.[33]

Later on, it is true, it became common to see the so-called "law of diminishing returns from land" of classical economics as the basis for Malthus's arithmetical ratio. But that theory—outside the work of James Anderson, one of Malthus's most formidable opponents—did not exist even in nascent form before the end of the Napoleonic Wars and does not appear, except in vague suggestions in relation to Anderson's views, in any of the six editions of Malthus's *Essay*. It therefore cannot be seen as the foundation of Malthus's argument. As the great conservative economist and historian of economic thought Joseph Schumpeter was to remark, The "'law' of diminishing returns from land ... was entirely absent from Malthus's *Essay*."[34]

It was only in Malthus's final work on population published near the end of his life in 1830—known as *A Summary View of the Principle of Population*—that this contradiction is removed in part and the analysis comes to be rooted in the presumed diminishing returns to the land. But here Malthus goes overboard, arguing that once all of the best land is cultivated, "The rate of the increase of food would certainly have a greater resemblance to a decreasing geometrical ratio than an increasing one. The yearly increment of food would, at any rate, have a constant tendency to diminish, and the amount of increase of each successive ten years would probably be less than that of the preceding."[35]

Here it is important to understand that Malthus's *Essay on Population* appeared some four decades before the emergence of modern soil science in the work of Justus von Liebig and others. Hence, along with his great contemporary David Ricardo, Malthus saw the fertility of the soil as subject to only very limited improvement. Nor was soil degradation an issue, as Marx, following Liebig, was later to argue. For Malthus, the properties of the soil were not subject to historical change, but were simply "gifts of nature to man" and, as Ricardo said, "indestructible." Nor were natural limits to be found in the area of raw materials. Rather Malthus argued that raw materials, in contrast to food, "are in great plenty" and "a demand ... will not fail to create them in as great a quantity as they are wanted."[36]

The fact that Malthus offered no basis for his arithmetical ratio, as well as the admission that he was forced to make in the course of his argument that there were occasions in which food had increased geometrically to match a geometric rise in population (as in North America)—thereby falsifying his own thesis—did not pass by Malthus's contemporary critics, who were unsparing in their denunciations of his doctrine. In the *Second Essay* (1806 edition) Malthus therefore resorted to sheer bombast in place of argument. As he put it, "It has been said that I have written a quarto volume to prove that population increases in a geometrical, and food in an arithmetical ratio; but this is not quite true. The first of these propositions I considered as proved the moment the American increase was related, and the second proposition as soon as it was enunciated." As one of his contemporary critics responded, "These phrases, if they mean any thing, must mean that the geometrical ratio was admitted on very slight proofs, the arithmetical ratio was asserted on no evidence at all."[37]

Equally questionable on both logical and empirical grounds was Malthus's contention that all checks upon the natural tendency toward population growth were reducible to vice or misery. Malthus had—perhaps with the intention of downplaying a logical break in his argument—used two different schemes for describing the checks on population. In his more neutral scheme he wrote of "preventative" and "positive" checks on population. Preventative checks generally acted by restricting births, and positive checks by increasing deaths. Under preventative checks Malthus hinted at the possibility of moral restraint, which, however, he thought applicable only to the higher classes; while under positive checks he addressed the effects of poverty and what he called "a hand to mouth" existence, which he thought applied almost exclusively to the lower classes. He went on to argue, however, that these checks were in turn reducible to his second scheme, that is, checks arising from vice and misery (the former being mainly associated with the preventative check, the latter mainly with the positive check).[38]

Malthus, it should be noted, does not say what he means precisely by "vice," or how this would constitute a preventative check, but he does say that restraints upon marriage "are but too conspicuous in the consequent vices that are produced in almost every part of the world, vices that are continuously involving both sexes in inextricable unhappiness." Further, he mentions "vicious customs with respect to women" as constituting such a vice (along with the growth of great cities, luxury, and "unwholesome manufactures"). Later on he criticizes Condorcet for alluding "either to a promiscuous concubinage, which would prevent breeding, or to something else as unnatural" with respect to the adjustment of morals surrounding the intercourse of the sexes and the prevention of birth.[39] In his *Second Essay* Malthus refers to "the licentious spirit of rapine" with respect to "wandering tribes" subject to Russia as constituting a preventative check on population growth. He also points to "irregular connexions with women" or "illicit intercourse between the sexes" as forms of vice associated with preventative checks on population; at the same time alluding to "promiscuous intercourse to such a degree as to prevent the birth of children."[40] From all of this one may surmise that Malthus held to the characteristic eighteenth-century belief—explicitly stated by Godwin—that "the promiscuous intercourse of the sexes" itself constituted a preventative check on population. John Avery has remarked with regard to Condorcet that "Probably this belief was based on observation, since what are today considered to be minor venereal diseases would often produce sterility in Condorcet's time."[41]

Vice could also generate misery, leading to increases in mortality. But vice that led to misery was to be distinguished from misery proper in that it was the consequence of vicious actions. "The vices of mankind," Malthus proceeded to argue,

> are active and able ministers of depopulation. They are the precursors in the great army of destruction; and often finish the dreadful work themselves. But should they fail in this war of extermination, sickly seasons, epidemics, pestilence, and plague, advance in terrific array, and sweep off their thousands and ten thousands. Should success be still incomplete, gigantic inevitable famine stalks in the rear, and with one mighty blow levels the population with the food of the world.[42]

More important than the mere vices among "depopulating causes," for Malthus, then, was "the grinding law of necessity, misery, and the fear of misery," which fell disproportionately on the poor. And if war, sickly seasons, epidemics, and the plague—all of which were encouraged by food shortages and overcrowding—failed to do the job, "famine seems to be the last, the most dreadful resource of nature."[43]

In his discussion of those positive checks that were generally reducible to misery, Malthus claimed that this was in effect a natural result of poverty, and that to interfere with it in any way, as in the case of the Poor Laws of England, was to court bigger disasters such as famine, and the lowering of the condition of the upper classes. "All cannot share alike in the bounties of nature," he wrote. It thus "appeared that from the inevitable laws of our nature some human beings must suffer from want. These are the unhappy persons who, in the great lottery of life, have drawn a blank."[44]

Misery, since it was a vital check on an overcharged population, was both necessary and inevitable. All that was left was to criticize those no doubt well-intentioned but misguided individuals who failed to recognize this. The Poor Laws of England, "though they may have alleviated a little the intensity of individual misfortune ... have spread the general evil over a much larger surface," tending "to depress the general condition of the poor." By handing out shares to the less deserving poor, Malthus argued, society thereby reduced the shares of the more deserving poor. Hence, if the Poor Laws were to be maintained, they should where possible consist of workhouses, thereby mitigating their ill effects.[45]

All of those who proposed either the amelioration of the conditions of the poor or a future society characterized by more general improvement were, in Malthus's view, simply denying the inexorable necessity of vice and misery. The most that could be expected, if early marriage was encouraged, was a kind of stagnation, as in China, where a "forced" growth of population had taken place by dividing the land in relatively egalitarian fashion in extremely small portions, so that few absolutely starved in normal years—though this was interrupted by periodic famines—and where population growth was prevented by such unnatural methods as the "exposure" of infants.[46]

Nevertheless, once the class issue entered in this way, and it became apparent that Malthus was distinguishing between high and low equilibrium situations, with the former including a level of luxury for the privileged, the argument lost its quality as a "geometric proof." Implicit in Malthus's argument from the start was a class element, in which the situations of the rich and the poor were seen as widely divergent. Thus Malthus had virtually admitted in his argument on preventative causes that human beings—in the case of the upper classes—were capable of some moral restraint—a moral restraint that was frequently exercised in England through delayed marriages. This of course was amply supported by the marriage pattern of the upper classes in England.[47] To be sure, for Malthus such delayed marriages among the privileged were mainly the product of the effects of unequal and uncertain property relations, which made it virtually impossible for many gentlemen of the upper classes to marry and raise a family until they had obtained a secure living (Malthus himself at this time was still a country curate with only a meager living). Such motives to moral restraint would be less available to a society that was not built on the inequality of property. Nevertheless, it was impossible to ignore the fact that moral restraint was often apparent here. Hence, Malthus was eventually forced to concede in response to criticisms that some form of "moral restraint" (especially among the upper classes) was indeed possible—a moral restraint that he was nevertheless to define in extremely restrictive terms as "temporary or final abstinence from marriage on prudential considerations [usually having to do with property], with strict chastity during the single state." For Malthus, the operation of such narrowly defined moral restraint was "not very powerful."[48] Yet once this much was admitted, even in a tentative way, Malthus's argument as to the impossibility of future improvement fell to the ground.[49]

The *Second Essay*

For this reason, Malthus's *Second Essay*, in which he admitted to the possibility of moral restraint, is a very different work from the *First Essay*. Reflecting this, the title itself is changed to *An Essay on the Principle of Population; or a View of its Past and Present Effects on Human Happiness; With an Inquiry into Our Prospects Respecting the Future Removal or Mitigation of the Evils which it Occasions*. No more is there any reference in the title to the question of "the future improvement of society" or to Godwin or Condorcet. The main thrust of the *Second Essay* is an attack on the English Poor Laws, a theme which played only a subordinate role in the *First Essay*.

According to the great Malthus scholar Patricia James (editor of the variorum edition of Malthus's *Essay*), "it was the 1803 essay [the earliest edition of the *Second Essay*] which made the greatest impression on contemporary thought."[50] This was because of the severity of the attack on the poor to be found in that work. Although Malthus said in the preface to the *Second Essay* that he had "endeavoured to soften some of the harshest conclusions of the first essay," this related mainly to the introduction of the possibility of moral restraint (applicable to the upper classes). In relation to the poor, who, he believed, were incapable of such moral restraint, his essay was even harsher than before. And it is here, particularly in the 1803 edition, that the most notorious passages are to be found. Thus he wrote that, "With regard to illegitimate children, after the proper notice has been given, they should on no account whatever be allowed to have any claim to parish allowance.... The infant is, comparatively speaking, of no value to the society, as others will immediately supply its place."[51]

In the same callous vein, Malthus wrote the following:

A man who is born into a world already possessed, if he cannot get subsistence from his parents on whom he has a just demand, and if the society do not want his labour, has no claim of *right* to the smallest portion of food, and, in fact, has no business to be where he is. At nature's mighty feast there is no vacant cover for him. She tells him to be gone, and will quickly execute her own orders, if he do not work upon the compassion of some of her guests. If these guests get up and make room for him, other intruders immediately appear demanding the same favour.... The order and harmony of the feast is disturbed, the plenty that before reigned is changed into scarcity.... The guests learn too late their error, in counteracting those strict orders to all intruders, issued by the great mistress of the feast, who, wishing that all her guests should have plenty, and knowing that she could not provide for unlimited numbers, humanely refused to admit fresh comers when her table was already full.[52]

This infamous passage, like the one quoted before it, was removed from later editions of the *Essay*. But the basic idea that it reflected—the claim that the poor were not entitled to the smallest portion of relief, and that any attempt to invite them to the "mighty feast" against the will of its "mistress" (who represented the nature of natural theology) would only come to grief—remained the central ideological thrust of the *Second Essay* throughout its numerous editions. "We cannot," in the nature of things, Malthus wrote, "assist the poor, in any way, without enabling them to rear up to manhood a greater number of their children."[53]

Nowhere were Malthus's narrow parsonic values more evident than in his view of women's indiscretions. Thus he sought to justify the double standard imposed on women who were "driven out of society for an offence ["a breach of chastity" outside of marriage, especially if resulting in an illegitimate birth] which men commit nearly with impunity" on the grounds that it was "the most obvious and effectual method of preventing the frequent recurrence of a serious inconvenience to the community."[54]

In attacking the English Poor Laws Malthus argued that while limitations in the growth of food impeded the growth of population, society could exist under either low-equilibrium, relatively egalitarian conditions, as in China, where population had been "forced" to such an extent that virtually everyone was reduced to near starvation, or it could exist under high-equilibrium conditions, such as pertained in England, where the aristocracy, gentry, and middle class were able to enjoy nature's "mighty feast"—though only if the poor were kept away—and where checks short of universal famine (and short of such practices as "exposure of infants") kept population down. His greatest fear—which he helped to instill in the oligarchy of Britain—was that as a result of excessive population growth combined with egalitarian notions "the middle classes of society would ... be blended with the poor."[55]

The solution to the problem of the rural poor was simply to remove them from the land, to turn them into proletarians. Thus Malthus responded to the issue of hunger and destitution in Ireland by arguing in a letter to Ricardo in August 1817 that the first object should not be poor relief but rather the dispossession of the peasantry: "the land in Ireland is infinitely more populous than in England; and to give full effect to the natural resources of the country, a great part of the population should be swept from the soil into large manufacturing and commercial Towns."[56]

Malthus died in 1834, the year of the passage of the New Poor Law, which was viewed as the triumph of Malthusianism. This legislation was aimed at ensuring that workers and the poor would look on exploitation in the workplace and even the prospect of slow starvation as in many ways preferable to seeking relief through the Poor Laws. Underlying it lay the idea, as Marx observed with respect to Malthus's *Essay* in 1844, that "charity ... itself fostered social evils." The very poverty that "was formerly attributed to a *deficiency of charity* was now ascribed to the *superabundance of charity*."[57]

It is no wonder, then, that the English working-class radicals generally looked on Malthusianism as their greatest enemy. Fighting on their behalf, William Cobbett had leveled the fiery accusation of "Parson!" against Malthus in 1819—an accusation both of class domination and narrow-minded moralistic subservience to the doctrines of natural theology and the established Protestant church. In Cobbett's own words, "I have, during my life, detested many men; but never any one so much as you.... No assemblage of words can give an appropriate designation of you; and, therefore, as being the single word which best suits the character of such a man, I call you *Parson*, which amongst other meanings, includes that of Borough-monger Tool."[58]

Among the harsher implications of Malthus's argument from its inception was that since there were limits to the means of subsistence for maintaining workers in any given period, any attempt to raise wages in general would only result in a rise of prices for this limited stock of provisions—it could not procure for the workers a larger portion of the necessities of life.[59] This erroneous doctrine—which in its more sophisticated versions became known as the "wages fund doctrine"—was then used to argue that improvement in the general conditions of workers by such means as trade-union organization was impossible.[60]

Indeed, one reason for the hatred that Cobbett and working-class radicals directed against Malthus had to do with the fact that Malthus's influence was so pervasive that it was not simply confined to middle-class reformers like John Stuart Mill, but extended into the ranks of working-class thinkers and activists such as Francis Place. For Place, who adopted the Malthusian wages fund theory, birth control became a kind of substitute for class organization—though this was conceived by Place as being not in the interests of capital, but, in his misguided way, in the interests of the working class. The Malthusian ideology thus served from the first to disorganize the working-class opposition to capital.[61]

It was because of this ideological service for the prevailing interests that, as Joseph Schumpeter said, "the teaching of Malthus' *Essay* became firmly entrenched in the system of economic orthodoxy of the time in spite of the fact that it should have been, and in a sense was, recognized as fundamentally untenable or worthless by 1803 and that further reasons for so considering it were speedily forthcoming." With the acknowledgement of moral restraint as a factor, Malthus did not so much improve his theory, Schumpeter added, as carry out an "orderly retreat with the artillery lost."[62]

Thomas Chalmers and the *Bridgewater Treatises*

Malthus's most important early disciple was the natural theologian and Scottish divine Thomas Chalmers (1780–1847).[63] More than a mere Malthusian political economist, Chalmers was professor of divinity at the University of Edinburgh, a parish minister, and an influential preacher and ecclesiastical reformer within the Established Church of Scotland. He was eventually to emerge as the leader of the evangelical party in the schism that led to the emergence of the Scottish Free Church in 1843. Chalmers was the author, most notably, of *On the Power, Wisdom and Goodness of God as Manifested in the Adaptation of External Nature to the Moral and Intellectual Constitution of Man* (1834). This work was to be the first volume of the *Bridgewater Treatises*, a series of eight treatises commissioned by the Earl of Bridgewater, which, taken together, constituted the greatest, most concerted attempt to defend natural theology against materialist and evolutionary heresies in the decades immediately prior to the emergence of Darwin's *The Origin of Species*. Paley's "conception of natural theology," as intellectual historian Robert Young has observed, "was shown to be untenable in a period of growing scientific detail and finally collapsed in the *Bridgewater Treatises*, the *reductio ad absurdum* of parading the details of all the sciences *seriatim* as a cumulative series of proofs of the wisdom, goodness and benevolence of God."[64]

Chalmers began his Bridgewater treatise by attacking materialism and atheism. "The tendency of atheistical writers," he observed,

> is to reason exclusively on the laws of matter, and to overlook its dispositions. Could all the beauties and benefits of the astronomical system be referred to the single law of gravitation, it would greatly reduce the argument for a designing

cause.... If we but say of matter that it is furnished with such powers as make it subservient to many useful results, we keep back the strongest and most unassailable part of the argument for a God. It is greatly more pertinent and convincing to say of matter, that it is distributed into such parts as to ensure a right direction and a beneficial application for its powers. It is not so much in the establishment of certain laws for matter, that we discern the aims or the purposes of intelligence, as in certain dispositions of matter, that put it in the way of being usefully operated upon by the laws.[65]

In Chalmers's view it was divine intelligence, evident in nature, that produced "the evolution of this chaos" of matter, endowing it "with right properties." In making this argument he utilized all of the Paleyian examples, referring to the watchmaker God, the superiority of the eye in comparison with a planetarium, and so on.[66]

The "signature of a Deity" was visible for Chalmers not merely in external nature as such, but also in moral and intellectual life—and particularly in the realm of the economy: "Had a legislator of supreme wisdom and armed with despotic power been free to establish the best scheme for augmenting the wealth and the comforts of human society—he could have devised nothing more effectual than the existing constitution of property, which obtains so generally throughout the world." For Chalmers, the world of trade and the market was "one of the animate machines of human society" and the mark of the "intellect that devised and gave it birth." The Smithian invisible hand by which self-interest promoted the general good through the market was, he insisted, the mark of a "higher agent." Similarly, God had instilled in humanity a strong "possessory feeling" against which unnatural human interventions, such as the Poor Laws, strove in vein.[67]

Perhaps no other political economist so strongly emphasized what he called the "self-regulating" character of the market or the need to keep it free from all outside regulation. According to Chalmers, "capital ever suits itself, in the way that is best possible, to the circumstances of the country—so as to leave uncalled for, any economic regulation by the wisdom of man; and that precisely because of a previous moral and mental regulation by the wisdom of God." Indeed, "if any thing can demonstrate the hand of a righteous Deity in the nature and workings of ... the very peculiar mechanism of trade; it is in the healthful impulse given to all of its movement."[68] On these righteous grounds, therefore, the attack on the Poor Laws and the Malthusian doctrine of population could be defended:

> However obnoxious the modern doctrine of population, as expounded by Mr. Malthus, may have been, and still is, to weak and limited sentimentalists, it is the truth which of all others sheds the greatest brightness over the earthly

prospects of humanity—and this in spite of the hideous, the yet sustained out-
cry which has risen against it. This is a pure case of adaptation, between the
external nature of the world in which we live, and the moral nature of man,
its chief occupier.[69]

In his later work, *On Political Economy in Connexion with the Moral State
and the Moral Prospects of Society* (1853), Chalmers wrote endlessly, in
Malthusian terms, on the "extinction of pauperism" through the elimination of all Poor Laws and all systems of state charity as the principal goal
of Christian political economy. Such systems of poor relief, he claimed,
had so undermined land rents, and hence the cultivation of the land, that
they represented clear violations of Nature, inviting "a judgement from
Heaven, till at length" the earth refused to produce wealth and nourish-
ment to those who had "abandoned her."[70]

Chalmers not only defended Malthusian political economy; he also
attacked the uniformitarian geology of Charles Lyell (Darwin's close friend
and mentor) for attributing geological change to "mere laws of nature,"
excluding the role of God, and downplaying catastrophism and successive
creation.[71] In Chalmers, natural theology and political economy are
perfectly fused—albeit crudely—into a defense of the existing social and
religious order.

It was this wedding of political economy with Christian natural
theology—embodied in Paley, Malthus, and Chalmers—which made the
parson naturalists such a powerful threat, not only to the working class
but also to all prospects for the unification of human beings with nature.
Radical opposition to such views was therefore to play a crucial role
from the very beginning in the development of the materialist conception
of history by Marx and Engels.

CHAPTER 4

THE MATERIALIST
CONCEPTION OF HISTORY

"With the exception of the Venetian monk Ortes, an original and clever writer, most of the population theorists," Marx wrote in *Capital*, "are Protestant clerics ... Parson Wallace, Parson Townsend, Parson Malthus and his pupil, the arch-Parson Thomas Chalmers, to say nothing of the lesser reverend scribblers in this line.... With the entry of 'the principle of population' [into political economy] the hour of the Protestant parsons struck."[1] Like William Cobbett, who had leveled the accusation of "*Parson*" against Malthus in 1819, Marx was an adamant critic of the intrusion of natural theology, the idea of providence and narrow, parsonic morality, into the political economy that Malthus, above all, represented. The critique of Malthus, and of the entire conception of the relation of population to the land that his work symbolized, was one of the central themes of Marx's political economy from 1844 until his death in 1883. Indeed, the rise of historical materialism as a distinctive approach to society can be viewed partly through this lens. The critique of Malthus with respect to land and of Pierre Joseph Proudhon in relation to industry—along with the break with the contemplative materialism of Feuerbach—become defining moments in the development of both Marx's materialist conception of history and his materialist conception of nature.

The Critique of Malthus and the
Origins of Historical Materialism

It was in Friedrich Engels's "Outlines for a Critique of Political Economy" that the Marxist critique of Malthusianism was first launched. Marx and Engels had first met in Cologne at the end of 1842, while Marx was the editor of the *Rheinische Zeitung*. Engels, who was the son of a German textile manufacturer, was on his way to England to become a clerk in the big Manchester cotton-spinning firm of Ermen and Engels, in which his father was a partner. This first meeting of the two founders of historical materialism was a cool one—arising from conflicts within the Young Hegelian movement—and it was only with the publication of Engels's "Outlines of a Critique of Political Economy" in the *Deutsch–Französische Jahrbücher* of 1844, edited by Marx, and the meeting of Marx and Engels again in Paris that same year that they began their life-long collaboration.

For Engels, in his "Outlines," the essence of Malthus's population theory lay in its religious conception of nature. "The Malthusian theory," he wrote, was but "the economic expression of the religious dogma, concerning the contradiction of spirit and nature and the resulting corruption of both." But more than a religious dogma it was an attempt to merge Protestant theology (and parsonic naturalism) with the economic necessity of bourgeois society. "The immediate consequence of private property," for Engels, "was the split of production into two opposing sides—the natural and the human sides, the soil which without fertilization by man is dead and sterile, and human activity, whose first condition is that very soil."[2] Bourgeois society had removed the population increasingly from the land, thereby preparing the way for the more intensive exploitation of both the natural and the human sides of production:

> To make earth an object of huckstering—the earth which is our one and all, the first condition of our existence—was the last step toward making oneself an object of huckstering. It was and is to this very day an immorality surpassed only by the immorality of self-alienation. And the original appropriation—the monopolization of the earth by a few, the exclusion of the rest from that which is the condition of their life—yields nothing in immorality to the subsequent huckstering of the earth.[3]

In order to defend this system of exploitation of human beings and nature, while denying any possibility of improvement, there arose the Malthusian population theory—"the crudest most barbarous theory that ever existed, a system of despair" expressly designed to compel human beings to accept the harsh laws of political economy. Reviewing Malthus's theory in close detail, Engels was sharply critical of the inexorable nature of its premises, which saw the same population principle as equally applicable at all times and places without regard to historical conditions. For Malthus, as he pointed out, the population principle was seen as applying just as much to colonial settlements in Australia and the Americas as to densely populated Europe. Indeed, the logic of Malthus's argument was such that "the earth was already over-populated when only one man existed." Further, "the implications of this line of thought are that since it is just the poor who are the surplus, nothing should be done for them except to make their starvation as easy as possible, to convince them that it cannot be helped and that there is no other salvation for their whole class than keeping propagation down to the absolute minimum."[4]

In contrast, Engels argued that it was necessary to reject "the crazy assertion that the earth lacks the power to feed men"—an assertion that he described as "the pinnacle of Christian economics"—at a time when only a third of the earth was cultivated, and when the productivity of the cultivation on that third alone might be increased sixfold. Moreover, "even if Malthus were completely right," Engels insisted, it only pointed to the urgent necessity of a transition to socialism, which "would have to be undertaken on the spot," since it alone "makes possible that moral restraint of the propagative instinct which Malthus himself presents as the most effective and easiest remedy for over-population." In this sense, Malthusian theory "has been an absolutely necessary transition," which points to the "deepest degradation of man," his dependence on private property and on a system of competition which systematically wastes human beings.

Malthus's doctrine also underscored the fact that, for all of its emphasis at times on "nature" and even materialism, bourgeois economics was "essentially Christian." Here it is important to note once again the incomplete nature of the eighteenth-century materialist revolt against religion, which had simply "posited Nature instead of the Christian God as the Absolute facing Man." It was this rejection of revolutionary materialism in the form of a utilitarianism of natural expediency, behind which lurked the old religious idea of providence, that made Malthusianism so dangerous, and that made "every proposition" of economics, according to Engels, Christian in character.[5]

The ahistorical nature of the Malthusian doctrine was revealed in its rejection of the notion of improvement, except of course in the narrow sense of the necessity of enclosures. In other words, Malthusianism rejected any notion of rapid and continual progress in the human cultivation of the earth or in animal husbandry, as well as all possibilities for social advance. For Engels, this eighteenth-century pessimism about improvement had been largely overturned by the scientific progress that had occurred since, particularly in relation to the development of soil science, where he pointed to the revolutionary breakthroughs of such figures as Humphry Davy and Liebig. Although Malthus had insisted that population tended to grow at a geometrical rate when not checked, while food supply only grew arithmetically, Engels pointed out that the whole doctrine fell apart when it came to the key arithmetical proposition, for which there was little basis. Following an argument advanced three years earlier by the British utopian socialist Robert Owen (also a strong critic of Malthusianism), Engels insisted that science tended to increase geometrically along with population, revolutionizing agricultural production along with production in general, and thus enhancing the ability to generate food. At a time when the whole valley of the Mississippi was largely uncultivated, and the whole of Europe might be transplanted there, these further possibilities of science meant that there was no reason to despair. Hence, the notion that the condition of the poor was a product of natural law (rooted in divine providence) was simply false. As Owen had said, Malthus's mistake was to attribute problems of subsistence "to a deficiency in Nature's stores, and not to man's laws, in opposition to Nature's laws!"[6]

Marx, too, directed critical attacks on Malthusian theory as early as 1844. His primary concern was how the attack on the English Poor Laws (reflected in the New Poor Law of 1834) was rooted in the idea of an "*eternal law of nature* in accordance with Malthus's theory." In this theory "the progressive increase in pauperism" was not "the inevitable consequence of modern *industry*" but rather that of "the *English Poor Law*"; it was not the lack of charity but its superabundance that was at fault. In the new welfare system represented by the New Poor Law of 1834 the English state no longer sought to eradicate pauperism, which it had come to understand was the basis of its power, but rather dispensed "its administrative gifts only to *that* pauperism which is induced by despair to allow itself to be caught and incarcerated." In this framework Malthus's parsonic naturalism, which had been carried over into the realm of political economy, constituted the essential, irreducible foundation.[7]

"The most open declaration of war of the bourgeoisie upon the proletariat," Engels wrote in *The Condition of the Working Class in England in 1844* (1845), "is Malthus' Law of Population and the New Poor Law framed in accordance with it." As Engels explained,

> The Old Poor Law which rested on the Act of 1601 (the 43rd of Elizabeth) naïvely started from the notion that it is the duty of the parish to provide for the maintenance of the poor. Whoever had no work received relief, and the poor man regarded the parish as pledged to protect him from starvation. He demanded his weekly relief as his right, not as a favour, and this became, at last, too much for the bourgeoisie.

The Malthusian law of population was designed to remove any notion that the relief of the poor was a "right" and to make the point that the pauperized elements of society were "superfluous" and therefore not to be protected from starvation. Malthusianism as the "pet theory" of the bourgeoisie thus became a rationalization for the construction of work-houses or "Poor Law Bastilles," which, while not abandoning the Poor Laws, ensured that they conformed as much as possible with the harsh requirements of the Malthusian doctrine.[8]

It was in response to Malthus's theory that Engels developed the reserve army of labor or relative surplus population concept which was to be central to Marxian political economy. "Malthus ... was ... right, in his way," Engels argued, "in asserting that there is always a surplus population; that there are always too many people in the world; he is wrong only when he asserts that there are more people on hand than can be main-tained from the available means of subsistence." It was not overpopulation in relation to food supply but overpopulation in relation to employment that explained low wages and poverty. An "unemployed reserve army of workers" existed at all times within industry, a reserve army that was larger or smaller depending on the extent to which the state of the market encouraged employment. It is in this way that a "surplus population" emerges. But the workers, far from actually thinking of themselves as superfluous, "have taken it into their heads that they, with their busy hands, are necessary, and the rich capitalists, who do nothing," constitute "the surplus population."[9]

Hence, it was in opposition to Malthusianism that the notion of the proletariat first clearly emerges within Marxism. Factory workers in England lived at this time in squalor and were plagued by hunger and disease. In the first-hand description of English proletarian existence in his *Condition of the Working Class in England*, Engels walked the reader through whole areas of Manchester, street by street, describing what was to be seen and arguing that the living environments of working-class Manchester and bourgeois Manchester were two different worlds. The homes of the "upper bourgeoisie" of Manchester were to be found "in remoter villas with gardens in Chorlton and Ardwick, or on the breezy heights of Cheetham Hill, Broughton, and Pendleton, in free, wholesome country air, in fine, comfortable homes, passed once every half or quarter hour by omnibuses going into the city. And the finest part of the arrange-ment," Engels observed, "is this, that the members of the money aris-tocracy can take the shortest road through the middle of all the labouring districts to their places of business, without ever seeing that they are in the midst of the grimy misery that lurks to the right and the left."[10]

In surveying the conditions of the working class in the industrial towns, the young Engels was particularly concerned with environmental toxins.

Relying on the reports of physicians and factory inspectors and on his own personal observations, Engels provided a detailed analysis of public health conditions. Using demographic data compiled by public health officials, he pioneered in arguing that mortality rates were inversely related to social class, which could be seen most dramatically by examining specific sections of each city. The poorly ventilated houses of the workers, he argued, did not allow for adequate ventilation of toxic substances, and carbon gases from combustion and human breathing remained trapped inside. Since there was no system for the disposal of human and animal waste, these accumulated and decomposed in apartments, courtyards, and streets, producing severe air and water pollution. The high mortality from infectious diseases, such as tuberculosis (an airborne disease) and typhus (carried by lice), was the result, he argued, of overcrowding, bad sanitation, and insufficient ventilation.

Engels also described the skeletal deformities caused by rickets as a nutrition-related problem, even though the specific dietary deficiency associated with this, the lack of vitamin D, was not yet known. He provided accounts of occupational illnesses, including detailed descriptions of orthopedic disorders, eye disorders, lead poisoning, and black lung disease.[11]

Nevertheless, there were many defenders of the factory system. When physicians called before a factory investigation committee testified that exposure to sunlight was essential to the physical development of children, Andrew Ure, a leading exponent of the principles of manufacturing, replied indignantly that the gas lighting of the factory was an adequate substitute for the sun.[12]

Marx's own vision of the proletariat developed in opposition to the inhumanity of the likes of classical liberal political economists such as Malthus and Ure. With the estrangement of general human needs that characterizes capitalism, according to Marx, "Light, air, etc.—the simplest *animal* cleanliness—ceases to be a need for man.... The Irishman has only one need left—the need to *eat*, to eat *potatoes*, and, more precisely, to eat *rotten potatoes*, the worst kind of potatoes. But England and France already have a *little* Ireland in each of their industrial cities." The "universal pollution" that, according to Marx, characterized the large industrial towns was the living environment of the working class. The proletariat thus became a universal class exposed to "universal pollution" and universal suffering, a class threatened with the total loss of humanity, and one that could emancipate itself only through the total emancipation of humanity.[13]

The New Materialism

Marx's increasing attention to the class struggle, the conditions of the proletariat, and the analysis of bourgeois political economy (represented in its most inhumane form by Malthusianism) meant that Feuerbachian naturalism, with its abstract, static conception of nature, was no longer sufficient, and increasingly appeared to be a dead end that had to be transcended. In their "fight against positive religion," Engels was to recall many years later, "the main body of the most determined Young Hegelians" were "driven back to Anglo-French materialism." But this had generated a contradiction among the radical Hegelians since the Hegelian system had stood opposed to materialism, viewing nature as nothing more than the alienated existence of the absolute idea, "so to say, a degradation of the idea." Feuerbach "pulverized" this contradiction, setting "materialism on the throne again. Nature, exists independently of all philosophy. It is the foundation upon which we human beings, ourselves the products of nature, have grown up. Nothing exists outside nature and man, and the higher beings our religious fantasies have created are only the fantastic reflection of our own essence." Hence, "the spell was broken. The [Hegelian] 'system' was exploded and cast aside."[14]

But the abstract materialism of Feuerbach, for all of its importance as a refutation of the Hegelian system, was nevertheless static, ahistorical in its conception, and seemed to lead nowhere. Its humanism lacked a concept of transformative practice (praxis). For Marx, who was then bent on understanding the historical basis of the class struggle, particularly the struggle between bourgeoisie and proletariat, it seemed empty, a mere inversion of the Hegelian system, lacking any content of its own, and hence forever in the shadow of the great system that it had refuted. Moreover, as the Young Hegelian Max Stirner (1806–1856) demonstrated in his *The Ego and its Own* (1844), Feuerbach's abstract humanism, since it lacked any genuine grounding, could be dialectically superseded, transformed into mere egoism and nihilism, the doctrine that "nothing is more to me than myself," and hence that "all things are nothing to me."[15]

Feuerbach, as Marx and Engels insisted in *The German Ideology*, both accepted and at the same time misunderstood existing reality. Being for Feuerbach was the same as essence, a contradiction between the two was therefore not allowed. In dissolving religious alienation into material existence Feuerbach thus lost sight of real earthly alienation. He therefore failed to develop a practical materialism. Feuerbachian nature and the Feuerbachian essence were abstractions, even if in the name of materialism.

"The 'essence,' of the fish," Marx and Engels were to write in *The German Ideology*,

> is its "being," water.... The "essence" of the freshwater fish is the water of a river. But the latter ceases to be the "essence" of the fish and is no longer a suitable medium of existence as soon as the river is made to serve industry, as soon as it is polluted by dyes and other waste products and navigated by steamboats, or as soon as its water is diverted into canals where simple drainage can deprive the fish of its medium of existence.

All this pointed to the fact that the fish's being was in a sense alienated as a result of human praxis. All such contradictions, between being and essence, thus demanded purely practical solutions.[16]

Marx's break with Feuerbachian materialism was therefore inevitable. It was in the context of this break, moreover, that Marx's more practical materialism, his materialist conception of history, is articulated for the first time. The break occurred in the spring of 1845, when Marx, having been expelled from France at the request of the Prussian government, was living in Brussels. It was there that Marx wrote the *Theses on Feuerbach*, which were found forty years later by Engels in an old notebook. According to Marx,

> the chief defect of all previous materialism—that of Feuerbach included—is that things, reality, sensuousness are conceived only in the form of the *object*, or of *contemplation*, but not as *human sensuous activity*, *practice*, not subjectively. Hence it happened that the *active* side, in contradistinction to materialism, was set forth by idealism—but only abstractly, since, of course, idealism does not know real, sensuous activity as such.

Materialism had been cut off from all sense of history and practical human agency, which, ironically, was better captured, though in abstract form, by idealist philosophy. The goal of the new materialism, Marx argued, must therefore be to "grasp the significance of 'revolutionary,' of practical-critical activity." The goal was to take over the active side of life, human freedom, from idealism, while retaining a materialist basis.[17]

In criticizing "all previous materialism" for its contemplative character, Marx, it should be noted, was criticizing Epicurean materialism too. For the Epicureans, Marx contended, "divine leisure is put forward as the ideal of life instead of 'active life.'"[18] Yet Epicurean materialism was nevertheless more practical, that is, more self-consciously political in its rejection of both the Platonic ideal of the *polis* and the Hellenistic state, than the materialism of Feuerbach, as Marx was clearly aware. Indeed, Epicurus, as Marx's doctoral thesis had argued, had sought to bring an *active* side, emphasizing contingency and hence human freedom, to materialism—which prior to Epicurus had been simply a form of mechanistic determinism.

Feuerbach, Marx argued, forgot that religious self-alienation, the formation of a duplicate, imaginary, religious world superimposed on a real one beneath it, also means that the secular forms are characterized by self-cleavage and must be criticized and transcended. "Thus, for instance, once the earthly family is discovered to be the secret of the holy family, the former must then itself be criticised in theory and transformed in practice."[19] The critique of the religious basis of thought was only the first step in the direction of the critique of real earthly contradictions. Applying this principle to Marx's materialist conception of nature, we can say that for Marx the elimination of teleological conceptions of nature, that is, the self-alienation of human beings from nature as expressed in Christian theology, was simply the first step in the critique of the real, material alienation of human beings from nature within production.

Rejecting all essentialism (apart from the practical, transformative nature of humanity itself, as *Homo faber*), Marx argued that "the human essence is no abstraction inherent in each single individual. In its reality it is the *ensemble* of social relations."[20] In other words, human beings did not consist of some fixed, *human nature* residing in each individual, but rather, as he was to argue later, all history was nothing but the development (that is, self-development) of human nature through social intercourse.

Exhibiting the effects of Stirner's critique of Feuerbach, which had shown that Feuerbach's abstract concept of humanism was defenseless before a critique that reduced that humanism to mere egoism, Marx wrote that "the highest point attained by contemplative materialism, that is, materialism which does not comprehend sensuousness as practical activity, is the contemplation of single individuals in 'civil society.' The standpoint of the old materialism is '*civil* society'; the standpoint of the new is *human* society, or associated humanity." A practical materialism therefore recognized that "the coincidence of the changing of circumstances and of human activity can be conceived and rationally understood only as revolutionising practice.... The philosophers have only *interpreted* the world in various ways; the point, however, is to *change* it."[21]

One consequence of Marx's new, practical materialism, however, was that the focus of materialist thought shifted from nature to history, without denying the ontological priority of the former. It is true that Marx tended to see his materialist conception of history as rooted in a materialist conception of nature, which together constituted the realm of natural history (in its Baconian sense, which included human production). Nevertheless his emphasis in his social critique was overwhelmingly on the historical development of humanity and its alienated relation to nature, and not on nature's own wider evolution.

If the materialist conception of nature and the materialist conception of history remained integrated in Marx's practical materialism, it was primarily, as he was later to suggest in *The Poverty of Philosophy*, through the concept of *"mors immortalis"* (immortal death), which he drew from Lucretius, and which expressed the idea that, in Marx's words, the only eternal, immutable fact was "the abstraction of movement," that is, "absolutely pure mortality." Natural and social history represented transitory developmental processes; there were no eternal essences, divine forms or teleological principles beyond this mortal world.[22]

At no point was the realm of external nature simply ignored in Marx's analysis. Yet in developing historical materialism he tended to deal with nature only to the extent to which it was brought within human history, since nature untouched by human history was more and more difficult to find. The strength of his analysis in this regard lay in its emphasis on the quality of the interaction between humanity and nature, or what he was eventually to call the "metabolism" of humanity with nature: through production.

The "new materialism" of the *Theses on Feuerbach* was developed much more systematically in Marx and Engels's great work *The German Ideology* (1846), in which they broke with the purely contemplative materialism, naturalism, and humanism of Feuerbach, replacing it with a practical materialism, naturalism, and humanism, that is, the materialist conception of history. Although the break with Feuerbach was the central feature of this work (which was to remain unpublished in Marx's and Engels's lifetime), it also included extensive critiques of Stirner's philosophy of egoism—which Stirner had offered as the dialectical answer to Feuerbachian humanism—and of the so-called "true socialists," who had tried to construct a socialism based on the abstract humanism and naturalism of Feuerbach. The Young Hegelian method had consisted in showing that religion, God, teleology, were contained, successively, in each category of the world and therefore were refuted as merely religious. Stirner took this the furthest in making "man" or humanity itself a religious concept and discarding it. The human world, that is, humanism, was therefore to be discarded *en bloc.*[23] For Marx and Engels, all of these abstract, speculative views of "critical criticism" needed to be countered through the development of a materialist conception of history. "The premises from which we begin," they wrote, are not arbitrary ones, not dogmas, but real premises from which abstraction can only be made in the imagination. They are the real individuals, their activity and the material conditions of their life, both those which they find already existing and those produced by their activity. These premises can thus be verified in a purely empirical way.

The first premise of all human history is, of course, the existence of living human individuals. Thus the first fact to be established is the physical organisation of these individuals and their consequent relation to the rest of nature. Of course, we cannot here go either into the actual physical nature of man, or into the natural conditions in which man finds himself—geological, oro-hydrographical, climatic and so on. All historical writing must set out from these natural bases and their modification in the course of history through the action of men.

Men can be distinguished from animals by consciousness, by religion or anything else you like. They themselves begin to distinguish themselves from animals as soon as they begin to *produce* their means of subsistence, a step which is conditioned by their physical organisation. By producing their means of subsistence men are indirectly producing their material life.

The way in which men produce their means of subsistence depends first of all on the nature of the means of subsistence they actually find in existence and have to reproduce.

This mode of production must not be considered simply as being the reproduction of the physical existence of the individuals. Rather it is a definite form of activity of these individuals, a definite form of expressing their life, a definite *mode of life* on their part. As individuals express their life, so they are. What they are, therefore, coincides with their production, both with *what* they produce and with *how* they produce. Hence what individuals are depends on the material conditions of their production.

This production only makes its appearance with the *increase of population*. In its turn this presupposes the *intercourse* of individuals with one another. The form of intercourse is again determined by production.[24]

Marx and Engels thus started out from a materialist or realist ontology, in which nature, the material world, was a precondition of human existence, and production of the means of subsistence was a precondition of human life in all its manifold determinations and hence human society. The analysis that follows is built up from this point, tracing the development of different modes of production, associated with different phases in the development of the division of labor and class over the long course of human history, and especially with the great eras represented by ancient, feudal, and capitalist society.

Feuerbach, Marx and Engels argued, "posits 'Man' instead of 'real historical man.'" Similarly, he posits nature rather than natural history. He recognizes the existing disharmony between humanity and nature and hence the alienation of nature. But his response is forever to seek out the "true essence" of things, of nature, humanity. He does not see nature as changing along with history. "He does not see that the sensuous world around him is not a thing given direct from all eternity ... [but] an historical product, the result of the activity of a whole succession of generations."

For Marx and Engels what Bruno Bauer had called "the antitheses in nature and history" reflected a tendency to see nature and history as "two separate 'things,'" as if historical nature and natural history were not two sides of a single material reality. In contrast to this, it could be said that "the celebrated 'unity of man with nature' has always existed in industry.... Even ... 'pure' natural science is provided with an aim, as with its material, only through trade and industry, through the sensuous activity of men." On the one hand, nature cannot be reduced to human history. On the other hand, nature as we perceive it cannot be easily divorced from human history and the sensuous activity of human beings as it develops with a given division of labor, involving specific relations to nature. "In all this," they underscore, "the priority of external nature remains unassailed, and all this has no application to the original men produced by *generatio aequivoca* [spontaneous generation—that is, not by God]." Still, it remains true that "matter, nature, the nature that preceded human history, is not by any means the nature in which Feuerbach lives, it is nature which today no longer exists anywhere (except perhaps on a few Australian coral islands of recent origin) and which, therefore, does not exist for Feuerbach either." Ultimately, the deficiency of Feuerbach's materialism is its divorce from activity, practice, and history. "As far as Feuerbach is a materialist he does not deal with history, and as far as he considers history he is not a materialist. With him materialism and history diverge completely."[25]

In contrast Marx and Engels posit as

> the first premise of all human existence and, therefore, of all history ... that men must be in a position to live in order to be able to "make history." But life involves before everything else eating and drinking, housing, clothing, and various other things ["geological, hydrographical, etc. conditions"]. The first historical act is thus the production of the means to satisfy these needs, the production of material life itself. And indeed this is an historical act, a fundamental condition of all history, which today, as thousands of years ago, must daily and hourly be fulfilled merely in order to sustain human life.

It follows that "the production of life, both of one's own in labour and of fresh life in procreation ... appears as a twofold relation: on the one hand as a natural, on the other hand as a social relation."[26]

In discussing the historical evolution of the division of labor Marx and Engels not only presented their well-known discussion of tribal property, ancient communal or state property, feudal or estate property, and bourgeois private property, but also placed considerable emphasis from the outset on the historical emergence of the antagonism of town and country. As they explained, "the division of labour inside a nation leads at first to the separation of industrial and commercial from agricultural labour, and hence to the separation of *town and country* and to the conflict of their interests." If ancient society was based primarily on the town—here they have in mind the Greek *polis*—feudal society was based on the country. It is only under capitalism, however, that the antagonism of town and country becomes fully developed, "the most important division of material and mental labour." Indeed, "the contradiction between town and country," Marx and Engels write, "can only exist within the framework of private property. It is the most crass expression of the subjection of the individual under the division of labour, under a definite activity forced upon him—a subjection which makes one man into a restricted town-animal, another into a restricted country-animal, and daily creates anew the conflict between their interests." It was this division, Marx and Engels insisted, that resulted in the severance of the rural population from "all world intercourse, and consequently, from all culture." Hence, "the abolition of the contradiction between town and country is one of the first conditions of communal life."[27]

Historical Geology and Historical Geography

In order to understand the nature of the competitive system of bourgeois property, it was first necessary to understand that such competition represented an advanced stage of the division between town and country, and that competitors operated through a world market and hence were able to take advantage of favorable geographical, geological, and hydrological conditions.[28] In presenting their materialist conception of history in *The German Ideology* Marx and Engels thus argued that fundamental conditions of geology and geography were part of the conditions of production, without which industry, and indeed living nature (such as the growth of plants), could not exist.[29] Marx had considerable knowledge of the development of geological science. In the gymnasium in Trier he had studied under the then famous German geologist Johann Steininger (1794–1874), a follower of the great German geologist—often considered to be the "father of historical geology"—Abraham Gottlob Werner (1749–1817).

Later at Berlin University Marx had attended lectures in anthropology given by Heinrich Steffens (1773–1845), a natural philosopher (in the tradition of Friedrich Schelling) and also an important geologist and mineralogist, who had attended lectures by Werner.[30] Hegel had also relied extensively on the Wernerian theory of historical geology (a field which Werner himself had called "geognosy," formed from the Greek words for earth and knowledge) in his own *Philosophy of Nature*.[31]

It was Werner, as the present-day historian of geology Rachel Laudan has written, "who made the formation the central concept of historical geology." Before Werner, rocks had been classified by geologists mainly in terms of miners' criteria of method of working, extent, and location, or mineralogists' emphasis on constituent minerals. Werner, however, insisted, in his words, that the "essential differences" between rocks of various kinds were to be found in their "mode and time of formation." As Laudan explains, "By making temporal restriction a defining characteristic of formations, by making time of the essence, Werner defined formations as unique, historical entities, not as natural kinds."[32]

The basic postulates of Werner's more speculative theory of long-term geological succession were that the earth had early on been enveloped by a universal ocean and that the important rocks that made up the earth's crust arose as precipitates or sediments of that ocean. More important than this perhaps was the fact that Werner early on emphasized the immensity of geological time, referring to the time separating the present from when the earth had been covered in water as "perhaps 1,000,000 years" (a number which, while ridiculously small by what geologists were to argue a generation or two later, was nonetheless a significant departure from earlier Christian accounts). In his lectures on geognosy, he spoke of the history of the earth "in contrast to which written history is only a point in time." Werner's argument on deep time was receiving support from other quarters as well. Kant in his great work *Universal Natural History and Theory of the Heavens* (1755), which addressed the creation of the solar system, wrote that "there had mayhap flown past a series of millions of years and centuries, before the sphere of the formed nature in which we find ourselves, attained to the perfection which is now embodied in it." Kant went on to speak of infinite time and space, recognizing that this conformed to Epicurean assumptions. Cognizant of the "deep abyss of time" to which his own researches pointed, Werner, writing at the same time as Kant, felt no need to relate his geology to the biblical story of creation. Indeed, his approach was decidedly materialist, residing in the principle of geological succession.[33]

Werner's work had enormous influence on the development of geology throughout Europe. In the generation after Werner, historical geology came in to its own, rooted in the concept of "formations," which replaced mineral classes as the key in reconstructing the past. As the English geologist W.H. Fitton (1780–1861) explained, Werner, in developing the concept of formations, was "the first to draw the attention of geologists, explicitly, to the *order of succession* which the various natural families of rocks are found in general to present."[34] It was this aspect of Werner's thought which was to have an immense impact on the work of the great French paleontologist Georges Cuvier (1769–1832), who was drawn to the German tradition of geognosy, in developing his own comparative anatomy and theory of the earth, which he pursued by examining the fossil record. Cuvier too referred quite casually, as early as 1804, to even comparatively recent fossils found around Paris as "thousands of centuries" old—thereby pointing to a concept of geological time that stretched back over immense, virtually unimaginable distances.[35]

Nevertheless, Werner's reputation within the history of geology was very much harmed by the theological disputes that developed around geology during this period. Since Werner's wider speculative theory had suggested that minerals had originated as precipitates or sediments from a universal ocean, his approach was seized upon by many of those seeking to defend the biblical account of Noah's flood. Proponents of this idea within the geological debate became known as "Neptunists" and were opposed by the "Vulcanists," whose scientific moorings were to be found in the work of the English geologist James Hutton (1726–1797). This approach was opposed to catastrophism, and led toward the "uniformitarian" geology later to be associated with Charles Lyell. The fact that Werner himself had not taken the theological stance promoted by Neptunism, and that the main contribution of his theoretical approach lay in carefully setting out the groundwork for a historical geology that in itself—through its emphasis on the immensity of geological time—undermined the biblical account, was frequently lost in many later histories of geology (particularly in the English tradition).[36]

In his *Philosophy of Nature* Hegel explicitly rejected the Neptunist hypothesis while nonetheless arguing that "the great merit of *Werner*" was that his theory had drawn attention to the "sequence of formations" in the history of the earth. Indeed, in Hegel's view the principal contribution of geognosy (that is, the Wernerian tradition) was that, in treating "the constitution of the Earth," it established for the first time that "it has had a *history*, and that its condition is a result of successive changes. It bears the marks of a series of prodigious revolutions, which belong to a remote past." For Hegel, following Werner, this was a process occurring over the immensity of geological time: millions of years. Hegel emphasized the phenomenon of "generatio aequivoca," the spontaneous generation of life out of non-living matter, as occurring at some point back in geological time: "the generatio aequivoca is the general mode of vitalization manifested by sea and land," a "revolution out of chaos."[37] (Here Hegel seems to have adopted a more evolutionary conception of nature than was typical of his thought.[38])

Marx, who was introduced to these ideas through Steininger and Hegel, and probably Steffens (whose lectures on anthropology doubtless touched on the question of earth history), was not only well acquainted with the Wernerian theory, but situated himself within it—as a science of historical geology, not in terms of the Neptunist idea. He grasped the revolution in the conception of time and evolution that it represented. In his *Economic and Philosophical Manuscripts* Marx thus wrote that "the creation of the *earth* has received a mighty blow from *geognosy*—i.e., from the science which presents the formation of the earth, the development of the earth, as a process, as a self-generation. *Generatio aequivoca* is the only practical refutation of the theory of creation."[39] In writing about the "*generatio aequivoca*" later on in *The German Ideology*, Marx and Engels insisted on a materialist ontology in approaching the question of the origin of life on earth. In this respect Marx remained true to Epicurus' view, related by Lucretius, that "The name of mother has rightly been bestowed on the earth, since out of the earth everything is born."[40]

Valentino Gerratana has argued that the notion of *generatio aequivoca* had by the early nineteenth century been turned into a *general* philosophic concept transcending any *specific* philosophical context. "The function of the idea of *generatio aequivoca* is therefore equivalent in the writings of the young Marx to the idea of evolutionism itself." It meant no more than the hypothesis of a materialist origin of life (which science had not yet been able to establish). Later on in *Anti-Dühring* (1877–1878) Engels, in criticizing "the more presumptuous advocates of spontaneous generation" within science, was to insist that, "with regard to the origin of life ... up to the present, science is only able to say with certainty that it must have arisen as a result of chemical action."[41] At the same time, Engels responded even more harshly to those who, on a creationist basis, rejected the whole materialist inquiry that lay behind the general idea of spontaneous generation—as the answer to the riddle of existence.

Today, based on a vastly greater scientific understanding, the issue of the origin of life on earth can be addressed with much greater precision. The dominant approach is similar to these early more speculative views arising out of the materialist conception of nature, in the sense that life is seen as having originated out of inanimate matter, not as a result of divine creation. It is now possible, however, to explain why life, if it originated from lifeless matter, has not continued to do so. Thus as noted scientists Richard Levins and Richard Lewontin write,

> The law that all life arises from life was enacted only about a billion years ago. Life originally arose from inanimate matter, but that origination made its continued occurrence impossible, because living organisms consume the complex organic molecules needed to recreate life *de novo*. Moreover, the reducing atmosphere that existed before the beginning of life has been converted, by living organisms themselves, to one that is rich in reactive oxygen.

In Rachel Carson's eloquent words, "The conditions on the young earth produced life; life then at once modified the conditions of the earth, so that this single extraordinary act of spontaneous generation could not be repeated."[42]

Carson's reference to "spontaneous generation" here reflects the fact that when a materialist explanation of the origins of life was finally presented in the 1920s in what is known as the Oparin–Haldane hypothesis—developed independently by two materialist and Marxist thinkers, Alexander Oparin in the Soviet Union and J.B.S. Haldane in Britain—the argument was constructed in the form of explaining how, if "spontaneous generation" is known to be impossible, life could have nonetheless originated spontaneously from nature. The answer lay partly in biochemistry, partly in the analysis already provided by the Russian ecologist V.I. Vernadsky in his theory in *The Biosphere* (1926) that the atmosphere, as we know it, was produced by life itself. By producing the atmosphere, life had altered the conditions from those that had made "spontaneous generation" possible.[43]

Beyond historical geology, Marx was also heavily influenced by the development of historical geography. As a student at the University of Berlin he had attended lectures by the great idealist historical geographer Karl Ritter (1779–1859), whose historical and teleological approach to geographical study had been an important influence on Hegel in the composition of his *Lectures on the Philosophy of History*. Hegel adopted, in addition to Ritter's specific geographical approach to the relations between the various continents, also the latter's inverse correlation between civilization and the degree of dependence on nature.[44] Ritter famously argued that

> Distances, natural influences, natural productions even, yield always to the victorious march of man, and disappear before his tread; or, in other words, the human race is more and more freed from the forces of nature; man is more and more disenthralled from the dominion of the earth which he inhabits. The history of specific districts and entire continents confirms this.

Ritter's approach to the history of the earth was ultimately teleological, traceable to the divine hand of providence. But it was more immediately evolutionary in character in the sense of reflecting a long-term process of organic development traceable to mechanical causes.

Hence, for Ritter, the earth—the object of geography—had to be viewed historically (as well as teleologically). "The history of the Earth displays, in all the monuments of the past, that it has been subjected in every feature, in every division of itself, to ceaseless transformation," demonstrating that "it is capable of that organic development on which I lay so much stress."[45] There was thus a rational core in the mystical shell of Ritter's geography.

Ritter's most important impact on environmental thought was to occur through his influence on the great New England conservationist George Perkins Marsh, the author of *Man and Nature* (1864)—a work which Lewis Mumford called "the fountainhead of the conservation movement." Marsh was to say of his book that it was a "a little volume showing that whereas Ritter and Guyot [a Swiss follower of Ritter who emigrated to the U.S.] think the earth made man, man in fact made the earth."[46] What Marsh meant by this was that it was necessary to incorporate Ritter's essential critical insight (departing from his normal geological determinism) that the disenthrallment of human beings from nature which progressed with civilization meant that humanity was now a potent force in the transformation of the globe, with often devastating consequences (Marsh's book was subtitled *The Earth as Transformed by Human Action*).

Hence Ritter's historical insights were used by Marsh to turn him on his head, in order to raise the question of the human domination of the earth. A similar process occurred in Ritter's pupil, Marx, who in *The German Ideology*, as we have seen, pointed to the fact that the earth that had existed prior to the rise of humanity was now exceedingly difficult to find. Moreover, the nature of this human transformation of nature— and its sometimes devastating consequences—gradually emerged as a major consideration in Marx's thought.

Critique of the True Socialists

With this long historical view of both natural and human history Marx and Engels were impatient with the ahistorical, mystifying conceptions of nature and humanity to be found in the work of the "true socialists" of the mid-1840s—an intellectual trend that was quite widespread but disappeared with the revolutions of 1848. This was a group of German writers who mixed an abstract humanism and abstract naturalism with various concepts drawn from political economy, in order to generate a notion of "socialism" predicated on the idea of reestablishing true humanity and true nature, all the while ignoring the material bases of human development and natural history. The expression "true socialism" itself was taken over by Marx and Engels from Karl Grün, one of the leading representatives of this trend.

A principal target for Marx and Engels was an article called "Cornerstones of Socialism" written by Rudolph Matthäi. Treating Matthäi not as an important intellectual in himself but simply as a representative of the tradition of "true socialism," Marx and Engels quoted him as lamenting "Can man greet the earth once more as the *land* of his happiness? Does he once more *recognize* earth as his original home? Why then should he still keep life and happiness apart? Why does he not break down the last barrier which cleaves earthly life into two hostile halves?" Wishing to reconcile humanity with nature, this true socialist invited the reader to take a walk in the realm of "free nature" in order to bridge the alienation of human beings from nature by spiritual means afforded by nature itself:

> [G]ay flowers ... tall and stately oaks ... their satisfaction, their happiness lie in their life, their growth and their blossoming ... an infinite multitude of tiny creatures in the meadows ... forest birds ... a mettlesome troop of young horses ... I see [says "man"] that these creatures neither know nor desire any other happiness than that which lies for them in the expression and enjoyment of their lives. When night falls, my eyes behold a countless host of worlds which revolve about each other in infinite space according to eternal laws. I see in their revolutions a unity of life, movement and happiness.[47]

The true socialist saw discord as entering into this world through the hand of "man," that is abstract humanity. For Marx and Engels, the error of this form of "philosophic mystification" lay in the notion that humanity should be reunited with a "free nature." The true socialist sees the answer in issuing a "summons" to nature "presupposing that this dichotomy [this alienation] does not exist in nature" as well. And since "man" too is a "natural body," it should not exist for humanity either. To this Marx and Engels hold up the struggle for existence that takes place within nature, which can no longer be seen as pure. Writing in what two decades later would be called "Darwinian" language, they remark that "'Man' could also observe a great many other things in nature, e.g., the bitterest competition between plants and animals." Indeed, they go on to say that "Hobbes had much better reasons [than the true socialist] for invoking nature as a proof of his *bellum omnium contra omnes*, and Hegel, on whose construction our true socialist depends, for perceiving in nature the cleavage, the slovenly period of the Absolute Idea, and even calling the animal the concrete anguish of God."[48]

The true socialist, as represented by Matthäi, then moves on to argue that in order for society to be free it must be made over in the image of nature. Matthäi had said that, "Just as the individual plant demands soil, warmth and sun, air and rain for its growth, so that it may bear leaves, blossoms and fruit, man too *desires* to find in society the *conditions* for the all-round development and satisfaction of all his needs, inclinations and capacities." To which Marx and Engels reply—from the standpoint of the materialist conception of nature—that

> the plant does not "demand" of nature all the conditions of existence enumer-
> ated above; unless it finds them already present it never becomes a plant at all;
> it remains a grain of seed. Moreover, the state of the "leaves, blossoms and
> fruit" depends to a great extent on the "soil," the "warmth" and so on, the
> climatic and geological conditions of its growth. Far from "demanding" any-
> thing, the plant is seen to depend utterly upon the actual conditions of existence.

The true socialist uses this mystifying view of nature to produce a mystifying few of society; so that society, that is, the creation of "true socialism," is also a mere question of desire, and not an issue of the conditions of its existence.

In this response to true socialism Marx and Engels thus presented in extremely clear terms the relation between the materialist conception of nature and the materialist conception of history. In failing to distinguish between human beings as natural beings and social beings—and by failing to comprehend that labor, through which humanity transforms nature and its social relations, is the essence of the human historical process— the true socialist simply reduces human beings to "equality with every flea, every wisp of straw, every stone." For Marx and Engels, responding to the sentimental, spiritualistic naturalism of the true socialists, it is necessary to acknowledge "man's struggle with nature," which is part of human history. The true socialists eliminated the social distinctions separating human beings from animals, while also failing to comprehend the real human bases of the alienation from nature.[49]

This critique of true socialism, and its purely spiritual and sentimentalist approach to nature, akin to nature worship, helps us to understand the response of Marx and Engels to George Friedrich Daumer's *The Religion of the New Age* (1850), which they reviewed in 1850. Daumer (1800–1875) not only criticized Christianity; he also sought to reestablish religion and society along lines that were, according to Marx and Engels, "reactionary even in comparison with Christianity." What they called Daumer's "cult of nature" could be seen in the following lines from the latter:

> Nature holy, Mother sweet,
> In Thy footsteps place my feet.
> My baby hand to Thy hand clings,
> Hold me as in leading strings!

For Marx and Engels this was simply too much. Moreover, they pointed out that Daumer's "cult of nature" in his works had a superficial, a-historical character to it. Indeed, it could be seen—though they did not say this—as peddling some of the same stock in trade as natural theology. Thus Daumer's sentimental observations regarding nature in his work, as they demonstrated by quoting volume and page, were confined to

> the Sunday walks of an inhabitant of a small provincial town who childishly wonders at the cuckoo laying its eggs in another bird's nest, at tears being designed to keep the surface of its eyes moist, and so on, and finally trembles with reverence as he recites Klopstock's *Ode to Spring* to his children. There is no question, of course, of modern sciences, which, with modern industry, have revolutionized the whole of nature and put an end to man's childish attitude towards nature.... But instead we get mysterious hints and astonished ... notions about Nostradamus's prophesies, and second sight in Scotsmen and animal magnetism. For the rest, it would be desirable that Bavaria's sluggish peasant economy, the ground on which priests and Daumers likewise grow, should at last be ploughed up by modern cultivation and modern machines.[50]

For Marx and Engels, reactionary sentimentalism about nature which sought to reestablish old feudal relations of hierarchy, while denying changing material conditions, were to be rejected. Better for the peasants that their relation to the land be transformed by more "modern" relations of production. Far from indicating a lack of sympathy for peasants or "the land," their dismissal here was simply a rejection of a reactionary relation to both. It was in this same year that Engels wrote his great work *The*

Peasant War in Germany (1850), which glorified the revolutionary peasantry of the sixteenth century and its struggle under the leadership of Thomas Müntzer to break with private property and construct a new communal relation to the land.

The Mechanistic "Prometheanism" of Proudhon

Marx was acquainted with the writings of French socialists as early as 1842 when he referred to the work of both Charles Fourier (1772–1837) and Pierre Joseph Proudhon (1809–1865) in an article for the *Rheinische Zeitung*. Fourier provided important insights in such areas as the condition of women, the degradation of nature, and the nature of associated labor. For Fourier, "the extension of privileges to women is the general principle of all social progress." On nature he wrote: "How our descendants will curse civilisation on seeing so many mountains despoiled and laid bare, like those in the South of France!" In his "associative regime" Fourier foresaw an increase in the catch of fish by a factor of twenty in ordinary years, "if an agreement could be made to fish only at the proper times, the quantity to be regulated by the requirements of reproduction, and if one-fourth of the time expended upon ruining the rivers were devoted to hunting the otter." Fourier, like the British utopian socialist Robert Owen, sought to address population issues through the dispersal of the population—in opposition to the increasing concentration of population in large urban centers in bourgeois society, accompanied by the depopulation of the countryside.[51]

But it was Proudhon who was to have a much larger influence—both positive and negative—on Marx's thought. Later followers of Proudhon have tended to be most influenced by his earlier work *What is Property?* (1840)—a work best known for its answer "It is theft." It was here that Proudhon displayed the anarchistic bent of his thought. Marx too was vastly impressed by this work. In his earliest article on communism, writing for the *Rheinische Zeitung* in 1842, Marx referred to "the sharp-witted work by Proudhon," which, along with other lesser theoretical works along similar lines, "cannot be criticised on the basis of superficial flashes of thought, but only after long and profound study."[52]

In *What is Property?* Proudhon had developed a theme that was later to become central to Marx's work: namely, the idea that the addition of labor to land or raw materials in the course of production did not justify (as in the Lockean theory of natural property right) private property in land, and the exclusion of the majority of the population from what ought to remain a communal relation to the earth. Writing on the state's selling of forests and other lands rightfully belonging to the whole population, Proudhon observed (in terms that were later to be echoed by Marx's critique in *Capital*) that,

> Even if the nation were proprietor, can the generation of today dispossess the generation of tomorrow? The people possess by title of usufruct; the government rules, superintends, protects them, and passes acts of distributive justice. If the nation also makes concessions of land, it concedes only their use; it has no right to sell it or to alienate them in any way whatsoever. Not being a proprietor, how can it alienate property? ... Destroy the land or (what is the same thing) sell it; and you not only alienate one, two, or more crops, but you annihilate all the products that you could derive from it—you and your children and your children's children.[53]

Marx and Engels continued to offer their highest praise for *What is Property?* in *The Holy Family*, saying that "Proudhon makes a critical investigation—the first resolute, ruthless, and at the same time scientific investigation—of the basis of political economy, *private property*. This is the great scientific advance he has made, an advance which revolutionises political economy and for the first time makes a real science of political economy possible."[54]

Only two years later, however, Marx was to respond quite differently to a later work by Proudhon. Since 1843 Marx had been studying British political economy at a relentless pace. The impact of these studies was already apparent in the *Economic and Philosophical Manuscripts*, *The Holy Family*, and *The German Ideology*. But it was *The Poverty of Philosophy* (1847) which was to be the first work by Marx that was concerned more with economics than philosophy. Ironically, this took the form of a critique of Proudhon's *System of Economical Contradictions: Or, The Philosophy of Misery* (1846).

The *System of Economical Contradictions* was an entirely different kind of work from *What is Property?* Better known by its subtitle *The Philosophy of Misery*, it constituted a peculiar mixture of an attempted critique of political economy, on the one hand, and an attempt to make bourgeois society more social, on the other—all wrapped up in allegories drawn from antiquity and teleological references to providence. For Marx it came to exemplify what he and Engels were to call in *The Communist Manifesto* "bourgeois socialism," which they defined as an attempt to construct bourgeois society without its miseries, and without the proletariat—or at least without the opposition of the proletarian.[55]

The *System of Economical Contradictions* opened and closed (in its first volume) with the concept of providence, whereby humanity was "assimilated to the absolute, implying identity of the laws of nature and the laws of reason." The "hypothesis of God" in a civilization that ends up denying God, Proudhon writes in an ironic tone, was necessary so that the providential nature of history could be understood. Just as God as the effective cause of providence cannot be affirmed by reason, so humanism, "which amounts to affirming, in social economy communism, in philosophy mysticism and the status quo," amounts to the development of the idea of providence (this time with humanity as its effective cause), which is nothing but a "religious restoration"—which likewise cannot be affirmed by reason. What we are left with, according to Proudhon, is a notion of providence, in the sense of order, progress, destiny—"a secret relation of our soul, and through it of entire nature, with the infinite."[56]

Within this peculiar, philosophical frame Proudhon sought to develop his "philosophy of poverty," which began with concepts of value and went on to examine such phenomena as the division of labor, machinery, competition, and monopoly. In order to explain his economic views Proudhon decided to depict society and to symbolize human activity by personifying both in the name of "Prometheus." "Prometheus, according to the fable," he writes, "is the symbol of human activity. Prometheus steals the fire from heaven and invents the early arts; Prometheus foresees the future, and aspires to equality with Jupiter; Prometheus is God. Then let us call society Prometheus." For Proudhon "Promethus ... extends his conquests over Nature." He learns that "justice is simply the proportionality of values." Indeed,

> Prometheus knows that such a product costs an hour's labor, such another a day's, a week's, a year's; he knows at the same time that all these products, arranged according to their cost, form the progression of wealth. First, then, he will assure his existence by providing himself with the least costly, and consequently most necessary, things; then, as fast as his position becomes secure, he will look forward to articles of luxury, proceeding always, if he is wise, according to the natural position of each article in the scale of prices.[57]

Hence, society, or "Prometheus," recognized that, according to "the law of proportion," commodities ranged in price from the cheapest goods, which were the basic necessities of life, to the most expensive, which were the luxury goods. This was because "society produces first *the least costly, and consequently most necessary things.*" The industries which were the simplest and involved the least costs arose with the beginning of civilization: "*gathering, pasturage, hunting, and fishing, which were followed long afterwards by agriculture*" (all forms of "extractive industry"). More advanced industries could only develop with further advances in productivity, the model of which was to be found in these, the simplest industries. For Proudhon, the determination of value/wealth was simply the proportionate distribution of costs determined by labor time. Productivity increases therefore when "Promethus [in whom the concepts of God, labor and proprietor are dissolved] finds a way of producing in one day as much of a certain object as he formerly produced in ten." Such innovations, Proudhon suggests, begin with the extractive industries, which are responsible for the development of the calendar and the manufacture of clocks and watches.[58]

Proudhon goes on to argue in myth-laden and biblical language that on the first day of creation "Promethus" emerges "from the womb of Nature" and begins to work; on the second day he discovers the division of labor; and on the third Prometheus "invents machinery, discovers new uses in things, new forces in Nature."[59] The goal of society, understood in such "Promethean" terms, is to create the greatest economic value and variety for society and to realize this proportionately for each individual according to the just distribution of economic rewards in accordance with labor time. This is, for Proudhon, the socialization of labor, which can be built on the foundations of the existing society. "Wherever labor has not been socialized ... there is irregularity and dishonesty in exchange" and society is inharmonious. Providence, represented not by God, but by Prometheus (who is both God and not-god, that is, alienated humanity, bourgeois and proletariat), points to a law of proportion that leads towards a more harmonious condition.[60]

For Proudhon, the essence of the antagonism between proletariat and society lay simply in the division of labor, which appeared to prevent a harmonious development. The problem then became one of demonstrating "the synthesis which, retaining the responsibility, the personality, in short, the specialty of the laborer, will unite extreme division and the greatest variety in one complex and harmonious whole." The answer was machinery, the embodiment of Proudhon's mechanistic Prometheanism, the key to progress and providence. "Every machine," he wrote,

> may be defined as a summary of several operations, a simplification of powers, a condensation of labor, a reduction of costs. In all these respects machinery is the counterpart of division. Therefore through machinery will come a restoration of the *parcellaire* laborer, a decrease of toil for the workman, a fall in the price of his product, a movement in the relation of values, progress towards new discoveries, advancement of the general welfare.

Hence, through machinery, "Prometheus, like Neptune, attains in three strides the confines of the world."[61]

This same tendency to discover harmony in the socialization of existing economic forms was to be found in Proudhon's analysis of rent, in which he argued, based on a muddled discussion of Ricardian rent theory, that it had become necessary at this point in development

> to *bind man more closely to nature.* Now rent was the price of this new contract.... In essence and by destination, then, rent is an instrument of distributive justice.... Rent, or rather property, has broken down agricultural egoism and created a solidarity that no power, no partition of the land could have brought into being.... The moral effect of property being secured, at present what remains to be done is to distribute the rent.[62]

For Marx, these ideas of the later Proudhon represented a direct theoretical challenge to the budding socialist movement and required a full-scale critique. In *The Poverty of Philosophy* Marx contested Proudhon's entire *System of Economical Contradictions* and in the context expanded much more fully than hitherto his own developing critique of political economy and materialist conception of history. Marx argued that Proudhon, rather than explaining the historical genesis of social relations, by recognizing that human beings are "actors and authors of their own drama," and that history is in this sense "profane," instead had recourse to reified notions: immutable laws and eternal principles such as his references to the laws of proportion, Prometheus (a "queer character," completely divorced from the original myth but representing Proudhon's own mythology), and above all providence. Proudhon's "way of explaining things," Marx writes (referring to Prometheus' creation of the social world in three biblical days), "savours both of Greek and of Hebrew, it is at once mystical and allegorical." Later, in the *Grundrisse*, Marx was to make this criticism even more explicit, by explaining that nothing was more convenient for a thinker like Proudhon than "to give a historico-philosophic account of the source of an economic relation, of whose historic origins he is ignorant, by inventing the myth that Adam or Prometheus stumbled on the idea ready-made, and then it was adopted, etc." Such commonplace thinking was in fact ahistorical since it ignored all historical *development* and hence historical specificity.[63] Mechanistic Prometheanism of this sort was therefore a form of reification (the translation of real human relations into relations between things) and hence a form of historical forgetting that reinforced the status quo.

In *The Poverty of Philosophy* Marx attacked Proudhon's whole emphasis on providence, arguing that "Providence, providential aim, this is the great word used today to explain the movement of history. In fact, this word explains nothing. It is at most a rhetorical form, one of the various ways of paraphrasing facts." If one were to say that the "providential aim of the institution of landed property in Scotland was to have men driven out by sheep," one could capture the form and substance of such "providential history." And yet behind the mere word "providence," Marx argued, lay a whole history of the expansion of landed property, the production of wool, arable land turned into pasturage, the abolition of small estates, the enclosures, the forcible removal of the peasants from the land—in fact, the real, material substance and course of history. In placing providence at the center of his analysis, Proudhon, Marx argued, despite his irreverent comments on God, essentially adopted a kind of theological position, or, in other words, had invented a teleological approach to nature and society.[64]

Marx was particularly critical of Proudhon's mechanistic Prometheanism, his derivation of machinery directly from the division of labor—and the treatment of this as the working out of a "providential aim." The "new Prometheus" of Proudhon is a god-like image that hides the purely metaphysical view of machinery offered by Proudhon, which detaches it from social relations of production and exploitation, and sees it following its own technological logic. Rejecting Proudhon's notion that machinery is "the synthesis," the solution to the division of labor, Marx goes into a lengthy and detailed account of the historical origins of machinery and its relation to the division of labor (including "the international division of labor"), the market, production, exploitation, and the degradation of the worker. "M. Proudhon has so little understood the problem of the division of labor," Marx wrote in a letter to P.V. Annenkov (December 28, 1846), "that he never even mentions the separation of town and country, which took place in Germany, for instance, from the ninth to the twelfth century." For Marx, Proudhon's fetishistic approach to machinery, which gives it a reified "Promethean" character, and discards its historical origins and conditions, only produces a false, mechanistic teleology, characteristic of the worst of bourgeois industrial ideology. "Nothing is more absurd," Marx writes, "than to see in machinery the *antithesis* of the division of labour, the *synthesis* restoring unity to divided labour."[65]

Social relations, technology, and ideas, in Marx's view, were constantly changing, and could only be viewed as fixed forms, through a process of reification in which their historical roots were forgotten. Ideas themselves, he wrote, "are as little eternal as the relations they express. They are *historical and transitory products.* There is a continual movement of growth in productive forces, of destruction in social relations, of formation in ideas; the only immutable thing is the abstraction of movement—*mors immortalis* [immortal death—Lucretius]."[66]

Marx also provided an extended critique of Proudhon's view that society produces its most basic needs first since these are the least costly and only then turns to the more costly luxury goods. In contrast to Proudhon, Marx argued that the price of manufactured goods has tended to fall while that of agricultural goods has risen—when compared to the Middle Ages. "In our age, the superfluous is easier to produce than the necessary." For Marx, the production and use of products was conditioned by social production, which was ultimately based in class antagonism. Cotton, potatoes, and spirits are the most commonly used objects; but potatoes have "engendered scrofula"; cotton has replaced wool and flax, although the latter are of "greater utility"; and, finally, spirits are produced in preference to beer and wine, though the much more poisonous character of the former is recognized. "Why are cotton, potatoes and spirits the pivots of bourgeois society? Because the least amount of labor is needed to produce them, and, consequently, they have the lowest price.... In a society founded on *poverty* the poorest products have the fatal prerogative of being used by the greatest number."[67]

Marx was no less critical when it came to Proudhon's notion that rent is a means of "binding man to nature." He wrote:

> Rent has so completely divorced the landed proprietor from the soil, from nature, that he has no need even to know his estates, as is to be seen in England. As for the farmer, the industrial capitalist and the agricultural worker, they are no more bound to the land they exploit than are the employer and the worker in the factories to the cotton and wool they manufacture; they feel an attachment only for the price of their production, the monetary product.

Rent for Marx cannot be an accurate gauge of the fertility of the land, Proudhon notwithstanding,

> since every moment the modern application of chemistry is changing the nature of the soil, and geological knowledge is just now, in our days, beginning to revolutionize all the old estimates of relative fertility.... Fertility is not so natural a quality as might be thought; it is closely bound up with the social relations of the time.

Contrary to Proudhon, then, "rent, instead of *binding man to nature,* has merely [under capitalist conditions of production] bound the exploitation of the land to competition."[68]

Proudhon's bourgeois socialism, or rather Proudhon's mistaken attempt to make bourgeois production more social, without altering its essential character, is revealed most explicitly, for Marx, by the former's position that justice has to do simply with proportional distribution of labor time, that is, the universalization of the principle of to each according to his labor. For Marx, in contrast, "the determination of value by labour time—the formula M. Proudhon gives us as the regenerating formula of the future—is ... merely the scientific expression of the economic relations of present-day society, as was clearly and precisely demonstrated by Ricardo long before Proudhon." For Marx, Proudhon's stance is an inadequate solution to the problems posed by capitalist society, since a revolutionary strategy demands a break with this system of production and distribution according to labor time (and hence with the law of value of capitalist society) and the determination of relations of production and distribution according to genuine human needs. As he was to explain many years later in the *Critique of the Gotha Programme*, the principle of "to each according to his labor" must be replaced with the principle "from each according to his ability, to each according to his need." Hence, what was required was a decisive break with the "law of value" of capitalism, not its generalization.[69]

For Marx, then, Proudhon's analysis was less than that of the scientific economist (such as Ricardo) since he had to resort to "magic" (Marx has in mind the recourse to Proudhon's new Prometheus) to explain—or rather explain away—relations of production and distribution under capitalism. At the same time Proudhon's *System of Economical Contradictions* fell short of the analysis of communism (which Proudhon had attacked) since it did not "rise, be it even speculatively, above the bourgeois horizon." Against Proudhon's confused mysticism, even idealism, Marx counterposed the materialist principle, drawn from Lucretius, of *"mors immortalis"* (immortal death) or absolute pure mortality—that is, practical materialism and the recognition of the historical, contingent, and transitory nature of reality—which could only be approached, according to Marx, from the standpoint of material production, or the struggle of human beings to exist.[70]

The View of *The Communist Manifesto*

The critiques of both Malthusianism and Proudhon's mechanistic "Prometheanism" were central to the argument of *The Communist Manifesto* (1848), which presented the materialist conception of history in the form of a revolutionary manifesto, for the first time. The *Manifesto* was commissioned in 1847 by the German Communist League. It had its origin

in "Principles of Communism," which Engels had drafted at the request
of the League to counter a proposed set of principles called "Confession
of Faith," modeled after Moses Hess's earlier Fourierist *Communist
Confession of Faith* (1844). (There were two "Confessions of Faith" written
in response to Hess in the struggle over what was to be the credo of the
Communist League. One of these, known as "The Communist
Confession of Faith," dated June 1847, was essentially a first draft, adopted
provisionally by the League and showing Engels's influence. The second,
in October 1847, was Engels's "Principles of Communism.") The success
of Engels's "Principles," and the overwhelming influence that Marx and
Engels exerted at the second congress of the Communist League in
London in November–December 1847, resulted in the request of the
League that Marx and Engels provide a final draft of the principles
adopted. Drawing on Engels's "Principles," Marx drafted the anonymous
masterpiece *The Manifesto of the Communist Party*, first published in London
in February 1848 (Marx and Engels were revealed as the authors in
1850).[71]

Given the nature of Marx's earlier critique of Proudhon's mechanistic
"Prometheanism," it is rather ironic that the *Manifesto*, when read from
an ecological perspective, is often viewed as the prime locus of Marx's
so-called "Promethean" view of the human–nature relation. According to
this very common criticism, Marx adopted what the socialist environmentalist Ted Benton—himself a critic of Marx in this respect—has called
"a 'productivist' 'Promethean' view of history." Reiner Grundmann,
writing in his *Marxism and Ecology*, contends that "Marx's basic premise"
was the "Promethean model" of the domination of nature—a position
that Grundmann attempts to defend. For liberal Victor Ferkiss, however,
no such defense is possible: "Marx's attitude toward the world always
retained that Promethean thrust, glorifying the human conquest of nature."
This view is supported by sociologist Anthony Giddens, who complains
of the "Promethean attitude" that characterized Marx's treatment of the
human–nature relation in his works overall (excluding his earliest writings),
which meant that "Marx's concern with transforming the exploitative
human social relations expressed in class systems does not extend to the
exploitation of nature." Social ecologist John Clark goes even further:

> Marx's Promethean ... "man" is a being who is not at home in nature, who
> does not see the earth as the 'household' of ecology. He is an indominable spirit
> who must subject nature in his quest for self-realization.... For such a being,
> the forces of nature, whether in the form of his own unmastered internal nature
> or the menacing powers of external nature, must be subdued.

Even the revolutionary socialist Michael Löwy charges that Marx adopted an "optimistic, 'promethean' conception of the limitless development of the productive forces" which was "totally indefensible ... above all from the standpoint of the threat to the ecological balance of the planet."[72]

This charge of "Prometheanism," it is important to understand, carries implicitly within it certain anti-modernist (postmodernist or premodernist) assumptions that have become sacrosanct within much of Green theory. True environmentalism, it would seem, demands nothing less than the rejection of modernity itself. The charge of Prometheanism is thus a roundabout way of branding Marx's work and Marxism as a whole as an extreme version of modernism, more easily condemned in this respect than liberalism itself. Thus postmodernist environmentalist Wade Sikorski writes that "Marx ... was one of our age's most devout worshippers of the machine. Capitalism was to be forgiven its sins because ... it was in the process of perfecting the machine."[73]

Ironically, this criticism of Marx as Promethean—which has a very long history within Marx criticism, extending back to the early years of the Cold War—seems to have emerged in a very roundabout way from Marx's own critique of Proudhon in this respect. Thus, Marx's critique of the mythico-religious bases of Proudhon's analysis of machinery and modernity has somehow been transposed (among those who have lost sight of the actual history of this critique) into a critique of Marx himself—as if such views were characteristic of him, rather than Proudhon. Such criticism, in fact, follows a well-established pattern. As Jean-Paul Sartre noted, "an 'anti-Marxist' argument is only the apparent rejuvenation of a pre-Marxist idea." Hence, nothing is more common among critics of Marx—ironic as this may seem—than to attribute to him the views of other radical thinkers (Proudhon, Blanqui, Lasalle, and so on) that he sought to transcend. In the case of so-called "Prometheanism," Marx's critique of Proudhon in this respect could not be more clear—except of course to those who failed to read Proudhon himself, and thus have no true understanding of the nature of Marx's critique.[74]

For Marx, the Prometheus to be admired was the revolutionary mythical figure of Aeschylus' *Prometheus Bound*, who defied the gods of Olympus and brought fire (light, enlightenment) to human beings. Like Bacon, he associated Prometheus with the appearance of science and materialism—and thus with the Enlightenment figure of antiquity, Epicurus.[75] The later image of Prometheus as a representative of mechanism was entirely absent from his writings—except in the context of his critique of the mechanistic Prometheanism of Proudhon.

The charge of "Prometheanism" leveled against Marx by thinkers like Benton and Giddens is directed above all at *The Communist Manifesto*, where Marx and Engels made reference to "the subjugation of nature to man" and the "idiocy of rural life"—points that, taken in isolation and at face value, may seem to reflect an inadequately critical, indeed "Promethean," standpoint. Yet, the *Manifesto*, despite its popular, polemical intent, already contained implicitly within it an understanding of the relationship between the materialist conception of nature and the materialist conception of history, as well as important ingredients of an ecological perspective—opposed to the mechanistic Prometheanism of the later Proudhon—that emphasized the necessary unity of human and natural existence.[76]

Part One of the *Manifesto* contained Marx and Engels's famous panegyric to the bourgeoisie, celebrating its revolutionary accomplishments through which "all that is solid melts into air," and pointing beyond these accomplishments to the main contradictions that it brought into being—periodic economic crises and the birth of its own heir apparent in the form of the industrial proletariat. It was in the context of the panegyric to the bourgeoisie that Marx and Engels referred to the fact that capitalism

> has subjected the country to the rule of the towns. It has created enormous cities, has greatly increased the urban population as compared with the rural, and thus has rescued a considerable part of the population from the idiocy of rural life. Just as it has made the country dependent on the towns, so it has made barbarian and semi-barbarian countries depend on the civilized ones, nations of peasants on nations of bourgeois, the East on the West.[77]

Simply because of the use of the phrase "idiocy of rural life," this has sometimes been characterized as an anti-ecological position. It is therefore worthwhile to look more carefully at the place of this statement in Marx and Engels's analysis. First, Marx had a classical education and hence knew that the meaning of "idiot" in ancient Athens came from "*Idiotes*," a citizen who was cut off from public life, and who, unlike those who participated in the public assembly, viewed public life (the life of the *polis*) from a narrow, parochial viewpoint, hence "idiotic." Second, and more important, Marx and Engels were saying no more here than what they had already said in *The German Ideology* in their discussion of the antagonistic division of labor between town and country. There they had observed that the division between town and country was "the most important division of material and mental labor": a form of "subjection which makes one man into a restricted town-animal, another into a restricted country-animal," and which serves to cut the rural population off from "all world intercourse, and consequently from all culture."[78]

Throughout his intellectual life Marx insisted that while the proletarian was deprived of air, of cleanliness, of the very physical means of life, the rural peasant under capitalism was deprived of all relation to world culture and the larger world of social intercourse. One portion of the exploited population had access to the world of social intercourse (as part of urban existence), but lacked physical health and well-being, the other frequently had physical health and well-being (due to the access to clean air, and so on), but lacked a link to world culture. Indeed, Marx took seriously David Urquhart's observation that society was increasingly divided into "clownish boors" and "emasculated dwarfs" as a result of the extreme division between rural and urban existence, which deprived one part of the working population of intellectual sustenance, the other of material sustenance.[79] All of this was used by Marx to explain why the proletariat was a greater revolutionary force than the peasantry. In being forced into the towns, the urban masses had lost their essential link to natural conditions, but gained forms of association that propelled them toward a more revolutionary social reality. One of the first tasks of any revolution against capitalism, Marx and Engels insisted, must therefore be the abolition of the antagonistic division between town and country. The point was not that nature was to be despised but rather that the antagonism between town and country was one of the chief manifestations of the alienated nature of bourgeois civilization.

Marx and Engels saw the dependence of the country on the towns as a product in part of the enormous "agglomerations of population" that emerged within cities during the bourgeois era—an issue that they discussed in the paragraph immediately following their statement on the rescue of the proletariat from the "idiocy of rural life." In Part Two of the *Manifesto*, which was devoted to the historically specific demands of proletarians and communists, they therefore insisted on the need to carry out "a gradual abolition of the distinction between town and country, by a more equable distribution of population over the country"—a possibility that could only be achieved through the "combination of agriculture with manufacturing industries." Marx and Engels thus sought to reconnect at a higher level what had been torn apart—what Marx was later to call the human metabolism with nature. Such measures were to be combined, further, with "the abolition of property in land and the application of all rents of land to public purposes" and "the bringing into cultivation of all waste lands, and the improvement of the soil generally in accordance with a common plan."[80] All of these measures could be seen as a response to the Malthusian approach to the relation of population to the land. In contrast to Malthus, who proposed to "sweep" the peasants from the land so that the number of urban workers would be increased, Marx and Engels (inspired to some extent by earlier suggestions by Fourier and Owen) proposed the *dispersal* of the population, overcoming the antagonism between town and country that they saw as constitutive of the bourgeois order.[81] Rather than insisting, along with Malthus, that improvements in cultivation were very limited (placing extreme restrictions on the pace if not the extent of progress), Marx and Engels argued that such improvements could be achieved, particularly if directed by associated labor under a "common plan." The main answer to Malthusianism, then, was the abolition of the alienation of human beings from nature.

Obviously, though, this was not a position that argued that nature should be left untouched by human beings. Marx and Engels had already rejected purely "sentimental" notions of nature based on the illusion that nature was still in a pristine condition and could be left untouched. Like nearly all other individuals in their time, they decried the existence of "waste lands" where food supply was still a question. Their position—which became clearer as their writings evolved—was rather that of encouraging a sustainable relation between human beings and nature through the organization of production in ways that took into account the metabolic relation between human beings and the earth.

The Communist Manifesto, as we have seen, is often criticized for its alleged straightforward *advocacy* of the mechanistic "Prometheanism" of Proudhon, which is often attributed to Marx and Engels themselves despite Marx's early critique of Proudhon in this respect. Such criticisms often turn on Marx and Engels's statement in their one-sided panegyric to the bourgeoisie that

> the bourgeoisie, during its rule of scarce one hundred years, has created more massive and more colossal productive forces than have all preceding generations together. Subjection of Nature's forces to man, machinery, application of chemistry to industry and agriculture, steam-navigation, railways, electric telegraphs, clearing of whole continents for cultivation, canalization of rivers, whole populations conjured out of the ground. What earlier century had even a presentiment that such productive forces slumbered in the lap of social labor?[82]

Based mainly on the reference here to "Subjection of Nature's forces to man" and to "the clearing of whole continents for cultivation," Marx and Engels have been frequently characterized as insufficiently critical, at the time that they wrote *The Communist Manifesto*, of the ecological contradictions of bourgeois production.[83] Certainly, they were sufficiently Baconian in their outlook to see the subjection of nature's forces to humanity, which they associated with the development of science and civilization, to be, on the whole, a good. Yet, this leaves open the whole question of sustainability which they did not address in their panegyric to the bourgeoisie in the first part of the *Manifesto*.

Here it should be noted that "Subjection of Nature's forces to man" is open to different interpretations, and is entirely compatible with Bacon's most famous injunction: "We can only command Nature by obeying her."[84] As for the "clearing of whole continents for cultivation"—this was something to celebrate, Marx and Engels believed, since famine, the Malthusian specter, had, by this and other means, been pushed back by bourgeois production. None of this, however, suggested a mechanistic Prometheanism in which the machine and industrialization were celebrated unreservedly at the expense of agriculture—though it did point to the fact that the preservation of wilderness was not Marx and Engels's primary concern.

Anyone who has read *The Communist Manifesto* has to be aware that the panegyric to bourgeois civilization that dominates the opening section of this work is merely a lead-in to a consideration of the social contradictions that capitalism has engendered and that will eventually lead to its downfall. No one would say that Marx in presenting the capitalist as a heroic figure, or in celebrating the advances in the division of labor, competition, globalization, and so on, in Part One of the *Manifesto*, simply dispensed with all critical perspective. Rather the one-sidedness of these developments is brought out in dialectical fashion in the subsequent argument. Just as Marx and Engels recognized that the wealth-generating characteristics of capitalism were accompanied by an increase in relative poverty for the greater portion of the population, so they understood that the "Subjection of Nature's forces to man" had been accompanied by the alienation of nature, manifested in the division between town and country, which they saw as central to capitalism. Hence, the *Manifesto* went on, albeit with desperate brevity, to address this problem—in their ten-point plan, included in the less well-known Part Two. In their later writings, significantly, Marx and Engels were to make the consideration of such ecological contradictions a central part of their critique of modern civilization (and particularly capitalist society).

Marx and Engels ended their panegyric to the bourgeoisie in the opening pages of Part One of the *Manifesto* with the observation that capitalism, with its gigantic means of production and exchange, was "like the sorcerer, who is no longer able to control the powers of the nether world whom he has called up by his spells." Although this referred ultimately to the proletariat, it also referred to the entire set of contradictions brought on by the one-sided nature of capitalist civilization.[85]

In the remainder of Part One of the *Manifesto* Marx and Engels confined their argument to the contradictions that they believed were to play a role in the revolutionary transition from capitalism to socialism. Here ecological factors, such as the division between town and country, seemed to play no part. And it is only in their proposals on how to begin to construct a society of associated producers, at the end of Part Two of the *Manifesto*, that Marx and Engels emphasize what can properly be called ecological factors.

The reason for this bifurcation of issues seems obvious. Marx and Engels did not generally treat environmental destruction (apart from the role that it played in the direct life of the proletariat—that is, the lack of air, of cleanliness, of the prerequisites for health, and so on) as a major factor in the revolutionary movement against capitalism that they saw as imminent. Where they emphasized ecological contradictions, they did not seem to believe that they were developed to such an extent that they were to play a central role in the transition to socialism. Rather such considerations with regard to the creation of a sustainable relation to nature were part of—even a distinguishing feature of—the later dialectic of the construction of communism.

Indeed, it was precisely because Marx and Engels placed so much emphasis on the dissolution of the contradiction between town and country, as the key to the transcendence of the alienation of humanity from nature, that they tended to see the ecological problem in terms that transcended both the horizons of bourgeois society and the immediate objectives of the proletarian movement. Careful to avoid falling into the trap of the utopian socialists of proposing blueprints for a future society that went too far beyond the existing movement, they nonetheless emphasized—like Fourier and some of the other utopian socialists—the need for the movement to address the alienation of nature in the attempt to create a sustainable society. In this sense, their analysis drew not only upon their materialist conception of history, but also on their deeper, materialist conception of nature. It therefore set the stage for Marx's mature ecological perspective—his theory of the metabolic interaction of nature and society.

CHAPTER 5

THE METABOLISM OF
NATURE AND SOCIETY

Before the ink was even dry on *The Communist Manifesto* a wave of revolutions broke out in Paris in 1848, quickly spreading across continental Europe. Although the *Manifesto* itself played no immediate part in this new phase of bourgeois revolution, its timing could scarcely have been better, and events seemed to underscore the importance of its revolutionary analysis. Both Marx and Engels participated in the uprisings then taking place in France and Germany, Marx starting up a revolutionary paper in Cologne, the *Neue Rheinishe Zeitung*, but the revolutions were quickly defeated and Marx, no longer welcome in Prussia, France or Belgium, took refuge with his family in England, taking up residence in London. It was here that he was to live for the rest of his life, and where he was to write his great work, *Capital: A Critique of Political Economy*.

It was in *Capital* that Marx's materialist conception of nature became fully integrated with his materialist conception of history.[1] In his developed political economy, as presented in *Capital*, Marx employed the concept of "metabolism" (*Stoffwechsel*) to define the labor process as "a process between man and nature, a process by which man, through his own actions, mediates, regulates and controls the metabolism between himself and nature." Yet an "irreparable rift" had emerged in this metabolism as a result of capitalist relations of production and the antagonistic separation of town and country. Hence under the society of associated producers it would be necessary to "govern the human metabolism with nature in a rational way," completely beyond the capabilities of bourgeois society.[2]

This conceptual framework was important because it allowed Marx to tie together his critique of the three principal emphases of bourgeois political economy: the analysis of the extraction of surplus product from the direct producer; the related theory of capitalist ground rent; and the Malthusian theory of population, which connected the two to each other. Moreover, Marx's concept of metabolic rift in the relation between town and country, human beings and the earth, allowed him to penetrate to the roots of what historians have sometimes called the "second agricultural revolution," occurring in the capitalism of his day, and the crisis in agriculture with which this was associated, thereby enabling him to develop a critique of environmental degradation that anticipated much of present-day ecological thought. Analytically, Marx's critique of capitalist agriculture passed through two stages: (1) the critique of Malthus and Ricardo (a critique in which James Anderson's analysis played a central role); and (2) a consideration of the second agricultural revolution and the implications of Justus von Liebig's soil chemistry, which compelled Marx to analyze the conditions underlying a sustainable relation to the earth.

Overpopulation and the Conditions of Reproduction of Human Beings

At the heart of Marx's analysis was always his critique of Malthusian population notions, which Malthus had propounded with what Marx called "clerical fanaticism." As Marx was to argue in the *Grundrisse* (1857–1858)—his great preliminary attempt to sketch out his whole critique of political economy—what was at issue here was the extremely complex historical and theoretical problem of "the conditions of reproduction of human beings," in which all human history was distilled, but which occurred under varying conditions in different social formations and different historic epochs.[3]

Malthus's theory, Marx contended, was significant for two reasons: first, because it gave "brutal expression to the brutal viewpoint of capital"; second, because it "*asserted* the fact of overpopulation in all forms of society." Although Marx did not deny—indeed he emphasized—the existence of overpopulation in earlier societies, he objected to Malthus's refusal to look at the "specific differences" that this assumed in different social formations at different phases of historical development, and his reduction of all these different cases to one numerical relation based in unchanging natural law. "In this way he transforms the historically distinct relations into an abstract numerical relation, which he has fished purely out of thin air, and which rests neither on natural nor historical laws."

Specifically, by reducing all questions of reproduction to two equations, one for plants and animals used for human subsistence, which Malthus insisted were limited to an arithmetical rate of increase, and the other for human beings, which Malthus claimed tended to grow by geometrical progression (when unchecked), Malthus had, according to Marx, committed both logical and historical errors. The claim that human population increased geometrically until checked externally (by such natural factors as high infant mortality, disease, and starvation) refused to acknowledge the historical and social character of human reproduction. At the same time Malthus sometimes wrote as if plants and animals had an immanent tendency to be limited to an arithmetical rate of population increase. (Indeed, Malthus initially had no explanation for his arithmetical ratio.) In contrast, Marx suggested, there was no such clear immanent limit to the demographic increase of plants and animals, which were checked only externally. If they encountered no external barrier, "The ferns would cover the entire earth. Their reproduction would stop only where space for them ceased." Hence, Malthus, according to Marx, had erroneously transformed "the immanent, historically changing limits of the human reproduction process into *outer barriers*; and the *outer barriers* [that is, the external checks on the growth of food] into *immanent limits* or *natural laws* of reproduction."

What was important in dealing with the question of overpopulation was the specific historical way it emerged in each case. "In different modes of social production," Marx wrote, "there are different laws of the increase of population and of overpopulation.... How small do the numbers which meant overpopulation for the Athenians appear to us!" Malthus's theory, Marx argued,

> abstracts from these specific historic laws of the movement of population, which are indeed the history of the nature of humanity, the *natural* laws, but natural laws of humanity only at a specific historic development.... Malthusian man, abstracted from historically determined man, exists only in his brain; hence also the geometric method of reproduction corresponding to this natural Malthusian man.[4]

Marx sided with Ricardo's criticism of Malthus, in which Ricardo had pointed out that it was not the amount of grain that was most significant in determining overpopulation, that is, the existence of paupers, but rather the amount of employment. But for Marx the point needed to "be conceived more generally, and relates to the *social mediation* as such, through which the individual gains access to the means of his reproduction and creates them; hence it relates to the *conditions of production* and his relation to them." Overpopulation under capitalism was therefore determined not simply by the existence of a relative surplus population of workers seeking employment and thereby means of subsistence; but more fundamentally by the relations of production that made the continual existence of such a relative surplus population necessary for the system.

A fuller critique of Malthus's population theory, however, required, as Marx realized, a critique of the classical theory of differential rent to which it was eventually linked. If Malthus did not offer any genuine explanation for his arithmetical ratio in any of the six editions of his *Essay on Population*, and hence, as Marx was wont to point out, the theory of rent was not "proper to Malthus at all," it is nevertheless true that Malthus was to turn to the classical theory of rent in order to defend his arithmetical ratio at the end of his life in his *A Summary View of the Principle of Population*, and that this was the basis on which classical Malthusianism eventually came to rest.

James Anderson and the Origins of Differential Fertility

Although it is often assumed that Marx simply followed Ricardo in the realm of rent theory and the analysis of agricultural development, he was in fact a sharp critic of this theory for its failure to understand the historical development of the cultivation of the earth or soil. The main weaknesses of the Ricardian theory of rent (sometimes known as the Malthusian/Ricardian theory of rent), in Marx's view, derived from its failure to incorporate a theory of historical development (and the fact that the subsequent historical development of agriculture had made this theory antiquated). In this respect, Marx argued that the work of the real originator of the classical theory of differential rent, the Scottish political economist and gentleman farmer James Anderson (1739–1808), was far superior to that of Malthus and Ricardo.[5]

Anderson developed all of the key theoretical propositions of the classical theory of rent as early as 1777 in *An Enquiry into the Nature of the Corn Laws*, and continued to expand upon this in subsequent works. Rent, he claimed, was a charge for the use of the more fertile soils. The least fertile soils in cultivation generate an income that simply covers the costs of production, while the more fertile soils receive a "certain premium for an exclusive right to cultivate them; which will be greater or smaller according to the more or less fertility of the soil. It is this premium which constitutes what we now call rent; a medium by means of which the expense of cultivating soils of very different degrees of fertility may be reduced to perfect equality."[6]

For Malthus and Ricardo, writing decades later, the source of this differential fertility came to be seen almost entirely in terms of conditions of natural productivity independent of human beings. As Ricardo wrote, rent could be defined as "that portion of the produce of the earth, which is paid to the landlord for the use of the original and indestructible powers of the soil."[7] Moreover, Malthus and Ricardo argued—with the presumed backing of natural law—that lands that were naturally the most fertile were the first to be brought into production, and that rising rent on these lands and diminishing agricultural productivity overall were the result of bringing lands of more and more marginal fertility into cultivation, in response to increasing population pressures.

In contrast, Anderson's earlier model had attributed the existence of differential rent primarily to historical changes in soil fertility, rather than to conditions of "absolute fertility." Continual improvement of the soil, through manuring, draining, and irrigating, was possible, and productivity of the least fertile land could rise to a point that brought it much closer to that of the most fertile land; yet the converse was also true, and human beings could degrade the soil. It was such changes in relative productivity of the soil, according to Anderson, that accounted for differential rent—and not the conditions of absolute fertility—as in the later arguments of Malthus and Ricardo.

Where general failures in the improvement of soil fertility occurred, these were largely a consequence, Anderson argued, of the failure to adopt rational and sustainable agricultural practices. The fact that the land in England was owned by landed proprietors and farmed by capitalist tenant farmers, he argued, placed major obstacles in the way of rational agriculture, since the farmer tended to avoid all improvements, the full return for which would not be received during the term of the lease.[8]

In *A Calm Investigation of the Circumstances that have Led to the Present Scarcity of Grain in Britain* (1801), Anderson contended that the growing division between town and country had led to the loss of natural sources of fertilizer. "Every person who has but heard of agriculture," he wrote, "knows that animal manure, when applied to the soil, tends to add to its fertility; of course he must be sensible that every circumstance that tends to deprive the soil of that manure ought to be accounted an uneconomical waste highly deserving of blame." Indeed, it was possible, Anderson contended, by the judicious application of animal and human wastes, to sustain the "*soil for ever after*, without the addition of any extraneous manures." Yet London, with its gargantuan waste of such natural sources of fertility, "which is daily carried to the Thames, in its passage to which it subjects the people in the lower part of the city to the most offensive effluvia," was an indication of how far society had moved from a sustainable agricultural economy.[9] Armed with this critical analysis, and a historical perspective, Anderson directly opposed the Malthusian view that the shortage of grain could be traced to rising human population and its pressures on a limited supply of land.[10]

Marx studied Anderson's work as early as 1851, incorporating brief excerpts from two of Anderson's works into his notebooks.[11] Writing in the 1850s and 1860s in *Theories of Surplus Value*, his long, three-part exegesis on the development of classical political economy, Marx argued that the core of Anderson's contribution lay in the fact that the latter had historicized the issue of soil fertility. "Anderson by no means assumes ... that different *degrees of fertility* are merely the product of nature." Instead, "the differential rent of the landlords is partly the result of the fertility that the farmer has given the land artificially."[12] Marx originally emphasized the significance of Anderson's model in understanding the possibility of agricultural improvement, and how this was consistent with the theory of differential rent. But it also followed from Anderson's *historical* perspective (as he himself demonstrated in his later writings) that a general decline in soil fertility ought to be attributed, not, as in the Ricardian theory, to decreases in the aggregate productivity of the soil due to the cultivation of marginal lands, but to such factors as the failure to invest in the improvement of the soil due to the class conflict between capitalist tenant farmer and landed proprietor, or the actual impoverishment of the soil associated with the failure to recycle manure (because of the growing division between town and country).[13]

Hence, in combining political economy with agronomy, Anderson developed at the end of the eighteenth century a body of thought that was unusually prescient—foreshadowing the concern with the interrelationship between soil fertility and soil chemistry (as well as such questions as the relationship between town and country, and between landed property and capitalist farming) that was come to the fore around four decades later as a result of the scientific revolution in soil chemistry. Anderson helped Marx to historicize the problem of capitalist ground rent, while more fully comprehending the conditions of the soil. It was the crisis of soil fertility in European and North American agriculture and the great advances in soil science in Marx's own day which were, however, to allow Marx to transform this historical approach to the question of agricultural improvement into an ecological critique of capitalist agriculture.[14]

Anderson not only developed a historically based analysis of rent and agricultural improvement (and degradation); he also emerged at the very end of his life as one of the leading critics of Malthus's 1798 *Essay on Population*. Anderson's *Calm Investigation* was written largely in response to

Malthus's *Essay on Population*—and probably in response as well to Malthus's pamphlet *An Investigation of the Cause of the Present High Price of Provisions* (1800). Anderson sent a copy of the *Calm Investigation* to Malthus, which was probably the latter's first introduction to the work of the former, and Malthus struggled repeatedly to answer Anderson in subsequent editions of his essay. (Marx was to contend that Malthus's acquaintance with the relatively little known work of Anderson, in the area of economics, allowed him to adopt without acknowledgement elements of Anderson's rent theory, without fully understanding it, in his own 1815 *Inquiry into the Nature and Progress of Rent.*)

Anderson's critique of Malthus's arithmetical ratio, which he also presented in the third volume of his *Recreations in Agriculture* (1801), was all the more devastating because in presenting this ratio (that is, the assumption that the rate of increase in food could never go beyond a fixed increment, which he claimed was at best equal to the entire agricultural production for the year 1798) Malthus had offered as "proof" the fact that no knowledgeable observer of agriculture would contradict this. Yet, Anderson, who was certainly one of the most knowledgeable analysts of agriculture in his day, set out to refute Malthus's argument. Indeed, Anderson argued that "if the population of any country shall advance, and if the people in it be chiefly employed in the cultivation of the soil, its productiveness will keep pace with that population, whatever it shall be; and they will have abundance at all times: and this the experience of all nations hath confirmed." Nevertheless, it was possible by the division of town and country, improper cultivation, and the failure to recycle organic wastes to create "an opposite state of progression, until, by a gradual process of deterioration, it [the soil] shall revert nearly to the original point from which it set out"—that is, the benefits of all improvement will have been lost. In this latter case the availability of food could prove insufficient due to the distortions produced within society and in the cultivation of the soil—rather than due to the inherent inadequacies of agriculture. Anderson went on to discuss the degradation of the soil in northern Africa, Sicily, and Italy itself in comparison to Roman times.[15]

Liebig, Marx, and the Second Agricultural Revolution

If Anderson's historical approach to the question of agriculture, which emphasized the possibility of improvement (and also degradation), was far superior to that of Malthus and Ricardo that followed, it is nonetheless true that all of these early classical economic theories suffered from the lack of a scientific understanding of the composition of the soil. This was most evident in Malthus and Ricardo, who relied almost exclusively on a natural law conception. Although it is true that Ricardo recognized the possibility of improvement of the land through better manuring, rotation of crops, and so on, he nevertheless placed little emphasis on this, stressing that the room for improvement was quite limited. His theory saw the properties of the soil as generally fixed. Hence, the failures of agriculture could be attributed almost entirely to the cultivation of inferior grades of land in response to increased demand emanating from increased populations.

Looking back in the mid-1860s at these early theories of agriculture and rent, when he was writing *Capital*, Marx was to place strong emphasis on the historical division separating such analyses from his own time, by observing that "the actual natural causes for the exhaustion of land ... were unknown to any of the economists who wrote about differential rent, on account of the state of agricultural chemistry in their time."[16] Marx made this observation after reading Liebig's assessment, in the seventh edition of his *Organic Chemistry in its Application to Agriculture and Physiology*, of the state of agricultural knowledge prior to 1840, the date at which the first edition of his landmark work had been published. According to Liebig, agricultural knowledge prior to the 1840s had emphasized the role of manure and the "latent power" in the land or soil. Since the chemical properties of the soil were unknown at that time, the nature of plant nutrition was also unknown. Hence, the latent power attributed to the soil was frequently seen as inherently limited and at the same time indestructible. In no way could the real problems of agriculture be ascertained.[17]

These observations by Liebig and Marx serve to underscore what some agricultural historians have called "the second agricultural revolution."[18] Although historians often still refer to a single agricultural revolution that occurred in Britain in the seventeenth and eighteenth centuries and that laid the foundations for industrial capitalism, agricultural historians sometimes refer to a second and even a third agricultural revolution. According to this conception, the first revolution was a gradual process taking place over several centuries, connected with the enclosures and the growing centrality of the market; technical changes included improvements in manuring, crop rotation, drainage, and livestock management. In contrast, the second agricultural revolution took place over a shorter period—1830–1880—and was characterized by the growth of a fertilizer industry and the development of soil chemistry, associated in particular with the work of Justus von Liebig.[19] The third agricultural revolution took place still later, in the twentieth century, and involved the replacement of animal traction with machine traction on the farm, followed by the concentration of animals in massive feedlots, coupled with the genetic alteration of plants (producing narrower monocultures) and the more intensive use of chemical inputs—such as fertilizers and pesticides.[20]

Marx's critique of capitalist agriculture and his contributions to ecological thought in this area have to be understood therefore in the context of the second agricultural revolution occurring in his time. The beginnings of this revolution correspond closely to the origins of Marx's thought. Already in 1844 in "Outlines for a Critique of Political Economy" Engels had referred to the scientific revolution associated with Liebig as a reason why Malthusian fears about the dearth of food for a growing population were misplaced. At the outset, Marx and Engels, like many other observers in their time, including Liebig himself, responded to this agricultural revolution by concluding that agricultural progress in the immediate future might outpace industry itself. Significantly, one of Marx's notebooks from 1851 opened with excerpts from Liebig, followed by excerpts from Malthus and various anti-Malthusian thinkers, and ended up (except for some very minor extracts that followed) with excerpts from James F.W. Johnston, a British soil chemist, whose work was closely related to that of Liebig. The overwhelming emphasis of Johnston's, as well as Liebig's, work at this time was the possibility of agricultural improvement—which Marx clearly regarded as a refutation of Malthusian assumptions about soil productivity. Yet, this optimistic assessment was to give way in the 1860s, in Marx's analysis—closely reflecting the changing views of Liebig—to a much more sophisticated understanding of ecological degradation within capitalist agriculture.[21]

Liebig and the degradation of the soil

During the nineteenth century the depletion of soil fertility was the chief environmental concern of capitalist society throughout Europe and North America, comparable only to concerns about the growing pollution of the cities, the deforestation of whole continents, and Malthusian fears of overpopulation. The critical nature of this problem of the relation to the soil can be seen quite clearly in the 1820s and 1830s, during the period of outright crisis that engendered the second agricultural revolution. But the problem did not simply end with the science of soil chemistry. Rather there was a growing recognition of the extent to which the new methods had only served to rationalize a process of ecological destruction.

In the 1820s and 1830s in Britain, and soon afterward in the other developing capitalist economies of Europe and North America, pervasive concerns about "soil exhaustion" led to a virtual panic, and a phenomenal increase in the demand for fertilizer. European farmers in this period raided the Napoleonic battlefields of Waterloo and Austerlitz and reportedly dug up catacombs, so desperate were they for bones to spread over their fields. The value of bone imports to Britain skyrocketed from £14,400 in 1823 to £254,600 in 1837. The first boat carrying Peruvian guano (accumulated dung of sea birds) arrived in Liverpool in 1835; by 1841 1,700 tons were imported, and by 1847 220,000.[22]

This second agricultural revolution associated with the origins of modern soil science was closely connected to the demand for increased soil fertility to support capitalist agriculture. The British Association for the Advancement of Science commissioned Liebig in 1837 to write a work on the relationship between agriculture and chemistry. The founding of the Royal Agricultural Society of England, a leading organization in the British high farming movement—a movement of wealthy landowners to improve farm management—took place in the following year. Two years later, in 1840, Liebig published his *Organic Chemistry in its Applications to Agriculture and Physiology* (known as his *Agricultural Chemistry*), which provided the first convincing explanation of the role of soil nutrients such as nitrogen, phosphorous, and potassium, in the growth of plants.[23] One of the figures most influenced by Liebig's ideas (as well as a rival whose discoveries challenged Liebig's own) was the wealthy English landowner and agronomist J.B. Lawes. In 1842 Lawes invented a means of making phosphate soluble, enabling him to develop the first agricultural fertilizer, and in 1843 he built a factory for the production of his new "superphosphates." Following the repeal of the Corn Laws in 1846, Liebig's organic chemistry, together with Lawes's new synthetic fertilizer, were seen by the large agricultural interests in Britain as offering the solution to the problem of obtaining larger crop yields.[24]

Nevertheless, the new technology represented by Lawes's fertilizer factory was slow to diffuse outside of Britain. The first factories for the production of superphosphates were introduced in Germany only in 1855; in the United States only after the Civil War; and in France only after the Franco-Prussian War. Moreover, the results obtained from the application of a single nutrient (such as phosphate) to the soil, though initially producing dramatic results, tended to diminish rapidly after that, since overall soil fertility is always limited by the nutrient in least abundance (Liebig's Law of the Minimum).

Hence, Liebig's discoveries at first only intensified the sense of crisis with capitalist agriculture, making farmers more aware of the depletion of soil minerals and the paucity of fertilizers. Moreover, capital's ability to take advantage of these breakthroughs in soil chemistry was limited by the development of the division of labor inherent in the system, specifically the growing antagonism between town and country. Hence by the 1860s, when he wrote *Capital*, Marx had become convinced of the unsustainable nature of capitalist agriculture, due to two historical developments in his time: (1) the widening sense of crisis in both European and North American agriculture associated with the depletion of the natural fertility of the soil—a sense of crisis which was in no way alleviated, but rather given added impetus, by the breakthroughs in soil science; and (2) a shift in Liebig's own work in the late 1850s and 1860s toward a strong ecological critique of capitalist development.

The contradictions within agriculture in this period were experienced with particular intensity in the United States—especially among farmers in upstate New York and in the Southeastern plantation economy. Blocked from easy, economical access to guano (which was high in both nitrogen and phosphates) by the British monopoly on Peruvian guano supplies, the United States undertook—first unofficially and then as part of a deliberate state policy—the imperial annexation of any islands thought to be rich in this natural fertilizer. Under the authority of what became the Guano Islands Act, passed by Congress in 1856, U.S. capitalists seized ninety-four islands, rocks, and keys around the globe between 1856 and 1903, sixty-six of which were officially recognized by the Department of State as U.S. appurtenances. "In the last ten years," Liebig was to observe in 1862, "British and American ships have searched through all Seas, and there is no small island, no coast, which has escaped their enquiries after guano." Nine of these guano islands remain U.S. possessions today. Yet guano imperialism was unsuccessful in providing the United States with the quantity and quality of natural fertilizer it needed.[25]

Meanwhile, Peruvian guano supplies had begun to run out in the 1860s and had to be replaced increasingly by Chilean nitrates. Although potassium salts discovered in Europe gave ready access to that mineral, and both natural and artificial supplies of phosphates made that nutrient more available, the limiting factor continued to be fertilizer nitrogen. (Synthetic nitrogen fertilizer was not developed until 1913, when the German chemist Fritz Haber, who was to go on to pioneer in the development of explosives and nerve gases for war production, originated such a process.)

The decline in natural fertility due to the disruption of the soil nutrient cycle accompanying capitalist agriculture, the growing knowledge of the need for specific soil nutrients, and limitations in the supply of both natural and synthetic fertilizers that would compensate for the loss of natural fertility all contributed, therefore, to a widespread sense of a crisis in soil fertility.

In the United States this was further complicated by geographical factors. In upstate New York, which by 1800 had displaced New England as a center for wheat cultivation, the relative exhaustion of the soil was brought into sharp relief by the steadily increasing competition from new farmlands to the West in the decades following the opening of the Erie Canal in 1825. Meanwhile the slave plantations of the Southeast experienced dramatic declines in fertility, particularly on lands devoted to the production of tobacco.

In New York farmers responded to the crisis by promoting a more rational agriculture through the creation of agricultural societies. In 1832 the New York Agricultural Society was formed. Two years later Jesse Buel, an Albany newspaper editor, started the *Cultivator*, which sought to promote the kind of improved farming already being introduced in Britain, concentrating on such issues as manures, draining wet soils, and crop rotation. With the publication of Liebig's *Agricultural Chemistry* in 1840, New York agriculturists turned to the new soil science as a savior. In 1850 the Scottish agricultural chemist James F.W. Johnston, whom Marx was to call "the English Liebig," traveled to North America, and in his influential work *Notes on North America* documented the loss of natural soil fertility, demonstrating in particular the depleted condition of the soil in New York as compared to the more fertile farmlands to the West.[26]

These issues were embraced in the 1850s by the U.S. political economist Henry Carey (1793–1879). In 1853 Carey observed in *The Slave Trade Domestic and Foreign*—a work that he sent to Marx—that "it is singular that all of the political economists of England have overlooked the fact that man is a mere borrower from the earth, and that when he does not pay his debts, she does as do all other creditors, that is, she expels him from his holding." On January 11, 1855, a young agronomist, George Waring (1833–1898), who began his career in the 1850s as an agriculturist and who later ended up as the leading sanitary engineer in the United States and the principal advocate and practitioner of the cleaning up of cities within the urban conservation movement, delivered a speech, entitled "The Agricultural Features of the Census for 1850," to the New York State Geographical Society in which he tried to demonstrate empirically that the soil was systematically being robbed of its nutrients. That speech was later published in the *Bulletin of the American Geographical and Statistical Association* in 1857. In an important essay in his *Letters to the President, on the Foreign and Domestic Policy of the Union* (1858) Carey quoted extensively from a speech by an "eminent agriculturist" (Waring, in the speech referred to above), who had provided some rough national estimates on the loss of soil nutrients through the shipment of food and fiber over long distances in a one-way movement from country to town. Waring had concluded his argument by declaring:

> [W]hat with our earth-butchery and prodigality, we are each year losing the intrinsic essence of our vitality.... The question of the economy should be, not how much do we annually produce, but how much of our annual production is saved to the soil. Labor employed in robbing the earth of its capital stock of fertilizing matter, is worse than labor thrown away. In the latter case, it is a loss to the present generation; in the former it becomes an inheritance of poverty for our successors. Man is but a tenant of the soil, and he is guilty of a crime when he reduces its value for other tenants who are to come after him.[27]

Throughout the late 1840s and 1850s Carey laid stress on the fact that long-distance trade arising from the separation of town and country (and agricultural producer and consumer) was a major factor in the net loss of soil nutrients and the growing crisis in agriculture—a point later developed further by Liebig and Marx.[28] "As the whole energies of the country," Carey wrote of the U.S. in his *Principles of Social Science* (1858)—quoting again from Waring—"are given to the enlargement of the trader's power, it is no matter of surprise that its people are everywhere seen employed in 'robbing the earth of its capital stock.'"[29]

Waring's and Carey's views were to have an important impact on Liebig. In his *Letters on Modern Agriculture* (1859) Liebig repeated the entire statement from the "eminent agriculturist" (Waring) that Carey had included in his *Letters to the President* and went on to argue that the "empirical agriculture" of the trader gave rise to a "spoliation system" in which the "conditions of reproduction" of the soil were undermined. "'A field from which something is permanently taken away,'" he wrote (quoting the practical acriculturalist Albrecht Block), "'cannot possibly increase or even continue in its productive power.'" In fact, "every system of farming based on the spoliation of the land leads to poverty." For Liebig, "*rational agriculture*, in contradistinction to the spoliation system of farming, is based upon the principle of *restitution*; by giving back to the fields the conditions of their fertility, the farmer insures the permanence of the latter." English "high farming," he argued, was "not the open system of robbery of the American farmer ... but it is a more refined species of spoliation which at first glance does not look like robbery." Following Carey, Liebig observed that there were hundreds, sometimes thousands, of miles in the United States between the centers of grain cultivation and their markets. The constituent elements of the soil were therefore shipped to locations distant from their points of origin, making the reproduction of soil fertility that much more difficult.[30] A few years later Liebig warned somewhat apocalyptically in the famous introduction to the 1862 edition of his *Agricultural Chemistry*, which influenced Marx, that, "if we do not succeed in making the farmer better aware of the conditions under which he produces and in giving him the means necessary for the increase of his output, wars, emigration, famines and epidemics will of necessity create the conditions of a new equilibrium which will undermine the welfare of everyone and finally lead to the ruin of agriculture."[31] What was needed, Liebig contended at another point in that same work, was the discovery of "deposits of manure or guano ... in volumes approximating to those of the English coalfields."[32] Ultimately, it was a question, as Liebig wrote in his *Familiar Letters on Chemistry*, of "the restoration of the elementary constituents of the soil," which had been withdrawn from it by the marketing over long distances of food and fiber and by the removal of cattle.[33]

The problem of the depletion of the soil was also tied, according to Liebig, to the pollution of the cities with human and animal wastes. The relation between Liebig's treatment of the soil nutrient cycle and the waste problem in the large cities had already been taken up by Edwin Chadwick as early as 1842 in his *Report on the Sanitary Condition of the Labouring Population of Great Britain*, which started the public health movement and greatly influenced Engels.[34] In his influential *Letters on the Subject of the Utilization of the Municipal Sewage* (1865) Liebig himself insisted—relying on an analysis of the condition of the Thames—that organic recycling that would return to the soil the nutrients contained in sewage was an indispensable part of a rational urban-agricultural system. "If it were practicable to collect, without the least loss, all the solid and fluid excrements of the inhabitants of towns," he was to write, "and to return to each farmer the portion arising from produce originally supplied by him to the town, the productiveness of his land might be maintained almost unimpaired for ages to come, and the existing store of mineral elements in every fertile field would be amply sufficient for the wants of the increasing populations."[35]

Marx's theory of metabolic rift

Marx was deeply affected by Liebig's analysis when writing *Capital* in the early 1860s. In 1866, the year before the first volume of *Capital* was published, he wrote to Engels that in developing his critique of ground rent in volume 3, "I had to plough through the new agricultural chemistry in Germany, in particular Liebig and Schönbein, which is more important for this matter than all the economists put together." Indeed, "to have developed from the point of view of natural science the negative, i.e. destructive side of modern agriculture," Marx noted in volume 1 of *Capital*, "is one of Liebig's immortal merits."[36]

Under the influence of Liebig, whom he studied attentively—making extensive extracts from Liebig's work in his scientific notebooks—Marx was to develop a systematic critique of capitalist "exploitation" (in the sense of robbery, that is, failing to maintain the means of reproduction) of the soil.[37] Hence, both of Marx's two main discussions of capitalist agriculture ended with explanations of how large-scale industry and large-scale agriculture combined to impoverish the soil and the worker. Much of this critique was distilled in a remarkable passage at the end of Marx's treatment of "The Genesis of Capitalist Ground Rent" in volume 3 of *Capital*, where he wrote:

> Large landed property reduces the agricultural population to an ever decreasing minimum and confronts it with an ever growing industrial population crammed together in large towns; in this way it produces conditions that provoke an irreparable rift in the interdependent process of social metabolism, a metabolism prescribed by the natural laws of life itself. The result of this is a squandering of the vitality of the soil, which is carried by trade far beyond the bounds of a single country. (Liebig.).... Large-scale industry and industrially pursued large-scale agriculture have the same effect. If they are originally distinguished by the fact that the former lays waste and ruins labour-power and thus the natural power of man, whereas the latter does the same to the natural power of the soil, they link up in the later course of development, since the industrial system applied to agriculture also enervates the workers there, while industry and trade for their part provide agriculture with the means of exhausting the soil.[38]

Marx provided a closely related and equally important distillation of his critique of capitalist agriculture in his discussion of "Large-scale Industry and Agriculture" in volume 1 of *Capital*:

> Capitalist production collects the population together in great centres, and causes the urban population to achieve an ever-growing preponderance. This has two results. On the one hand it concentrates the historical motive force of society; on the other hand, it disturbs the metabolic interaction between man and the earth, i.e. it prevents the return to the soil of its constituent elements consumed

by man in the form of food and clothing; hence it hinders the operation of the eternal natural condition for the lasting fertility of the soil.... But by destroying the circumstances surrounding that metabolism ... it compels its systematic restoration as a regulative law of social production, and in a form adequate to the full development of the human race.... [A]ll progress in capitalist agriculture is a progress in the art, not only of robbing the worker, but of robbing the soil; all progress in increasing the fertility of the soil for a given time is a progress toward ruining the more long-lasting sources of that fertility.... Capitalist production, therefore, only develops the technique and the degree of combination of the social process of production by simultaneously undermining the original sources of all wealth—the soil and the worker.[39]

What is common to both of these passages from Marx's *Capital*—the first ending his discussion of capitalist ground rent in volume 3 and the second concluding his treatment of large-scale agriculture and industry in volume 1—is the central theoretical concept of a "rift" in the "metabolic interaction between man and the earth," that is, the "social metabolism prescribed by the natural laws of life," through the "robbing" of the soil of its constituent elements, requiring its "systematic restoration." This contradiction develops through the growth simultaneously of large-scale industry and large-scale agriculture under capitalism, with the former providing the latter with the means of the intensive exploitation of the soil. Like Liebig, Marx argued that long-distance trade in food and fiber for clothing made the problem of the alienation of the constituent elements of the soil that much more of an "irreparable rift." For Marx, this was part of the natural course of capitalist development. As he wrote in 1852, "the soil is to be a marketable commodity, and the exploitation of the soil is to be carried on according to the common commercial laws. There are to be manufactures of food as well as manufacturers of twist and cottons, but no longer any lords of the land."[40]

Moreover, the contradictions associated with this development were global in character. As Marx observed in *Capital*, volume 1, the fact that the "blind desire for profit" had "exhausted the soil" of England could be seen daily in the conditions that "forced the manuring of English fields with guano" imported from Peru.[41] The mere fact that seeds, guano, and so on, were imported "from distant countries," Marx noted in the *Grundrisse* (1857–1858), indicated that agriculture under capitalism had ceased to be "self-sustaining," that it "no longer finds the natural conditions of its own production within itself, naturally arisen, spontaneous, and ready to hand, but these exist as an independent industry separate from it."[42] A central part of Marx's argument was the thesis that the inherent character of large-scale agriculture under capitalism prevents any truly rational application of the new science of soil management. Despite all of the scientific and technological development in agriculture, capital was unable to maintain those conditions necessary for the recycling of the constituent elements of the soil.

The key conceptual category in Marx's theoretical analysis in this area is the concept of metabolism (*Stoffwechsel*). The German word "*Stoffwechsel*" directly sets out in its elements the notion of "material exchange" that underlies the notion of structured processes of biological growth and decay captured in the term "metabolism." In his definition of the labor process Marx made the concept of metabolism central to his entire system of analysis by rooting his understanding of the labor process upon it. Thus in his definition of the labor process in general (as opposed to its historically specific manifestations), Marx utilized the concept of metabolism to describe the human relation to nature through labor:

> Labour is, first of all, a process between man and nature, a process by which man, through his own actions, mediates, regulates and controls the metabolism between himself and nature. He confronts the materials of nature as a force of nature. He sets in motion the natural forces which belong to his own body, his arms, legs, head and hands, in order to appropriate the materials of nature in a form adapted to his own needs. Through this movement he acts upon external nature and changes it, and in this way he simultaneously changes his own nature.... It [the labor process] is the universal condition for the metabolic interaction [*Stoffwechsel*] between man and nature, the everlasting nature-imposed condition of human existence.[43]

A few years previous to this Marx had written in his *Economic Manuscript of 1861–63* that "actual labour is the appropriation of nature for the satisfaction of human needs, the activity through which the metabolism between man and nature is mediated." It followed that the actual activity of labor was never independent of nature's own wealth-creating potential, "since material wealth, the world of use values, exclusively consists of natural materials modified by labour."[44]

Marx utilized the concept of metabolism throughout his mature works, though the context varied. As late as 1880 in his *Notes on Adolph Wagner*, his last economic work, Marx highlighted the centrality of the concept of *Stoffwechsel* to his overall critique of political economy, indicating that "I have employed the word ... for the 'natural' process of production as the material exchange [*Stoffwechsel*] between man and nature." "Interruptions of the formal exchange" in the circulation of commodities, he emphasized, "are later designated as interruptions of the material exchange." The economic circular flow then was closely bound up, in Marx's analysis, with the material exchange (ecological circular flow) associated with the metabolic interaction between human beings and nature. "The chemical process regulated by labour," he wrote, "has everywhere consisted of an exchange of (natural) equivalents." Building on the universal character of material exchange, upon which the formal exchange of economic equivalents in the capitalist economy was a mere alienated expression, Marx referred in the *Grundrisse* to the concept of metabolism (*Stoffwechsel*) in the wider sense of "a system of general social metabolism, of universal relations, of all-round needs and universal capacities ... formed for the first time" under generalized commodity production.[45]

Marx therefore employed the concept both to refer to the actual metabolic interaction between nature and society through human labor (the usual context in which the term was used in his works), and in a wider sense (particularly in the *Grundrisse*) to describe the complex, dynamic, interdependent set of needs and relations brought into being and constantly reproduced in alienated form under capitalism, and the question of human freedom it raised—all of which could be seen as being connected to the way in which the human metabolism with nature was expressed through the concrete organization of human labor. The concept of metabolism thus took on both a specific ecological meaning and a wider social meaning.[46]

Much of Marx's discussion of the metabolic relation between human beings and nature can be seen as building on the early Marx's more directly philosophical attempts to account for the complex interdependence between human beings and nature. In 1844 in his *Economic and Philosophical Manuscripts* Marx had explained that "Man *lives* from nature, i.e. nature is his *body*, and he must maintain a continuing dialogue with it if he is not to die. To say that man's physical and mental life is linked to nature simply means that nature is linked to itself, for man is a part of nature."[47] Marx's later concept of metabolism, however, allowed him to give a more solid and scientific expression of this fundamental relationship, depicting the complex, dynamic interchange between human beings and nature resulting from human labor. The concept of metabolism, with its attendant notions of material exchanges and regulatory action, allowed him to express the human relation to nature as one that encompassed both "nature-imposed conditions" and the capacity of human beings to affect this process.

Most importantly, the concept of metabolism provided Marx with a concrete way of expressing the notion of the alienation of nature (and its relation to the alienation of labor) that was central to his critique from his earliest writings on. As he explained in the *Grundrisse*,

It is not the *unity* of living and active humanity with the natural, inorganic conditions of their metabolic exchange with nature, and hence their appropriation of nature, which requires explanation, or is the result of a historic process, but rather the *separation* between these inorganic conditions of human existence and this active existence, a separation which is completely posited only in the relation of wage labour and capital.[48]

Herein was contained the essence of Marx's entire critique of the alienated character of bourgeois society.

According to Tim Hayward, Marx's notion of socio-ecological metabolism

captures fundamental aspects of humans' existence as both natural and physical beings: these include the energetic and material exchanges which occur between human beings and their natural environment ... This metabolism is regulated from the side of nature by natural laws governing the various physical processes involved, and from the side of society by institutionalized norms governing the division of labour and distribution of wealth etc.[49]

Given the centrality that he assigned to the concept of metabolism—constituting the complex, interdependent process linking human beings to nature through labor—it should not surprise us that this concept also plays a central role in Marx's vision of a future society of associated producers: "Freedom in this sphere [the realm of natural necessity]," he wrote in volume 3 of *Capital*, "can consist only in this, that socialized man, the associated producers, govern the human metabolism with nature in a rational way, bringing it under their own collective control instead of being dominated by it as a blind power; accomplishing it with the least expenditure of energy and in conditions most worthy and appropriate for their human nature."[50]

To understand more fully the significance of Marx's use of the concept of metabolism to account for the human–nature relation through social production, it is necessary to look briefly at how this concept emerged. The term "metabolism" (*Stoffwechsel*) was introduced as early as 1815 and was adopted by German physiologists during the 1830s and 1840s to refer primarily to material exchanges within the body, related to respiration. But the term was given a somewhat wider application (and therefore greater currency) by Liebig's use of it in 1842 in his *Animal Chemistry*, the great work that followed his 1840 *Agricultural Chemistry*. In *Animal Chemistry* Liebig introduced the notion of metabolic process in the context of tissue degradation. It was later generalized still further and emerged as one of the key concepts, applicable both at the cellular level and in the analysis of entire organisms, in the development of biochemistry.[51]

In Liebig's *Animal Chemistry* the material concept of metabolism was mixed rather inconsistently with the notion of "vital force," in which Liebig hearkened back to an earlier vitalism, identifying physiological motion with unknown, even mystical, sources (imponderables) that could not be reduced to material exchange. (Liebig's contribution here fed into a whole tradition of analysis that has been called "vital materialism," which tried to avoid mechanistic approaches to biochemistry.) His analysis in this respect came under attack in 1845 from the German scientist Julius Robert Mayer, one of the four co-discoverers in the early 1840s of the law of the conservation of energy. In a paper entitled "The Motion of Organisms and their Relation to Metabolism" Mayer argued, in opposition to Liebig, that the notion of "vital force" was unnecessary, and that metabolism (*Stoffwechsel*) was explicable entirely in terms of a scientific materialism emphasizing energetics (the conservation of energy and its exchange). Hence, the whole notion of metabolism came to be linked in this way with the more general shift toward energetics in science, and was thus essential for the development of "quantitative ecology." Marx's own use of the concept in the 1860s in order to explain the relation of human labor to its environment was consistent with this general shift toward energetics in science.[52]

Nor was this merely fortuitous, since Marx was well aware of these scientific debates. He was a close follower of the work of the British physicist John Tyndall, who championed Mayer's work in the 1860s. Engels was also familiar with Mayer's contributions and the general scientific discussions in this area, no doubt imparting some of this knowledge to Marx. In addition, Marx in 1864 had studied, and was deeply impressed by, the work of the German physiologist Theodor Schwann, who in 1839 had introduced the notion of cellular metabolism, thereby influencing Liebig, Mayer, and others.[53]

Beginning in the 1840s down to the present day, the concept of metabolism has been used as a key category in the systems theory approach to the interaction of organisms to their environments. It captures the complex biochemical process of metabolic exchange, through which an organism (or a given cell) draws upon materials and energy from its environment and converts these by way of various metabolic reactions into the building blocks of growth. In addition, the concept of metabolism is used to refer to the specific *regulatory processes* that govern this complex interchange between organisms and their environment. Eugene Odum and other leading system ecologists now employ the concept of "metabolism" to refer to all biological levels, starting with the single cell and ending with the ecosystem.[54]

Given all of this, it is somewhat surprising to discover that in his *Concept of Nature in Marx* (1962) Alfred Schmidt claimed that Marx simply took over the German chemist Jakob "Moleschott's theory of metabolism," though not without changing it somewhat. As his evidence for this, Schmidt quoted from a work by Moleschott, authored in 1857, in which Moleschott stated that

> The name "metabolism" has been given to this exchange of material [between different forms of life]. We are right not to mention the word without a feeling of reverence. For just as trade is the soul of commerce, the external circulation of material is the soul of the world.... I make no bones about stating this: the pivot about which the wisdom of the present-day world turns is the theory of metabolism.[55]

Yet, Schmidt's inference here, with respect to Moleschott's direct influence on Marx, has little actual basis in logic or evidence. The term "metabolism" (*Stoffwechsel*) was already well established in the scientific literature by the time Moleschott wrote this. Although Marx was aware of Moleschott's work (in London he attended lectures by Moleschott as well as Liebig, Tyndall, and Thomas Huxley), and this may have played into his use of the term, there is no evidence that he took it particularly seriously.[56] In contrast, Marx studied Liebig closely, and was undoubtedly familiar with his earlier, more influential use of the concept. Moreover, in his use of the concept in *Capital* Marx always stayed close to Liebig's argument, and generally did so within a context that included direct allusions to Liebig's work. Given Moleschott's tendency to shift back and forth between mechanistic materialism and mysticism, Marx is unlikely to have found his analysis congenial.

The widespread use of the concept of metabolism during these decades—a usage that cannot be attributed to any one thinker, although Liebig clearly played an important role—was pointed out by Engels in *Anti-Dühring* (1877–1878). The fact that "metabolism" or "the organic exchange of matter," Engels wrote, "is the most general and characteristic phenomenon of life has been said times without number during the last thirty years by physiological chemists and chemical physiologists." Later he added in The *Dialectics of Nature*—in a discussion of Liebig, Helmholtz, and Tyndall, all of whom had contributed to the shift to energetics in science in the 1840s and 1850s—that "Life is the mode of existence of protein bodies, the essential element of which consists in *continual metabolic interchange with the natural environment outside them*, and which ceases with the cessation of this metabolism, bringing about the decomposition of the protein." (For Engels, such metabolic exchange constituted a primary condition of life, even in a sense its "definition"—"but neither an exact nor an exhaustive one." Moreover, exchange of matter was also encountered in the absence of life.) There would therefore seem to be no genuine basis for assuming that Marx, in employing this concept in the late 1850s and 1860s, was drawing primarily on Moleschott (or indeed on Moleschott at all).[57]

More peculiar still, Marina Fischer-Kowalski, basing her remarks on Schmidt's interpretation, has stated that, "according to Schmidt, Marx drew much of his understanding of metabolism from this source [Moleschott] and imported a notion of trophical hierarchy, food chains and nutrient cycling rather than an organismic, biochemical interpretation of metabolism." The fact that Marx's analysis in this area was primarily derived from Liebig (and was undoubtedly influenced by Mayer, Tyndall, and Schwann), however, contradicts the claim that his analysis was neither biochemical nor organismic in nature. Indeed, it is undoubtedly a mistake to try to separate issues such as "nutrient cycling" from "the biochemical interpretation of metabolism," as Fischer-Kowalski has done, since the former is part of the metabolic process in the life of organisms. Thus Marx referred to "man's natural metabolism" when discussing the complex, interdependent biochemical process involved in the intake of nutrients and the production of human wastes or excrement.[58]

More usefully, Marina Fischer-Kowalski has recently referred to the concept of metabolism as "a rising conceptual star" within socio-ecological thought because of the emergence of cross-disciplinary research on "industrial metabolism"—dealing with the regulatory processes governing the throughput of materials and energy for a given industrial complex.[59] Further, the concept of metabolism is frequently employed in a more global context to analyze the material interchange between city and country, in much the same fashion as Liebig and Marx used the concept. For scholars working in these areas, it is now common to recognize, as Fischer-Kowalski has stated, that "within the nineteenth-century foundations of social theory, it was Marx and Engels who applied the term 'metabolism' to society."[60]

Environmental theorists working with the concept of "industrial metabolism" in recent years have often insisted that, just as the materials that birds use to build nests are commonly viewed as material flows associated with the metabolism of birds, so analogous material flows within human production can be seen as constituting part of the human metabolism. For example, Fischer-Kowalski includes "as part of the metabolism of a social system *those material and energetic flows that sustain the material compart-*

ments of the system."[61] Nevertheless, how such a system is regulated, particularly in the case of human society, is the big question. In Marx's case the answer was human labor and its development within historically specific social formations.

Marx's analysis of sustainability

An essential component of the concept of metabolism has always been the notion that it constitutes the basis on which the complex web of interactions necessary to life is sustained, and growth becomes possible. Marx employed the concept of a "rift" in the metabolic relation between human beings and the earth to capture the material estrangement of human beings within capitalist society from the natural conditions which formed the basis for their existence—what he called "the everlasting nature-imposed condition[s] of human existence."

To insist that large-scale capitalist society created such a metabolic rift between human beings and the soil was to argue that the nature-imposed conditions of sustainability had been violated. "Capitalist production," Marx observed, "turns towards the land only after its influence has exhausted it and after it has devastated its natural qualities." Further, this could be viewed in relation not only to the soil but also to the antagonistic relation between town and country. For Marx, like Liebig, the failure to return to the soil the nutrients that had been removed in the form of food and fiber had its counterpart in the pollution of the cities and the irrationality of modern sewerage systems. In the third volume of *Capital* he noted that "In London ... they can do nothing better with the excrement produced by 4 1/2 million people than pollute the Thames with it, at monstrous expense." Engels was no less explicit on this point. In addressing the need to transcend the antagonistic division of labor between town and country in *The Housing Question*, he referred, following Liebig, to the fact that "in London alone a greater quantity of manure than is produced by the whole kingdom of Saxony is poured away every day into the sea with an expenditure of enormous sums." It was therefore necessary, he argued, to reestablish an "intimate connection between industrial and agricultural production" together with "as uniform a distribution as possible of the population over the whole country" (an argument that Marx and Engels had made in *The Communist Manifesto*). Writing in volume 3 of *Capital*, Marx was adamant in insisting that the "excrement produced by man's natural metabolism," along with the waste of industrial production and consumption, needed to be returned to the soil, as part of a complete metabolic cycle.[62]

For Marx, the metabolic rift associated at the social level with the antagonistic division between town and country was also evident on a more global level: whole colonies saw their land, resources, *and soil* robbed to support the industrialization of the colonizing countries. Following Liebig, who had contended that "Great Britain robs all countries of the conditions of their fertility" and had pointed to Ireland as an extreme example, Marx wrote, "England has indirectly exported the soil of Ireland, without even allowing its cultivators the means for replacing the constituents of the exhausted soil."[63]

Hence, it is impossible to avoid the conclusion that Marx's view of capitalist agriculture and of the metabolic rift in the nature-imposed relations between human beings and the soil led him to a wider concept of ecological sustainability—a notion that he thought of very limited practical relevance to capitalist society, which was incapable of applying rational scientific methods in this area, but essential for a society of associated producers.

> The way that the cultivation of particular crops depends on fluctuations in market prices and the constant changes in cultivation with these price fluctuations—the entire spirit of capitalist production, which is oriented towards the most immediate monetary profits—stands in contradiction to agriculture, which has to concern itself with the whole gamut of permanent conditions of life required by the chain of human generations.[64]

Marx's emphasis on the need to maintain the earth for the sake of "the chain of human generations" (an idea that he had encountered in the early 1840s in Proudhon's *What is Property?*) captured the very essence of the present-day notion of sustainable development, famously defined by the Brundtland Commission as "development which meets the needs of the present without compromising the ability of future generations to meet their needs." Or, as Marx, capturing the same essential idea, put it at another point, the "conscious and rational treatment of the land as permanent communal property" is "the inalienable condition for the existence and reproduction of the chain of human generations."[65] Indeed, in a truly remarkable passage in *Capital*, Marx wrote:

> From the standpoint of a higher socio-economic formation, the private property of particular individuals in the earth will appear just as absurd as the private property of one man in other men. Even an entire society, a nation, or all simultaneously existing societies taken together, are not owners of the earth. They are simply its possessors, its beneficiaries, and have to bequeath it in an improved state to succeeding generations as *boni patres familias* [good heads of the household].[66]

These issues became increasingly important to Marx near the end of his life, when, as a result of his investigations into the revolutionary potential of the archaic Russian commune, he developed the argument that it would be possible to form an agricultural system "organized on a vast scale and managed by cooperative labor" through the use of modern "agronomic methods" not fully or rationally employed under capitalism. The merit of such a system, he contended, would be that it would be "in a position to incorporate all the positive acquisitions devised by the capitalist system" without falling prey to the purely exploitative relation to the soil, that is, the robbery, that characterized the latter. Marx's focus on the literature of the Russian populists near the end of his life, and his growing conviction that revolution against capitalism would emerge first in Russia—where economic, and more specifically agricultural, abundance could not be taken for granted—compelled him to focus on agricultural underdevelopment, and the ecological requirements of a more rational agricultural system.[67]

Marx did not believe, though such views are commonly attributed to him, that the answer to problems of agricultural development was simply to increase the scale of production. Rather his analysis taught him the dangers of large-scale agriculture, while also teaching him that the main issue was metabolic interaction between human beings and the earth. Hence, agriculture could occur on a fairly large scale only where conditions of sustainability were maintained—something that he believed was impossible under large-scale capitalist agriculture. "The moral of the tale," Marx wrote in volume 3 of *Capital*, "...is that the capitalist system runs counter to a rational agriculture, or that a rational agriculture is incompatible with the capitalist system (even if the latter promotes technical development in agriculture) and needs either small farmers working for themselves or the control of the associated producers." Marx and Engels consistently argued in their writings that large landholders were invariably more destructive in their relation to the earth than free farmers. Thus Engels wrote in *Anti-Dühring* that in North America "the big landlords of the South, with their slaves and their rapacious tilling of the land, exhausted the soil until it could only grow firs."[68]

Although focusing to a considerable extent on the contradictions of the second agricultural revolution and its relation to the antagonistic division between town and country, Marx and Engels's materialist conception of nature meant that they also addressed (though much more briefly) other ecological problems, including the depletion of coal reserves, the destruction of forests, and so on. As Engels noted in a letter to Marx, "the working individual is not only a stabiliser of the *present* but also, and to a far greater extent, a squanderer of *past*, solar heat. As to what we have done in the way of squandering our reserves of energy, our coal, ore, forests, etc., you are better informed than I am."[69] Marx himself referred to the "devastating" effects of "deforestation" and viewed this as a long-term, historical result of the exploitative relation to nature that had characterized all civilization, not just capitalism, up to that point: "the development of civilization and industry in general," he wrote, "has always shown itself so active in the destruction of forests that everything that has been done for their conservation and production is completely insignificant in comparison."[70] Marx also decried the fact that the forests in England were not "true forests" since "the deer in the parks of the great are demure domestic cattle, as fat as London aldermen"; while in Scotland "the so-called "deer forests" that had been set up for the benefit of huntsmen (at the expense of rural laborers) encompassed deer but no trees.[71] Under the influence of the ancient materialists and Darwin, Marx and Engels repudiated the age-old conception that had placed human beings at the center of the natural universe. Thus Engels professed "a withering contempt for the idealistic exaltation of man over the other animals." There is no trace in Marx and Engels of the Cartesian reduction of animals to mere machines.[72]

In recent years ecological economics has focused heavily on energetics and the entropy law. In this context it has sometimes been argued that Marx and Engels were in error in refusing to acknowledge the importance of energy and material flows for a theory of economic value, in the context of their rejection of the work of the early ecological economist Sergei Podolinsky, who, beginning in 1880, had made some pioneering contributions in this area, and who considered himself a follower of Marx. This criticism has been leveled in particular by Juan Martinez-Alier in a series of works.[73]

Nevertheless, the entire body of "evidence" offered for this interpretation consists of two letters that Engels wrote to Marx, at the latter's request, assessing Podolinsky's analysis, three months before Marx's death. In these letters Engels accepted the general scientific basis upon which Podolinsky's analysis was erected, but criticized the shortcomings of his analysis of energy transfers, which failed to take into account energy transferred by fertilizers in agriculture and the importance of fossil fuels. In general, Engels believed that the obstacles to calculating accurately the energy transfers involved in economic transactions were so enormous as to make them impractical. This was far from constituting a rejection of the entropy law.

Marx himself never replied to this letter from Engels nor commented on Podlinsky's work, and, given the fact that he died a few months later, even his silence tells us nothing.[74] If Marx was thus unable to take advantage of Podolinsky's work, however, the same was not true with respect to his incorporation of Liebig's insights into his analysis. Hence, it is significant that some ecological economists have seen Marx's work, in line with Liebig's, as offering the essential elements of a thermodynamic critique of capitalist agriculture.[75]

A more prominent criticism of Marx, deriving from a failure to understand his approach to the question of sustainability, is that he allegedly denied the role of nature in the creation of wealth by constructing a labor theory of value that saw all value derived from nature, and by referring to nature as a "free gift" to capital.[76] Yet this criticism is based on fundamental misunderstanding of Marx's economics. The idea that the earth was a "gift" of nature to capital was propounded by Malthus long before Marx. Marx, while accepting this as a reality of capitalist production, nonetheless was aware of the social and ecological contradictions embedded in such a view. In his *Economic Manuscript of 1861–63* he repeatedly attacked Malthus for falling back on this "physiocratic notion" that the environment was "a gift of nature to man," while failing to perceive how this was connected to historically specific social relations brought into being by capital.[77]

Nevertheless, this tenet of classical liberal political economy was carried forward into neoclassical economics in the work of the great economic theorist Alfred Marshall and persisted in neoclassical economics textbooks well into the 1980s. Hence the tenth (1987) edition of a widely used introductory textbook in economics by Campbell McConnell states the following: "Land refers to all natural resources—all 'free gifts of nature'— which are usable in the production process." And further along we find: "Land has no production cost; it is a 'free and nonreproducible gift of nature.'"[78]

To be sure, Marx agreed with classical liberal political economy that *under the law of value of capitalism* nature was accorded no value. "The earth," he wrote, "…is active as an agent of production in the production of a use-value, a material product, say wheat. But it has nothing to do with producing the *value of the wheat*."[79] The *value* of the wheat, as with any commodity under capitalism, arose from labor. For Marx, however, this merely pointed to the very narrow, limited conception of wealth associated with capitalist commodity relations and a system built around exchange value. Genuine wealth, he argued, consisted of use values—the characteristic of production in general, transcending its specifically capitalist form. Indeed, it was the contradiction between use value and exchange value engendered by capitalism that Marx considered to be one of the foremost contradictions of the entire dialectic of capital. Nature, which contributed to the production of use values, was just as much a source of wealth as labor—even though its contribution to wealth was neglected by the system. Indeed, labor itself was ultimately reducible to such natural properties—a proposition deeply embedded in the materialist tradition going back as far as Epicurus. "What Lucretius says," Marx wrote in *Capital*, "is self-evident: *nil posse creari de nihilo*, out of nothing, nothing can be created. 'Creation of value' is the transposition of labour-power into labour. Labour-power itself is, above all else, the material of nature transformed into a human organism."[80]

"Nature," Marx wrote, "builds no machines, no locomotives, railways, electric telegraphs, self-acting mules, etc. These are products of human industry; natural material transformed into organs of the human will over nature, or of human participation in nature. They are *organs of the human brain, created by the human hand*; the power of knowledge, objectified." Hence, human beings through their production give new form, that is, actively transform, already existing material nature. "Labour is the living, form-giving fire; it is the transitoriness of things, their temporality, as their formation by living time."[81] (Here Marx was building on Epicurus' notion of the transitory nature of things, of matter as mere "embodied time," as Marx had put it in his doctoral thesis; see Chapter Two above.)

In line with this conception, which took into account both material nature and the transformative role of human labor, Marx insisted that "labour," as he stated at the beginning of *Capital*, "is not the only source of material wealth, i.e. of the use-values it produces. As William Petty says, labour is the father of material wealth, the earth is its mother." In the *Critique of the Gotha Programme* Marx offered a trenchant criticism of those socialists such as Ferdinand Lassalle who had attributed what Marx called "*supernatural creative power* to labour" by viewing it as the sole source of wealth and setting aside nature's contribution.[82] Under communism, he insisted, wealth would need to be viewed in far more universal terms, as consisting of those material use values that constituted the foundations for the full development of human creativity, "the development of the rich individuality which is all sided in its production as in its consumption"—expanding the wealth of connections allowed for by nature, while at the same time reflecting the complex and changing human metabolism with nature.[83]

An even more important criticism frequently leveled at Marx in this area is that he had an extremely optimistic, cornucopian view of the conditions that would exist in post-capitalist society due to the development of the forces of production under capitalism. In this interpretation Marx relied so much on the assumption of abundance in his vision of a future society that ecological considerations such as the scarcity of natural resources and external limits to production simply vanished. Thus Alec Nove has contended that Marx believed that "the problem of production had been 'solved'" by capitalism, and that the future society of associated producers would not have to "take seriously the problem of the allocation of scarce resources," which also implied that there was no need for an "ecologically conscious" socialism.[84]

Yet, rather than arguing, as Nove contends, that natural resources were "inexhaustible" and that ecological abundance was simply assured by the development of capitalist forces of production, Marx insisted again and again that capitalism was beset with a chronic problem of production in agriculture, which could ultimately be traced to the unsustainable way in which production was organized. Agriculture in general, Marx argued, "when it progresses spontaneously and is not *consciously controlled* ... leaves deserts behind it—Persia, Mesopotamia, etc., Greece."[85]

Within industry Marx was aware of the enormous waste generated, and stressed the need for the "reduction" and "re-use" of waste, especially in a section of volume 3 of *Capital* entitled "Utilization of the Refuse of Production." Further, he gave every indication that these difficulties would continue to plague any society attempting to construct socialism or communism. Thus, although some critics, such as Andrew McLaughlin, argue that Marx envisioned "a general material abundance as the substratum of communism," and hence saw "no basis for recognizing any interest in the liberation of nature from human domination," this is contradicted by overwhelming evidence from Marx's texts themselves, where he demonstrates a deep concern for issues of ecological limits and sustainability.[86]

Further, there is simply no indication at any point in Marx's vast intellectual corpus that he believed that a sustainable relation to the earth would come about automatically with the transition to socialism. Rather he stressed the need for planning in this area, beginning with measures aimed at the elimination of the antagonistic division of labor between town and country. This included the more even dispersal of population, the integration of industry and agriculture, and the restoration and improvement of the soil through the recycling of soil nutrients. All of this obviously required a revolutionary transformation in the human relation to the earth. Capitalism, Marx observed, "creates the material conditions for a new and higher synthesis, a union of agriculture and industry on the basis of the forms that have developed during the period of their antagonistic isolation." Yet in order to achieve this "higher synthesis," he argued, it would be necessary for the associated producers in the new society to "govern the human metabolism with nature in a rational way"— a requirement that raised fundamental and continuing challenges for post-revolutionary society.[87]

Toward the society of associated producers

For Marx, capitalism was a class society characterized by an extreme division of the population within society, which was rooted in a no less extreme division of the population from the earth. "All production," under all forms of society, he wrote in the *Grundrisse*, "is appropriation of nature on the part of an individual within and through a specific form of society." Yet, the system of capitalist private property, as distinguished both from communal property and from private property rooted in individual worker-farmer proprietorship over the land, arises through the severing of any direct connection between the mass of the population and the earth—often by forcible removal. Hence, a "presupposition" for the development of capitalist wage labor "is the separation of free labour from the objective conditions of its realization—from the means of labour and the material for labour. Thus, above all, release of the worker from the soil as his natural workshop." The very existence of capital, for Marx, therefore presupposed "a process of history which dissolves the various forms in which the worker is a proprietor, or in which the proprietor works. Thus above all (1) *Dissolution* of the relation to the earth—land and soil—as natural condition of production—to which he relates as to his own organic being.... (2) *Dissolution of the relations* in which he appears as *proprietor*." This dissolution of the organic relation between human labour and the earth took the form of what the classical economists, including Marx, called "original," "primary," or "primitive" accumulation. In this process lay the genesis of the capitalist system.[88]

At the end of *Capital*, volume 1, Marx devoted Part 8 of his book, consisting of eight chapters, to the description of "So-Called Primitive Accumulation," in which he described the lengthy historical process, beginning as early as the fourteenth century, whereby the great mass of the population was removed, often by force, from the soil and "hurled onto the labour-market as free, unprotected and rightless proletarians." Moreover, this historical process of "the expropriation of the agricultural producer, the peasant," went hand in hand with the genesis of the capitalist farmer and the industrial capitalist.[89]

In England, where this process had reached its highest development at the time that Marx was writing, and which he took therefore as the classic form of primitive accumulation, the nobility, which had metamorphosed early on into a moneyed nobility, made "transformation of arable land into sheep-walks ... its slogan." The process of dispossessing the peasantry took the form of enclosures of common lands, thus separating the free agricultural laborers from the means of their production, turning them into paupers and proletarians who could survive only by selling their labour power in the towns. In developing his critique of this historical movement, Marx gave pride of place to Bacon's criticism of the "depopulating inclosures" in his *The Reign of Henry VII*, and to Thomas More's *Utopia*, where it was said that England was a "curious land where 'sheep ... swallow down the very men themselves.'" The Reformation, and the seizure of church lands, gave new impetus to this whole process. "The Catholic church," at the time of the Reformation, was, Marx remarked, "the feudal proprietor of a great part of the soil of England." With the seizure of church lands, innumerable peasants were driven out. So great was the increase in pauperization that Queen Elizabeth was forced to acknowledge it directly by the introduction of the poor rate— the beginning of the Poor Laws. "In fact, the usurpation of the common lands and the accompanying revolution in agriculture," Marx noted, "had such an acute effect on the agricultural labourers that ... their wages began to fall below the minimum between 1765 and 1780, and to be supplemented by official Poor Law relief."[90]

These changes also spelled the end of the yeomanry, which were, as late as the seventeenth century, much more numerous than the class of farmers, and had constituted the backbone of Cromwell's New Model Army. By the eighteenth century the yeomanry had simply disappeared. Numerous parliamentary "Bills for Inclosure of Commons" were introduced to make lawful the seizure of the common lands. "By the nineteenth century, the very memory of the connection between the agricultural labourer and communal property had ... vanished."[91] The process of enclosure, however, continued into the nineteenth century. "As an example of the method used in the nineteenth century," Marx wrote,

the "clearings" made by the Duchess of Sutherland will suffice here. This person, who had been well instructed in economics, resolved, when she succeeded to the headship of the clan, to undertake a radical economic cure, and to turn the whole county of Sutherland, the population of which had already been reduced

to 15,000 by similar processes, into a sheep-walk. Between 1814 and 1820 these
15,000 inhabitants, about 3,000 families, were systematically hunted and rooted
out. All their villages were destroyed and burnt, all their fields turned into
pasturage. British soldiers enforced this mass of evictions, and came to blows
with the inhabitants. One old woman was burnt to death in the flames of the
hut she refused to leave. It was in this manner that this fine lady appropriated
794,000 acres of land which had belonged to the clan from time immemorial.
She assigned to the expelled inhabitants some 6,000 acres on the sea-shore—2
acres per family. The 6,000 acres had until this time lain waste, and brought in
no income to their owners. The Duchess, in the nobility of her heart, actually
went so far as to let these waste lands at an average rent of 2s 6d. per acre to
the clansmen, who for centuries had shed their blood for her family. She divided
the whole of the stolen land of the clan into twenty-nine huge sheep farms,
each inhabited by a single family, for the most part imported English farm-
servants. By 1825 the 15,000 Gaels had already been replaced by 131,000 sheep.
The remnant of the original inhabitants, who had been flung onto the sea-shore,
tried to live by catching fish. They became amphibious, and lived, as an English
writer says, half on land and half on water, and withal only half on both.[92]

All of this meant that it became possible to "incorporate the soil into
capital," while creating the necessary army of surplus labor to feed urban
industry.[93]

However, "where," Marx asks, "did the capitalists originally spring from?
For the only class created directly by the expropriation of the agricultural
peasant is that of the great landed proprietors." Marx divides his answer
to this question into two parts: the origin of the capitalist farmer and the
origin of the industrial capitalist. The former emerged slowly, and can be
said to have emerged out of the earlier form of the bailiff in the second
half of the fourteenth century. It is at this point that the landlord begins
providing seed, cattle, and farm implements so that the farmer can carry
on the real work of agriculture. Eventually this takes the form of the
developed system based on ground rent. The whole process was greatly
facilitated, moreover, by the agricultural revolution that began in the late
fifteenth century, and the enclosures. "The usurpation of the common
lands allowed the farmer to augment greatly his stock of cattle, almost
without cost, while the cattle themselves yielded a richer supply of manure
for the cultivation of the soil."[94]

The degree of the division of labor is, as Adam Smith had pointed
out, partly dependent on the extent of the market. For Marx, the "genesis
of the industrial capitalist" was a story not so much of English history as
of world history. It took place not gradually but all at once. This took
the form of the pillage of the non-capitalist world and the creation of the
triangle trade of the trans-Atlantic slave system. As Marx famously put it:

The discovery of gold and silver in America, the extirpation, enslavement and entombment in mines of the indigenous population of that continent, the beginnings of the conquest and plunder of India, and the conversion of Africa into a preserve for the commercial hunting of blackskins, are all things which characterize the dawn of the era of capitalist production. These idyllic proceedings are the chief moments of primitive accumulation.[95]

The trade in scalps promoted by the British and the Puritans of New England, the slave trade in Java, the conquest and plunder of India, the opium trade, and so on, were all means in which capital created a world system under its control that extracted wealth and raw materials for capitalist industry for the benefit of Europe, while destroying communal systems of property elsewhere. All of this is part of the larger, global expropriation that provided the primary accumulation for the genesis of industrial capital. Hence, in Marx's words, it was "not without reason" that Carey accused England "of trying to turn every other country into a purely agricultural nation, whose manufacturer is to be England." Within England itself, soon to be known as "the workshop of the world," the change was profound. It transformed "at one pole, the social means of production and subsistence into capital, and at the opposite pole, the mass of the population into wage-labourers, into the free 'labouring poor,' that artificial product of modern history."[96]

Primitive accumulation ("so-called") constitutes the prehistory and the precondition of capital. The metamorphosis that it represents ushers in the system of capitalist appropriation, which rests on the exploitation of alienated, but formally free labor. And from this arises the whole historical tendency of capitalist accumulation— its "immanent laws" of development. For Marx, this is expressed most succinctly in terms of the new laws that govern population itself under these conditions, that is, what he calls the "absolute general law" of capitalist accumulation: the tendency of capitalist class society, built on the exploitation of the proletariat, to polarize so that more and more wealth is concentrated in fewer and fewer hands, while the great mass of the population, kept down by the continual reproduction of an industrial reserve army of the unemployed, finds itself in a situation of relative impoverishment and degradation. As Marx himself puts it:

The greater the social wealth, the functioning capital, the extent and energy of its growth, and therefore also the greater the absolute mass of the proletariat and the productivity of its labor, the greater is the industrial reserve army.... But the greater this reserve army in proportion to the active labour-army, the greater is the mass of a consolidated surplus population, whose misery is in inverse ratio to the amount of torture it has to undergo in the form of labour.

The more extensive, finally, the pauperized sections of the working class and the industrial reserve army, the greater is official pauperism. *This is the absolute general law of capitalist accumulation.* Like all other laws, it is modified in its working by many circumstances, the analysis of which does not concern us here.[97]

In this way Marx points, in the last two parts of volume 1 of *Capital*, to laws of population—though ones very different from the transhistorical (and essentially non-developmental) form which they take in Malthus's theory. The precondition of capitalism is the removal of the mass of the population from the soil, which makes possible the historical development of capital itself. This takes the form of the increasing class polarization of the population between rich and poor, the antagonistic separation of town from country (replicated on a world scale by the fact that some countries are turned into mere agricultural feeding grounds, mere sources of raw materials for the industrial development at the center of the system).

For Marx, all of this was inseparable from, and indeed is a logical outgrowth of, what he called the "*differentia specifica*" of the system of capitalist private property—the fact that it was built on systematic alienation from all forms of naturally based need. Hence, under the artificial regime of capital it is the search for exchange value (that is, profit), rather than the servicing of genuine, universal, natural needs, which constitutes the object, the motive, for production. The resulting extreme polarization between wealth that knows no bounds, at one pole, and an alienated, exploited, degraded existence which constitutes the denial of all that is most human, on the other, creates a contradiction that runs like a fault-line through the capitalist system. Eventually the capitalist "integument" that so distorts and restricts the development of social labor "is burst asunder, the knell of capitalist private property sounds. The expropriators are expropriated."[98]

In all of this, however, Marx continually insists that the alienation from the earth is *sine qua non* of the capitalist system. Thus in his frequently disregarded last chapter to volume 1 of *Capital*, "On the Modern Theory of Colonization," Marx points to Edward Wakefield's theory of colonization, whereby Wakefield argued that the only way in which to maintain a cheap proletarian workforce for industry in the colonies was to find a way of artificially raising the price of the land. Otherwise workers would quickly leave industry for the land and set themselves up as small proprietors. For Marx, this pointed to the contradiction of the separation and estrangement of the population from the land that constituted the foundation on which the whole system of formally free labor rested. The transformation of property in the land by capital, Marx wrote in the *Grundrisse*, "'clears,' as Steuart says, the land of its excess mouths, tears the children of the earth from the breast on which they were raised, and thus transforms labour on the soil itself, which appears by its nature as the direct wellspring of subsistence, into a mediated source of subsistence, a source purely dependent on social relations." The transformation of capitalism, the abolition of wage labor, and the creation of a society of associated producers thus necessitated the abolition of this alienation of human beings from the earth.[99]

Hence, from the 1840s on, both Marx and Engels insisted on the need to transcend this form of alienation from nature upon which capitalism rested. Always their argument involved the abolition of the antagonistic relation between town and country through the integration of agriculture and industry, the dispersal of population, and what Marx referred to as "the restoration" of the metabolic relation between human beings and the earth. Marx quoted Hippolyte Colins as saying, "It is thanks to the individual appropriation of the soil that there exist men who only possess the strength of their arms.... When you put a man in a vacuum, you rob him of the air. You do the same when you take the soil away from him ... for you are putting him in a space void of wealth, so as to leave him no way of living except according to your wishes."[100]

For Engels, following Liebig, the transcendence of the antagonism between town and country was expressed in ecological terms:

> Abolition of the antithesis between town and country is not merely possible. It has become a direct necessity of industrial production itself, just as it has become a necessity of agricultural production and, besides, of public health. The present poisoning of the air, water and land can be put an end to only by the fusion of town and country; and only such fusion will change the situation of the masses now languishing in the towns, and enable their excrement to be used for the production of plants instead of for the production of disease.[101]

Hence, in their conception of a future society Marx and Engels proposed a higher synthesis in the relation between town and country that, as Bertell Ollman has observed, appeared "to involve moving some industries to the country as well as greatly expanding the amount of unencumbered land inside cities for parks, woodlands, and garden plots. I suspect, too, that Marx would like to see the number of people living in any one city reduced, and more small and medium size cities set up throughout the countryside."[102]

The close connection between Marx's vision of communism and ecological sustainability is evident in the utopian conceptions of the acclaimed nineteenth-century English artist, master-craftsperson, designer, poet, and socialist activist William Morris (1834–1896), who was not only a firm advocate of Marxian socialism but also one of the formative Green thinkers in the English context. In his celebrated utopian novel *News from Nowhere* Morris described a society in which the overthrow of the World Market had led to the demise of wasteful forms of economic production geared to artificial necessities for the sake of profit, and the subsequent reorganization of production in such a way that "nothing *can* be made but for genuine use." Free time for the pursuit of intellectual inquiry and independent craftsmanship was more readily available—because society had given up its narrowly defined, instrumentalist ends—whereas work itself was seen as serving the needs of both human creativity and the fulfillment of social needs. In this postrevolutionary utopian social order, Morris wrote in the spirit of Marx, "the difference between town and country grew less and less." Initially, following the revolution, people had flocked from town to country but "yielded to the influence of their surroundings, and became country people"—with the population of the country more numerous than that of the towns. England in the nineteenth century, it was explained, had become "a country of huge and foul workshops, and fouler gambling-dens, surrounded by an ill-kept, poverty-stricken farm, pillaged by the masters of workshops. It is now a garden, where nothing is wasted and nothing is spoilt, with the necessary dwellings, sheds, and workshops scattered up and down the country, all trim and neat and pretty." The existence of this garden did not, however, preclude the preservation of wilderness areas, which were maintained for their intrinsic value. Population, meanwhile, had stabilized and been spread about (part of the program enunciated by Marx and Engels in *The Communist Manifesto*).[103]

Morris's vision, so close to that of Marx (whom he read and reread), reminds us of the fully revolutionary character of Marx's analysis, which, from his very earliest writings on, took account of the alienation of human beings from the earth under capitalism, as a precondition for alienation within the regime of capital accumulation. Marx never moved very far in this respect from the Epicurean notions that nothing came from nothing and nothing could be reduced to nothing, that is, that all human production involved the transformation and conservation of matter.[104] Likewise he adhered consistently to the proposition, arising from this analysis, that the land needed to be conserved and cultivated—for the sake of future generations. These constituted naturally imposed conditions of human production and existence, and the most general expression of the alienation of capitalism from the conditions of production in general. The revolution against capitalism required therefore not only the overturning of its specific relations of exploitation of labor, but also the transcendence—through the rational regulation of the metabolic relation between human beings and nature by means of modern science and industry—of the alienation from the earth: the ultimate foundation/precondition for capitalism. Only in these terms does Marx's frequent call for the "abolition of wage labor" make any sense.

CHAPTER 6

THE BASIS IN NATURAL
HISTORY FOR OUR VIEW

Darwin wrote the first short draft of his theory of the transmutation of species in soft pencil in 1842. Two years later he wrote a much longer draft, of about fifty thousand words, and gave strict instructions to his wife Emma that it should be published upon his death. It was not until 1858—two decades after he first articulated his theory in his *Notebooks*—that he made it public in a joint presentation of papers with his young rival Alfred Russell Wallace (publishing *The Origin of Species* itself in the following year). And he only did so then when it appeared that Wallace would scoop him. This has raised the issue (as we saw in Chapter Two) of what Stephen Jay Gould has called "Darwin's Delay"—a question which has been of increasing interest to Darwin scholars, particularly with the publication of his early transmutation notebooks.

The traditional interpretation for the delay has been that as a rational scientist Darwin had simply been slowly accumulating evidence in order to construct a much stronger theory. But such an interpretation must explain why during these years he was engaged in activities such as the writing of a multi-volume work on the taxonomy and natural history of barnacles. Based on the evidence provided in Darwin's *Notebooks*, historians of science have recently arrived at quite different conclusions, now almost universally held by Darwin scholars: that Darwin was a "tormented evolutionist," "reluctant revolutionist," and alarmed materialist, trying to reconcile his scientific discoveries with his traditional Whig and Anglican beliefs, fearful as well as of losing his respectability and his position within elite circles.[1] Still, it would be a serious mistake to attribute Darwin's delay to cowardice. Rather he needs to be understood not simply as a scientist, but as a complex social actor in a time of turbulent social change, trying to advance his scientific views, which were rooted in materialism, while defending a particular class position. The grandson on his maternal side of industrialist Josiah Wedgwood, living on his estate at Down House in

Kent, his money (and his wife's money) invested in railroad stock, Darwin was a strong believer in the bourgeois order. His science was revolutionary but Darwin the man was not, and therein lay his inner dilemma.[2]

England in Darwin's day was a seething cauldron of discontent. In August 1839 when he was attending a meeting of the British Association for the Advancement of Science in Birmingham he found a city on the verge of martial law. The Chartist Convention was being held in the town and socialists and red-Lamarckian evolutionists were in attendance—with half a million pamphlets denouncing property, marriage, and the uncooperative state being distributed. In 1842, while Darwin worked on his evolutionary sketch, the entire country was paralyzed by a general strike organized by the Chartists. The Riot Act was read in many of the industrial towns, and in some demonstrators were shot and killed. Meanwhile the atheists had recently founded an illegal penny paper, the *Oracle of Reason*, which was selling in the thousands. It attacked religion with geological tidbits and revolutionary Lamarckianism. William Chilton, writing for the *Oracle*, presented materialism in revolutionary class terms, coupling this with evolutionary concepts: "Man was just a collection of organized atoms." The *Oracle* attacked Paley's natural theology as a "pernicious" justification of the status quo. In August 1842 the *Oracle* editor, George Holyoake, was tried publicly and uttered such blasphemies as the non-existence of God and the inability of the poor to support parsons during economic bad times. Darwin meanwhile had been reading William Cobbett's *Rural Rides*, with its attacks on Parson Malthus and the Corn Laws. With an uprising feared, the old "Iron Duke," the Duke of Wellington, called up the Guards and special units of the police. The zoologist Richard Owen, a colleague and collaborator of Darwin's, drilled with the Honourable Artillery Company and was called out to reinforce the police. Day after day, up to ten thousand demonstrators massed on the commons all over the capital. Darwin and his wife Emma, in relief, left London in the fourth week of the general strike to take up residence in the rural surroundings of their new home at Down House in Kent.[3]

The new setting did not, however, lessen the magnitude of the dilemma in which Darwin was caught, when writing up his theory for the first time. As Adrian Desmond and James Moore observe in their biography, *Darwin: The Life and Times of a Tormented Evolutionist* (1991),

> *Of course* Darwin could not publish. Materialism petrified him, and one can see why, with it condemned by the forces of Church-and-State as a blasphemous derision of the Christian law of the land. He was too worldly-wise not to sense the danger, the damning class implications. He had no illusions about how he

would be treated.... By netting man and ape together he risked being identified with atheistic-low-life, or with extreme Dissenters cursing the "fornicating" Church. The "whole fabric" was ready to be ripped apart without his help. As the old world "totters & falls," he could not be seen aiding the demolition. Ultimately he was frightened for his respectability. For a gentleman among the Oxbridge set, priming itself to guard man's soul against the socialist levellers, publishing would have been tantamount to treachery—a betrayal of the old order.[4]

Evolutionary ideas had long been associated with materialism—each implying the other—and were seen as first arising from the ancient materialists Empedocles, Epicurus, and Lucretius. It was in Lucretius that the notion of species survival through adaptation to the environment, and more importantly the idea of the extinction of species that failed to adapt (known as "the elimination theory"), was most clearly stated in antiquity. Lucretius died in 55 B.C. and evolutionary thinking on the origins of life did not reemerge until the mid-eighteenth century. Hence, as Paul Sears states in his book *Charles Darwin: The Naturalist as a Cultural Force* (1950), "after Lucretius, speculations as to the origin and development of life lay dormant for eighteen centuries," only to be revived by thinkers like Jean Baptiste Lamarck (1744–1829) and Erasmus Darwin. Until the publication of Darwin's *Origin* itself, however, such views were mostly confined to the materialist underground, excluded from the realm of respectable science and establishment thought. Moreover, they lacked any clear explanation of the mechanism of evolution.[5]

We now know that Darwin was exposed to materialist theories of evolution by his walking companion and early mentor, the Lamarckian biologist Robert Grant, while he was still a young medical student in Edinburgh. It was at Edinburgh, moreover, that he saw materialist views raised and then censored within the Pliny Society. Although later on, at Cambridge, Darwin found himself still attracted to Paley's *Natural Theology*—entranced by the logic of the argument and the emphasis on the perfect adaptation of species to their environment (which was viewed as evidence of design)—these materialist-evolutionary doubts lingered with him.

In his Cambridge years Darwin had considered himself to be a devout Christian, but there is no doubt that his immediate family background gave impetus to the tendency toward free-thinking that he was always to display—and that became stronger subsequent to his voyage on the *Beagle*. His grandfather Erasmus was a weak deist, his father Robert an unbeliever, his uncle Josiah Wedgwood a Unitarian, and his brother Erasmus (by the time that Darwin returned from his voyage on the *Beagle*) was also an unbeliever. Darwin's free-thinking family background thus placed him in potential conflict with the leading naturalists in his day since, in the words of Ernst Mayr, "virtually all the naturalists in England at that time were ordained ministers, as were the professors at Cambridge who taught botany (J.S. Henslow) and geology (Adam Sedgwick)."[6]

Darwin's evolutionary speculations had been strengthened enormously by his reading of Charles Lyell's *Principles of Geology*, the first volume of which he took on his voyage on the *Beagle*, where he served as the ship's naturalist. It was Lyell's conception of an extremely slow, uniform process of geological change over what then seemed to be almost interminable time that provided the basis on which Darwin was able gradually to erect his notions of transmutation of species (although Lyell himself at that time rejected the hypothesis of the transmutation of species). In his *Notebooks* Darwin continued these speculations, and drafting and redrafting his theory, in the early 1840s, but conditions did not seem propitious for publication. Hence, while building up his scientific reputation—publishing his *Journal* on the voyage around the world on the HMS *Beagle* (which immediately made him famous in both scientific and non-scientific circles), and authoring works on the geology of South America, coral reefs, and volcanic islands—Darwin continued to develop his most important idea, the theory of natural selection, in the hope of eventual publication. The botanist Joseph Hooker, one of Darwin's few confidants, had written to him in 1847 saying that no one has a right to "examine the question of species who has not minutely described many." Although Hooker did not actually have Darwin himself in mind in writing this, the latter nonetheless took it personally, and felt partly compelled for this reason to carry out his comprehensive study of barnacles—thereby earning the right to pronounce on species transmutation. Contemplating a theoretical scientific revolution that was as significant, and as threatening to established views, as the Copernican revolution had been, Darwin sought first to create a reputation for himself as an empirical scientific investigator that was unassailable. This in itself, though, was a delaying tactic of sorts, since Darwin's chief problem was that he felt unable to publish his theory due to the social implications and the climate of the time.[7]

By 1854 Darwin had finished his study of barnacles and returned once again to his work on natural selection. He commenced writing a work on the transmutation of species in 1856. His task was made easier this time around by the fact that historical conditions had changed considerably since he had first drafted his theory. By 1851 when the Great Exhibition was held in London, "the age of revolution" appeared to be gone, replaced by "the age of capital." The Great Exhibition celebrated Britain's hegemonic position as the industrial workshop of the world. The abolition of the Corn Laws five years earlier reflected the increasing dominance of the British economy by manufacturing capital. These conditions meant that materialist-evolutionary science, insofar as it was compatible with the system of industrial capitalism, could no longer be as easily suppressed.

As Thomas Huxley (1825–1895) wrote in 1859 at the time of the first publication of the *Origin*, "the transmutation theory, as it has been called, has been a 'skeleton in the closet'" always threatening to break out into the open. Why, it was frequently asked, did the realm of biology, of life, not conform, as part of a "consistent whole," with those material laws that had been shown to govern astronomy, physics, chemistry, and medicine?

In the decade of the 1850s the question of transmutation would not go away. One way in which it was raised was through the anonymous publication *The Vestiges of the Natural History of Creation* (1844) by Edinburgh publisher Robert Chambers (1802–1871). Chambers's book quickly became a best seller—four editions appeared in the first seven months and it eventually went through ten editions. By 1860 it had sold 24,000 copies. Chambers aimed the *Vestiges* not at the scientists, much less at those that he referred to as "the dogs of clergy," but at the ordinary educated Victorian. His arguments, though flawed, were impressive—convincing enough that for the first time the evolutionary doctrine became an open topic of discussion among the educated public at large. The *Vestiges* was of course full of weaknesses, and was savaged, not only by the likes of Sam Wilberforce, the Bishop of Oxford, and Adam Sedgwick, the Cambridge geologist and defender of natural theology, but also by Thomas Huxley, later to be known as "Darwin's bulldog." Nevertheless, its role in drawing the poison, and thus preparing the way for Darwin's later success, is not to be underestimated. "By the mid-forties," Desmond and Moore write with the *Vestiges* in mind, "transmutation was moving off the streets, out of the shabby dissecting theatres, and into the drawing-rooms." The great English Romantic John Ruskin had at one time seen nature in teleological terms but by the early 1850s was suffering doubts: "If only the Geologists would let me alone," he wrote in a letter in 1851, "I could do very well, but those dreadful Hammers! I hear the clink of them at the end of every cadence of the Bible verses."[8]

Darwin in the late 1850s had decided to publish his ideas on a grand scale, overcoming all opposition through the massive nature of his research. By 1858 he had written a number of chapters of what was intended to be his great work on *Natural Selection*. But in June 1858 the mail brought a score of pages from Alfred Russell Wallace outlining his own theory of natural selection, developed independently, providing an argument very similar to Darwin's 1842 sketch. A panic-stricken Darwin was thus forced to present his theory, together with Wallace's, in a joint presentation of papers (carried out by Charles Lyell and Joseph Hooker with the two principals absent) that very year, followed by the rapid completion of *The Origin of Species*, which Darwin persisted in viewing as a mere "abstract" of a longer work that never materialized, in the following year.

The Origin of Species

Like many great discoveries, the essential idea of Darwin's work, the full title of which was *On the Origin of Species by Means of Natural Selection; Or the Preservation of Favoured Races in the Struggle for Life*, was quite simple—though endlessly complex in its inner workings and ramifications. The fundamental theory laid out in the opening chapters of the work was developed as follows: All organisms are characterized by "superfecundity," or the tendency to produce many more offspring than can survive. These offspring vary among themselves, and are not simply replicas of an original type. Part of this variation is passed down to future generations. (Darwin did not know the laws of heredity at this time prior to the development of genetics, but the fact of heredity was of course well known.) Since not all offspring survive, Darwin concluded, there must necessarily be a struggle for existence among these numerous offspring, and those best fitted by this process of innate variation to the limited conditions of the local environment in which they lived would tend, statistically, to have a higher survival rate, thereby passing on these variations (at least to some extent) to their offspring. The accumulation of such favorable variations over the very long span of geological time would result in the evolution of species—or descent with modification.[9]

Darwin made it clear in the introduction that the chief contribution of his work lay not in the mere postulate of transmutation of species, which had already been proposed numerous times, such as in the work of the author of the *Vestiges*, but in explaining the specific mechanism—natural selection by means of innate variation—through which such transmutation occurred. Moreover, the aim of his theory was to account for the marvelous adaptation (and coadaptation) to the environment to be found everywhere in nature—and so heavily emphasized by the natural-theological tradition.

Darwin's strategy of presentation was simple and elegant. He started in Chapter 1 with what his readers knew best—the conditions of the

"Variation Under Domestication" of plants and animals, drawing on the long human history of horticulture and animal husbandry. Here he demonstrated that artificial selection had produced variations that were often greater than those separating what were generally recognized as different species, and at the same time that these variations could be traced to a common ancestry. He then turned, in Chapter 2, to the question of "Variation Under Nature." Not only was there enormous variation in nature; the question arose as to whether there was some mechanism in nature, equivalent to the action of the breeder, which would produce the same result—although on a greater scale over immense periods of time.

The answer came in Chapter 3, entitled "The Struggle for Existence," in which Darwin began to articulate the workings of such a mechanism. This was elaborated more fully in Chapter 4 in terms of the principle of "Natural Selection." The remainder of the work was then devoted to exploring the full complexity of the issues raised by the general principle of natural selection in the context of a struggle for existence. In Chapter 6, for example, Darwin examined the issue of the evolution of organs of extreme perfection—such as the eye—upon which Paleyian natural theologians had placed so much emphasis. And in Chapter 7 he took up the question of the development of complex instinctual behavior, such as that of hive-making bees. In each case he explained how all of this could have originated in innumerable gradations by means of natural selection. As a result, the natural-theological argument on the fineness of adaptation as constituting irrefutable evidence for divine intervention in nature was at last laid to rest. Darwin's argument went further than natural theology itself in recognizing the variation and adaptation of organisms in nature. Yet it did so without resorting to final causes.

Central to the whole argument was the idea of "The Struggle for Existence," an idea that had to a considerable extent been inspired by Malthus. As Darwin stated in the introduction to the *Origin*,

> This is the doctrine of Malthus, applied to the whole animal and vegetable kingdoms. As many more individuals of each species are born than can possibly survive; and as, consequently, there is a frequently recurring struggle for existence, it follows that any being, if it vary however slightly in any manner profitable to itself, under the complex and sometimes varying contributions of life, will have a better chance of surviving, and thus be *naturally selected*. From the strong principle of inheritance, any selected variety will tend to propagate its new and modified form.[10]

This principle was stated somewhat differently in the chapter on "The Struggle for Existence" itself. There Darwin wrote:

A struggle for existence inevitably follows from the high rate at which all organic beings tend to increase. Every being, which during its natural lifetime produces several eggs or seeds, must suffer destruction during some period of its life, and during some season or occasional year, otherwise, on the principle of geometrical increase, its numbers would quickly become so inordinately great that no country could support the product. Hence, as more individuals are produced than can possibly survive, there must in every case be a struggle for existence, either one individual with another of the same species, or with the individuals of different species, or with the physical conditions of life. It is the doctrine of Malthus applied with manifold force to the whole animal and vegetable kingdoms; for in this case [as opposed to the human case with which Malthus was concerned] there can be no artificial increase of food, and no prudential restraint from marriage. Although some species may be now increasing, more or less rapidly, in numbers, all cannot do so, for the world would not hold them. There is no exception to the rule that every organic being naturally increases at so high a rate, that if not destroyed, the earth would soon be covered by the progeny of a single pair. Even slow-breeding man has doubled in twenty-five years, and at this rate, in a few thousand years, there would literally not be standing room for his progeny.[11]

So intense was the struggle for existence within nature that Darwin was unable to explain it except by means of a dramatic metaphor (first used in his *Notebooks*): "The face of Nature may be compared to a yielding surface, with ten thousand sharp wedges packed close together and driven inwards by incessant blows, sometimes one wedge being struck, and then another with greater force." The wedge image, which Darwin used repeatedly, was, in the words of Stephen Jay Gould, "the image of a surface absolutely chock-full with wedges, representing species in an economy of nature sporting a No Vacancy sign. Evolutionary change can only occur when one species manages to insinuate itself into this fullness by driving (wedging) another species out." All organic beings, Darwin argued, were "striving to increase at a geometrical ratio," and each of these organic beings was forced "at some period of its life, during some season of the year, during each generation or at intervals ... to struggle for life and to suffer great destruction."[12]

Darwin was careful, however, to explain that the notion of the "struggle for existence" should not be seen as simply (or even mainly) representing a direct struggle between individual organisms and/or species. "I use the term Struggle for Existence," he noted,

in a large and metaphorical sense, including dependence of one being on another, and including (which is more important) not only the life of the individual, but success in leaving progeny. Two canine animals in a time of dearth, may be truly said to struggle with each other over which shall get food and live.

But a plant on the edge of a desert is said to struggle for life against the drought, though more properly it should be said to be dependent on the moisture.... The missletoe is dependent on the apple and a few other trees, but can only in a far-fetched sense be said to struggle with these trees, for if too many of these parasites grow on the same tree, it will languish and die. But several seedling missletoes, growing close together on the same branch, may more truly be said to struggle with each other. As the missletoe is disseminated by birds, its existence depends on birds; and it may metaphorically be said to struggle with other fruit-bearing plants, in order to tempt birds to devour and disseminate its seeds rather than those of other plants. In these several senses, which pass into each other, I use for convenience sake the general term of struggle for existence.[13]

The use of the concept of "struggle for existence," which Darwin understood often in a metaphorical, rather than literal, sense, gave a "Malthusian" tone to his theory—which was in large part misleading. Although the reading of Malthus's *Essay on Population* certainly inspired Darwin, his direct intellectual debt to Malthus was extremely limited— scarcely going beyond the hypothesis that a geometrical rate of natural increase must be subject to some external check associated with the struggle for existence.

To be sure, Malthus seems to have inspired Darwin to engage in what evolutionary biologists refer to as "population thinking." In the words of Ernst Mayr, one of the foremost contributors to the neo-Darwinian synthesis (referred to by Stephen Jay Gould as "our greatest living evolutionist"), population thinking is "a viewpoint which emphasizes the uniqueness of every individual in populations of a sexually reproducing species and therefore the real variability of populations." Malthus's discussion of the geometric rate of population increase (when unchecked) had highlighted the struggle among individuals of a single species, and the application of this even to the dominant species, human beings—since, as the human species suggested, there was no exception to the general rule. By combining this insight with population thinking and focusing on variation and hence the struggle for existence within a given population (and not simply between different species), Darwin was able to visualize the full force of an evolutionary process enacted by means of innumerable small, innate variations, or what he called "descent with modification." But although Darwin himself attributed his intellectual breakthrough (his moment of inspiration) to reading Malthus, the latter, as Mayr has pointed out, rejected the notion of variability of species beyond certain very strict limits, and hence the very possibility of "improvement" in adaptation. Indeed, Malthus's crucial arithmetical ratio—which he applied to plants and animals—was based initially (to the extent that it had a basis) on this very negative assumption: namely, that productivity in agriculture was limited by the inability to improve (except very marginally) either the condition of the soil or the plant and animal species upon which human subsistence depended. In Malthus's natural-theological view, adaptation was a divine gift to nature—part of the fixed design of God—not a product of species transformation. Hence, there is no trace of evolutionary analysis in his thinking. Moreover, "population thinking," as it is now conceived within biology, was completely missing from Malthus. Mayr himself is explicit on this point: "Curiously, when we go through Malthus's writings we find no trace of population thinking. There is nothing whatsoever even faintly relating to the subject in those chapters of Malthus that gave Darwin the idea of exponential growth."[14]

If the direct theoretical influence of Malthus on Darwin was very small, there is nonetheless no denying that Darwin's articulation of his views in terms of Malthusian metaphors had a significant effect on the reception of his doctrines. As Marx was to say, it was the discovery of "Hobbes' *bellum omnium contra omnes*" applied to the natural world.[15] Indeed, given the pervasiveness of Malthusian views among the upper class in Britain, a Malthusian interpretation of the struggle for existence was perhaps inevitable. Darwin's own acquaintance with Malthusianism was an intimate family one (reflecting the class to which he belonged), as well an intellectual one: Harriet Martineau, a leading Malthusian and close acquaintance of Malthus himself, had a long relationship with Darwin's brother Erasmus. Darwin's cousin (and his wife Emma's brother— Emma was a Wedgwood and Darwin's first cousin) Hensleigh Wedgwood had married Fanny Mackintosh, the daughter of economist Sir James Mackintosh, Malthus's close friend and fellow lecturer at the East India College at Haileybury. Malthus's daughter, Emily, had been a bridesmaid at the wedding for Fanny and Hensleigh. All of this virtually guaranteed that Malthus was a persistent topic of discussion at the dinner table of the extended Wedgwood–Darwin clan.[16]

Darwin was to contribute even further to the Malthusian interpretation of his theory—pointing the way to what eventually came to be known as "social Darwinism"—by reluctantly adopting, in the 1869 edition of the *Origin*, the concept of "survival of the fittest"—a term first introduced by Herbert Spencer in 1864—as roughly synonymous with "natural selection."[17] In biology the notion of the "fittest" eventually came to mean survival of an individual organism to the point that it could pass on its genes to its progeny. In the Spencerian/Malthusian, that is, social Darwinist, sense in which the concept came to be applied to human society, however, it seemed to offer a justification for the law of the stronger, and for the superiority of those on top. Malthus's theory had been an equilibrium theory of an eighteenth-century kind, designed to show that improvement or progress in the social realm was made impossible by strict natural laws enforcing a struggle for existence meant to keep population growth in equilibrium with the means of subsistence. Yet Spencer, as J.W. Burrow, in his introduction to Darwin's *The Origin of Species*, has pointed out, "turned Malthus upside down by making his [Malthus's] theory the basis of a theory of human progress based on the elimination of the 'unfit.'"[18]

In the United States this view was taken up by the social Darwinist William Graham Sumner, who argued that "the millionaires are a product of natural selection." This outlook was extremely attractive to robber barons such as John D. Rockefeller, James J. Hill, and Andrew Carnegie. Rockefeller told a Sunday school class that "the growth of a large business is merely a survival of the fittest ... merely the working out of a law of nature and a law of God." Internationally social Darwinism was used to justify the imperialist policy of mass violence and annihilation succinctly summarized by Kurtz in Joseph Conrad's *Heart of Darkness*—"exterminate all the brutes."[19] All of this was anathema to Darwin himself, and opposed to his theory, properly understood. Yet, so powerful was this image, and so widespread, that it has dominated the popular image of Darwinism up to this day.

If the idea of the "survival of the fittest" and Spencerian-Malthusianism seemed at times to overwhelm Darwin's scientific message, so did the concept of "evolution," which, like "survival of the fittest," did not appear in the first edition of *The Origin of Species*. In that initial edition Darwin had referred simply to "natural selection," the "mutability" of species, and "descent with modification" (only once does he use the term "evolve"— never "evolution"). "Evolution," with its sense of "unrolling" and "progress," contained an almost teleological view—a sense of direction, toward ever greater perfection, in the overall organic process—which was opposed to Darwin's decidedly materialistic views. "Never higher or lower," he had written epigrammatically in the margins of his copy of *The Vestiges of Creation*.

Natural selection in Darwin's theory related only to adaptation to local environments; if the environment changed, a species (say the woolly mammoth) that was superbly adapted to the old environment might not be to the new one. In no way did adaptability to changing local environments suggest superiority/inferiority. Nevertheless, here too a more

Spencerian view, which explicitly associated evolution with general progress, triumphed. Darwin's theory was thus rapidly converted into what it was not—a theory that reinforced specifically bourgeois ideals of progress. The more revolutionary materialistic aspects of his theory were thus curtailed, and indeed had to be rediscovered by later biologists. Today biologists no longer think of evolution in terms of higher or lower, but the general public continues to use the term in its Spencerian sense.[20]

Unfortunately, Darwin occasionally allowed such inconsistencies to creep into his analysis—inconsistencies that can be traced to his class position. Thus he himself contributed to the view of evolution as constituting progress. In the second to last paragraph of The Origin of Species (a paragraph that was devoted to downplaying the revolutionary nature of his doctrines and calming his shaken readers), he wrote that, "As natural selection works solely by and for the good of each being, all corporeal and mental endowments will tend to progress towards perfection." For a thinker who had previously taken such a decidedly materialist, that is, anti-essentialist/anti-teleological stance—not only in his book but even more so in his theoretical notebooks—this was a case of dissimulation on a grand scale.

Darwin, Huxley, and the Defeat of Teleology

Nevertheless, the revolutionary character of Darwin's thought was not easily buried, and stood out starkly in the beginning. In June 1860 the British Association for the Advancement of Science met in Oxford, ushering in one of the most memorable encounters in the history of science. On Saturday June 30, roughly seven months after the publication of The Origin of Species, a large public crowd of between seven hundred and a thousand packed into Oxford's new Gothic-revival museum. Both Thomas Huxley and Joseph Hooker, leading Darwinists, were in attendance. The white chokers of the clergy dominated the center of the room. On the podium was the Bishop of Oxford, Sam Wilberforce (nicknamed by his Oxford students "Soapy Sam" in reference to his oratorical skills), a mathematician and ornithologist and a BAAS vice-president. After speaking at length on Darwin's Origin, the Bishop aimed a sarcastic shot at Huxley, who was in the audience, asking him whether the apes were on the maternal or paternal side of his family. The intent was clearly to score a point by showing that Huxley had impugned the inviolability of the Victorian lady. Rather than simply denying (or affirming) the implications and getting trapped in what would have seemed to have been a vulgarity, Huxley replied (as he later recounted the affair in a letter):

> That it would not have occurred to me to bring forward such a topic as that for discussion myself, but that I was quite ready to meet the Right Rev. prelate even on that ground. If then, said I the question is put to me would I rather have a miserable ape for a grandfather or a man highly endowed by nature and possessed of great means of influence and yet who employs these faculties and that influence for the mere purpose of introducing ridicule into a grave scientific discussion, I unhesitatingly affirm my preference for the ape.

The students in the hall burst into inextinguishable laughter. The attack on rank and wealth as adjudicator of science could not have been more clearly expressed. Robert Fitzroy, who had captained the HMS *Beagle* when Darwin had made his famous voyage, and afterward had become mentally unhinged, blaming himself for the Darwinian attack on teleology, stalked about during this great confrontation holding the Bible about his head and shouting "The Book, the Book." In all the pandemonium perceptions of what had transpired naturally differed greatly, but Huxley, Joseph Hooker, and the "new model army" of Darwinists left the affray convinced that they had triumphed—and quickly informed Darwin at Down House of their victory. Natural theology, history would record, had suffered a decisive defeat.[21]

The Darwinian revolution struck blows at two fundamental tenets of traditional thought: essentialism and teleology. Mayr has written:

> Of the ... ideologies challenged by Darwin's theories, none was more deeply entrenched than the philosophy of essentialism.... Essentialism, as a definite philosophy, is usually credited to Plato, even though he was not as dogmatic about it as some of his later followers.... Plato's cave allegory of the world is well known: What we see of the phenomena of the world corresponds to the shadows of the real objects cast on the cave wall by a fire. We can never see the real essences. Variation is the manifestation of imperfect reflections of the underlying constant essences.[22]

Darwin's Cambridge teachers were all essentialists (as well as teleologists) schooled in Platonism and scholasticism and conforming to natural theology. Even Charles Lyell, the great geologist and Darwin's later mentor, argued that "There are fixed limits beyond which the descendants from common parents can never deviate from a certain type." Likewise John Stuart Mill wrote that species were natural "kinds ... between which there is an impassable barrier." For Darwin, in contrast, all species were mutable, and there were in fact no firm divisions—species designations were heuristically useful but inherently arbitrary and changing. "A race, once produced," Huxley wrote, "is no more a fixed and immutable entity than the stock whence it sprang"—the same applying to species themselves. This was in fact the essence of the "transmutation hypothesis."[23] Moreover, the ultimate implications of Darwin's critique of essentialism went even further—questioning the supposedly fixed, exalted position of human beings and the permanence of "human nature."

Darwin's revolutionary critique of teleology was of even greater importance in that it was directed at the central tenet of natural theology. As Thomas Huxley put it in 1864, "teleology, as commonly understood, had received its deathblow at Mr. Darwin's hands." The teleological argument, according to Huxley, ran as follows:

> an organ or organism (A) is precisely fitted to perform a function or purpose (B); therefore it was specially constructed to perform that function. In Paley's famous illustration, the adaptation of all the parts of the watch to the function, or purpose, of showing the time, is held to be the evidence that the watch was specially contrived to that end; on the ground, that the only cause we know of, competent to produce such an effect as a watch which shall keep time, is a contriving intelligence adapting the means directly to that end.

But if it could be shown that there was an entirely contingent natural process producing the same set of results without intention or a contriver, then the teleological argument from design for the "doctrine of special creation" would be extinguished. This, according to Huxley, constituted the enormity of Darwin's achievement.[24]

The teleological position had argued that cats were so well adapted to catching mice because they had been specially contrived to do so, as their primary purpose. Yet, such teleological arguments, from Huxley's standpoint, were, "as a question of dialectics ... not very formidable." "Far from imagining that cats exist *in order* to catch mice well, Darwinism," Huxley declared, "supposes that cats exist *because* they catch mice well— mousing being not the end, but the condition, of their existence." Responding to those who wanted to find a way to make Darwin compatible with teleology—and who based their arguments on Darwin's misleading statement on the tendency of organisms to evolve toward "perfection" at the end of the *Origin*—Huxley insisted that "if we apprehend the spirit of the 'Origin of Species' rightly, then nothing can be more entirely and absolutely opposed to Teleology, as it is commonly understood, than the Darwinian Theory." Downplaying Darwin's reference to the tendency of organisms to advance "toward perfection," Huxley insisted that Darwin's theory, properly understood, was independent of any linear conception of progress, or purposive teleological process:

> So far from a gradual progress towards perfection forming any necessary part of the Darwinian creed, it appears to us that it is perfectly consistent with indefinite persistence in one state, or with a gradual retrogression. Suppose, for example, a return of the glacial epoch and a spread of polar climatal conditions over the whole globe. The operation of natural selection under these circumstances would tend, on the whole, to the weeding out of the higher organisms and the cherishing of the lower forms of life.

The fact that environments could change radically, thus making an organism that was previously superbly adapted to its environment, such as the woolly mammoth, no longer so well adapted (actually driving it into extinction), in itself contradicted any simple notion of progression.[25]

For Huxley, the significance of the Darwinian revolution, from the first, was the annihilation of the "doctrine of final causes." Further, it did so without relying on Lamarckian assumptions as to "modification through exercise" and the hereditary transmission of such modifications once produced. (Lamarck, for example, had erroneously observed that "the efforts of some short-necked bird to catch fish without wetting himself have, with time and perseverance, given rise to all our herons and long-necked waders.") Yet, there always remained the question, voiced by Huxley in his earliest discussions of *The Origin of Species*, of whether Darwin had "overestimated" the role of natural selection. In Huxley's view,

> Mr. Darwin's position might, we think, have been even stronger than it is if he had not embarrassed himself with the aphorism, "*Natura non facit saltum*" [Nature makes no leaps], which turns up so often in his pages. We believe … that Nature does make jumps now and then, and a recognition of the fact is of no small importance in disposing of many minor objections to the doctrine of transmutation.[26]

Such doubts about Darwin's exclusive emphasis on the slow process of natural selection as the sole mechanism of evolution persisted—even among Darwin's greatest followers—and these doubts were to become greater over the remainder of his lifetime. By the end of his life Darwin himself had retreated from reliance on natural selection as an exclusive cause of evolutionary development. This was due to three objections that came to be leveled at his theory. The first of these objections centered on the incompleteness of the fossil record and the absence of intermediate types between species. Relying on Lyell's uniformitarian geology, which ruled out catastrophic events in the explanation of geological change— thereby extending enormously the length of geological time which had to work by way of slow, incremental changes—Darwin ruled out any "leaps" in nature. Yet, the paleontological record which was then rapidly being revealed seemed to indicate vast, unbridgeable gaps. (Nowadays scientists acknowledge sudden abrupt shifts in evolutionary history but integrate this with the theory of evolution by means of natural selection through concepts such as "punctuated equilibrium.")

A second criticism arose from physics. The greatest physicist of Darwin's day, William Thomson (later Lord Kelvin), argued, based on calculations regarding the supposed rate of cooling of the earth's crust (in which it was assumed that the sun was like a huge figurative coal pile), that the earth was around a hundred million years old (given the simplifying assumptions in his estimates, he sometimes widened his net to 20 million to 400 million years); far more, to be sure, than the biblical view of six thousand years, but far less than what was needed to explain the evolution of all known species by means of a slow accumulation of chance variations as in Darwin's theory of natural selection. (Following the discovery of radioactivity by the French physicist Antoine Henri Becquerel in 1896, Thomson's estimates were shown to have been incorrect—based on insufficient knowledge—and the estimated age of the earth was once again increased to Lyellian proportions.)

Finally, in 1867 a professor of engineering, Fleeming Jenkin, introduced the argument that if, as was then assumed, the inherited characteristics of each parent were blended in the offspring, then the actual chances that an important variation would be repeated in the offspring were minute, since the chances were halved in the next generation, halved again in the succeeding generation, and so on—the assumption being that the variation would distribute itself in steadily diminishing amounts and would be swamped out and obliterated in any given population. (Ironically, the answer to this had already been provided, but was unknown or unrecognized by the scientific community until the beginning of the twentieth century, in the form of Mendelian genetics, which demonstrated that genetic factors behaved as if they were indivisible particles that did not dilute themselves when inherited.[27])

Faced with the criticism of the physicist Thomson, Huxley struck a counterblow by arguing that "Biology takes her time from Geology. The only reason we have for believing in the slow rate of the change in living forms is the fact that they persist through a series of deposits which, geology informs us, have taken a long while to make. If the geological clock is wrong, all the naturalist will have to do is to modify his notions of the rapidity of change accordingly." This defense was, however, a mere delaying action at best, since Huxley had at hand no theory to replace that of natural selection in accounting for the evolutionary process. With respect to geology he hinted at the need to retreat from an absolutely pure uniformitarianism with respect to geological change and to add in elements traditionally associated with catastrophism. As for biological evolution, the only alternatives to replace natural selection and to speed up the clock of evolutionary change at the time seemed to be Lamarckianism or some theory of macro-mutations or saltations. But Huxley, in his response to Thomson, addressed neither.[28]

Darwin himself was unimpressed by this rhetorical game and was compelled by the Thomson and Jenkin nightmares to retreat more and more back into the Lamarckian notions of his youth (and of his grandfather). Increasingly he adopted Lamarck's notion of inheritance of acquired characteristics, although always struggling to maintain as much as seemed possible of his theory of natural selection. Even in the first edition of *The Origin of Species* such Lamarckian views had not been entirely absent; but they had been very much in the background, the center stage being occupied by natural selection. By the sixth edition, however, Lamarckianism had come to play a large role in Darwin's argument, for the simple reason that in this way he was able to speed up the biological clock to conform to the much shorter time allowed by geology, which was falling into line with Thomson's physics.[29]

Yet, despite the fact that Darwin's theory of natural selection had, by the end of his life, been abandoned to a large extent by even his most prominent followers—and even to a degree by himself—and was to continue to decline in influence through the remainder of the century (not fully revived until the neo-Darwinian synthesis later in the twentieth century), the general evolutionary view had nonetheless triumphed, and natural theology had been vanquished. "Extinguished theologians," the materialist Huxley had declared in 1860, "lie about the cradle of every science as the strangled snakes beside that of Hercules." Huxley's bellicose advance of Darwin's theory of descent with modification was waged, in the words of one of Huxley's biographers, as "an onslaught on 'Parsonism.'" Charles Lyell, though a less belligerent advocate than Huxley and a late convert to evolutionism, saw matters in those terms as well, once complaining to friends in the United States that his own country was "more parson-ridden than any in Europe except Spain." Geological questions, he objected, were subject to the pronouncements of thirty thousand clergymen. Hence, the Darwinian revolution was regarded by its leading protagonists as a victory of science (and for some of materialism) over natural theology, which had sought to bind science to religion. Rather than overthrowing religion, this scientific revolution, like others before it, sought only to push it into the background (like the Gods confined to the *intermundia* in Epicurus' philosophy), leaving science as the sole arbiter of the material world.[30]

For materialist scientists such as Thomas Huxley and the British physicist John Tyndall, "the magnificent poem of Lucretius," as Paul Shorey writes in *Platonism: Ancient and Modern*, was "the truest expression of the spirit and poetry of science." At the time of the great Victorian poet Alfred Lord Tennyson's death in 1892, Huxley, who joined the Royal Society elite at Tennyon's funeral, declared that Tennyson, who was known for supposedly anticipating "Darwinian" ideas (with his famous reference to "Nature, red in tooth and claw"), had a right to such scientific honors "as the first poet since Lucretius who has understood the drift of science." Attacked many years before by Richard Owen for being a "Lucretian" upstart, Huxley, ever the combatant, chose to commemorate Tennyson's lifetime of achievement by reminding the world (via Lucretius) of the great materialist victory over teleology that Darwinism had represented. As Huxley was to state on another occasion, Lucretius had "drunk deeper in the scientific spirit than any poet of ancient or modern times except Goethe."[31]

Another thinker with whom Huxley had strong connections, and who viewed Lucretius as one of his own scientific forebears, was Darwin's leading follower in Germany, Ernst Haeckel (1834–1919).[32] Haeckel coined the word "*Ökologie*" or "ecology" in his *Generelle Morphologie der Organismen* in 1866, the year before the publication of Marx's *Capital*. In doing so he drew on the same Greek root, *oikos*, for household, out of which had arisen the word "economy." For Haeckel, ecology related to what Darwin in *The Origin of Species* had called "the economy of nature." Thus in defining the word "ecology" in 1866, Haeckel wrote,

> By ecology we mean the body of knowledge concerning the economy of nature—the investigation of the total relations of the animal both to its inorganic and its organic environment; including above all, its friendly and inimical relations with those animals and plants with which it comes directly and indirectly into contact—in a word, ecology is the study of all those complex interrelations referred to by Darwin as the conditions of the struggle for existence. This science of ecology, often inaccurately referred to as "biology" in a narrow sense, has thus far formed the principal component of what is commonly referred to as "Natural History."[33]

Haeckel's concept of "ecology" caught on slowly and was not immediately embraced by the Darwinian literature, not coming into fashion until the twentieth century. Marx and Engels, who were well acquainted with Haeckel's work, and who saw the human species in evolutionary terms as part of the animal world (rejecting the teleological view that put human beings at the center of creation), were to embrace the older concept of "natural history" (the equivalent, as Haeckel said, of his new word "ecology") rather than the newer one of "ecology" itself. At the same time they applied the notion of "natural history" in a Baconian fashion, which focused on the "natural history" of human beings in relation to production. In contrast, Haeckel imbued his concept of "ecology" with social Darwinist connotations associated with his philosophical "monism." This was brought out clearly later on, in his *Monism as Connecting Religion and Science: The Confession of Faith of a Man of Science* (1892), where he wrote:

> We now know that the whole of organic nature on our planet exists only by a relentless war of all against all. Thousands of animals and plants must daily perish in every part of the earth, in order that a few chosen individuals may continue to subsist and enjoy life.... The raging war of interests in human society is only a feeble picture of the unceasing and terrible war of existence which reigns throughout the whole of the living world. The beautiful dream of God's goodness and wisdom in nature, to which as children we listened so devoutly fifty years ago, no longer finds credit now—at least among educated people who think. It has disappeared before our deeper acquaintance with the mutual relations of organisms, the advancement of oecology and sociology, and our knowledge of parasite life and pathology.[34]

These social Darwinist views meant that Haeckel's ideas were eventually to exert influence in a tragic direction, on national socialism. As Stephen Jay Gould has written,

> his evolutionary racism; his call to the German people for racial purity and unflinching devotion to a "just" state; his belief that harsh, inexorable laws of evolution ruled human civilization and nature alike, conferring upon favored races the right to dominate others; the irrational mysticism that had always stood in strange communion with his brave words about objective science—all contributed to the rise of Nazism. The Monist League that he had founded and led, though it included a wing of pacifists and leftists, made a comfortable transition to active support for Hitler.[35]

Marx and Engels: Labor and Human Evolution

As Marx began the most productive period of his life (his *Contribution to the Critique of Political Economy* was published in 1859 and *Capital*, volume 1, in 1867), all of England was rocked by the Darwinian revolution. Unable to ignore this revolution in science, Marx was to use the occasion to add specificity to his materialist conception of nature (or approach to natural history), making more concrete its relation to the materialist conception of history. For Marx, the impact of what he was to call Darwin's "epoch-making work" ultimately had to do with the conception of human evolution that it necessitated, leading Marx to form a definite hypothesis on the relation of human labor to human evolution. In order to appreciate the complex, critical nature of this response it is essential to view Marx's thinking on Darwin step by step from 1859 to 1867 (from the date at which *The Origin of Species* appeared to the date at which the first volume of *Capital* was published—in which Marx codified his relation to Darwin), followed by an elaboration of how this theoretical position was developed subsequently (mainly by Engels).

The first edition of *The Origin of Species* was published in late November 1859. It consisted of just 1,250 copies and sold out on its day of publication. On December 12, 1859 Engels, who had one of these 1,250 copies in his hands, reported to Marx,

> Darwin, by the way, whom I'm just reading just now, is absolutely splendid. There was one aspect of teleology that had yet to be demolished, and that has now been done. Never before has so grandiose an attempt been made to demonstrate historical evolution in Nature, and certainly never to such good effect. One does, of course, have to put up with the crude English method.

A year later Marx himself took up the study of Darwin, writing back to his friend on December 19, 1860, "During my time of trial, these last four weeks [Marx had been nursing his wife, Jenny, through a severe illness], I have read all sorts of things. Among others Darwin's book on *Natural Selection*. Although it is developed in the crude English style, this is the book which contains the basis in natural history for our view." A month later Marx observed to the German socialist Ferdinand Lassalle that,

> Darwin's work is most important and suits my purpose in that it provides a basis in natural science for the historical class struggle. One does, of course, have to put up with the clumsy English style of argument. Despite all shortcomings, it is here that, for the first time, "teleology" in natural science is not only dealt a mortal blow but its rational meaning is empirically explained.[36]

The impact of Darwin's work on Marx was so great that, as his German Communist friend and fellow émigré Wilhelm Liebknecht recalled, "When Darwin drew the conclusions from his research work and brought them to the knowledge of the public, we [Marx and Liebknecht] spoke of nothing else for months but Darwin and the enormous significance of his scientific discoveries."[37]

Paul Heyer has suggested in his *Nature, Human Nature and Society* (1982) that Marx's attraction to the open-ended materialism of Epicurus "that allowed [for] freedom as well as determinism" helps to explain his enormous enthusiasm for Darwin. "One aspect of Darwin's theory of evolution by natural selection that must have pleased Marx's philosophical sensibility," Heyer points out, "was its stress on the interplay of random chance, opportunism and environmental determinism. While many of Darwin's critics wrongly referred to his approach as being mechanistic—what philosophers sometimes label mechanistic materialism—Marx believed that Darwin provided a materialistic perspective compatible with his own, although it was being applied to a different set of phenomena."[38]

In June 1862, Marx returned to *The Origin of Species*, writing to Engels that

> I'm amused that Darwin, at whom I have been taking another look, should say that he *also* applies the "Malthusian" theory to plants and animals, as though in Mr. Malthus's case the whole thing didn't lie in its *not* being applied to plants and animals, but only—with its geometric progression—to humans as against plants and animals. It is remarkable how Darwin rediscovers among the beasts and plants, the society of England with its division of labour, competition, opening up of new markets, "inventions," and the Malthusian "struggle for existence." It is Hobbes' *bellum omnium contra omnes*.[39]

During this period, Marx, along with his German communist friend Wilhem Liebknecht, attended some of the "popular lectures" that Thomas Huxley delivered on Darwin and evolutionary theory to audiences of English workers. These lectures, despite the fact that they were delivered to workers, were extremely erudite and Huxley was satisfied enough with those of 1863 to include them in his collection of *Darwiniana* at the end of his life. Moreover, Marx, along with Friedrich Lessner, a German friend from the International Working Men's Association, occasionally attended lectures by Huxley and Tyndall at London University between 1860 and 1864. Although Marx admired Huxley's materialism, he was critical of the latter's tendency always to leave a "loophole" for a religious point of view—actually going so far as to deny philosophical materialism as speculative (no better than religion in this respect), while affirming materialism as absolute in all scientific analysis. It was in this convoluted context that Huxley was to declare, in seeming contradiction to many earlier statements, that "I, individually, am no materialist, but, on the contrary, believe materialism to involve grave philosophical error."[40] Ultimately, Huxley seems to have adopted a view that subsumed materialism within a Kantian viewpoint, as in Lange's *History of Materialism*.[41]

Continuing his own studies of the Darwinian revolution, and of the breakthroughs in paleontology and ethnology that were then occurring, Engels devoted part of the spring of 1863 to reading Charles Lyell's *Geological Evidences of the Antiquity of Man* and Thomas Huxley's *Evidence as to Man's Place in Nature*, both published that same year and both of which he considered "very good."[42] Huxley's book demonstrated the anatomical similarity—close genealogical relation—between human beings and apes. Lyell's book presented the revolution in ethnological time occurring parallel with the Darwinian revolution. In this work Lyell provided evidence that the human species was very ancient. Contrary to the scientific consensus up to that time—which included his own *Principles of Geology*—Lyell was reluctantly forced to admit that human beings had existed on the earth not for a few thousand years only, but for thousands of centuries.[43]

In August 1866 Marx read a book, entitled *Origine et transformations de l'homme et des autres êtres* (Origin and transformation of man and other beings), published in Paris by Pierre Trémaux. Although Trémaux's work turned out to contain many egregious errors and to be of little scientific importance, Marx was initially impressed by his attempt to see biological evolution as patterned by conditions of geological succession and the changing condition of the soil. For Marx, this represented, despite all of its shortcomings, "a *very significant* advance over Darwin" in that it explained both progress and "degeneration, which Darwin cannot explain," as a result of geological change. It also pointed to "the rapid extinction of merely transitional forms," compared with the much slower development of species, "so that the gaps in paleontology, which Darwin finds disturbing, are necessary here." From these tentative remarks it seems that Marx was looking for a theory of evolutionary change that would be connected to geological succession, and that emphasized the influence of the soil; and that he saw the gaps in the paleontological record as a major problem for evolutionary theory. Yet Engels, who was sharply critical of Trémaux for his poor knowledge of geology and his absurd ideas about race, seems to have convinced Marx in this respect since all mention of Trémaux ceases after October 1866.[44]

Up to the time of the publication of the first volume of *Capital*, therefore, Marx and Engels had discussed the following aspects of Darwin's work in their correspondence: the fact that Darwin had dealt the death blow to teleology in the realm of natural history; the irony of Darwin's discovery of Malthusian/Hobbesian relations in the plant and animal kingdom (as well as Darwin's failure to understand that Malthusian theory demanded that the plant and animal kingdom not evolve); and the fact that Darwin's theory provided the natural-historical "basis for our view." (In addition, such issues as the relation of geological succession to evolution and the problem of the incompleteness of the paleontological record had been alluded to.)

For some present-day critics the fact that Marx emphasized that Darwin's theory provided the "basis" in natural history for his own analysis has presented a serious enigma, since Marx did not actually specify in his letters what he meant by this, leading to all sorts of speculations about the relation of natural selection and "survival of the fittest" to the class struggle. "How, precisely," the Darwin scholar Ralph Colp has asked, "can the theory of Natural Selection be shown to be the 'basis' for the theory of the Class Struggle?"[45]

The key to answering this question is to be found in *Capital*, volume 1, where Marx theorizes briefly (in two footnotes) on the relation of Darwin's theory to his own analysis of the development of human history through changing production and technology. Referring to Darwin's "epoch-making work," Marx uses Darwin's comparison of the development of specialized organs in plants and animals to that of specialized tools (in chapter 5 of the *Origin* on "Laws of Variation") to help explain his own notion of how the historical process of manufacturing "multiplies the implements of labour by adapting them to the exclusive and special functions of each kind of worker" (already separated by the division of labor). Further along in *Capital*, Marx draws on the same distinction in Darwin to differentiate between the development of "natural technology" in the process of the natural evolution of plants and animals and the development of human technology in the process of human history (human evolution):

> Darwin has directed attention to the history of natural technology, i.e. the formation of the organs of plants and animals, which serve as the instruments of production for sustaining their life. Does not the history of the productive organs of man in society, of organs that are the material basis of every particular organization of society, deserve equal attention? And would not such a history be easier to compile, since, as Vico says, human history differs from natural history in that we have made the former, but not the latter? Technology reveals the active relation of man to nature, the direct process of the production of his life, and thereby it also lays bare the process of the production of the social relations of his life, and the mental conceptions that flow from those relations.[46]

In drawing this comparison between "natural technology" and human technology, Marx was of course aware that the Greek word "organ" (*organon*) also meant tool, and that organs were initially viewed as "grown-on" tools of animals—tools, as the artificial organs of human beings.[47] As Engels stated, "animals in the narrower sense also have tools, but only as limbs of their body."[48] Human technology was thus distinguished from natural technology in that it did not consist of such adnated organs, but rather occurred through the social production of tools: the "productive organs of man in society." Building both on a conception of the human relation to nature that was already evident as early as the *Economic and Philosophical Manuscripts*—where he had viewed tools as the external extension of human beings, that is, "man's inorganic body"—and on the results of Darwin's analysis, Marx, writing in *Capital*, was able to define the labor process and the human relation to nature (eventually leading to his notion of the metabolic interaction between human beings and nature) in terms that were both materialist and evolutionary:

> Leaving out of consideration such ready-made means of subsistence as fruits, in the gathering of which a man's bodily organs alone serve as the instruments of his labour, the object the worker directly takes possession of is not the object of labour but its instrument. Thus nature becomes one of the organs of his activity, which he annexes to his own bodily organs, adding stature to himself in spite of the Bible. As the earth is his original larder, so too it is his original tool house. It supplies him, for instance, with stones for throwing, grinding, pressing, cutting, etc. The earth itself is an instrument of labour, but its use in this way, in agriculture, presupposes a whole series of other instruments and a comparatively high stage of development of labour-power. As soon as the labour process has undergone the slightest development, it requires specially prepared instruments. Thus we find stone implements and weapons in the oldest caves. In the earliest period of human history, domesticated animals, i.e., animals that have undergone modification by means of labour, that have been bred specially, play the chief part as instruments of labour along with stones, wood, bones and shells, which have also had work done on them. The use and construction of instruments of labour, although present in germ among certain species of animals, is characteristic of the specifically human labour process, and Franklin therefore defines man as a "tool-making animal." Relics of bygone instruments of labour possess the same importance for the investigation of extinct economic formations of society as do fossil bones for the determination of extinct species of animals.[49]

Human evolution then, for Marx, had to be traced through the development of tools, much more than fossils. This was because tools represented the development of human productive organs—the evolution of the human relation to nature—just as animal organs represented the instruments by which animals had adapted to their local environments. In this very sophisticated way, Marx, eight years after the publication of Darwin's *The Origin of Species*, and four years before the publication of

Darwin's *Descent of Man* (1871), sought to specify the distinctive nature of human development and evolution. Such analysis, moreover, was based on close study. Marx carefully read and took marginal notes on Lyell's *Geological Evidence of the Antiquity of Man*, scrutinizing Lyell's analysis of the development of tool-making in prehistory, and questioning his assumption of "the reluctance of savage tribes to adopt new inventions."[50]

To put all of this into historical perspective, it is useful to note that in 1864 Alfred Russell Wallace, the co-discoverer with Darwin of the theory of natural selection, had written an influential paper on "The Origin of the Human Races and the Antiquity of Man Deduced from the Theory of 'Natural Selection.'" Wallace argued, in terms that had already been suggested by Darwin and that were later more widely adopted within Darwinian theory, that animals can only adapt to changes in their environment through alterations in bodily structure. "For an animal to alter its food, its clothing, or its weapons, it can only do so by a corresponding change in its bodily structure and internal organization." However, human beings, he contended, were able to change their relation to their environment, by "making weapons and tools," thus taking "away from nature that power of changing the external form and structure which she exercises over all other animals." In Wallace's view, the human body (as distinct from the mind) was relatively immune to evolutionary processes, as a result of this tool-making ability—or human technology—which gave impetus to the development of the "mind." (Even at this early stage of his thought Wallace demonstrated a tendency to view the mind or intellect as separated from the physical body—so that he did not talk about the evolution of the brain as such—a tendency that was later to lead him in the direction of spiritualism and a radical break with Darwin's consistently materialist standpoint.[51])

Writing only three years later, but in terms that were closer to Darwin than Wallace, Marx had sought to distinguish between natural and human technology, by pointing to the distinctiveness of tool making—recognizing even then that certain animals had shown such capacity, but that tool making was "characteristic" only of human beings. In this way, Marx sought to provide a natural-historical basis, linked to Darwin, for his own general theory of the role of labor (which was of course related to the development of tool making) in the development of human society.

Engels was to develop this analysis even further in his pathbreaking essay "The Part Played by Labour in the Transition from the Ape to Man" (written in 1876, first published posthumously in 1896). According to Engels's analysis—which derived from his materialist philosophy but which was also influenced by views voiced by Haeckel a few years before—when the primates, who constituted the ancestors of human beings, descended from the trees, erect posture developed first (prior to the evolution of the human brain), freeing the hands for tool making:

> *The hand became free* and could henceforth attain ever greater dexterity and skill, and the greater flexibility thus acquired was inherited and increased from generation to generation. Thus the hand is not only the organ of labour, *it is also the product of labour.* Only by labour, by adaptation to ever new operations, by inheritance of the resulting special development of muscles, ligaments, and, over longer periods of times, bones as well, and by the ever renewed employment of these inherited improvements in new, more and more complicated operations, has the human hand attained the high degree of perfection that has enabled it to conjure into being the pictures of Raphael, the statues of Thorwaldsen, the music of Paganini.[52]

As a result early humans (hominids) were able to alter their relation to their local environment, radically improving their adaptability. Those who were most ingenious in making and using tools were most likely to survive, which meant that the evolutionary process exerted selective pressures toward the enlargement of the brain and the development of speech (necessary for the social process of labor), leading eventually to the rise of modern humans. Thus the human brain, like the hand, in Engels's view, evolved through a complex, interactive set of relations, now referred to by evolutionary biologists as "gene–culture coevolution." All scientific explanations of the evolution of the human brain, Stephen Jay Gould has argued, have thus far been theories of gene–culture coevolution, and "the best nineteenth-century case for gene–culture coevolution was made by Friedrich Engels."[53]

Up until the early twentieth century the consensus of the scientific community was radically opposed to the kind of explanation provided by Engels (although largely unaware of Engels's speculations, which unfortunately had little discernible influence on the development of evolutionary science). The cerebral focus of most biological thought (which Engels had attributed to the dominance of idealist notions) placed overwhelming emphasis rather on the development of the brain as the impetus behind human evolution. The expectation was that the "missing links" between primates and human beings, when they were discovered, would exhibit a brain at an intermediate level of development. These expectations collapsed with the discovery beginning in the 1920s of the genus *Australopithecus*, dating back as much as four million years ago. The brain of *Australopithecus* was enlarged only very slightly, and was generally of ape-proportion in relation to the body. Nevertheless, the australopithecines were clearly hominid species, standing erect, exhibiting evolved hands (and feet) and already tool makers.[54]

In recent decades the great paleontological discoveries associated with the uncovering of various remains of the australopithecines in the twentieth century have led to the development of theories of human evolution in close accord with Engels's nineteenth-century analysis. Anthropologist Sherwood L. Washburn exhibited the shock produced by these discoveries in his essay "Tools and Human Evolution" in *Scientific American* in September 1960:

> A series of recent discoveries has linked prehuman primates of half a million years ago with stone tools. For some years investigators have been uncovering tools of the simplest kinds from ancient deposits in Africa. At first they assumed that these tools constituted evidence of the existence of large-brained, fully bipedal men. Now the tools have been found in association with much more primitive creatures, the not-fully bipedal, small-brained near-men, or man-apes. Prior to these finds the prevailing view held that man evolved nearly to his preset structural state and then discovered tools and the new ways of life that they made possible. Now it appears that man-apes—creatures able to run but not yet walk on two legs, and with brains no larger than those of apes now living—had already learned to make and to use tools. It follows that the structure of modern man must be the result of the change in the terms of natural selection that came with the tool-using way of life.[55]

The analysis later evolved into the thesis, expressed by Sherwood Washburn and Ruth Moore in 1974, that "Tools Makyth the Man." "As a few apes left the jungle," these writers explain,

> and the most bipedal and upright survived in the new terrain, their legs grew longer and the foot and pelvis changed. But at first there was little change in the low dome of the head, in the small brain, and almost no change in the trunk, in its breadth, in the shortness of the lumbar region, or in the length of the arms. Most bones, joints, and muscles remained as they had been through most of the time of the apes. Hands then began to change. Those best able to manipulate the chipped stone tools and win themselves more food had a decided advantage. The hand bones found by Leakey at Olduvai Gorge are about half-way in form between those of contemporary man and the modern apes. The thumb was growing longer and was capable of a powerful grasp.[56]

The key to the understanding of human evolution, according to Washburn and Moore, is to be explained in the development of the hand associated with tool making, and labour in general. In this way much of modern anthropological theory has come around to the materialist-coevolutionary view pioneered by Engels in the nineteenth century. It was labor that constituted the secret, from the very first, not only to the development of human society but also to "the transition of ape to man." It was labor, moreover, that defined the distinctive ecological niche occupied by humanity. Marx and Engels thus saw the human relation to the earth in coevolutionary terms—a perspective that is crucial to an ecological understanding, since it allows us to recognize that human beings transform their environment not entirely in accordance with their choosing, but based on conditions provided by natural history.

In subsequent writings Engels continued to see natural history in terms of Darwin's theory of natural selection, remaining a strong defender of Darwin's theory even as the attacks on it grew. In his critique of Eugen Dühring's "revolution of science" in 1878 and in other works (including *The Dialectics of Nature*), Engels sought to defend Darwin's views against distortions and to counter social Darwinist tendencies (the use of Darwin to promote Malthusian viewpoints in the social realm)—particularly where these developments affected the nascent socialist movement. In his response to Dühring (the whole of which he read to Marx prior to publication), Engels defended Darwin against Dühring's *charges* that Darwin had simply transferred Malthusian theory to the plant and animal realm; that he never got past the viewpoint of an animal breeder; and that whatever was useful in *The Origin of Species* actually came from Lamarck.

Rather than objecting to the view of the plant and animal kingdom that saw it as a struggle for existence, Engels strongly supported this. Nevertheless, he argued, in Darwininian terms, that "struggle for existence" should not be viewed simply in terms of direct struggle between individuals or species, but also (more importantly) in terms of the struggle for life, symbolized by the plant's struggle to obtain space and light. "Darwin," Engels goes on to point out,

> would not dream of saying that the *origin* of the idea of the struggle for existence is to be found in Malthus. He only says that his theory of the struggle for existence is the theory of Malthus applied to the animal and plant world as a whole. However great the blunder made by Darwin in accepting the Malthusian theory so naïvely and uncritically, nevertheless anyone can see at the first glance that no Malthusian spectacles are required to perceive the struggle for existence in Nature.

Defending Darwin against Dühring's charge that he never rose above the perspective of an "animal breeder," Engels proceeds to a step-by-step discussion of the development of Darwin's thought, explaining how the origins of his thinking were to be found in his voyage on the *Beagle*, how he used variation under domestication to introduce his idea, but that the real analysis focused on natural variation and natural selection not domestic variation and artificial selection. Finally, Engels provides a crushing attack on Dühring's attempt to argue that Darwin was second to Lamarck. Lamarck's importance, Engels argued, was only fully appreciated once Darwin's revolution had occurred. But Lamarck's views of inheritance of acquired characteristics were deficient. In Lamarck's time embryology and paleontology had not developed sufficiently to make a correct scientific theory of evolution possible. Ironically, Dühring's own approach (despite its invocation of Lamarck), Engels contends, still smacks of the teleology of natural theology: of a "parson's mode of thought."[57]

Engels's close adherence to Darwin's theory was even more evident in his response to Russian populist theorists who sought to move in the direction of cooperation and mutualism in the analysis of nature—a movement that eventually came to be identified with the work of Prince Petr Alekseevich Kropotkin (1842–1921). In 1873 a leading Russian populist thinker, Pyotr Lavrovich Lavrov (1823–1900), published an article entitled "Socialism and the Struggle for Existence" in the radical émigré journal *Vpered* (*Forward*). Lavrov sought to expel Malthusianism from Darwin's theory and to counter those critiques of socialism that were based on the notion that the struggle for existence was the law of life and therefore made socialism impossible. In order to accomplish this, Lavrov deconstructed Darwin's notion of the "struggle for existence," arguing that this struggle occurred on various levels; that the lowest level was the struggle for existence between individuals of the same species or family. In this struggle, he wrote, "the casualties are incalculable, nature is full of bodies." The highest form of the struggle for existence, however, was that which occurred between species, organized as societies, such as "societies of insects." In such "societies" the main characteristics were "solidarity" and "mutual aid." Such mutual aid, Lavrov contended, was the ultimate answer to those who argued on Darwinian grounds that socialism was impossible.[58]

Lavrov discussed his analysis with Friedrich Engels and in 1875 the latter wrote a letter back that, while sympathizing with Lavrov's desire to counter Malthusianism and social Darwinism, nevertheless warned against getting too distracted by one-sided expressions such as "struggle for existence" or "cooperation," while losing sight of the dialectical interconnections. In this regard Engels pointed out how "*co-operation* in organic nature, the way in which the plant kingdom supplies oxygen and food to the animal kingdom and, conversely, the latter supplies plants with carbonic acid and manure, as indicated by Liebig," had, prior to Darwin, been stressed by some of the same scientists—"Vogt, Büchner, Moleschott, and others"—who now "see nothing but the *struggle* for existence." "Both conceptions," Engels argued—that is, the one derived mainly from Liebig and the one derived mainly from Darwin—"are to some extent justified, but each is as one-sided and narrow as the other. The interaction of natural bodies—both dead and living—comprises harmony as well as strife, struggle as well as competition." For Engels, the real problem, once again, was not the idea that a struggle for existence existed in nature, that is, the extrapolation of Malthusianism or of Hobbes's *bellum omnium contra omnes* to the plant and animal kingdoms (although this tended to produce a one-sided understanding of nature), but rather the attempt of some theorists to "re-extrapolate the same theories from organic nature to history, and then claim to have proved their validity as eternal laws of human society."[59] In the kind of dialectical, coevolutionary perspective that Marx and Engels advocated, then, organic nature (and the human relation to nature) was characterized by both harmony and strife: a perspective that brought out the insights associated with both Liebig and Darwin.

In 1873 the second German edition of *Capital*, volume 1, was published, two years after the appearance of Darwin's *Descent of Man*. Marx sent a copy of the new edition to Darwin inscribed: "Mr. Charles Darwin/ On the part of his sincere admirer/ (signed) Karl Marx/ London 16 June 1873 [1] Modena Villas/ Maitland Park." In October Darwin wrote back to Marx:

> Dear Sir:
>
> I thank you for the honor which you have done me by sending me your great work on Capital; & I heartily wish that I was more worthy to receive it, by understanding more of the deep & important subject of political economy. Though our studies have been so different, I believe that we both earnestly desire the extension of Knowledge, & ["that" added] this in the long run is sure to add to the happiness of Mankind.
>
> I remain Dear Sir/ Yours faithfully/ Charles Darwin.[60]

The Plight of the Materialists

In 1874 in his Inaugural Address in Belfast as President of the British Association for the Advancement of Science, John Tyndall (1820–1893), the "archdemocrat of science" and Huxley's closest friend, declared war on the establishment and delivered a lengthy exegesis on the development of materialism from Epicurus to Darwin. Tyndall and Huxley went to

Ireland, as Tyndall was to say, "as Luther did to Worms," and were to meet "all the devils in Hell there."[61]

Tyndall was born an Irish Protestant and started out as a railroad surveyor. He subsequently studied chemistry in Germany under the great Bunsen, and became acquainted, superficially at least, with German philosophy. In 1851 he went to London, where he soon became the assistant of Michael Faraday at the Royal Institution, eventually taking Faraday's place. Tyndall emerged as a leading physicist and chemist and was reputed to be the greatest teacher and popularizer of science in England. As Huxley's comrade in arms, he was part of the small group of materialist scientists who promoted Darwin's theory of evolution in the turbulent atmosphere of the 1860s and 1870s. Tyndall was known for his Alpine mountaineering, and for being a poetic materialist, who gave a humanist cast to his thought, even while presenting views that had frequently been associated with mechanism.[62]

In his "Belfast Address" Tyndall presented what Friedrich Engels was to call "the boldest speech to have been delivered in England [sic] to such an audience." He sought to provide a coherent materialist philosophy, reaching back to Epicurus, to support the revolutionary developments in science. Influenced by Frederick Albert Lange's *History of Materialism* (1865), Tyndall retraced the entire history of science. He pointed to Bacon's "high appreciation of Democritus" and to the fact that "Bacon considered Democritus to be a man of weightier metal than either Plato or Aristotle." It was Empedocles, among the pre-Socratics, who had first introduced the notions of adaptation and "survival of the fittest." For Tyndall, however, ancient materialism developed to its highest point in the work of Epicurus and Lucretius. Like Bacon in *Of the Dignity and Advancement of Learning*, and like Marx in the preface to his doctoral thesis, Tyndall saw the essence of Epicurus' defiance of orthodox religion as lying in the statement that "Not he is godless who rejects the gods of the crowd, but rather he who accepts them."[63]

For Tyndall, Epicurus, through Lucretius, had provided the essence of the modern scientific view in his treatment of atoms and void and his recognition that matter could be neither created nor destroyed. Giordono Bruno had become one of the earliest converts to Copernican astronomy as result of the influence that Epicurus (through Lucretius) exerted on his thought, opening him up, Tyndall contended, to "the notion of the infinity of worlds." Epicurus' "vaguely grand conception of the atoms falling eternally through space suggested the nebular hypothesis to Kant, its first propounder." To be sure, the ancient atomists had no notion of magnetism or electricity and thus had no way of understanding molecular force: the fact that "molecules are endowed with attractive and repellent poles." In postulating the swerve, Lucretius quit the domain of physics in order to have the atoms move together, but in doing so he was not entirely at fault, since his instincts led him in the right direction from the standpoint of modern science. The initial ground for the discoveries of Thomas Mayer and other nineteenth-century scientists regarding the conservation of energy was first established by the notion of the indestructibility of matter so clearly enunciated by the ancient materialists.[64]

Although Tyndall celebrated the work of Descartes and Hobbes in the seventeenth century, it was Gassendi, he explained, who, despite his Catholicism, had first provided a solid philosophical basis for modern materialism based on Epicurus. In Gassendi, he writes, "the principle of every change resides in matter. In artificial productions the moving principle is different from the material worked upon; but in nature the agent works within, being the most active and mobile part of the material itself. Thus this bold ecclesiastic, without incurring the censure of the church or of the world, contrives to outstrip Mr. Darwin."[65]

Darwin's great achievement, in Tyndall's conception, was that, while considering all those details that had supposedly constituted the evidence of the teleologist, he nonetheless "rejects teleology, seeking to refer these wonders to natural causes." The problem that Darwin left behind, however, was the "primordial form": out of what did life arise, if not from a Creator? Insisting on Lucretius' view that "Nature is seen to do all things spontaneously of herself without the meddling of the gods," and on Bruno's claim that matter was the "universal mother," Tyndall went on to affirm the need for purely materialist explanations in science and to identify this with the development of science itself. "The impregnable position of science may be described in a few words. We claim, and we shall wrest from theology, the entire domain of cosmological theory."[66]

Although famous for contributing, along with Pasteur, the definitive scientific critique of spontaneous generation, Tyndall nevertheless insisted on numerous occasions that in the deep abyss of time life had emerged out of matter, and that the origins of life were connected to the origins of the solar system—to be explained by the nebular hypothesis of Kant and Laplace. Thus life had at one time emerged from non-life, though the conditions that made that possible belonged to the history of the solar system and no longer pertained. Only four years before, Huxley had adopted a similar position, though not so clearly connected to the nebular hypothesis (and strikingly similar in outline to scientific views held to-day), in his 1870 Presidential Address to the British Association for the Advancement of Science, in which he had declared: "If it were given to me to look beyond the abyss of geologically recorded time to the still more remote period when the earth was passing through physical and chemical conditions, which it can no more see again than a man can recall his infancy, I should expect to be a witness of the evolution of living protoplasm from not living matter." William Thomson, Darwin's nemesis, had responded by unfairly accusing Huxley of advocating "spontaneous generation."[67]

Tyndall's "Belfast Address" created a storm of protest. He was attacked in particular for discerning in "Matter ... the promise and potency of every form and quality of life." He was accused of hastening the "ruin" of mankind and of promoting blasphemy. He found himself defending himself against a myriad of blows.[68] Engels, reading the addresses that Tyndall and Huxley had delivered in Belfast, reported to Marx, who was in Germany at the time, that all of this had once again revealed "the plight of these people, and the way they are stuck fast in the thing-in-itself and their cry of anguish for a philosophy to rescue them." Writing of the "tremendous impression and panic" created by Tyndall's address, Engels told Marx of Tyndall's courageous defiance of the establishment, adding that "his acknowledgement to Epicurus will amuse you. So much is certain: the return to a genuinely reflective view of nature is making much more serious progress here in England than in Germany, and people here seek salvation at least in Epicurus, Descartes, Hume and Kant.... The French thinkers of the eighteenth century, of course, are still taboo." Engels pondered how to transcend the difficulties that such adamant materialists as Tyndall and Huxley had found themselves caught up in, and suggested that the way out lay in Hegel's dialectics, especially the *Encyclopedia*, where, because of the more "popular" presentation, much of the analysis was comparatively free of idealism and "tailor-made for these people." There can be little doubt that it was at this point that Engels began to formulate his own great project, which was to take the form of his unfinished *Dialectics of Nature*.[69]

Engels's larger project was evident in 1878 in his "Old Preface to *Anti-Dühring on Dialectics*," his original, draft preface to the first edition of *Anti-Dühring*, which he decided to use only in a shortened version. In the "Old Preface" Engels, relying in part on notes that had been provided for him by Marx, observed that natural scientists wrote frequently in ignorance of the history of philosophy. As a result, propositions which were advanced in philosophy centuries ago, which often enough have long been disposed of philosophically, are frequently put forward by theorizing natural scientists as brand new wisdom and even become fashionable for a while.... Since physics and chemistry once more operate almost exclusively with molecules and atoms, the atomic philosophy of ancient Greece has of necessity come to the fore again. But how superficially it is treated by the best of them! Thus Kekulé tells us ... that Democritus, instead of Leucippus, originated it, and he maintains that Dalton was the first to assume the existence of qualitatively different elementary atoms and was the first to ascribe to them different weights characteristic of the different elements. Yet anyone can read in Diogenes Laertius ... that already Epicurus had ascribed to atoms differences not only of magnitude and form but also of weight, that is, he was already acquainted in his own way with atomic weight and atomic volume.[70]

For Engels, this ignorance of ancient Greek philosophy was tied to the failure since 1848 in Germany (as elsewhere) to comprehend the significance of the dialectic and Hegelianism. The two great sources of dialectical knowledge had been the ancient Greeks and Hegel. Failure to understand their philosophies and hence the dialectic was the main obstacle to the development of a philosophy adequate to the needs of modern natural science. Engels noted how it was becoming "increasingly rare" for natural scientists "to look down upon the Greeks," particularly those fragments of Greek atomic philosophy (namely, Democritus, Epicurus, and Lucretius), simply because the Greeks had "no empirical natural science"; the strength of the holistic view of the Greeks was at last beginning to force itself on contemporary natural science. So far, however, natural scientists had failed to make even the first steps in embracing the second great source of dialectical knowledge, that of Hegel.[71]

The object of course, from Engels's standpoint, was the creation of a materialist dialectics applicable to natural science. By the time he wrote *Anti-Dühring* he had concluded that the French materialists of the eighteenth century were useless for this purpose since they had developed a materialism that was "exclusively *mechanical*." The answers, to the extent that they were to be found in the history of philosophy, lay in the Greek materialists and Aristotle, Kant, and Hegel. With respect to Epicurus, the old contention, presented by Diogenes Laertius, that he had scorned dialectics no doubt was a stumbling block. All of this helps explain Engels's enormous enthusiasm at the end of his life for Marx's dissertation on Epicurus with its explanation of the "immanent dialectics" of the latter.[72]

For Engels, the brilliant intuition of the ancient Greeks, although vastly inferior in its empirical knowledge to the science of the eighteenth century, was still superior to the latter in its general conception, because of its intuitive understanding of the material world as evolving out of chaos, as developing, coming into being. Only in the nineteenth century, in particular with the Darwinian revolution, was this general conception surpassed within science. Yet, the Darwinian materialists were nonetheless philosophically weak, and surrounded at every point by philosophical and theological opponents. Hence they needed the dialectical heritage which constituted the main legacy of Greek philosophy and of classical German philosophy.[73]

The Revolution in Ethnological Time: Morgan and Marx

The year 1859 saw not only the publication of Darwin's *On the Origin of Species*, which for the first time provided a strong theory of evolution, but also a closely related "revolution in ethnological time," which had sources independent of Darwin's analysis—and which was in many ways as important in altering the Victorian conceptions of self and the world as Darwin's work itself. This was the discovery and acceptance within the scientific community of conclusive evidence found in Brixham cave near Torquay in southwestern England that human beings had existed on earth in periods of "great antiquity," extending back, as Lyell was later to conclude, as much as thousands of centuries.[74]

To understand the significance of this revolution it is important to understand that although the development of geology and the understanding of paleontological succession had long since destroyed the old biblical clock of Genesis, creating a sense of almost infinite time, and thus making possible Darwin's theory of evolution, the paleontological view up until 1859, with few exceptions, did not extend to human beings: humanity was still viewed as appearing on the earth recently, that is, only a few thousand years ago. Hence, the fossil record did not apply to human beings. "There are no fossil human bones," Cuvier had argued. More to the point, perhaps, there was no such thing as antediluvian man.[75]

It is true that various human remains (sometimes accompanied by primitive implements) had been found in caves in Europe, including the discovery of the first Neanderthal remains in the Neander Valley in 1856. Some of these remains were examined by leading geological authorities of the nineteenth century, including William Buckland and Charles Lyell, but the significance of these discoveries was doubted. Although evidence was accumulating as to the antiquity of humanity, this was still questionable enough to be denied. The poor way in which these discoveries were excavated, deviating from the slow, careful process required by geological work, often failing to preserve the proper stratigraphic context, allowed scientific observers to conclude that remains from distinct geological strata had been mingled with one another. In 1837 Buckland, author of one of the *Bridgewater Treatises*, concluded that no human remains had yet been found in conjunction with extinct animals. This view was reiterated by Lyell as late as 1855.

It was the discoveries at Brixham cave, the excavation of which was supervised by the Geological Society of London, rather than the ultimately more important paleontological discovery associated with the unearthing of Neanderthal man near Düsseldorf in Germany, that was to change Lyell's view, and that, given his authority, was to bring about a revolution in ethnological time. After examining the Brixham discoveries Lyell announced, in a presidential address to the Geological Section of the British Association for the Advancement of Science in September 1859, his own conversion to the view that human beings had existed on the earth in ages of great antiquity. This was followed by a three year intensive search for further evidence, in which Lyell reconsidered evidence found in caves in France, leading to the publication of his formidable work *Geological Evidences of the Antiquity of Man* (1863), which made clear this revolution in the understanding of ethnological time. Lyell's book was published in the same year as Huxley's important work in comparative anatomy, *Evidence as to Man's Place in Nature*, in which Huxley examined the anatomical evidence from the Neanderthal skulls and concluded that man had descended from the same stock as the apes. Both of these developments reinforced in different ways the effects of the Darwinian revolution, making clear that this revolution extended to human beings themselves.[76]

It would be difficult to exaggerate the importance that the revolution in ethnological time had on mid-nineteenth-century thinkers. John Lubbock, a leading Darwinian who contributed to the development of ethnology, wrote on the first page of his *Prehistoric Times* (1865) that "The first appearance of man in Europe dates from a period so remote, that neither history, nor even tradition, can throw any light on his origin, or mode of life.... [A] new Science has ... been born among us, which deals with times and events far more ancient than any which have yet fallen within the province of the archaeologist."[77] Looking back on these developments in 1881, the influential geologist James Geikie wrote,

> When the announcement was made some years ago that rude stone implements of undoubted human workmanship had been discovered in certain alluvial deposits in the valley of the river Somme under circumstances which argued for

the human race a very high antiquity, geologists generally received the news with incredulity. That the advent of man was an occurrence merely of yesterday, as it were, and a matter to be discussed properly by chronologists and historians alone, most of us until lately were taught to believe. So ingrained, indeed, had this belief become, that although evidence of the antiquity of our race similar to those subsequent French discoveries, which succeeded at last in routing the skeptical indifference of geologists ... had been noted from time to time ..., yet it was noted only to be explained away.[78]

No thinker understood the significance of the revolution in ethnological time better than American anthropologist Lewis Henry Morgan (1818–1881), often viewed as the founder of social anthropology. In the preface to his *Ancient Society, Or Researches in the Lines of Human Progress from Savagery through Barbarism to Civilization* (1877), Morgan wrote:

The great antiquity of mankind upon the earth has been conclusively established. It seems singular that the proofs should have been discovered as recently as within the last thirty years, and that the present generation should be the first called upon to recognize so important a fact.

Mankind are now known to have existed in Europe in the glacial period, and even back of its commencement, with every probability of their origination in a prior geological age. They have survived many races of animals with whom they were contemporaneous, and passed through a process of development, in the several branches of the human family, as remarkable in its courses as in its progress.

Since the probable length of their career is connected with geological periods, a limited measure of time is excluded. One hundred or two hundred thousand years would be an unextravagant estimate of the period from the disappearance of the glaciers in the northern hemisphere to the present time. Whatever doubts may attend any estimate of a period, the actual duration of which is unknown, the existence of mankind extends backward immeasurably, and loses itself in a vast and profound antiquity.[79]

In his *Ancient Society* Morgan attempted to provide a general theory of human social development, encompassing this longer conception of ethnological time, in which he sought to transcend regional particularities of development, and to seek out at a theoretical level, informed by ethnological data, the common basis of the development of human institutions and ideas, focusing on three branches of human institutions: government, family, and property. In doing so, however, Morgan took a decidedly materialist historical approach, rooting his understanding of the evolution of these spheres in material conditions, namely the growth of "the arts of subsistence"—and within this various inventions and implements—which he took as indicators revealed by the ethnological record.[80] Like other thinkers who sought to reconceptualize the development of human beings over vast reaches of time, Morgan reached back to Lucretius' broad contention that human beings had first relied on nails, teeth, wood, and stones in their struggle for existence and then had learned—following their forming of "mutual alliances" and the mastery of fire—to forge implements and weapons, successively, from copper, bronze, and iron. In his own division of human development in terms of three ages of stone, bronze, and iron, Lubbock, in his *Pre-historic Times* (1865), had quoted from Lucretius, who, he observed, "mentions the three ages."[81]

Morgan delineated various "ethnical periods": the great epochs of Savagery and Barbarism—each of which could be divided into lower, upper, and middle periods—and the stage of Civilization. In Lower Savagery, humankind, he argued (referring to Lucretius as his classical source on the arts of subsistence at this stage), subsisted mainly on fruits and nuts— a primitive gathering basis of subsistence. Though little could be said with certainty, Morgan cited Lucretius' contention that human beings at the earliest stage of their existence had existed in groves and caves, the possession of which they disputed with the beasts.[82] This was followed, in Middle Savagery, by the growth of a fish subsistence, made possible by "the knowledge of the use of fire." Upper Savagery, in contrast, was defined by the introduction of the bow and arrow.

The main indicator of the great change of subsistence represented by Lower Barbarism was the practice of the art of pottery. Middle Barbarism, according to Morgan, was characterized by domestication of animals in the Eastern hemisphere and by the use of irrigation in the growing of crops and of adobe-brick and stone in architecture in the Western hemisphere (where large animals suitable for domestication were much more scarce). Upper Barbarism began with the manufacture of iron and ended with the invention of the phonetic alphabet, and the use of writing in literary composition.

The great transition from Barbarism to Civilization represented a period of enormous cultural advance, according to Morgan. Yet, grand barbarism already supported a rich literary tradition. "Language had attained such development that poetry of the highest structural form was about to embody the inspirations of genius," he observed, with the Heroic Age of Greece in mind. Language, like everything else, had developed with human culture. "Human speech," he observed, "seems to have developed from the rudest and simplest forms of expression. Gesture or sign language, as intimated by Lucretius, must have preceded articulate language, as thought preceded articulate language, as thought preceded speech.... This great subject, a department of knowledge by itself, does not fall within the scope of the present investigation."[83]

Instead, Morgan's analysis in *Ancient Society* consistently focused on the material basis for human institutions established at the level of subsistence. The iron plow, he insisted, unleashed a period of "unlimited subsistence," which was, in addition to writing, to characterize the stage of Civilization. With the introduction of the iron plow, Morgan observed, citing Lucretius, arose "the thought of reducing the forest, and bringing wide fields under cultivation." Arriving at exaggerated conclusions from this, Morgan contended that "mankind are the only beings who may be said to have gained an absolute control over the production of food; which at the outset they did not possess above other animals."[84]

The stages that Morgan described are still generally employed in anthropology, although the names have been changed, reflecting the negative connotations associated with the terms "savagery" and "barbarism." Morgan's "savagery" is now generally referred to as gathering (with marginal hunting) society—a form of subsistence that obtained throughout the Paleolithic period. Instead of "barbarism," today, reference is made to societies practicing horticulture. Domestication of plants is usually associated with the Neolithic revolution around ten thousand years ago. (The terms "Paleolithic" and "Neolithic," or "New" and "Old Stone Ages," were originally introduced by Lubbock to distinguish between an age of crude, chipped stone implements, followed by a later age of polished stone implements. Nowadays, however, the emphasis is much more on Morgan's changing forms of subsistence.[85])

Morgan hinted at a rudimentary theory of gene–culture coevolution, focusing on the development of tools or "inventions."

> With the production of inventions and discoveries, and with the growth of institutions, the human mind necessarily grew and expanded; and we are led to recognize a gradual enlargement of the brain itself, particularly of the cerebral portion. The slowness of this mental growth was inevitable, in the period of savagery, from the extreme difficulty of compassing the simplest invention out of nothing.

The argument closely paralleled that of Darwin in *The Descent of Man*.[86]

For a long time it was assumed that Morgan's evolutionary approach to the development of human society was derived mainly from Darwin, whom Morgan knew, and who clearly influenced his thought. More recent scholarship, however, has focused on the crucial role that Lucretius (hence Epicurus) exerted on the development of his view of the evolution of human society. As Thomas R. Trautmann states in *Lewis Henry*

Morgan and the Invention of Kinship, Morgan regarded "Darwin's theory as a special case of evolutionism that, so far from being a novelty, is traceable to Horace and above all to Lucretius, who is for Morgan evolution's first theorist." The basis for this contention is the Morgan papers themselves. The first manuscript version of *Ancient Society* (MS dated 1872–1873) included a chapter entitled "The Roman Genesis of Human Development" which presented Lucretius' system. In this early manuscript version of *Ancient Society* Morgan wrote:

> Those who adopt the Darwinian theory of the descent of man from a quadruped, and those who, stopping short of this, adopt the theory of evolution, equally recognise the fact that man commenced at the bottom of the scale and worked his way up to civilization through the slow accumulation of experimental knowledge. That early state of man, on either alternative, was one of extreme rudeness and savagism, the precise conditions of which, though not wholly inconceivable, are difficult of apprehension.[87]

According to Trautmann, this

> passage makes it clear that in Morgan's conception the Darwinian theory was but a special case of the theory of evolution. In his own view again the intellectual charter of the work he had just undertaken was the invention not of Darwin but of Horace and Lucretius, the latter above all, and he devoted the second chapter of the draft of *Ancient Society* to an appreciation of the "'Roman genesis of human development,' as precursor of modern evolutionism.[88]

Essentially the same point was made earlier by Carl Resak in his important biography of Morgan. Referring to the early draft manuscript of *Ancient Society*, Resak wrote: "The theory of evolution, he [Morgan] went on to say, did not really belong to Darwin. Ancient philosophers like Horace and Lucretius recognized the fact that man started in savagery and went through a slow and tortuous ascent."[89]

Upon these foundations Morgan went on to develop his analysis of the origin of the idea of government, the idea of family, and the idea of property—the three parts into which the remainder of his work was divided. Morgan's analysis was to interest Marx, who had carefully read Lyell's great work on *Antiquity of Man*, scrutinizing its treatment of prehistory, and making critical comments in the margins of the book.[90] As early as 1857–1858, in the *Grundrisse*, Marx had already observed that "One can determine *a priori* a people's degree of civilization if one knows no more than the metal, gold, copper, silver or iron which it uses for weapons, tools or ornamentation." Here he had quoted Lucretius on the fact that bronze was known before iron.[91] Later, in *Capital*, volume 1,

Marx noted (probably referring to Lyell here) how in the study of "pre-historic times" classification was being made "on the basis of the investigations of natural science, rather than utilizing the methods of so-called historical research. Prehistory has been divided, according to the materials used to make tools and weapons, into the Stone Age, the Bronze Age and the Iron Age." For Marx, this approach of writers of prehistory was superior to the classificatory schemes that "writers of history" had thus far employed, since the latter tended to pay "little attention to the development of material production, which is the basis of all social life, and therefore of all real history."[92]

Marx took down extensive extracts in his *Ethnological Notebooks* in 1880–1882, which were devoted principally to Morgan, but also to the work of John Budd Phear, Henry Sumner Maine, and John Lubbock. In the year following Marx's death, Engels used these notebooks of Marx, together with Morgan's work, in developing his own argument in *The Origin of the Family, Private Property and the State* (1884). "Morgan in his own way," Engels wrote, "had discovered afresh in America the material-istic conception of history discovered by Marx forty years ago, and in his comparison of barbarism and civilization it had led him, in the main points, to the same conclusions as Marx." For Engels, following Morgan, private property and class struggle now dominated only hitherto existing *written history*; before that, in what Lubbock and others in the 1860s had begun to call "prehistory," society had been organized around kinship groups. Nevertheless it was "the production and reproduction of immediate life ... on the one side, the production of the means of existence, of food, clothing and shelter and the tools necessary for production, on the other side, the production of human beings themselves, the propagation of the species," which always constituted the decisive set of conditions defining a given historical epoch.[93]

The importance of the debates over the origins of the family, private property, and the state that arose from this analysis, however, tended to obscure certain crucial elements governing Marx's (and even Engels's) work in this area. It is crucial to understand that Marx and Engels, like other early analysts of "prehistory," were impelled toward these studies by the revolution in ethnological time that began in 1859. Moreover, in Marx's case this was tied very closely to concerns about the development of agriculture, that is, the long-term relation to the soil, which was a continual focus of his studies in his last decade (he continued to take hundreds of pages of notes on geology and agricultural chemistry in the late 1860s and 1870s), both in relation to the third volume of *Capital* and due to his concerns over the direction of Russian development, as reflected in the populist debates in Russia. At issue with respect to Russia was the fate of the archaic Russian communal land system, and how all of this related to the prospects of revolution. Finally, there was the question of the roots in historical development of the materialist conception of history, which needed now to be extended back before ancient Greece, before written history, and before philological analysis. What was at issue, then, was the origins of human beings and of human institutions over the long ages of "prehistory." In these latter years Marx also sought to break out of the literature of colonialism, through which he had naturally been compelled to view the development of the rest of the world, becoming increasingly critical of the history of capitalist penetration into what is now called the "periphery." He thus tried to construct a massive radical chronology of world history, breaking with dominant conceptions. All of these preoccupations have come to be seen as defining the last decade of Marx's life, which Teodor Shanin famously described as "late Marx."[94]

We can better understand Marx's struggle and its relation to his times if we understand how close, and overlapping, were these debates about human evolution and the origins of human society. In 1871 Darwin had published his long-awaited *Descent of Man*, which attempted to account for human biological evolution and in the process referred to important ethnological questions. *The Descent of Man* had less impact than it might have had, however, because it had already been preceded by Huxley's *Evidences as to Man's Place in Nature* (1863), Lyell's *Geological Evidences of the Antiquity of Man* (1863), Lubbock's *Pre-historic Times* (1865), as well as other works, which within a decade of the publication of *The Origin of Species* and the Brixham cave discoveries had revolutionized thinking about human development. Of the four thinkers on whom Marx concentrated in his *Ethnological Notebooks*, the three most important—Morgan, Lubbock, and Maine—had all been referred to by Darwin in *The Descent of Man*.

How, then, was one to think about the question of human development, prior to written history? Marx studied geology and paleontology as well as agricultural chemistry and ethnology with a fervor in this period. He was attracted to *Ancient Society* undoubtedly because of Morgan's emphasis on the arts of subsistence. Morgan, who had adopted a materialist approach to ethnology that was independent of (but took into account) Darwin's analysis, focused on the development of the arts of subsistence—even embracing Darwin's hint that there was a relation between inventions necessary for subsistence and the development of the brain. The outline of the arts of subsistence was crafted in relation to

Lucretius' analysis in *De rerum natura*. Marx, with his deep understanding of Lucretius, carefully noted Morgan's references to Lucretius and was aware of the deep implications of this way of approaching the problem of subsistence—the relation between the materialist conception of nature and the materialist conception of history that it entailed. This focus on the arts of subsistence—the human relation to nature through the transformation of production and reproduction—as it was developed by Morgan (inspired by Lucretius, and ultimately Epicurus) was deeply ecological, in the sense that it focused on human coevolution with the environment. Already in *Capital* Marx had said that tools as "relics of bygone instruments of labour possess the same importance for the investigation of extinct economic formations of society as do fossil bones for the determination of extinct species of animals."[95] Morgan's focus on the arts of subsistence, in which he singled out the development of tools, ensured that his analysis followed a similar track—while connecting this to changes in family/kinship relations, property and the state.

Marx dissented, however, from Morgan's contention that human beings had developed "absolute control over the production of food." Rather, the ecological problem associated with the development of the arts of subsistence existed into the capitalist period (where the contradictions had become quite extreme) and would outlast capitalism itself—posing problems that the society of associated producers would have to approach rationally and based on an understanding of the metabolic relation between human beings and the earth.

Since the 1950s we have seen the rise of the field of ethnoecology within anthropology, as anthropologists have sought to understand "traditional environmental knowledge" embedded in now extinct or threatened cultures; not only in order to retrieve that essential knowledge in a time characterized by ecological crisis, but also in order to emphasize the importance of cultural survival for those indigenous communities now threatened by the penetration of capitalism. Within this literature, subsistence is understood by leading ethnoecologists such as Eugene Hunn as the long-term relationship between community and land base. This knowledge of basic subsistence relations is also, it is argued, an invaluable heritage of ecological understanding, not based on the severance of human beings from nature. Marx's continual emphasis, throughout his work—particularly in the *Grundrisse* and in the work of his last decade—on traditional communal relations and the importance of a non-alienated relation to the earth has been seen by some ethnoecologists as the essential critical standpoint from which this new field must proceed. As Hunn has recently argued in "The Value of Subsistence for the Future of the World," Marx "valued the organic unity of a community of human beings tied to their land by their own labor with which they produced their livelihood and in so doing reproduced their community."[96] For Marx, a crucial part of his materialist conception of history—linked in this way to his materialist conception of nature, that is, to its basis in natural history—was always how the alienation from the land had developed in relation to the alienation from labor—a problem addressed today by radical ethnoecology (and by cultural materialist ecology more generally). The most important problem facing the society of associated producers, Marx emphasized again and again in his work, would be to address the problem of the metabolic relation between human beings and nature, under the more advanced industrial conditions prevailing in the wake of the final revolutionary crisis of capitalist society. To this end it was clearly necessary to learn more about the human relation to nature and subsistence, through the development of property forms, over the great span of ethnological time. Marx was thus driven back, by the materialist precepts of his analysis, to a consideration of the origins of human society and the human relation to nature—as a means for envisioning the potential for a more complete transcendence of an alienated existence.

In 1882, the year before Marx's death, Marx and Engels raised the question, in the "Preface to the Second Russian Edition of *The Manifesto of the Communist Party*," of whether the archaic Russian commune could provide the basis for a proletarian revolution, rooted in communal land ownership, that would "serve as the point of departure for a communist development." What was at issue, they emphasized, was the existence not simply of communal social forms, but of a non-alienated relation to nature that would stand in sharp contrast to the system of "giant farms" of capitalist America. The question of the material development of society was thus linked to the material development of the human relation to nature—in both cases history was not simply linear, but followed a complex, contradictory, dialectical pattern. In this complex, contradictory development lay the entire potential for revolutionary transformation.[97]

A Young Darwinian and Karl Marx

Marx's interest in ethnological issues in the last few years of his life may help to explain the mystery of his close friendship in these last years with the young Darwinian E. Ray Lankester (1847–1929), already a prominent evolutionary biologist and a Fellow of the Royal Society, later to become one of the most celebrated of all British scientists in his day—serving from 1898 to 1907 as the director of the British Museum (Natural History), at the very apex of his field. Lankester knew Darwin, Huxley, and Hooker intimately from childhood and had met Lyell, Haeckel, and Tyndall. He patterned himself after Huxley, who viewed Lankester as his protégé. Although primarily a scientist, Lankester was something of a nonconformist politically, revealing himself as an intellectual aristocrat with progressive sympathies during the most active part of his life (becoming more conservative in his old age). Thus Lankester exhibited socialist sympathies at times and counted numerous radicals among his friends (including in his youth Marx, and later H.G. Wells and J.B.S. Haldane; he also knew and admired William Morris). Fluent in German, he read Marx's *Capital* in 1880 with enthusiasm, observing in a letter to Marx that he was absorbing "your great work on Capital ... with the greatest pleasure and profit." Decades later, after the *Titanic* disaster, Lankester wrote to the *Times* that business associations were "necessarily by their nature, devoid of conscience," and were impersonal mechanisms "driven by laws of supply and demand." In the notes for his influential "Nature and Man" talks of 1905 he declared that "the capitalist wants cheap labour, and he would rather see the English people poor and ready to do his work for him, than better off." He greeted the February 1917 revolution in Russia with enthusiasm—though the October revolution that followed had him bewildered. Eventually, like his friend Wells, he became very anti-Bolshevik. As an intellectual aristocrat, Lankester was often elitist, even conservative, in his views, particularly in the cultural domain. In the words of his biographer, "he did not believe that women should have the vote, and indeed thought that the fewer people who could vote the better." Still, Lankester's more general commitment to a "militant humanism" is evident throughout his published writings.[98]

As a scientist Lankester was a convinced materialist, a Darwinian, and an opponent of religion and superstition. Like Marx in his last years he was particularly interested in the early ethnological development of human beings. In his youth he visited Boucher de Perthes, the French pioneer in the field of prehistory. Lankester was thus caught up early on by the revolution in ethnological time, an interest that was to persist throughout his career. His *Kingdom of Man* (1907) sought to extend estimates of human antiquity, based on the discovery of what were believed to be extremely primitive stone age tools (or eoliths). Lankester's materialism and Darwinism put him frequently in conflict not only with religion but also with other scientists, notably William Thomson (Lord Kelvin) and Alfred Russell

Wallace. Lankester opposed Thomson's recourse to vitalism in his discussion of life. More importantly, he was one of the first Darwinian scientists to note that the discovery of radioactivity overturned Thomson's estimate of the age of the earth—a fact that Lankester emphasized in his presidential address to the British Association for the Advancement of Science in 1906. Lankester criticized Alfred Russell Wallace for his resort to "metaphysical" explanations for the evolution of the human brain, arguing that these developments could be explained in materialist terms (an argument that paralleled that of Engels in the manuscripts for *The Dialectics of Nature*).[99]

Among scientists of his day Lankester was notable for his protests against the human ecological degradation of the earth. In his popular essay "The Effacement of Nature by Man" he wrote one of the most powerful ecological critiques of his (or any) time, pointing to "a vast destruction and defacement of the living world by the uncalculating reckless procedure of both savage and civilised man." Lankester was particularly concerned about extinction of species and the relationship of this to the destruction of habitat. "The most repulsive of the destructive results of human expansion," he wrote,

> is the poisoning of rivers, and the consequent extinction in them of fish and of well-nigh every living thing, save mould and putrefactive bacteria. In the Thames it will soon be a hundred years since man, by his filthy proceedings, banished the glorious salmon, and murdered the innocents of the eel-fare. Even at its foulest time, however, the Thames mud was blood-red (really 'blood-red,' since the colour was due to the same blood-crystals which colour our own blood) with the swarms of a delicate little worm like the earth-worm, which has an exceptional power of living in foul water, and nourishing itself upon putrid mud.... In smaller streams especially in the mining and manufacturing districts of England, progressive money-making man has converted the most beautiful things of nature—trout-streams—into absolutely dead corrosive chemical sewers. The sight of one of these death-stricken black filth-gutters makes one shudder as the picture rises, in one's mind, of a world in which all the rivers and waters of the sea-shore will be thus dedicated to acrid sterility, and the meadows and hill-sides will be drenched with nauseating chemical manures. Such a state of things is possibly in store for future generations of men! It is not "science" that will be to blame for these horrors, but should they come about they will be due to the reckless greed and the mere insect-like increase of humanity.[100]

Marx met Lankester in 1880 and a firm friendship seems to have been developed between the two men during the final three years of Marx's life. It is not known how Marx and Lankester were introduced, but they had a number of friends and acquaintances in common, including

Lankester's colleague at University College, professor of history E.S. Beesly, who had been for many years a close friend of the Marx family. We do know that Marx approached Lankester in September 1880 for medical help for his wife, Jenny, who was dying of breast cancer. Lankester recommended his close friend, the physician H.B. Donkin. Donkin treated Jenny Marx and eventually Marx himself in their final illnesses. Lankester subsequently became a fairly regular visitor at the Marx home, and both Marx and his daughter Eleanor were invited to visit Lankester at his residence. When Marx died in 1883 Lankester was one of the small group of mourners at his funeral. Since Marx was, during the time that he knew Lankester, hard at work on his *Ethnological Notebooks*, which addressed issues of human antiquity, and delved into the work of figures whose ethnological studies overlapped with Darwin's speculations in *The Descent of Man*—namely, Lubbock, Morgan, and Maine—it is fairly certain that they discussed some of these issues, as well as more general questions of materialism and evolution. Marx made inquiries on Lankester's behalf as to whether the latter's short Darwinian tract on *Degeneration* had been translated into Russian. Although Marx's relation to Lankester has long been seen as a mystery, nothing could be more natural, given Marx's lifelong interest in materialism and science. As Stephen Jay Gould has indicated, Marx in his declining years clearly derived enjoyment from befriending a younger man of great promise, one whom Darwin had seen as the flower of his generation. But the friendship with Lankester also symbolizes Marx's strong commitment to the materialist conception of nature, and his enduring conviction that Darwin (when disentangled from Malthus) had provided "the basis in natural history for our view."[101]

On September 28, 1881, Darwin hosted Edward Aveling (who was later to become the common-law husband of Marx's daughter Eleanor) and a group of freethinkers, the most distinguished of whom was Ludwig Büchner of Germany, at Down House. In the discussion that followed, Darwin admitted that he had finally given up completely on Christianity at forty years of age. But he insisted that he was "agnostic" on the issue of God and was unwilling to attack religion from the standpoint of science. In the following spring, on April 19, 1882, Darwin died. To the end of his days he remained a consistent materialist in his approach to natural history but refused to pronounce on religion, instead adopting the precept which Stephen Jay Gould has called "Non-Overlapping Magisteria" (NOMA), whereby it is recognized that science and religion operate in essentially different spheres, one material, the other moral.[102]

Darwin's death was followed in less than a year by the death of Marx, on March 14, 1883. In a letter written the day after Marx's death, Engels stated that he had been in the habit of referring to a passage from Epicurus: "'Death is not a misfortune for him who dies, but for him who survives,' he used to say, quoting from Epicurus."[103] Marx thus remained true to the very end to the fundamental materialist doctrine of Epicurus as expressed by Lucretius: *mors immortalis*. Where Marx differed from that philosophy was in his call for the revolutionary transformation of the world—of the human material relation to nature and society—extending beyond mere contemplation. "The philosophers have only *interpreted* the world, in various ways; the point, however, is to *change* it."

EPILOGUE

We know only one science, the science of history. History can be viewed from two sides: it can be divided into the history of nature and that of man. The two sides, however, are not to be seen as independent entities. As long as man has existed, nature and man have affected each other.

Karl Marx and Friedrich Engels, *The German Ideology*[1]

In February 1937 Nikolai Bukharin (1888–1938), one of the leading figures of the Russian Revolution, whom Lenin had called "the golden boy of the revolution," the "favorite of the entire party," and its "biggest theorist," was arrested on Stalin's orders and placed in Lubyanka Prison. Except when taken to the interrogation room, he was confined to a tiny cell lit by a single bare bulb, alone for months, but for a time sharing his cell with an informer. For more than a year he awaited trial and possible execution, fearful for the survival of his family. In March 1938 he was forced to stand trial publicly, with not only his own life but that of his family as well at stake, and to confess to being a vile enemy of the Revolution. Two days later he was shot in a secret execution cell. His biography was systematically removed from the history of the Revolution, and he was officially remembered only as an enemy of the people.

Bukharin had fought despair during his time of terror in Lubyanka by writing four book-length manuscripts, mostly at night (the interrogations increasingly occupied his days), including an autobiographical novel (*How It All Began*), a book of poetry (*The Transformation of the World*), a treatise on socialism (*Socialism and its Culture*), and a wide-ranging philosophical-theoretical work (*Philosophical Arabesques*). Only Stalin and a few jailers knew of the existence of the four manuscripts. Recognizing that execution probably awaited him, Bukharin fought hard to have the manuscripts preserved, sending letters to Stalin pleading that they be saved even if his own life were to be taken. In the end, Stalin did not burn the manuscripts but instead consigned them to his personal archive, the deepest repository of the Terror, where they were only rediscovered in the late 1980s under Gorbachev. Their existence was first revealed to Stephen Cohen in 1988 by an aide to Gorbachev. Not until 1992, however, was Cohen able to obtain copies of the manuscripts. Both *How It All Began* and *Philosophical Arabesques* were published soon after in Russian.[2]

Bukharin believed *Philosophical Arabesques* to be his most important and mature intellectual work. In it he sought to reassess philosophy from the standpoint of dialectical materialism and the development of science. His aim was to construct a more philosophically advanced, humanistic Marxism, based on Marx's practical materialism, in order to transcend some of the cruder elements of mechanical materialism, and at the same time providing a weapon against solipsism, mysticism, and fascism. For Bukharin, as he indicted in *Philosophical Arabesques*, the ultimate basis of materialism was to be found in ecology, in the theory, emanating from V.I. Vernadsky, of the "earth's biosphere, full of infinitely varied life, from the smallest microorganisms in water, on land and in the air, to human beings. Many people do not imagine the vast richness of these forms, or their direct participation in the physical and chemical processes of nature." "Human beings," he went on to observe,

> are both products of nature and part of it; if they have a biological basis when their social existence is excluded from account (it cannot be abolished!); if they are themselves the summits of nature and its products, and if they live within nature (however much they may be divided off from it by particular social and historical conditions of life and by the so-called "artistic environment"), then what is surprising in the fact that human beings share in the rhythm of nature and its cycles?[3]

Although it may seem startling today to hear these words coming from the Marxism of the 1930s, the deep ecological character of Bukharin's work would not have surprised Bukharin's more informed readers if *Philosophical Arabaseques* had been published at the time that it was written, instead of being consigned to Stalin's deepest, darkest, most secret archive. Of the leading Marxist theorists of that time, Bukharin was the one with the closest ties to natural science. His important work of the 1920s, *Historical Materialism* (1921), had contained a chapter on "The Equilibrium Between Society and Nature" which had analyzed "the material process of 'metabolism' between society and nature," which he saw as "the fundamental relation between environment and system, between 'external conditions' and human society." Here Bukharin built his analysis on Marx's concept of the metabolic interaction between nature and society; with the result that Stephen Cohen, whose landmark biography of Bukharin played a role in the political thaw in the Soviet Union under Gorbachev, has characterized Bukharin's theory as one of "naturalistic materialism."[4]

Already in 1931, six years before his arrest, Bukharin was arguing that the real living, breathing human subject was not the stenographer providing "'convenient' signs in shorthand," as in Wittgenstein and other "seekers after solipsism," but rather an active, transformative being who has "changed the face of the whole of the earth. Living and working in the biosphere, social man has radically remoulded the surface of the planet."[5] V.I. Vernadsky's work *The Biosphere* (1926) had made a deep impression on Bukharin, who came to believe that placing human history within the larger context of the biosphere was an essential element in bringing Marx's practical materialism up to date.

Although mechanistic explanations entered into his analysis of the "equilibrium" between nature and society, along with what seemed at times to be a "triumphalist" view of the human relation to nature, Bukharin was well aware of the complex, reciprocal relation associated with coevolution; the possibility of ecological degradation (especially, following Marx, in relation to the soil); and the need to avoid a radical social constructionism that failed to consider the natural-physical conditions of existence. Yet, this way of thinking, which might be characterized as "dialectical naturalism" (to distinguish it from the greater mechanism or positivism that came to characterize "dialectical materialism"), perished for the most part within Marxism with Bukharin's fall, which was accompanied by the purge of some of the greatest Russian ecologists. Hence, Bukharin's fate can be taken as symbolic of the grand tragedy that befell Marxist ecological thinking after Marx.

Although the seeming absence of ecological thinking within Soviet Marxism (and within Marxian social science in the West prior to the 1970s) has long reinforced the view that Marx's legacy in this area was at best a very weak one, such conclusions ignore the real struggles that took place. The story of what happened to Marx's ecology in the decades immediately following his death is a very complex one, involving as it does the most controversial stage in the development of Marxist theory: Engels's attempt to develop a "dialectics of nature," followed by the development of "dialectical materialism" in its various post-Engels phases, eventually metamorphosing into Soviet ideology (as well as its dialectical twin in the West in the rejection of all connection to science and nature).

In this brief "Epilogue" only a rough sketch of some of these developments can be provided. An attempt will be made to understand what happened to Marx's materialism; and how Engels's own very important,

never completed efforts to elaborate a dialectal materialism that encompassed the materialist conception of nature were appropriated (and
misappropriated) by later theorists. The roles played by Morris, Bebel,
Kautsky, Luxemburg, Lenin, and Bukharin in keeping alive some of Marx's
ecological notions will be examined. The enormous vitality of Russian
ecology of the 1920s and early 1930s will be considered, along with its
rapid decline under Stalinism. Finally, attention will be given to the
Marxist theorist in the West in the 1930s who came closest to developing
an analysis that dialectically bridged the epistemological divide, and that
pointed to a coevolutionary theory of human history and nature, rooted
in both Marx and Darwin. But herein too lay a tragedy: that of Christopher Caudwell, who died in the Spanish Civil War at age twenty-nine.

If a Marxism armed with a materialist conception of nature (and a
dialectics of nature) was eventually to reemerge in the West in the 1970s,
it will be argued, it was only by way of natural science, where the legacy
of the materialist conception of nature had not been extinguished.

Dialectical Naturalism

The responsibility for carrying forward Marx's vision after his death
initially fell on Engels. It was Engels who provided the most direct
connection between Marxism and science. Moreover, it was Engels who
initially defined the relation of Marxism to philosophy, since Marx's most
important philosophical writings, namely, the *Economic and Philosophical
Manuscripts* of 1844, were unknown, even to Engels. Here it is important
to note that although in referring to Engels's contributions to the later
development of Marxist theory it has become common, in recent years,
to cite mainly the *Dialectics of Nature*, this work was not published *until
1927, after Lenin's death*. The initial conceptions of Marxism within the
Second and Third Internationals were therefore influenced not by that
work but by Engels's *Anti-Dühring* (1877–1878) and *Ludwig Feuerbach and
the Outcome of Classical German Philosophy* (1886). Engels had read all of
Anti-Dühring to Marx, who wrote one chapter for it and clearly approved
of the general argument. *Ludwig Feuerbach* was Engels's attempt to explain
the origins of Marxism in the critique of the Hegelian system (by way of
Feuerbach), to argue for the necessity of a materialist conception of nature,
and to insist on a dialectical approach to materialism, opposed to its
mechanical interpretation. Although it has frequently been argued that
these works were marred by positivism, that mechanistic assumptions were
embedded within Engels's analysis, a close inspection reveals the extent to

which Engels managed to transcend the mechanistic forms of thinking, based on a dialectical critique and a knowledge of evolution. The latter was critical, since in Engels's view (like Marx's) it was the conception of natural *history* that emerged from Darwin's analysis that allowed one to understand nature dialectically, that is, in terms of its *emergence*. It was this that became, in his thought, the key to the understanding of the relation between what he called "the materialist conception of nature" and the materialist conception of history.

Yet, what was principally missing in Engels's analysis was a deep enough understanding of the philosophical bases of Marx's own materialist conception of nature as this had emerged through his confrontation with Epicurus and Hegel. If Kant had treated Epicurus as "the foremost philosopher of sensibility, and Plato that of the intellectual," Marx, as we have seen, substituted Hegel for Plato in his own antinomy, thus struggling to comprehend the relation between the immanent dialectics of the foremost materialist philosopher and the foremost idealist philosopher. From this critical, dialectical inquiry arose Marx's synthesis of materialism and dialectics, overlapping with a similar synthesis being carried out by Feuerbach at the time, but going beyond the latter (and beyond Epicurus) in shifting from a purely contemplative to a more practical materialism. Epicurus, Marx argued, was the first to discover the alienation embedded via religion in the human conception of nature. Hegel was the first to discover the alienation of labor (but only in an idealist mode as the alienation of thought). Marx's goal *within the history of philosophy* was simply to combine within a larger dialectical synthesis the conception of alienation within praxis, associated with Hegel, and the materialist conception of alienation of human beings from nature to be found in Epicurus.

It is clear that in the last years of his life Engels had begun to recognize the importance of Marx's doctoral thesis on Epicurus, and its relation to the development of a materialist dialectic. He had clearly expected Alexei Voden, with whom he discussed these issues, to carry the message to the Russian Marxist Georg Valentinovich Plekhanov (1856–1918) that it was here, and not in the study of the mechanistic French materialists, that the basis for a dialectical approach to materialism (that is, the materialist conception of nature) was to be found. Plekhanov, who developed his own conception of materialism based on a critical analysis of the materialism of the French Enlightenment, and who fell into various positivist traps, clearly did not get the message. As Voden put it, "Plekhanov was of the opinion that when Engels spoke of the materialists Democritus and Epicurus I should have shifted the conversation on to the 'more interesting'

French materialists of the eighteenth century. I noted that I could not forgo the delight of hearing Engels's account of Marx's first philosophical work."[6]

For Engels, like Marx, the origins of materialism (its natural basis) was to be found *not* in the French materialists of the eighteenth century, who developed a materialism that was "exclusively *mechanical*," but in ancient Greece.

> The materialist outlook on nature means no more than simply conceiving nature just as it exists without any foreign admixture, and as such it was understood originally among the Greek philosophers as a matter of course. But between those old Greeks and us lie more than two thousand years of an essentially idealist world outlook, and hence the return to the self-evident is more difficult than it seems at first glance.[7]

This failure to recognize these deeper philosophical roots of materialism to be found in both Marx and Engels had important consequences for subsequent Marxist thought (after Engels), which all too often fell prey to mechanistic conceptions, and to a simple *reflective* (or correspondence) view of knowledge, even while supposedly emphasizing dialectical perspectives that rejected both mechanism and idealism. Thus theorists like Plekhanov produced some of the worst forms of Marxist positivism. Lenin's materialism (particularly the Lenin of the *Philosophical Notebooks*) was more philosophically sophisticated but was caught up in the same difficulties, which posed genuine problems for the development of dialectical materialism. In the 1920s the positivistic influence within Marxism became more and more apparent, prompting the revolt of such Western Marxists as Lukács, Korsch, and Gramsci. But if these thinkers, and the subsequent Frankfurt School, resisted the invasion of positivism into Marxism, they did so, as E.P. Thompson emphasized, "at a very heavy cost," opening the way to "a fashionable Marxist epistemology which has become locked into an idealist theoretical practice." It was one that represented a "serious regression"—when compared not only to Marx and Engels but also to a figure like Caudwell, who still integrated within his analysis both a materialist conception of history and a realist emphasis on the natural-physical basis of existence—rooted in an understanding of the necessary interconnection between nature and society.[8]

Engels, as we have noted, has been criticized by Western Marxists both for being mechanistic and reductionist in his materialism and for attempting to impose an idealist philosophy of nature derived from Hegel on to science.[9] Thus one possible interpretation is that Engels drew too heavily on Hegel's *Philosophy of Nature* and *Logic*, superimposing a despiritualized

Hegelian dialectic on top of an otherwise mechanical view of the universe.[10] Engels's application of a simplified notion of dialectics, conceived in terms of three general laws, directly to natural phenomena seems to reinforce this view.

Yet, such an interpretation of the synthesis that Engels was aiming at is unsatisfactory for a number of reasons. First, because of the extent of his critique of Hegel for his idealism and of mechanical materialism for its mechanism, and his clear adherence to Marx's practical materialism. Second, because of the very strong emphasis that Engels placed on Kant of the third critique, specifically, the "Critique of Teleological Judgment," which he came to believe provided a basis for understanding not only the critique of teleological thinking, but also how this could be integrated with Darwinism. Third, and most importantly, because of his clear intention to develop a dialectic of *emergence* in which Darwin's theory of evolution played the crucial part. For Engels (as for Marx), a materialist and dialectical conception of nature was not only possible, but had actually been provided in large part for the natural world by Darwin's *The Origin of Species*.

The difficulty in reading Engels's unfinished *Dialectics of Nature* is that there is an unresolved tension within it reflecting its unfinished state that seems to allow for more than one interpretation: a strong dialectics of nature and a weak dialectics of nature. Engels sometimes writes as if the dialectic was an ontological property of nature itself; at other times he appears to be leaning toward the more defensible, critical postulate that the dialectic, in this realm, is a necessary heuristic device for human reasoning with regard to nature. In fact, the two arguments may be regarded as consistent. As Hegel wrote, "the truth is the whole." But he immediately added that it can only be understood therefore in terms of its "development."[11] Hence, we can know reason (or the world) only in the context of its emergence. Marx himself took from Epicurus the materialist conception that we perceive nature through our senses only as it "passes away," that is, in a temporal process; hence the "free movement of matter" is part of our cognition, inasmuch as we are part of nature and perceive it sensuously, and in accordance with the concepts that we abstract from this sensuous perception. Dialectical reasoning can thus be viewed as a necessary element of our cognition, arising from the *emergent, transitory* character of reality as we perceive it. "'The free movement of matter,'" Marx wrote, "is nothing but a paraphrase for the *method* of dealing with matter: that is, the *dialectic method*."[12] The dialectical method thus presents a more radical alternative to Kant's argument, in his third critique, that even though teleology could not be defended on the grounds of pure reason, it was nonetheless necessary to use teleological (that is, purposive) accounts for heuristic purposes *in order to describe nature at all.* Here dialectical reasoning, *the logic of emergence,* plays the same necessary, heuristic role for our cognition that teleology played for Kant. But the reasons for this, in the case of Marx and Engels, are themselves *material,* rooted in a *materialist ontology of emergence*—one that encompasses human beings themselves. The material world as it is given to us, the world of objective appearance, is, Marx believed, nothing other than "embodied time": *mors immortalis.*[13]

Given the fact that that an immanent materialist dialectic of this sort was conceived by Marx (and also Engels) as an alternative to both teleology and mechanism, it should come as no surprise that it is in his evolutionary-ecological understanding, arising out of Darwin, that Engels provides the most sophisticated version of his own dialectical *naturalism.* Here we see his complex understanding of evolution, in which the "Darwinian theory" was "to be demonstrated as the practical proof of Hegel's account of the inner connection between necessity and chance." Thus *"hard and fast lines,"* Engels argued,

> are incompatible with the theory of evolution. Even the border-line between vertebrates and invertebrates is now no longer rigid, just as little is that between fishes and amphibians, while that between birds and reptiles dwindles more and more every day.... Dialectics, which likewise knows no *hard and fast lines,* no unconditional, universally valid "either–or" and which bridges the fixed metaphysical differences, and besides "either–or" recognizes also in the right place "both this—and that" and reconciles the opposites, is the sole method of thought appropriate in the highest degree to this stage [in the development of science].[14]

In his plan for the *Dialectics of Nature* Engels had indicated that the discussion of the "limits of knowledge" in regard to biology would begin with the German scientist (electrophysiologist) Emil Du Bois-Reymond (1818–1896), who had argued in the 1870s and 1880s that evolutionary theory could provide the answer to "the origin of life"—a world-mystery that was not "transcendent" but rather "soluble"—precisely because the relation of life to matter is one of emergence. In this respect Du Bois-Reymond was following a tradition that went back to Epicurus (and even further back—to Empedocles and Democritus). In Engels's view this was an essential part of immanent materialist dialectic.[15] The philosophy of emergence, moreover, was applicable beyond mere organic evolution, to the realm of the inorganic as well—to cosmogony and cosmology. "Engels' position," Ted Benton has written (in his more mature assessment of

Engels's ecology), "can be seen as a first approximation to a view of emergent properties consequent upon successive levels of organization of matter in motion."[16]

Such a dialectical view, focusing on emergence, Engels argued, was opposed to the "determinism" which he associated with the French materialists, who had sought to "dispose of chance by denying it altogether." Rather necessity, as Hegel taught (and as Marx also discovered in Epicurus), was grounded in chance (or contingency). "Darwin, in his epoch-making work," Engels wrote,

> set out from the widest existing basis of chance. Precisely the infinite, accidental differences between individuals within a single species, differences which become accentuated until they break through the character of the species, and whose immediate causes even can be demonstrated only in extremely few cases (the material on chance occurrences accumulated in the meantime has suppressed and shattered the old idea of necessity), compelled him to question the previous basis of all regularity in biology, viz., the concept of species in its previous metaphysical rigidity, and unchangeability. Without the concept of species, however, all science was nothing. All its branches needed the concept of species as basis: human anatomy and comparative anatomy—embryology, zoology, paleontology, botany, etc., what were they without the concept of species? All of their results were not only put in question but directly set aside. Chance overthrows necessity, as conceived hitherto. The previous idea of necessity breaks down. To retain it means dictatorially to impose on nature as a law a human arbitrary determination that is in contradistinction to itself and to reality, it means to deny thereby all inner necessity in living nature.[17]

The fact that Darwin had started from chance in no way took away from the fact that evolution generated a necessity compatible with emergent development. "Each advance in organic evolution," Engels wrote, "is at the same time a regression, fixing *one-sided* evolution and excluding the possibility of evolution in many other directions." This evolutionary development needed, Engels insisted, to be seen both from the standpoint of the "harmonious co-operative working of organic nature" as in theories of metabolic exchange, and in terms of the struggle for existence within nature.[18] It was these two elements, taken together, that, as Marx understood, created the possibility of "rifts" in nature, particularly with the growth of the human ecology.

It was this complex, dialectical naturalism, in which nature was seen as "the proof of dialectics," that accounts for the brilliant array of ecological insights that pervade Engels's later thought.[19] The Darwinian revolution and the discovery of prehistory, he argued, had made possible, for the first time, an analysis of the "pre-history of the human mind ... following its various stages of evolution from the protoplasm, simple and structureless yet responsive to stimuli, of the lower organisms right up to the thinking human brain. Without this pre-history … the existence of the thinking human brain remains a mystery."[20] The understanding of the evolution of human beings from their primate ancestors could be explained as arising from labor, that is, from the conditions of human subsistence, and from its transformation by means of tool making, simply because it was at this level that human beings interacted with nature, as real, material, active beings who must eat, breathe, and struggle for survival. In this way Engels developed his distinctive theory of gene–culture coevolution, whereby the development in prehistory of the human species—of erect posture, the human hand, and finally the human brain—could be seen as arising dialectically out of the material process of labor, whereby human beings satisfied their subsistence needs by transforming their relation to nature through tool making and production.

From the moment human beings begin to *produce*, human history begins, distinguishing itself from the history of animals—though here too there are no hard and fast distinctions. Animals too relate to the natural world in way that is coevolutionary, changing their environments as well as being affected by it.

> We have seen how goats have prevented the regeneration of forests in Greece; on the island of St. Helena, goats and pigs brought by the first arrivals have succeeded in exterminating its old vegetation almost completely, and so have prepared the ground for the plants brought by later sailors and colonists. But animals exert a lasting effect on their environment unintentionally and, as far as the animals themselves are concerned, accidentally.

Although animals can in some cases plan responses to their environment, "all the planned action of all animals has never succeeded in impressing the stamp of their will upon the earth. That was left for man."[21]

But the human capacity to place its stamp on nature is limited by the continuing dependence of human beings on a natural system of which humanity is a part. Hence, human history, according to Engels, continually comes up against ecological problems that represent contradictions in the human relation to nature; contradictions that can only be addressed by relating to nature rationally through the understanding of nature's laws, and thus organizing production accordingly:

> Let us not, however, flatter ourselves overmuch on account of our human victories over nature. For each such victory nature takes its revenge on us. Each victory, it is true, in the first place brings about the results we expected, but in

the second and third places it has quite different, unforeseen effects which only too often cancel the first. The people who, in Mesopotamia, Greece, Asia Minor and elsewhere, destroyed the forests to obtain cultivable land, never dreamed that by removing along with the forests the collecting centres and reservoirs of moisture they were laying the basis for the present forlorn state of those countries. When the Italians of the Alps used up the pine forests on the southern slopes, so carefully cherished on the northern slopes, they had no inkling that by doing so they were cutting at the roots of the dairy industry of their region; they had still less inkling that they were thereby depriving their mountain springs of water for the greater part of the year, and making possible for them to pour still more furious torrents on the plains during the rainy season.... Thus at every step we are reminded that we by no means rule over nature like a conqueror over a foreign people, like someone standing outside nature—but that we, with flesh, blood and brain, belong to nature, and exist in its midst, and that all our mastery of it consists in the fact that we have the advantage of all other creatures of being able to learn its laws and apply them correctly.[22]

Marxism and Ecology after Engels

It is often contended that Marxism after Marx and Engels contributed very little to ecological analysis, at least prior to the 1970s, and that whatever legacy that the founders of historical materialism left in this area had no influence on the next few generations of Marxist theorists. The truth, however, is that Marx's ecological critique, together with that of Engels, was fairly well known (though its philosophical foundations were more obscure), and had a direct impact on Marxism in the decades immediately following his death. It was discarded only later on, particularly within the Soviet Union under Stalin, as the expansion of production for production's sake became the overriding goal of Soviet society. This can be understood in terms of two major themes arising out of Marx's (and Engels's) ecological critique: the concept of sustainable development, associated with Liebig; and the coevolutionary analysis, emanating from Darwin.

Even while Engels was still alive, the close connection between Marx's vision of communism and ecological sustainability was already evident in the utopian Marxist conceptions of William Morris. Morris first read Marx's *Capital* in 1883, the year of Marx's death, and openly declared himself a socialist at the same time. In addition to his argument on the dispersal of population in order to transcend the antagonism between town and country and his defense of wilderness (see Chapter Six), he is to be remembered (within environmental analysis) for his emphasis on production only for art or use—not for profit.[23]

Morris was alarmed by the pollution in the cities and the toxic environment in which industrial workers were compelled to labor. As he wrote in *Commonweal* in 1886:

> A case of white-lead poisoning reported in the press this week is worth a little notice by workmen generally. Stripped of its verbiage it amounts to this, that a man was killed by being compelled to work in a place where white-lead was flying about and that no precautions were taken to prevent his dying speedily. A shilling-a-week extra was the handsome sum given to the poor man thus murdered in compensation for his being killed. It is quite impossible that the man's employers did not know the risk he ran of speedier death, and the certainty of his being poisoned sooner or later, and yet all that the jury durst say about the matter was "to express a hope that Mr. Lakeman (the factory supervisor) would be able to make representations to the Home Office with reference to the case, to show the necessity of some extra precaution being taken for people working in mixing factories."
>
> Yet, further, this is only an exaggerated example of the way in which the lives of working-people are played with. Under present conditions, almost the whole labour imposed by civilisation on the "lower classes' is unwholesome; that is to say that people's lives are shortened by it; and yet because we don't see people's throats cut before our eyes we think nothing of it.[24]

In "A Factory as It Might Be," Morris envisioned a socialism in which factories would be set amidst gardens, cultivated by means of the voluntary labor of workers:

> Impossible I hear an anti-Socialist say. My friend, please to remember that most factories sustain to-day large and handsome gardens; and not seldom parks and woods of many acres in extent; with due appurtenances of highly-paid Scotch professional gardeners, wood reeves, bailiffs, gamekeepers, and the like, the whole being managed in the most wasteful way conceivable; *only* the said gardens, etc., are, say, twenty miles away from the factory, *out of the smoke*, and are kept up for *one member of the factory only*, the sleeping partner to wit, who may, indeed, double that part by organising its labour (for his own profit), in which case he receives ridiculously disproportionate pay additional.[25]

Such a factory of the future, Morris suggested, "must make no sordid litter, befoul no water, nor poison the air with smoke. I need say nothing more on that point, as 'profit' apart, it would be easy enough."[26]

The Socialist League, which Morris, along with Eleanor Marx, helped to found, and which was the focus of his activities in this respect, was, however, short-lived, and was to be overwhelmed by more mechanistic, reformist, and non-ecological varieties of British socialism.

It was not just a utopian Marxist like Morris who was to build on the ecological components of Marx's thought (such as the need to transcend the contradictions between use value and exchange value, between town and country), but also the mainline of the Marxist tradition, represented by thinkers such as Bebel, Kautsky, Lenin, Luxemburg, and Bukharin.

First published in 1879, and republished in an improved edition in 1884, August Bebel's *Woman Under Socialism* (later retitled *Woman in the Past, Present and Future*) was one of the most important early works of German social democracy and Marxism. Indeed, Bebel (1840–1913), who was a close associate of Marx and Engels, was also one of the *political founders* of German social democracy. Bebel's *Woman*, as it was called, was his most influential theoretical work. It was known principally for its critical discussion of the exploitation of women, and the centrality of women's emancipation to the future of socialism. Bebel's discussion of the prospects for the creation of socialism, however, incorporated aspects of Marx's analysis of the ecological crisis of the soil in capitalist society, and the need to remedy this in the rational reorganization of production under socialism. At the same time he wrote an extensive critique of Malthusian overpopulation theory. Hence, his work contained important ecological elements. "The mad sacrifice of forest, for the sake of 'profit,'" he wrote,

> is said to be the cause of the appreciable deterioration of climate and decline in the fertility of the soil in the provinces of Prussia and Pomerania, in Styria, Italy, France, and Spain. Frequent inundations are the consequence of stripping high ground of trees. The inundations of the Rhine and Vistula are chiefly attributed to the devastation of forest land in Switzerland and Poland.

Drawing on Liebig's (and Marx's) analysis of the need to restore nutrients taken from the soil, Bebel wrote that

> Manure is precisely the same to the land as food to man, and every kind of manure is just as far from being of the same value for the land as every kind of food is from being equally nutritive for man. The ground must receive exactly the same chemical ingredients as those which have been extracted from it by the previous crops, and it must especially receive those chemical ingredients which the crop to be next sown requires.... Animal and human refuse and excrements principally contain the chemical ingredients which are the most appropriate for the reconstruction of human food. It is therefore desirable to obtain this manure to as large an extent as possible. This rule is being constantly transgressed at the present day, especially in large towns, which receive enormous quantities of food, but only restore a small portion of the valuable refuse and excrements to the land. The consequence is, that all farms at a distance from the towns to which they annually send the greater part of their produce, suffer considerably from want of manure; that obtained from the human inmates and from the cattle of the farm is insufficient, because they consume only

a small portion of the crops, and a ruinous system of cultivation ensues, by which the soil is impoverished, the harvests lessened, and the price of food is raised. All those countries which principally export produce of the soil, but receive no materials for manuring in return, are being gradually but inevitably ruined, Hungary, Russia, the Danubian Principalities, and America. It is true, artificial manure, especially guano, replaces that of men and cattle, but few farmers are able to buy it in sufficient quantities on account of its price, and in any case it is reversing the natural order of things to import manure from a distance of many thousands of miles, whilst that which one has close at hand is wasted.[27]

Karl Kautsky's landmark work *The Agrarian Question* (1899) developed these themes more systematically. It included a section on "The Exploitation of the Countryside by the Town" in which he argued that the net flow of value from country to town

corresponds to a constantly mounting loss of nutrients in the form of corn, meat, milk and so forth which the farmer has to sell to pay taxes, debt-interest and rent.... Although such a flow does not signify an exploitation of agriculture in terms of the law of value [of capitalism], it does nevertheless lead ... to its material exploitation, to the impoverishment of the land of its nutrients.

Arguing at a time when the fertilizer industry had advanced beyond that of Marx's day, Kautsky presented a critique of the fertilizer treadmill resulting from the metabolic rift:

Supplementary fertilisers ... allow the reduction in soil fertility to be avoided, but the necessity of using them in larger and larger amounts simply adds a further burden to agriculture—not one unavoidably imposed by nature, but a direct result of current social organisation. By overcoming the antithesis between town and country ... the materials removed from the soil would be able to flow back in full. Supplementary fertilisers would then, at most, have the task of enriching the soil, not staving off its impoverishment. Advances in cultivation would signify an increase in the amount of soluble nutrients in the soil without the need to add artificial fertilisers[28]

Following the general outline of Marx's argument, Kautksy went on to argue that "the growth of towns and the expansion of industry, which increasingly exhausts the soil and imposes burdens on agriculture in the form of the fertilisers needed to combat this exhaustion, does not rest content with this achievement. It also robs agriculture of its *labour-power*" through the "depopulation of the countryside."[29]

Kautsky went on to discuss the increasing use of pesticides, attributing the growth of pests to the killing of insect-eating birds due to the extension of cultivation, to the replacement of natural selection with artificial selection in the growth of plants (tending to reduce resistance to diseases and pests), and to the characteristics of "modern large-scale operations"—whereby in forestry, for example, the destruction of forests is encouraged by "the elimination of slow growing deciduous trees by rapid-growing, and more rapidly exploitable, conifers." Hence "the costs of fertilizers are joined by those of pesticides."[30]

Related concerns were expressed in Lenin's work. In *The Agrarian Question and the "Critics of Marx"* (1901), he wrote that

> the possibility of substituting artificial for natural manures and the fact that this is already being done (*partly*) do not in the least refute the irrationality of wasting natural fertilisers and thereby polluting the rivers and the air in suburban and factory districts. Even at the present time there are sewage farms in the vicinity of large cities which utilise city refuse with enormous benefit to agriculture; but by this system only an infinitesimal part of the refuse is utilised.[31]

In prison in May 1917 Rosa Luxemburg also demonstrated her concern in this area. She wrote to her friend Sonja Liebknecht that she was studying "natural science":

> geography of plants and animals. Only yesterday I read why the warblers are disappearing from Germany. Increasingly systematic forestry, gardening and agriculture are, step by step, destroying all natural nesting and breeding places: hollow trees, fallow land, thickets of shrubs, withered leaves on the garden grounds. It pained me so when I read that. Not because of the song they sing for people, but rather it was the picture of the silent, irresistible extinction of these defenseless little creatures which hurt me to the point where I had to cry. It reminded me of a Russian book which I read while still in Zurich, a book by Professor Sieber about the ravage of the redskins in North America. In exactly the same way, step by step, they have been pursued from their land by civilized men and abandoned to perish silently and cruelly.[32]

It was Bukharin among the early followers of Marx and Engels, however, who was to go furthest in applying Marx's concept of the metabolic interaction of human beings and nature—at least on a general level. "The material process of 'metabolism' between society and nature," Bukharin wrote in *Historical Materialism*,

> is the fundamental relation between environment and system, between "external conditions" and human society.... The metabolism between man and nature consists, as we have seen, in the transfer of material energy from external nature to society.... Thus, the interrelation between society and nature is a process of social reproduction. In this process, society applies its human labor energy and obtains a certain quantity of energy from nature ("nature's material," in the words of Marx). The *balance* between expenditures and receipts is here obviously

the decisive element for the growth of society. If what is obtained exceeds the loss by labor, important consequences obviously follow for society, which vary with the amount of this excess.[33]

It was technology that, for Bukharin, was the principal mediating force in this metabolic exchange. The social metabolism with nature was therefore an "unstable equilibrium," which could be either progressive or regressive from a social standpoint. "The productivity of labor," he wrote, "is a precise measure of the 'balance' between society and nature." An increase in social productivity arising from this relation was seen as a progressive development; conversely, a decrease in social productivity due to an ill-adapted metabolic relation—here Bukharin cited "the exhaustion of the soil" as a possible cause of such a decrease—meant that the relationship was a regressive one. Such a decline, he argued, could lead to society being "barbarianized."[34]

The whole "process of social production," he insisted, "is an adaptation of human society to external nature." Consequently, "nothing could be more incorrect than to regard nature from the teleological point of view: man, the lord of creation, with nature created for his use, and all things adapted to human needs." Instead human beings were engaged in a constant, active struggle to adapt. "Man, as an animal form, as well as human society, are products of nature, part of this great, endless whole. Man can never escape from nature, and even when he 'controls' nature, he is merely making use of the laws of *nature* for his own ends."[35] "No system," including that of human society," Bukharin stressed, "can exist in empty space; it is surrounded by an 'environment,' on which all its conditions ultimately depend. If human society is not adapted to its environment, it is not meant for this world." To be sure, the human relation to nature is less direct than that of other species since it is mediated by society, and society is the immediate human environment. But society has nature as its environment: "For the tree in the forest," as Bukharin himself put it, "the environment means all the other trees, the brook, the earth, the ferns, the grass, the bushes, together with all their properties. Man's environment is society, in the midst of which he lives; the environment of human society is external nature."[36] Indeed, human beings, as Bukharin emphasized in 1931 at the London conference on the history of science and again in 1937 in *Philosophical Arabesques*, needed to be conceived as "living and working in the biosphere."

Soviet ecology in the 1920s was arguably the most advanced in the world. While Western models of ecology still tended to rely on reductionist, linear, teleologically oriented models, geared to natural succession, Soviet ecology was pioneering in the development of more dialectically complex, dynamic, holistic, coevolutionary models. The two greatest Russian ecologists of the 1920s and 1930s were V.I. Vernadsky (1863–1945) and N.I. Vavilov (1887–1943). Vernadsky achieved international renown both for his analysis of the biosphere and as the founder of the science of geochemistry (or biogeochemistry). In 1926 Vernadsky published *The Biosphere*. As Lynn Margulis et al. have written in the Foreword to the English translation of his book, he was "the first person in history [to] come to grips with the real implications of the fact that Earth is a self-contained sphere." It was only as a result of Vernadsky's work on the biosphere, with its holistic approach, that a solution to the problem of the origins of life from inanimate matter finally became available to science (through discussions between British and Soviet scientists).[37]

More closely connected than Vernadsky to the proletarian revolution was the brilliant plant geneticist Vavilov, who was the first President of the Lenin Agricultural Academy and who, with the support of the Soviet state, applied a materialist method to the question of the origins of agriculture. It was Vavilov who in the 1920s determined that there were a number of centers of great plant gene diversity—the richest banks of germplasm, the basis for all human cultivation—located in the underdeveloped countries "in tropical and subtropical mountain regions." For Vavilov, who adopted a dialectical, coevolutionary perspective, these centers of plant genetic diversity were the product of human culture, which arose in "seven principal centres" out of which all of the principal crops originated, and in which the richest genetic stock, the product of millennia of cultivation, are consequently to be found. "The fundamental centres of origin of cultivated plants," he wrote, "…very frequently play the role of accumulators of an astonishing diversity of varieties."[38] For many years now, since Vavilov's discovery, scientists, particularly in the West, have been returning to these genetic "reservoirs" (in places such as Mexico, Peru, Ethiopia, Turkey, and Tibet) for new germplasm to use in breeding resistance in commercial varieties. Today there is an international struggle between countries in the periphery (where these sources of germplasm are located) and the center of the capitalist system over the control of these genetic resources.[39]

Other Soviet scientists, connected to Bukharin, shared his view of the ecological roots of human society. In a book entitled *Marxism and Modern Thought*, introduced by Bukharin, V.L. Komrov quoted at length from the long passage on illusions of the human "conquest of nature" in Engels's

Dialectics of Nature and went on to note that "the private owner or employer, however necessary it may be to make the changing of the world comply with the laws of Nature, cannot do so since he aims at profit and only profit. By creating crisis upon crisis in industry he lays waste natural wealth in agriculture, leaving behind a barren soil and in mountain districts bare rocks and stony slopes." Similarly, Y.M. Uranovsky placed heavy emphasis, in a discussion of Marxism and science in the same book, on Marx's research into Liebig and "the theory of the exhaustion of the soil."[40]

All of these contributions to ecology were products of the early Soviet era, and of the dialectical, revolutionary forms of thinking that it engendered. The ultimate tragedy of the Soviet relation to the environment, which eventually took a form that has been characterized as "ecocide," has tended to obscure the enormous dynamism of early Soviet ecology of the 1920s, and the role that Lenin personally played in promoting conservation.[41] Lenin was a sophisticated materialist, whose materialism (especially as developed in his *Philosophical Notebooks*) was dialectical and non-reductionist. He was a close student of Hegel, and of Hegel's analysis of Epicurus, and saw Epicurus' philosophy as embodying "the guess works of genius and *signposts* for science, but not for clericalism."[42]

In his writings and political pronouncements Lenin insisted that human labor could not simply substitute for the forces of nature and that a "rational exploitation" of the environment, or the scientific management of natural resources in accord with the principles of conservation, was essential. As the leader of the young Soviet state he argued for "preservation of the monuments of nature." He appointed the dedicated environmentalist Anatiolii Vasil'evich Lunacharskii as head of the People's Commissariat of Education (Enlightenment), which was put in charge of conservation for all of Soviet Russia.[43] Lenin had enormous respect for Vernadsky, to whom he had referred favorably in *Materialism and Empirio-Criticism*. In response to the urging of Vernadsky and the mineralogist E.A. Fersman, Lenin in 1920 established in the southern Urals the first nature preserve in the Soviet Union—the first reserve anywhere by a government exclusively aimed at the scientific study of nature. Hence, under Lenin's protection the Soviet conservation movement prospered in the 1920s, particularly during the New Economic Policy period (1921–1928).

But with the early death of Lenin in 1924, and the subsequent triumph of Stalinism, conservationists were increasingly attacked for being "bourgeois." To make matters worse, the rise of Trofim Denisovich

Lysenko as an arbiter of biological science meant that "scientific" attacks were launched on ecology and genetics.[44] By the late 1930s the Soviet conservation movement had been completely decimated. Many of the more ecological thinkers has been purged, including Bukharin, Vavilov, and Uranovsky. As a crowning irony, ecological factors were eventually to play a major role in the precipitous decline of Soviet economic growth rates and the onset of stagnation in the 1970s.[45]

Caudwell's Dialectics

Western Marxism as a distinctive tradition arising in the 1920s was characterized by its unrelenting war against positivism in the social sciences, which unfortunately carried a very heavy cost, due to a tendency to create a fissure between nature and society, resulting in a neglect of all of those aspects of existence related to ecology and the coevolution of human beings and nature. Thus both Lukács and Gramsci were harshly critical of Bukharin's *Historical Materialism*. For Lukács, Bukharin's weakness was his "preoccupation with the natural sciences," which created a "false methodology," leading him, like Engels before him, to "attempt to make a 'science' out of the dialectic." Indeed, "the closeness of Bukharin's theory to bourgeois natural-scientific materialism," Lukács wrote, "derives from his use of 'science' ... as a model." By applying dialectics to nature, Bukharin had allowed positivism to intrude into the study of society.[46]

Both Bukharin's *Historical Materialism* and his later introduction to *Science at the Cross Roads* (his 1931 paper presented to the International Conference of the History of Science and Technology held in London) were criticized in Gramsci's *Prison Notebooks*, where Bukharin was in many ways Gramsci's principal target. Gramsci objected to any tendency to "make science the base of life" and to neglect the fact that "science is a superstructure." Such a view would suggest that the philosophy of praxis needed "philosophical supports outside of itself."[47] Nevertheless, Gramsci was somewhat less inclined than Lukács to exclude the dialectic from nature. In criticism of the latter he wrote:

> It would appear that Lukács maintains that one can speak of the dialectic only for the history of men and not for nature. He might be right and he might be wrong. If his assertion presupposes a dualism between nature and man he is wrong because he is falling into a conception of nature proper to religion and to Graeco-Christian philosophy and also to idealism which does not in reality succeed in unifying and relating man and nature to each other except verbally. But if human history should be conceived also as the history of nature (also by

means of the history of science) how can dialectic be separated from nature? Perhaps Lukács, in reaction to the baroque theories of the *Popular Manual* [Bukharin's *Historical Materialism*], has fallen into the opposite error, into a form of idealism.[48]

Yet Gramsci, like Lukács, failed to perceive the strengths (as well as the weaknesses) evident in Bukharin's analysis—strengths which derived from the attempt to connect the materialist conception of history to a materialist conception of nature. Although a certain mechanism intruded itself into Bukharin's analysis, which took "equilibrium" as one of its defining characteristics, the often profound understanding of ecological connections, including a coevolutionary perspective, was a crucial aspect of Bukharin's synthesis which was lost within the Western Marxist tradition. The Frankfurt School, which followed the lead of Lukács in this respect, developed an "ecological" critique which was almost entirely culturalist in form, lacking any knowledge of ecological science (or any ecological content), and generally attributing the alienation of human beings from nature to science and the Enlightenment—an analysis that arose more from Romantic roots and from Weber's critique of rationalization and the "disenchantment" of the world than from Marx.[49] In this perspective the alienation was grasped one-sidedly in terms of the alienation of the idea of nature. What was lacking, however, was any analysis of the real, material alienation of nature, for example, Marx's theory of metabolic rift.

Alfred Schmidt's very influential book *The Concept of Nature in Marx* (1962) extends this one-sided perspective of Lukács and the Frankfurt School. The central contradiction that pervades Schmidt's analysis lies in his repeated contention that materialism and dialectics are "incompatible."[50] Although Schmidt continually stresses the significance of Marx's concept of "metabolism," this is removed from all relation to natural-material conditions, other than labor itself *in its most abstract form*, that is, devoid of metabolic relations to the earth. Consequently, barely any mention is made in his book of the metabolic rift in the soil nutrient cycle or the Marx–Liebig critique of capitalist agriculture, despite the fact that this was the *material context* in which Marx's concept of metabolic exchange was developed. Having failed to perceive Marx's concept of metabolism in the terms in which Marx actually applied it, that is, to the real earthly problems of capitalist agriculture, and thereby missing Marx's materialist dialectic (the real coevolutionary bases of his thinking), Schmidt ends up concluding that Marx simply fell prey in the end to his materialism, and thus to a "Promethean" view, emphasizing the domination of nature.[51]

Hence, direct ecological analysis was almost non-existent in Marxian social science (as was also the case for social science in general, with only a few exceptions) from the late 1930s to the 1960s, when the publication of Rachel Carson's *Silent Spring* helped to rekindle environmental struggle. The destruction of Soviet ecology in the "East" had been accompanied in the "West" by the rejection of any attempt to apply the dialectical method of Marxist analysis to nature and science.

The one figure within Western Marxism in the 1930s who, as we now know, managed to transcend these contradictions in large part—if only for a brief, glorious moment—was Christopher St. John Sprigg (better known by his pen name of Christopher Caudwell). Yet Caudwell was to die at the age of twenty-nine on February 12, 1937, in the Spanish Civil War, at his machine gun guarding the retreat of his fellows, in the British Battalion of the International Brigade. Caudwell's breathtaking intellectual achievements in a brief period of time, the years 1935–1936, in which all of his major works were written, ranged widely over the cultural and scientific landscape, resulting in such brilliant (if somewhat rough) works as *Illusion and Reality, Studies and Further Studies in a Dying Culture, The Crisis in Physics, Romance and Reaction*, a volume of *Poems*, and *Heredity and Development*—all published posthumously. His general viewpoint is best expressed by his famous statement in the foreword to *Studies and Further Studies*: "Either the Devil has come amongst us having great power, or there is a causal explanation for a disease common to economics, science and art."[52] Caudwell saw the central problem as the atomized, alienated world of bourgeois science and culture, characterized by dialectical rifts between nature and society, idealism and mechanism, and mechanism and vitalism within science. These dualisms and partial, one-sided rationalities so characteristic of bourgeois society arose, in his perspective, out of the necessary defenses of a dying culture.

For Caudwell, as E.P. Thompson wrote, bourgeois culture was characterized by "the repeated generation of idealism and mechanical materialism, not as true antagonists but as pseudo-antitheses, generated as twins in the same moment of conception, or, rather, as positive and negative aspects of the same fractured moment of thought."[53] But Caudwell opposed not merely these dualisms; he also opposed that form of positivism which simply denied the antithesis, by adopting a crude "reflective" view of the subject–object relation within knowledge. He thus directed much of his fire at the crude "epistemological" position of what was then the dominant school of "dialectical materialism."

The central element in Caudwell's thought was rather the mutual determination (or conditioning) of subject–object within what now might be called a "critical-realist" standpoint, emphasizing *dialectic as emergence.* Concretely, this took the form of a constant insistence on the co-evolutionary character of the relation between human beings and nature. For Caudwell, the triumph of Marx's materialism, which was active and dialectical in character, over earlier mechanical, reductionist, and contem-plative forms of materialism, could be explained in part as a product of the greater materialist and dialectical coherence within science itself that arose with the development of evolutionary theories. Thus, "the rise of the evolutionary sciences from 1750 to 1850 [preceding the Darwinian revolution] was what altered the mechanical materialism of Condillac, d'Holbach and Diderot to the dialectical materialism of Marx and Engels and made it capable of including all the active side of the subject–object relation developed by idealism."[54]

If this central theme, running through Caudwell's thought, was not easily perceived by subsequent analysts, it was no doubt because Caudwell's *Heredity and Development*, his critical study of biology, was not published, as Caudwell had clearly intended it would be, along with the other studies that made up *Studies and Further Studies in a Dying Culture* and *The Crisis in Physics.* Rather *Heredity and Development* remained unpublished until mid-1986, a half-century after it was written.[55]

In this extraordinary work, Caudwell attempted to deal with the epistemological and ideological problems associated with the "crisis of biology," which was also a crisis of Darwinian theory at a time of renewed Larmarckianism and the growth of genetics. Although his analysis some-times contains errors—a product of the crisis and disorder within biology itself prior to the development of the neo-Darwinian synthesis—in the main his analysis points towards a complex coevolutionary synthesis that anticipates much of the most sophisticated biological and ecological analysis that was to follow. For Caudwell, the new field of ecology, like biology itself, was characterized by a dichotomous conception of the relationship between organism and environment; one which was un-dialectical, in the sense that it denied the mutual determination of subject–object, of organism and environment.

Teleology, Caudwell argued, was a form of subjective mechanism ("the Universe is God's machine"), the counterpart of the objective mechanism more commonly associated with positivism. Rather than simply rejecting teleology, positivism, as its dialectical twin, had in a sense naturalized it, creating a one-sided, purposive conception of evolution. Although science, insofar as it was materialist and dialectical, opposed teleology, and "no scientist believes in the determinism of phenomena by a God as a methodological rule, yet he does to-day—in a 'tired' part of biology—admit the possibility of phenomena being determined by a purpose not life's own consciousness of purpose, nor the necessity of matter, but a purpose, or pattern, or plan, or entelechy outside both." The failure of science to remain materialist and dialectical is manifested therefore in "the bourgeois self-contradiction as to the relation of individual and environment—expressed as a myth about the machine." This "gives us the basic biological metaphysic of Cartesian materialism or mechanism, which eventually reappears in its apparently contradictory but really twin forms of vitalistic idealism or teleology."[56]

The value of Darwin's own work, according to Caudwell, is that it largely eluded such one-sided viewpoints, pointing toward a coevolutionary perspective. For the first time Darwinism had taught people to view nature *historically*. "If we picture life diagrammatically," Caudwell wrote (falling somewhat into a metaphor of linear progression),

> as a series of steps, then at each step the environment has become different—there are different problems, different laws, different obstacles at each step even though any series of steps besides its differences has certain general problems, laws and obstacles in common. Each new step of evolution is itself a new quality, and this involves a newness which affects both terms—organism and environment.[57]

Caudwell rejected the crude notion that the environment was simply "inimical," to be understood one-sidedly in terms of the natural generation of overpopulation and a struggle for existence within and between species. Rather the environment had to be seen as enabling as well as limiting. "An earlier society," he points out, relying on anthropological discoveries, "saw Nature as a system, in which the whole world of life co-operated in mutual assistance." Although in many ways just as illusory (or even more so because of the teleological conceptions adopted), this view of nature as cooperative captured a part of reality that the crude Darwinian view of nature—not to be confused with Darwin's own work or that of his immediate followers such as Huxley—as a world of unbridled competition and survival of the fittest all too often missed.

Caudwell argued convincingly that the same breaks in the dialectic that characterized the bourgeois approach to economics also characterized the conception of biology (and ecology), and some of the same general type of criticisms thereby applied. Namely: (1) "It is not possible to separate organism from environment as mutually distinct opposites. Life is the relation between opposed poles which have separated themselves out of reality, but remain in relation throughout the web of becoming." (2) "The evolution of life cannot be determined by the wills of living matter alone, or by the obstacles of non-living matter alone." (3) "The laws of the environment, in so far as they constrain the operations of life, are not given in the environment, but given in the relation between environment and life." (4) "The development of life is determined by the tendencies of life. But history does not realise the wills of individuals; it is only determined by them, and in turn determines them." (5) "The relation within a species or between species is not solely inimical, in the sense of individuals fighting for individual possession of a limited food supply. The food supply is itself an outcome of the particular relations between life and nature.... Similarly the multiplication of one species is not inimical to another, if it is the food of that species. Or the relation between species may be beneficial but indirect, as when birds distribute seeds, bees pollen, and coral polyps form reefs."[58]

The very fact that the relation between organisms and environment was a *relation*, according to Caudwell, meant that, like all relations, it was a mutually determining one, connected to "*material* change." Indeed, "a material becoming is what reality is."[59] This complex materialist, dialectical, coevolutionary perspective captured the essence of an ecological worldview. As E.P. Thompson argued four decades after Caudwell's death, Caudwell had managed to transcend positivism while also avoiding paying the "heavy cost" associated with "Western Marxism" after the 1920s, in which materialism was rejected once again as inherently mechanical in favor of a dialectical approach that was essentially idealist.[60] In this way he maintained a critical, dialectical realism and the possibility of naturalism—avoiding the tearing apart of the Marxian dialectic and the bifurcation of the human and natural realms.

The Dialectical Ecologist

Caudwell's great contribution, as we have seen, did not escape the tragedy that beset Marxist ecological analysis during this period. Caudwell died before the age of thirty, and *Heredity and Development*, his most co-evolutionary, ecologically oriented work, remained unpublished—unlike all of his other studies that made up *Studies and Further Studies in a Dying Culture*—because of its explicit criticism of Lysenkoism, which went against the ideology of the British Communists at that time, who took responsibility for the publication of Caudwell's manuscripts.[61]

Yet, despite the virtual disappearance of ecological discussions within

Marxian social theory from the 1930s to the 1970s, all was not lost. Ecological understandings permeated the British cultural-materialist tradition
represented by Raymond Williams and E.P. Thompson. Thompson, in
particular, was deeply influenced by the ecological socialism of William
Morris, as well as by the materialism of Caudwell.[62] Some recognition of
ecological issues was retained within certain schools of Marxian political
economy, particularly the Monthly Review school, which (unlike most of
the "Western Marxist" tradition) retained a strong materialist orientation.
An emphasis on the critique of economic waste under the regime of
monopoly capital (which was related to the contradiction between use
value and exchange value) gave an ecological cast to Paul Sweezy's analysis
as early as the 1940s—a theme that was to be strengthened in his work of
the 1960s to 1990s.[63]

Of greater significance, however, was the fact that a second foundation
of Marxist ecological thinking existed in the West within science itself
(particularly biology), where a deep commitment to both materialism and
dialectics was found among leading scientists influenced by Marxism—
even constituting, in some cases, the fundamental philosophical bases for
their scientific discoveries. In England in the 1930s a strong tradition of
left-wing scientists emerged, including J.D. Bernal, J.B.S. Haldane, and
Joseph Needham. For Bernal and Needham, the presentations of the
Soviet delegation, including Bukharin, Vavilov, and Boris Hessen, at the
Second International Conference on the History of Science and Technology in London in 1931 were crucial in the formation of their views.
Bernal was to become famous principally for his histories of science,
most notably his four-volume *Science in History*. In this work he took a
decided materialist perspective, though one that has been criticized for
occasionally exhibiting mechanistic views. For Bernal, the greatest ancient
expression of materialism to survive was

> Lucretius' *De Rerum Natura*, (On the nature of things), which shows both its
> power and danger to established order. It is essentially a philosophy of objects
> and their movements, an explanation of Nature and society from below and not
> above. It emphasizes the inexhaustible stability of the ever-moving material
> world and man's power to change it by learning its rules. The classical materi-
> alists could go no further because, as we shall see, of their divorce from the
> manual arts; nor could, in later days, the great re-formulator of materialism,
> Francis Bacon.

Bernal was the first to suggest that in criticizing contemplative materialism in his *Theses on Feuerbach* Marx was thinking not simply about
Feuerbach, but even more about "his old favourite Epicurus."[64]

The Cambridge biochemist Joseph Needham, a member of the Royal Society, adopted a dialectical perspective arguing that "Marx and Engels were bold enough to assert that it [the dialectic] happens in evolving nature itself." Moreover, "the undoubted fact that it happens in our thought about nature is because we and our thought are a part of nature."[65] Needham explicitly rejected both mechanistic and vitalistic views, favoring a dialectical and materialist approach.

More important than either Bernal or Needham was Haldane, also a member of the Royal Society, who was a leading figure in the development of the neo-Darwinian synthesis within biology. Haldane in 1929 (a year after a trip to the Soviet Union), working along parallel lines with but independently from the Soviet biochemist A.I. Oparin, was the "codiscoverer," as we have already seen in Chapter Five, of the first genuine materialist explanation for the emergence of living organisms from the inorganic world—a hypothesis which is now known as the Oparin–Haldane hypothesis, and was made possible in part by Vernadsky's analysis of the biosphere. Commenting on this materialist theory of the origins of life (now widely adhered to in science), Bernal wrote in his monumental work *The Origins of Life* (1967) that "The great liberation of the human mind, of the realization first stressed by Vico and then put into practice by Marx and his followers that *man makes himself*, will now be enlarged with the essential philosophical content of the new knowledge of the origin of life and the realization of its self-creative character."[66]

Haldane himself was a strong adherent of Engels's dialectical naturalism and wrote a "Preface" to *The Dialectics of Nature*. According to Haldane, "had Engels' method of thinking been more familiar, the transformations of our ideas on physics which have occurred during the last thirty years would have been much smoother. Had his remarks on Darwinism been generally known, I for one would have been saved a certain amount of muddled thinking."[67]

Although there were all sorts of discontinuities, this tradition of materialist and dialectical research by Marxist-influenced thinkers within the life sciences continued, and even gained a new impetus between the 1970s and the 1990s in the work of such important figures as Richard Lewontin, Stephen Jay Gould, and Richard Levins (all professors at Harvard). The materialism of these thinkers is derived as much or more from Darwin as from Marx. Yet the debt to Marx is clear. Significantly, an understanding of the long debate over materialism and teleology, which philosophers now have generally lost sight of, is retained in the work of these thinkers—providing the basis for a thoroughgoing ecological materialism.

Indeed, the very prominence of these scientists—Gould in paleontology and natural history, Lewontin in genetics, and Levins in ecology—points to the continuing importance of Marx, Darwin, materialism, and dialectical reasoning in the analysis of what can broadly be termed ecological phenomena.

A general attempt to outline a new dialectical naturalism was developed in Levins and Lewontin's now classic work, *The Dialectical Biologist* (1985). The hallmark of this work, which was dedicated to none other than Friedrich Engels ("who got it wrong a lot of the time but who got it right where it counted"), is its complex, non-teleological, coevolutionary perspective. "A commitment to the evolutionary world view," Levins and Lewontin write, "is a commitment to a belief in the instability and constant motion of systems in the past, present and future; such motion is assumed to be their essential characteristic." At the heart of Levins and Lewontin's analysis (like Engels and Caudwell but on a far sounder scientific basis) is the notion of "the organism as the subject and object of evolution." What this means is that organisms do not simply adapt to their environment; they also change it. "It is often forgotten that the seedling is the 'environment' of the soil, in that the soil undergoes great and lasting evolutionary changes as a direct consequence of the activity of the plants growing in it, and these changes in turn feed back on the organisms' conditions of existence." This essentially dialectical point of view is then used to critique ecological reductionism, which dominates much of ecological science; namely, the traditional view of Clementsian ecology that ecosystems demonstrate properties of growing diversity, stability, and complexity and pass through stages of succession—as if they were in effect "superorganisms." For Levins and Lewontin, in contrast, all such analysis is "idealistic," and non-dialectical.[68]

In *Humanity and Nature: Ecology, Science and Society* (1992) Yrjö Haila and Richard Levins united this view with a wide-ranging analysis of the problems of ecology that included the "social history of nature" as seen from a Marxist perspective. Here they introduced the concept of "eco-historical periods" to explain the complex, changing specificity of the human coevolutionary relation to nature. Such works emphasize the importance of a sustainable human relation to nature, not within a static framework, but within a larger perspective that attempts to focus on the processes of change inherent in both nature and society—and in their interaction.[69]

Stephen Jay Gould reflects continually in his writings on the principles of materialism and dialectical reasoning that inspire his own understanding of science and its development. His work is based principally on Darwin, but also occasionally draws on Engels and even Marx. The result is a dynamic materialist and dialectical treatment of nature and human society as a *process of natural history* that is apparent in everything that he writes, whatever the subject. Most important have been his treatments of chance/contingency and "punctuated equilibrium."[70]

If the Darwin–Marx relation is evident in the work of such thinkers as Lewontin, Levins, and Gould, the Liebig–Marx relation is also evident in contemporary work within science. The way in which Marx's analysis in this area prefigured some of the more advanced ecological analysis of the late twentieth century is nothing less than startling. Some of the more important recent scientific research on the ecology of the soil, in particular the work of Fred Magdoff, Less Lanyon, and Bill Liebhardt, has focused on successive historical breaks in nutrient cycling. The first such break, traceable to the second agricultural revolution, is conceived, in this analysis, in generally the same terms in which it was originally discussed by Liebig and Marx, and is seen as arising out of the physical removal of human beings from the land, as well as from the associated rift in the metabolic cycle and the net loss of nutrients to the soil arising from the transfer of organic products (food and fiber) over hundreds and thousands of miles. The result was the creation of a fertilizer industry, external to the farm economy, that sought to replace these nutrients.

> A subsequent break occurred with the third agricultural revolution (the rise of agribusiness), which was associated in its early stages with the removal of large animals from the farms, the development of centralized feedlots, and the replacement of animal traction with tractors. No longer was it necessary to grow legumes, which naturally fixed nitrogen in the soil, in order to feed ruminant animals. Hence, the dependence on fertilizer nitrogen, the product of the fertilizer industry, increased, with all sorts of negative environmental effects, including the contamination of ground water, the "death" of lakes, etc. These developments, and other closely related processes, are now seen as connected to the distorted pattern of development that has characterized capitalism (and other social systems such as that of the Soviet Union that replicated this pattern of development), taking the form of an ever more extreme rift between city and country—between what is now a mechanized humanity opposed to a mechanized nature.[71]

Unfortunately, the recent revival of Marxist ecological thinking in social science, which has been centered primarily in the political economy of ecological relations, has taken little notice thus far of the deeper materialism (deeper in its philosophical as well as its scientific standpoint), and more developed *ecological* materialism, that has often been maintained

among radical materialists within science.[72] Despite great advances in ecological thought within Marxist political economy, and the rediscovery of
much of Marx's argument, the issue of the relation of the materialist
conception of nature to the materialist conception of history (that is, of
the alienation of labor to the alienation of nature) is barely broached in
such discussions.[73] The barrier set up by the dominant philosophic critique
of the "dialectics of nature" remains hegemonic within Marxist social
theory itself; so much so that all creative inquiry in this direction seems
to be stymied at the outset. (One exception to this is the work of socialist
ecofeminists, such as Ariel Salleh and Mary Mellor, with their notions of
"embodied nature."[74]) All too often the environmental socialists focus
simply on the capitalist economy, viewing ecological problems one-sidedly
from the standpoint of their effect on the capitalist economy, rather than
focusing on the larger problem of the "fate of the earth" and its species.
Where connections with science are made within this analysis it is frequently within the realm of thermodynamics, that is, energetics and its
effects on the economy, while the whole issue of evolutionary biology is
curiously viewed as separate from ecological issues and Darwin is seldom
discussed.

In this respect a wider theory of ecology as a process of change involving contingency and coevolution is necessary if we are not only to
understand the world but to change it in conformity with the needs of
human freedom and ecological sustainability. "What matters is not whether
we modify nature or not"—Haila and Levins write—"but how, and for
what purpose, we do so."[75] What matters is whether nature is to be
dominated one-sidedly for narrow human ends, or whether, in a society
of associated producers, the alienation of human beings from nature and
from each other will be no longer be the *precondition* for human existence, but will be recognized for what it is: the estrangement of all that is
human.

The Principle of Conservation

Nothing comes from nothing and nothing being destroyed can be reduced
to nothing, Epicurus had said. Epicurus, Diogenes Laertius tells us, "was
a most prolific author and eclipsed all before him in the number of his
writings: for they amount to about three hundred rolls." Nevertheless,
only a few fragments of Epicurus' voluminous writing survived into early
modern times—the three letters preserved by Diogenes Laertius as the
epitome of his system, the *Principal Doctrines* (also preserved by Diogenes),

the poem of Lucretius, which faithfully rendered Epicurus' system, and various quotations in the works of other writers. Despite the widespread influence of Epicureanism in Hellenistic and Roman times, most of the writings of Epicurus and his followers perished or were destroyed long before the seventeenth-century revival of his thought. The discovery in the eighteenth century of a whole library of charred fragments in Philodemus' library in Herculaneum (which had been buried by the eruption of Mount Vesuvius in A.D. 79) seemed to suggest that some of these writings would be recovered. But so slow and laborious was the process of recovery from the charred remains that Hegel concluded in his *History of Philosophy* "that the fragment of one of Epicurus's own writings, found some years ago in Herculaneum, and reprinted by Orelli ... has neither extended nor enriched our knowledge; so that we must in all earnestness deprecate the finding of the remaining writings."[76] Marx wrote without the benefit of any more writings than had been available to Hegel.

Still the effort of recovery persisted throughout the nineteenth and twentieth centuries. The charred remains have metamorphosed into significant fragmentary sections from Epicurus' *On Nature*, with a broad outline of the greater part of this massive work, which took up thirty-seven volumes, emerging only now. This is coupled with other discoveries that have occurred since Hegel and Marx wrote. Only a year after Marx's death the remains of the great wall of Diogenes of Oenoanda, carrying inscriptions from Epicurus' writings meant to last through the ages, were discovered; followed by the discovery of the Vatican manuscript of Epicurus' sayings.

What has emerged from all of this is a view of Epicurus that conflicts with much of previous thought. He is now revealed as a non-reductionist, non-mechanistic, non-deterministic thinker concerned with the issue of human freedom and embodying a dialectical perspective. In general, the picture of Epicurus that has arisen over the last century is one that conforms startlingly to what Marx argued (and Kant suspected): a thinker who struggled against both the determinism of mechanistic physics and the teleology of idealist philosophy, against Democritus as well as Plato, in order to allow room for contingency and freedom.

Moreover, he did so within a standpoint that was critical-materialist; one that arose from materialist postulates and yet recognized in his concept of "anticipations" (or preconceptions) the importance of *a priori* certain knowledge, not derived directly from the senses. The picture of Epicurus' *On Nature* that has arisen in recent years is one that David Sedley, the leading authority on that work, has referred to as methodologically rigorous and "dialectical."[77] Epicurus' materialism extended freedom and contingency to human beings and all of nature, while not losing sight of the realm of material necessity. In doing so, it provided the basis for a humanistic and ecological world-view. "When all the evidence is duly considered," Long and Sedley write (taking into account the materials recovered from Philodemus' library in Herculaneum), "Epicureanism would be better regarded as a radical but selective critique of contemporary politics, rather than the apolitical posture with which it is frequently identified."[78]

Marx was deeply influenced by the non-deterministic materialism that he thought he had found in Epicurus (but couldn't quite prove given the sources then available). He transformed this view while absorbing it within his larger dialectical synthesis, which also included Hegel, political economy, French socialism, and nineteenth-century evolutionary science. Epicurus, according to Marx, had discovered alienation from nature; but Hegel revealed the alienation of human beings from their own labor, and hence from both society and the specifically human relation to nature. Marx forged these insights, together with the critical knowledge obtained from Ricardo's economics, Liebig's chemistry, and Darwin's evolutionary theory, into a revolutionary philosophy that aimed at nothing less than the transcendence of alienation in all of its aspects: a world of rational ecology and human freedom with an earthly basis—the society of associated producers.

NOTES

Introduction

1. Karl Marx, *Grundrisse* (New York: Vintage, 1973), 489.
2. The significance of Epicurus for Marx's ecology, as well as the importance of Liebig and Darwin, was pointed out some years ago in a remarkable outline on the development of Marx's ecological views authored by Jean-Guy Vaillancourt. Vaillancourt was clearly pointing in the direction of the kind of analysis offered in this book. See Jean-Guy Vaillancourt, "Marxism and Ecology: More Benedictine than Franciscan," in Ted Benton, ed., *The Greening of Marxism* (New York: Guilford, 1996), 50–63.
3. Bertrand Russell, "Introduction," in Frederick Albert Lange, *The History of Materialism* (New York: Humanities Press, 1950), v.
4. Roy Bhaskar, "Materialism," in Tom Bottomore, ed., *A Dictionary of Marxist Thought* (Oxford: Blackwell, 1983), 324.
5. Karl Marx, *Texts on Method* (Oxford: Basil Blackwell, 1975), 190.
6. Bertrand Russell, *A History of Western Philosophy* (New York: Simon & Schuster, 1945), 246. See also George E. McCarthy, *Marx and the Ancients* (Savage, Md.: Rowman & Littlefield, 1990), 42–43.
7. Georg Wilhelm Friedrich Hegel, *Lectures on the History of Philosophy* (Lincoln: University of Nebraska Press, 1995), vol. 2, 295–98.
8. Friedrich Engels, *Ludwig Feurbach and the Outcome of Classical German Philosophy* (New York: International Publishers, 1941), 17, 21.
9. Heinrich Heine, *Selected Prose* (Harmondsworth: Penguin Books, 1993), 238–40.
10. Immanuel Kant, *Critique of Pure Reason* (Cambridge: Cambridge University Press, 1997), 702–3, and *Critique of Practical Reason* (Cambridge: Cambridge University Press, 1997), 117.
11. On the role of the Hegelian dialectic in transcending the Kantian thing-in-itself, see Charles Taylor, *Hegel and Modern Society* (Cambridge: Cambridge University Press, 1979), 47–49.
12. Georg Wilhelm Friedrich Hegel, *Science of Logic* (New York: Humanities Press, 1969), 154–55.
13. Karl Marx and Friedrich Engels, *Collected Works* (New York: International Publishers, 1975), vol. 4, 125.
14. Marx and Engels, *Collected Works*, vol. 1, 30, 64. In terms of pure philosophy, Marx wrote to Ferdinand Lassalle that he preferred Aristotle and Heraclitus

among the ancients to the "easier" Epicurus. It was to Epicurus, however, that Marx had devoted "special study," because of his "[political]" significance—presumably Epicurus' concept of freedom and his connection to the Enlightenment. Marx to Lassalle, December 21, 1857 and May 31, 1858, in Marx and Engels, *Collected Works*, vol. 40, 226, 316. (The word "political" is bracketed in the quote above because it is an editorial reconstruction—the actual wording used by Marx is not clear due to damage to the manuscript.)

15. Marx and Engels, *Collected Works*, vol. 1, 62; Lucretius, *On the Nature of the Universe* (Oxford verse translation) (New York: Oxford University Press, 1999), 93 (1.865–70).

16. The reference to an "active principle" here is meant to be associated with *practical* materialism and contrasted to its more *contemplative* form. In no way is it meant to suggest that nature imposes relations on human beings in which they are simply "passive," that there is a "passive element in experience," as in the unfortunate terminology adopted by Sebastiano Timpanaro in his otherwise valuable critique in *On Materialism*. This error finds its dialectical counterpart in Timpanaro's thought in his tendency to view nature itself as in a sense "passive," reduced to a set of limiting conditions on human beings. The deterministic nature of such assumptions feeds into the extreme pessimism that characterizes Timpanaro's outlook. See S. Timpanaro, *On Materialism* (London: Verso, 1975), 34; Raymond Williams, *Problems in Materialism and Culture* (London: Verso, 1980), 107–9; Perry Anderson, *Considerations on Western Marxism* (London: Verso, 1979), 60, 91.

17. Roy Bhaskar, *The Possibility of Naturalism* (Atlantic Highlands, N.J.: Humanities Press, 1979), 100.

18. Karl Marx, *Capital*, vol. 1 (New York: Vintage, 1976), 92.

19. Bhaskar, *The Possibility of Naturalism*, 3; Roy Bhaskar, "General Introduction," in Margaret Archer, Roy Bhaskar, Andrew Collier, Tony Lawson, and Alan Norrie, eds., *Critical Realism* (New York: Routledge, 1998), xiii.

20. This was explicitly stated in Georg Lukács's great work, *History and Class Consciousness* (1922). In Lukács's words,

> The misunderstandings that arise from Engels' account of dialectics can in the main be put down to the fact that Engels—following Hegel's mistaken lead—extended the method to apply also to nature. However, the crucial determinants of dialectics—the interaction of subject and object, the unity of theory and practice, the historical changes in the reality underlying the categories as the root cause of changes in thought, etc.— are absent from our knowledge of nature.

As important as these points were, the consequence for Lukács's own work was the radical severance of social science from natural science and history from nature—as if the natural-physical realm could be ceded to positivism. Georg Lukács, *History and Class Consciousness* (London: Merlin Press, 1971), 24. In this way, Lukács, in Bhaskar's words, "inaugurates a long tradition within Marxism which confounds science with its positivistic misinterpretation." Bhaskar, *Reclaiming Reality* (London: Verso, 1989), 139.

21. Williams, *Problems in Materialism and Culture*, 104.

22. Ibid., 105. See also E.P. Thompson, *Making History* (New York: New Press, 1994), 98.

23. See Stephen Jay Gould, *The Mismeasure of Man* (New York: W.W. Norton, 1996); R.C. Lewontin, Steven Rose, and Leon J. Kamin, eds., *Not in Our Genes* (New York: Pantheon, 1984).

24. Massimo Quaini, *Geography and Marxism* (Totowa, N.J.: Barnes & Noble, 1982), 136.

25. David Goldblatt, *Social Theory and the Environment* (Boulder, Colo.: Westview Press, 1996), 5.

26. Anthony Giddens, *A Contemporary Critique of Historical Materialism* (Berkeley: University of California Press, 1981), 59–60. See also Ted Benton, "Marxism and Natural Limits," *New Left Review*, no. 178 (November–December 1989), 51–86.

27. Alec Nove, "Socialism," in John Eatwell, Murray Milgate, and Peter Newman, eds., *The New Palgrave Dictionary of Economics*, vol. 4 (New York: Stockton, 1987), 399.

28. Michael Redclift and Graham Woodgate, "Sociology and the Environment," in Michael Redclift and Ted Benton, eds., *Social Theory and the Global Environment* (New York: Routledge, 1994), 53.

29. Anna Bramwell, *Ecology in the Twentieth Century* (New Haven, Conn.: Yale University Press, 1989), 34.

30. Jean-Paul Sartre, *The Search for a Method* (New York: Vintage, 1963), 7. See also John Bellamy Foster, "Introduction," in Ernst Fischer, *How to Read Karl Marx* (New York: Monthly Review Press, 1996), 7–30.

31. Marx and Engels, *Collected Works*, vol. 5, 36.

32. For a classic, brilliant example of this, see Carolyn Merchant, *The Death of Nature* (New York: Harper & Row, 1980)—a work that is indispensable, despite its one-sided treatment of the Baconian tradition, for its profound critique of the mechanistic and patriarchal tendencies of much of seventeenth-century science.

33. Christopher Caudwell, *Scenes and Actions: Unpublished Manuscripts* (New York: Routledge & Kegan Paul, 1986), 199.

34. See, for example, Wade Sikorski, *Modernity and Technology* (Tuscaloosa: University of Alabama Press, 1993).

35. On the complex nature of the concept of "the domination of nature" as it grew out of Bacon, and the even more complex, dialectical way in which this was perceived by Marx, see William Leiss, *The Domination of Nature* (Boston: Beacon Press, 1974). On Marx's critique of the Baconian-style "ruse" see Marx, *Grundrisse*, 409–10.

36. Christopher Caudwell, *Illusion and Reality* (New York: International Publishers, 1937), 279.

37. See John Bellamy Foster, "Introduction to John Eveyln's *Fumifugium*," *Organization & Environment*, vol. 12, no. 2 (June 1999), 184–87.

38. For a historical analysis of Baconian improvement and the concept of "natural history" in the seventeenth century, see Charles Webster, *The Great Instauration* (London: Duckworth, 1975).

39. Caudwell, *Scenes and Actions*, 187–88.

40. Rachel Carson, *Lost Woods* (Boston: Beacon Press, 1998), 245.

41. Barry Commoner, *The Closing Circle* (New York: Knopf, 1971), 37–41. Although Commoner himself referred to the fourth informal law as "there's no such thing as a free lunch," the Russian ecologist Alexei Yablokov has translated this more generally as "nothing comes from nothing." Rolf Edberg

and Alexei Yablokov, *Tomorrow Will Be Too Late* (Tucson: University of Arizona Press, 1991), 89.

42. The close connection between Epicurus (and Lucretius) and Commoner was highlighted in Vaillancourt, "Marxism and Ecology," 52.

43. Carson, *Lost Woods*, 230–31.

44. Richard Levins and Richard Lewontin, *The Dialectical Biologist* (Cambridge, Mass.: Harvard University Press, 1985), 134.

45. Marx, *Texts on Method*, 191. Such a complex, dialectical perspective is to be distinguished from traditional, Clementsian ecology with its mechanistic, teleological, systems-theory modeling of ecosystems as superorganisms evolving in a unilinear direction—toward stability and diversity.

46. Levins and Lewontin, *The Dialectical Biologist*, 160.

47. Contemporary environmental sociology can be said to have emerged with the introduction by William Catton and Riley Dunlap in 1978 of the distinction between the "human exemptionalist paradigm" (originally referred to as the "human exceptionalist paradigm"), which they said characterized most of post-Second World War sociology, and which denied that human beings were dependent on nature, and the "new environmental paradigm," which they themselves proposed, which recognized such dependence. The former was understood as a form of radical constructionism in the human relation to nature, the latter as reflecting realism. Ironically, this realism, which characterized environmental sociology in the U.S., has recently found itself on the defensive with respect to more extreme, constructionist accounts emanating from Europe (reflecting the growth of radical culturalist and postmodernist thought), forcing the former to redefine itself as a weak or "cautious constructionism" (as opposed to the strong contructionism of the latter). Still, what is noticeably missing from this whole debate so far is any genuine attempt to comprehend the dialectical, coevolutionary nature of the interaction between human beings and their natural-physical environment. See William Catton and Riley Dunlap, "Environmental Sociology: A New Paradigm," *The American Sociologist*, vol. 13, no. 4 (November 1978), 252–56.

48. This argument is developed more fully in John Bellamy Foster, "Marx's Theory of Metabolic Rift: Classical Foundations for Environmental Sociology," *American Journal of Sociology*, vol. 104, no. 2 (September 1999), 370. For a discussion of the general state of environmental sociology, see Fred Buttel, "New Directions in Environmental Sociology," *Annual Review of Sociology*, vol. 13 (1987), 465–88.

49. Raymond Murphy, *Sociology and Nature* (Boulder, Colo.: Westview Press, 1996), 10.

50. Riley Dunlap, "The Evolution of Environmental Sociology," in Michael Redclift and Graham Woodgate, eds., *International Handbook of Environmental Sociology* (Northampton, Mass.: Edward Elgar, 1997), 31–32.

51. See, for example, Robyn Eckersley, *Environmentalism and Political Theory* (New York: State University of New York Press, 1992).

52. The traditional difficulty in ascertaining Marx's relation to the subsequent "dialectics of nature" debate is well stated by Bhaskar, who writes: "While the evidence indicates that Marx agreed with the general thrust of Engels's intervention, his own critique of political economy neither presupposes nor entails any dialectics of nature." Bhaskar, *Reclaiming Reality*, 122.

53. Karl Marx, letter of December 19, 1860, in Karl Marx and Friedrich Engels, *Selected Correspondence, 1846–1895* (New York: International Publishers, 1936), 126.

1. The Materialist Conception of Nature

1. Charles Darwin, *Notebooks, 1836–1844* (Ithaca, N.Y.: Cornell University Press, 1987), 375.
2. Charles Darwin, *Autobiography* (New York: Harcourt, Brace, 1958), 120.
3. Stephen Jay Gould addresses this question in an admirable essay entitled "Darwin's Delay," in Gould, *Ever Since Darwin* (New York: W.W. Norton, 1977), 21–27.
4. Ibid., 24–25.
5. Petty cited in Arthur O. Lovejoy, *The Great Chain of Being* (Cambridge, Mass.: Harvard University Press, 1964), 190.
6. On the whole history of the idea of the Scale of Nature, including the propensity in the eighteenth and early nineteenth centuries to "temporalize" it, see Loren Eiseley, *Darwin's Century* (New York: Doubleday, 1958).
7. Ibid., 66–69, 88–89, 94, 353.
8. John Hedley Brooke, *Science and Religion* (New York: Cambridge University Press, 1991), 193–94.
9. See Margaret C. Jacob, *The Radical Enlightenment: Pantheists, Freemasons and Republicans* (Boston: George Allen & Unwin, 1981), and *Scientific Culture and the Making of the Industrial West* (New York: Oxford University Press, 1997).
10. John Locke, *An Essay Concerning Human Understanding* (New York: Dover, 1959), vol. 2, 193.
11. Charles Coulston Gillispie, *Genesis and Geology* (Cambridge, Mass.: Harvard University Press, 1996), 33–35.
12. Abraham Wolf, *A History of Science, Technology and Philosophy in the 18th Century*, second edition revised by Douglas McKie (New York: Harper & Brothers, 1952, 784–87; John W. Yolton, *Thinking Matter: Materialism in Eighteenth-Century Britain* (Minneapolis: University of Minnesota Press, 1983), xi, 14, 107–25.
13. Paul Henry Thiery, Baron d'Holbach, *The System of Nature* (New York: Garland Publishing, 1984), vol. 1, 138.
14. Wolf, *A History of Science,* 787–91.
15. Ibid., 791–93.
16. William Paley, *Natural Theology* (London: R. Faulder, 1803), 473.
17. Howard E. Gruber, *Darwin on Man* (Chicago: University of Chicago Press, 1981), 37; John Hedley Brooke, *Science and Religion: Some Historical Perspectives* (New York: Cambridge University Press, 1991), 74–75; Thomas S. Kuhn, *The Copernican Revolution* (Cambridge, Mass.: Harvard University Press, 1985), 199, 235–37. Kuhn emphasizes Bruno's discovery of "the affinity" of Copernicanism to Epicurean atomism as his greatest contribution to science, but seems unaware of the extent to which the heresy of Epicureanism (viewed by the Christian church of the day as the greatest heresy against religion) was a central element in the church's condemnation of him. Hence, Kuhn himself questions whether Bruno was actually a "martyr to science" rather than to mysticism. Here Brooke's treatment is important.
18. Gruber, *Darwin on Man,* 204–5.

19. Janet Browne, *Charles Darwin: Voyaging* (Princeton, N.J.: Princeton University Press, 1995), 72–78.
20. Gruber, *Darwin on Man*, 204.
21. Sandra Herbert and Paul H. Barrett, "Introduction to Notebook M," in Darwin, *Notebooks, 1836–1844*, 519; Darwin, *Notebooks, 1836–1844*, 291, 638.
22. Darwin, *Notebooks, 1836–1844*, 551.
23. Francis Bacon, *Philosophical Works* (New York: Freeport, 1905), 473; Darwin, *Notebooks, 1836–1844*, 637. Darwin was partly reacting to the natural theologian William Whewell's Bridgewater treatise, which had commented on Bacon's statement. See William Whewell, *Astronomy and General Physics Considered with Reference to Natural Theology* (London: William Pickering, 1834), 355–56.
24. Darwin, *Notebooks, 1836–1844*, 614.
25. James R. Moore, "Darwin of Down," in David Kohn, ed., *The Darwinian Heritage* (Princeton, N.J.: Princeton University Press, 1985), 452; Adrian Desmond, *The Politics of Evolution: Morphology, Medicine and Reform in Radical London* (Chicago: University of Chicago Press, 1989), 412–14.
26. Darwin, *Notebooks, 1836–1844*, 532–33.
27. Ibid., 213.
28. John R. Durant, "The Ascent of Nature in Darwin's *Descent of Man*," in Kohn, ed., *The Darwinian Heritage*, 301.
29. Marx's doctoral thesis has come down to us in incomplete form. The most critical gap is the loss of the final two chapters (Chapters 4 and 5) of Part One of his thesis, which we know from the table of contents were entitled "General Difference in Principle Between the Democritean and Epicurean Philosophy of Nature" and "Result." (We do, however, have the notes to Chapter 4.) In addition, we are missing all but a fragment of the Appendix to his thesis, entitled "Critique of Plutarch's Polemic Against the Theology of Epicurus" (though here again we have the notes to the Appendix).
30. For the traditional interpretation, see H.P. Adams, *Karl Marx in His Earlier Writings* (London: George Allen & Unwin, 1940), 27–41; and David McLellan, *Marx Before Marxism* (New York: Harper & Row, 1970), 52–68. McLellan's interpretation, which sees Marx as never going beyond the viewpoint of Hegel in his thesis, is predicated on McLellan's prior claim of Marx's "conversion to Hegelianism"—an interpretation that, by reducing Marx to a mere "convert," clearly understates (as the doctoral thesis itself serves to highlight) the intellectual struggle in which he was engaged. *Marx Before Marxism*, 46–52. McLellan's interpretation here is similar in some ways to that of Franz Mehring, who argued in his classic biography that Marx's doctoral thesis remained "completely on the idealist basis of the Hegelian philosophy." Mehring's only evidence for this was that Marx rejected Democritus' mechanistic materialism, preferring the materialist model of Epicurus, with its greater emphasis on free activity, instead. Yet, far from proving that he was a Hegelian idealist, Marx's admiration for Epicurus, which continues in his later writings, only points to a much more complex relation to materialism, even at this very early stage, than is generally supposed. See Franz Mehring, *Karl Marx* (Ann Arbor: University of Michigan Press, 1962), 30.
31. The view that Marx was already leaning toward materialism when he wrote his doctoral dissertation is indicated by the following epigram, written in

1837: "Kant and Fichte soar to heaven's blue/ Seeking for some distant land,/ I but seek to grasp profound and true/ That which—in the street I find." Karl Marx and Friedrich Engels, *Collected Works* (New York: International Publishers, 1975), vol. 1, 577.

32. Ibid., 18–19.

33. James D. White, *Karl Marx and the Intellectual Origins of Dialectical Materialism* (New York: St. Martin's Press, 1996), 42. As Norman Livergood has noted, "Marx was interested in materialism as early as the writing of his doctoral dissertation.... It is the concept of free activity which Marx considers Epicurus' most significant contribution to materialism." Norman D. Livergood, *Activity in Marx's Philosophy* (The Hague: Martinus Nijhoff, 1967), 1.

34. Maximilian Rubel and Margaret Manale, *Marx Without Myth: A Chronological Study of His Life and Work* (Oxford: Basil Blackwell, 1975), 16–17. Marx presented Epicurean materialism as the enemy of Christian theology as early as his youthful examinations in the gymnasium. See Karl Marx, "On the Union of the Faithful with Christ According to John," in Robert Payne, ed., *The Unknown Karl Marx* (New York: New York University Press, 1971), 43.

35. The main body of the extant work of Epicurus can be found in Cyril Bailey, *Epicurus: The Extant Remains* (Oxford: Oxford University Press, 1926). Whitney J. Oates has provided a convenient edition that includes Bailey's translation of the extant remains of Epicurus, *The Stoic and Epicurean Philosophers: The Complete Extant Writings of Epicurus, Epicteus, Lucretius, Marcus Aurelius* (New York: Random House, 1940). Lucretius' *De rerum natura* has been translated into English numerous times in both verse and prose. Owing to the difficulties in the translation of a long didactic poem, the English-speaking reader will find both verse and prose translations of value. For verse, see the translation by Ronald Melville, *On the Nature of the Universe* (New York: Oxford University Press, 1999). For prose, see the translation by R.E. Latham (revised by John Godwin): Lucretius, *On the Nature of the Universe* (Harmondsworth: Penguin Books, 1994). In what follows, the prose translation by Latham (and Godwin) will normally be referred to with occasional quotations from the verse translation of Melville, cited as the Oxford verse translation. (The classical reference system, indicating the books and lines of Lucretius' text, will also be used.) Since Marx's time, it should be noted, some additional sources of Epicurus' work have been discovered. In 1884, the year after Marx's death, a philosophical inscription of Epicurus' teaching containing extensive fragments of his work was found by French and Austrian archaeologists on the remains of a great stone wall in the interior of modern Turkey. The inscription was carved in the form of 120 or more columns of text, stretching along the wall for over 40 meters, at the instigation of one of Epicurus' followers, Diogenes of Oenoanda, around A.D. 200. See Diogenes of Oenoanda, *The Fragments* (New York: Oxford University Press, 1971). In addition the library of the school of the leading proponent of Epicurus' ideas in Italy, Philodemus of Gadara in Palestine, who lived in Herculaneum, was overwhelmed by the eruption of Vesuvius in A.D. 79. The patient excavation of hundreds of charred papyrus rolls, which were found when his library was rediscovered in the excavation of Herculaneum in the eighteenth century, has been gradually giving rise to bits of information over the last

two centuries. Much of Epicurus' work *On Nature* has been found among the remains and is now being carefully reconstructed from the charred papyrus rolls. For a full-scale evaluation and synopsis of Epicurus' *On Nature*, see David Sedley, *Lucretius and the Transformation of Greek Wisdom* (New York: Cambridge University Press, 1998), 94–133. Sedley demonstrates, through a close examination of Lucretius' poem against Epicurus' text, what has long been assumed by scholars, that Lucretius was an Epicurean "fundamentalist" duplicating the arguments and even the language of the master, though departing in a few places from the overall structure (the dialectical ordering of arguments) in Epicurus' great treatise. See also Benjamin Farrington, *The Faith of Epicurus* (New York: Basic Books, 1967), xi–xiii; Marcello Gigante, *Philodemus in Italy: The Books from Herculaneum* (Ann Arbor: University of Michigan Press, 1990). A third source, not available to Marx, were the fragments of the Vatican Collection, a series of doctrinal statements, primarily epigrams, presenting Epicurus' ethical theory. This collection, also known as "The Sayings of Epicurus," was discovered in 1888 (five years after Marx's death) in a fourteenth-century Vatican manuscript which also contained Epicteus' *Manual* and Marcus Aurelius' *Meditations*. See Epicurus, *Letters, Principal Doctrines and Vatican Sayings* (Indianapolis: Bobbs-Merrill, 1964), 89 (translator's note).

36. See Cyril Bailey, *The Greek Atomists and Epicurus* (Oxford: Oxford University Press, 1928), 128–33, 287–317; A.A. Long, *Hellenistic Philosophy: Stoics, Epicureans and Sceptics* (Berkeley: University of California Press, 1986), 14–74. The swerve has never actually been found in Epicurus' extant writings themselves. Rather knowledge of it is based entirely on Lucretius and various secondary sources. Most editors of Epicurus' "Letter to Heredotus" insert the swerve at a certain point in the text (in accordance with their reading of Lucretius) to make the text more understandable. The discovery of Epicurus' *On Nature* in Philodemus' library at Herculaneum has raised the hope that Epicurus' own discussion of the swerve will be discovered, but so far the restoration of the book has not produced this result. See Epicurus, *Letters, Principal Doctrines, and Vatican Sayings*, 12 (translator's note); Gigante, *Philodemus in Italy*, 43.

37. Georg Wilhelm Friedrich Hegel, *Lectures on the History of Philosophy* (Lincoln: University of Nebraska Press, 1995), vol. 1, 306.

38. Lucretius, *On the Nature of the Universe*, 13–15 (1.145–214); A.A. Long and D.N. Sedley, eds., *The Hellenistic Philosophers: Translations of the Principal Sources with Philosophical Commentary* (Cambridge: Cambridge University Press, 1987), 25–27. The principle of conservation was not original to Epicurus. Farrington points out that Democritus was "the first to put it in its proper place as the first principle of all scientific thought about the physical world." Benjamin Farrington, *Science in Antiquity* (New York: Oxford University Press, 1969), 46.

39. Epicurus, "Letter to Menoeceus," in Oates, ed., *The Stoic and Epicurean Philosophers*, 33; Cyril Bailey, *The Greek Atomists and Epicurus* (Oxford: Oxford University Press, 1928), 318.

40. Lucretius, *On the Nature of the Universe* (Oxford verse translation), 17 (1.475–85).

41. Long and Sedley, eds., *The Hellenistic Philosophers*, 88–89. Marx took careful

note of Epicurus' concept of *prolēpsis* (anticipation, preconception) at the
very beginning of his *Notebooks on Epicurean Philosophy*, as well as later on in
his notes from Sextus Empiricus and Clement of Alexandria. See Marx and
Engels, *Collected Works*, vol. 1, 405–6, 428, 487.

42. Cicero, in Long and Sedley, eds., *The Hellenistic Philosophers*, 141. See also
Epicurus, *The Epicurus Reader* (Indianapolis: Hackett, 1994), 51.

43. Farrington, *The Faith of Epicurus*, 108–9. See also Diogenes Laertius, *Lives of
Eminent Philosophers*, (Cambridge, Mass.: Harvard University Press, Loeb Classical Library, 1925), vol. 2, 563; Bailey, *The Greek Atomists and Epicurus*, 245–
48; Long, *Hellenistic Philosophy*, 23–24. For Gassendi's interpretation of
Epicurus' concept of "anticipations," see Lynn Sumida Joy, *Gassendi the Atomist*
(Cambridge: Cambridge University Press, 1987), 169. For a recent interpretation, see Gisela Striker, *Essays on Hellenistic Epistemology and Ethics* (Cambridge: Cambridge University Press, 1996), 150–65.

44. Immanuel Kant, *Critique of Pure Reason* (Cambridge: Cambridge University
Press, 1998), 290–91; Howard Caygill, *A Kant Dictionary* (Oxford: Blackwell,
1995), 74–75.

45. Marx and Engels, *Collected Works*, vol. 5, 139; Lucretius, *On the Nature of the
Universe*, 88.

46. Oates, ed., *The Stoic and Epicurean Philosophers*, 35.

47. George A. Panichas, *Epicurus* (New York: Twayne, 1967), 83; Brad Inwood
and L.P. Gerson, eds., *Hellenistic Philosophy* (Indianapolis: Hackett, 1988), 65;
Oates, ed., *The Stoic and Epicurean Philosophers*, 35–39.

48. Ibid.; Panichas, *Epicurus*, 116–17; Long and Sedley, eds., *The Hellenistic Philosophers*, 137. Marx and Engels, *Collected Works*, vol. 5, 141.

49. J. Donald Hughes, *Pan's Travail: Environmental Problems of the Ancient Greeks
and Romans* (Baltimore: Johns Hopkins University Press, 1994), 60, 123–24,
130–31, 144, 196. Clarence J. Glacken places heavy emphasis on Epicurus
and Lucretius in his discussion of the nature–culture relation (and the whole
issue of environmental history) in ancient thought in his *Traces on the Rhodian
Shore: Nature and Culture in Western Thought from Ancient Times to the End of
the Eighteenth Century* (Berkeley: University of California Press, 1967), 62–
67, 134–40 As early as the late sixteenth century the French Renaissance
essayist, sceptic, humanist, and natural-theologian Michel de Montaigne
referred repeatedly to Lucretius' arguments on the essential likeness between
human beings and animals in his *Apology for Raymond Sebond* (Harmondsworth:
Penguin Books, 1993).

50. Long and Sedley, eds., *The Hellenistic Philosophers*, 134.

51. Epicurus, "Letter to Heredotus," in Oates, ed., *The Stoic and Epicurean Philosophers*, 13.

52. Lucretius, *On the Nature of the Universe*, 154–55 (5.1011–27). On Empedocles,
see Farrington, *Science in Antiquity*, 40–43.

53. Aristotle, *Basic Works* (New York: Random House, 1941), 249 (Book II,
Chapter 8, section 198b).

54. Ibid., 251.

55. Lucretius, *On the Nature of the Universe*, 149–51 (5.791–895); Robert J.
Richards, "Evolution," in Evelyn Fox Keller and Elisabeth A. Lloyd, eds.,
Keywords in Evolutionary Biology (Cambridge, Mass.: Harvard University Press,
1992), 99; Sedley, *Lucretius and the Transformation of Greek Wisdom*, 19–20;

Henry Fairfield Osborn, *From the Greeks to Darwin* (New York: Charles Scribner's Sons, 1927), 36–68.

56. Lucretius, *On the Nature of the Universe*, 149 (5.791–800); W.K.C. Guthrie, *In the Beginning: Some Greek Views of the Origin of Life and the Early State of Man* (Ithaca, N.Y.: Cornell University Press, 1957), 28.

57. Thomas S. Hall, *Ideas of Life and Matter: Studies in the History of General Physiology 600 B.C. to 1900 A.D.* (Chicago: University of Chicago Press, 1969), vol. 1, 19–20, 128. See also Lucretius, *On the Nature of the Universe*, 59 (2.865–85).

58. Lucretius, *On the Nature of the Universe*, 152–66 (5.916–1448).

59. Lucretius, *On the Nature of the Universe* (Oxford verse translation), 7 (1.145–50); Michael R. Rose, *Darwin's Spectre* (Princeton, N.J.: Princeton University Press, 1998), 217.

60. As Jonathan Kemp wrote: "The work of Epicurus dominates the history of early materialism." Editor's notes in Jonathan Kemp, *Diderot, Interpreter of Nature* (New York: International Publishers, 1963), 343.

61. Hall, *Ideas of Life and Matter*, vol. 1, 136.

62. Robert Hugh Kargon, *Atomism in England from Hariot to Newton* (Oxford: Oxford University Press, 1966).

63. Hariot, cited in ibid., 24.

64. Ibid., 27–29; J.A. Lohue, "Harriot (or Hariot) Thomas," *Dictionary of Scientific Biography*, vol. 6, 124–29.

65. Francis Bacon, *Philosophical Works,* ed. John M. Robertson (Freeport, N.Y.: Books for Libraries Press, 1905), 754. See also Thomas Franklin Mayo, *Epicurus in England (1650–1725)* (Dallas: Southwest Press, 1934), 19–23.

66. Bacon, *Philosophical Works*, 471–72.

67. Ibid., 848–53, 444–46; Diogenes Laertius, *Lives of Eminent Philosophers*, vol. 2, 649–51 (X, 123–24). The above argument on Bacon's interpretation of Prometheus owes much to the brilliant analysis in Reid Barbour, *English Epicures and Stoics: Ancient Legacies in Early Stuart Culture* (Amherst: University of Massachusetts Press, 1998), 79–91. On Bacon's materialism, see F.H. Anderson, *The Philosophy of Francis Bacon* (Chicago: University of Chicago Press, 1948).

68. Francis Bacon, *Philosophical Works* (London: Longman, 1857), vol. 2, 507.

69. See Carolyn Merchant, *The Death of Nature* (New York: Harper & Row, 1980), 201–2; Howard Jones, *The Epicurean Tradition* (New York: Routledge, 1992), 166–85; Alfred Cobban, *In Search of Humanity: The Role of the Enlightenment in Modern History* (New York: George Braziller, 1960), 75.

70. Marx and Engels, *Collected Works*, vol. 1, 57.

71. Pierre Gassendi, *Selected Works* (New York: Johnson Reprint, 1972), 207; René Descartes, *Discourse on Method and the Meditations* (Harmondsworth: Penguin Books, 1968).

72. George A. Panichas, *Epicurus* (New York: Twayne Publishers, 1967), 140–41. Both Hobbes and Locke were influenced by Gassendi's restoration of Epicurean atomism. See Bernard Pullman, *The Atom in the History of Human Thought* (New York: Oxford University Press, 1998), 144–45, 166.

73. Howard Jones, *The Epicurean Tradition* (New York: Routledge, 1992), 204–5.

74. John Evelyn, *Sylva, Or a Discourse of Forest-Trees and the Propagation of Timber*

in His Majesties Dominions (London: Royal Society, 1664), 2–3; John Evelyn, *Fumifugium: Or, the Inconvenience of the Aer and Smoake of London Dissipated,* in James P. Lodge, ed., *The Smoake of London: Two Prophesies* (Elmstead, New York: Maxwell Reprint, 1969), 15–17, 22; Lucretius, *On the Nature of the Universe,* 187, 194 (6.808–29, 1065–91); Merchant, *The Death of Nature,* 236–42.

75. Waller, quoted in Kargon, *Atomism in England,* 92.

76. Ibid., 95.

77. Jacob, *The Radical Enlightenment,* 70, 81. See also J.J. MacIntosh, "Robert Boyle on Epicurean Atheism and Atomism," in Margaret J. Osler, ed., *Atoms, Pneuma, and Tranquility: Epicurean and Stoic Themes in European Thought* (New York: Cambridge University Press, 1991), 197–217.

78. Boyle, quoted in John C. Greene, *The Death of Adam* (Ames, Iowa: Iowa State University Press, 1959), 11–12.

79. Robert Boyle, *Works* (London: A. Millar, 1744), vol. 4, 515.

80. Stephen Jay Gould, *Leonardo's Mountain of Clams and the Diet of Worms* (New York: Crown Publishers, 1998), 287–98; Mitchell Salem Fisher, *Robert Boyle, Devout Naturalist* (Philadelphia: Oshiver Studio Press, 1945).

81. Greene, *The Death of Adam,* 12.

82. See Richard Bentley, *Sermons Preached at Boyle's Lecture* (London: Francis Macpherson, 1838), 1–50, 146–216. When Boyle died in 1691 he left a will providing fifty pounds a year to found a lectureship for the purpose of demonstrating that science constituted the best evidence for and truest defense of the Christian religion. The sums were to be allocated to "some divine and preaching minister" who would be enjoined to give eight sermons over the course of a year attacking "notorious infidels, *viz.,* Atheists, Deists, Pagans, Jews, and Mahometans." Richard Bentley was selected as the first lecturer under the terms of this bequest and delivered a series of eight sermons under the title of *A Confutation of Atheism* in which Epicurus and Lucretius were the primary targets. Bentley later became a Doctor of Divinity and Master of Trinity College, Cambridge. See H.S. Thayer, ed., *Newton's Philosophy of Nature* (New York: Hafner Publishing Company, 1953), 63–64. 187–88; Stephen Jay Gould, *Dinosaur in a Haystack* (New York: Random House, 1995), 25–26.

83. Kargon, *Atomism in England,* 129; Jacob, *Scientific Culture and the Making of the Industrial West,* 69; J.T. Dobbs, "Stoic and Epicurean Doctrines in Newton's System of the World," in Osler, ed., *Atoms, Pneuma, and Tranquility,* 221–38.

84. Alan Cook, *Edmund Halley: Charting the Heavens and the Seas* (Oxford: Oxford University Press, 1998), 198.

85. Peter Gay, *The Enlightenment* (New York: Alfred A. Knopf, 1966), vol. 1, 306.

86. Mayo, *Epicurus in England,* 129.

87. Margaret J. Osler and Letizia A. Panizza, "Introduction," in Osler, ed., *Atoms, Pneuma, and Tranquility,* 9.

88. Paolo Rossi, *The Dark Abyss of Time: The History of the Earth and the History of Nations from Hooke to Vico* (Chicago: University of Chicago Press, 1984), 25–28, 217–27, 251; Lucretius, *On the Nature of the Universe,* 137 (5.326–36).

89. Gino Bedani, *Vico Revisited* (Oxford: Berg, 1989), 132.

90. Cobban, *In Search of Humanity,* 140.

91. David Hume, *Enquiries Concerning Human Understanding and Concerning the*

Principles of Morals (Oxford: Oxford University Press, 1975), 132–42. Lucian (*c.* 120–*c.* 180) was a Greek satirist and master of narrative, known especially for his witty satires on religion. He was an admirer of Epicurus, although not himself an Epicurean.

92. Gay, *The Enlightenment*, vol. 1, 98–107, 356.

93. Ibid., 102–3. As we shall see, Marx in his doctoral dissertation pointed to the same conclusion, depicting Epicurus as the great enlightener of antiquity and pointedly associating this with the Greek myth of Prometheus as depicted in Aeschylus' *Prometheus Bound*, in which Prometheus *brought fire* (light) to humanity and openly defied the gods of Olympus.

94. Shirley A. Roe, "Voltaire versus Needham: Atheism, Materialism, and the Generation of Life," in John W. Yolton, ed., *Philosophy, Religion and Science in the Seventeenth and Eighteenth Centuries* (Rochester, New York: University of Rochester Press, 1990), 417–39.

95. Julien Offray de La Mettrie, *Machine Man and Other Writings* (New York: Cambridge University Press, 1996), 91–115; Kemp, ed., *Diderot, Interpreter of Nature*, 21; Pullman, *The Atom in the History of Human Thought*, 153.

96. Immanuel Kant, *Cosmogony* (New York: Greenwood, 1968), 12–13; James W. Ellington, "Kant, Immanuel," *Dictionary of Scientific Biography*, vol. 7, 224–35.

97. Ibid., 14. Kant was to adopt a somewhat more critical view of Greek atomism, without entirely repudiating it, in his *Metaphysical Foundations of Natural Science* (1758). See Immanuel Kant, *Philosophy of Material Nature* (Indianapolis: Hackett Publishing, 1985), Book II, 90–93.

98. Immanual Kant, *Critique of Judgement* (Indianapolis: Hackett, 1987), 257–317, 324–36, 369–81; Frederick Copleston, *A History of Philosophy*, vol. 6 (London: Burnes & Oates, 1960), 349–56, 370–79; James G. Lennox, "Teleology," in Fox Keller and Lloyd, eds., *Keywords in Evolutionary Biology*, 324–33.

99. Kant, *Critique of Judgement*, 272; Daniel O. Dahlstrom, "Hegel's Appropriation of Kant's Account of Teleology in Nature," in Stephen Houlgate, ed., *Hegel and the Philosophy of Nature* (Albany: State University of New York Press, 1998), 172.

100. Kant, *Critique of Pure Reason*, 702–3; Immanuel Kant, *Critique of Practical Reason* (Cambridge: Cambridge University Press, 1997), 117.

101. Immanuel Kant, *Logic* (New York: Dover, 1988), 34–36. In his *Anthropology* (1798) Kant argued for the superiority of the Epicurean over the Stoic approach to the satisfaction of the senses, that is, the pursuit of pleasure. See Immanuel Kant, *Anthropology from a Pragmatic Point of View* (Carbondale: Southern Illinois University Press, 1978), 54, 136.

102. See Josiah Royce, *The Spirit of Modern Philosophy* (Boston: Houghton Mifflin, 1920), 186–89, where Schelling's poem is quoted at length.

103. Hegel, *Lectures on the History of Philosophy*, vol. 2, 232–36.

104. Ibid., 235–36, 295–98. Michael Inwood contends, with some justification, that Marx wrote his doctoral thesis "to redress Hegel's injustice to Epicurus." See Michael Inwood, *A Hegel Dictionary* (Oxford: Basil Blackwell, 1992), 262.

105. In this regard it is noteworthy that Gay writes that, as a philosopher, Voltaire was "an Eclectic who had synthesized the ideas of the Stoics, Epicureans, and Skeptics, and brought them up to date." Peter Gay, *The Party of the*

Enlightenment (New York: W.W. Norton, 1963), 11.

106. Heinrich Heine, *Selected Prose* (Harmondsworth: Penguin Books, 1993), 256; Schlegel and Köppen, quoted in White, *Karl Marx and the Intellectual Origins of Dialectical Materialism*, 122–23; Adams, *Karl Marx in His Earlier Writings*, 26. On the significant impact that Epicureanism had on the German Enlightenment, where the response, however, tended to be pantheistic and deist rather than materialist, see Thomas P. Saine, *The Problem of Being Modern: Or the German Pursuit of Enlightenment from Leibniz to the French Revolution* (Detroit: Wayne State University Press, 1997).

107. Marx and Engels, *Collected Works*, vol. 1, 73.

108. Lucretius, *On the Nature of the Universe*, 167–68.

109. "Is not their essence so full of character, so intense and eternal, that the modern world itself has to admit them to spiritual citizenship?" Marx and Engels, *Collected Works*, vol. 1, 35.

110. Bacon, *Philosophical Works*, 443–44.

111. Ibid., 47–72.

112. Marx and Engels, *Collected Works*, vol. 1, 19; Hermann Samuel Reimarus, *The Principal Truths of Natural Religion Defended and Illustrated, in Nine Dissertations; Wherein the Objections of Lucretius, Buffon, Maupertius, Rousseau, La Mettrie, and other Ancient and Modern Followers of Epicurus are Considered, and their Doctrines Refuted* (London: B. Law, 1766); Charles H. Talbert, "Introduction," in Hermann Reimarus, *Fragments* (Chico, Calif.: Scholar's Press, 1970), 6; Frederick Lange, *The History of Materialism* (New York: Humanities Press, 1950), 140; Copleston, *A History of Philosophy*, 123–24; Saine, *The Problem of Being Modern*, 193–205.

113. Cyril Bailey, "Karl Marx on Greek Atomism," *Classical Quarterly*, vol. 22, nos. 3 and 4 (July–October 1928), 205–6. Bailey emphasizes Marx's reference in his *Notebooks* to "The Immanent Dialectic of the Epicurean System."

114. Farrington, *The Faith of Epicurus*, 7–9, 113–19; Farrington, *Science in Antiquity*, 123.

115. Oates, ed., *The Stoic and Epicurean Philosophers*, 13; Benjamin Farrington, *Science and Politics in the Ancient World* (New York: Barnes & Noble, 1965), 146, 159, 173.

116. A.H. Armstrong, "The Gods in Plato, Plotinus, Epicurus," *Classical Quarterly*, vol. 32, nos. 3 & 4 (July–October 1938), 191–92.

117. Marx and Engels, *Collected Works*, vol. 1, 29–30.

118. Ibid., 40.

119. Ibid., 43. Ludwig Feuerbach, whose *History of Modern Philosophy from Bacon to Spinoza* (1833) Marx studied in the course of writing his doctoral thesis, had emphasized the role of chance in the atomism of Epicurus and Gassendi. "To make the atom the principle of things is to make chance the world principle." Quoted in Mark W. Wartofsky, *Feuerbach* (New York: Cambridge University Press, 1977), 72.

120. Marx and Engels, *Collected Works*, vol. 1, 36, 49–53. On the issue of the swerve, which in Epicurean philosophy allowed for chance/contingency, without which the nature of the universe as evident to our senses would actually be unintelligible, George Strodach has noted in his edited volume, *The Philosophy of Epicurus* (Evanston, Ill.: Northwestern University Press, 1963), 88, that, "It so happens that the swerve theory has a perfect modern

analogue in the Heisenberg Uncertainty Principle of modern physics. According to this principle there is a basic uncertainty (sometimes interpreted as a-causality) at the heart of matter. The behavior of subatomic particles is not uniform nor wholly predictable, even under identical conditions of experimentation."

121. Marx and Engels, *Collected Works,* vol. 1, 49–53.

122. Ibid., 63–65. Today we might capture the meaning of all of this by saying that for Epicurus our knowledge through our senses of the material world is simultaneously the recognition of "the arrow of time"—of a material passing away.

123. Sidney Hook, *Towards the Understanding of Karl Marx* (New York: John Day Company, 1933), 93–96; Marx and Engels, *Collected Works,* vol. 1, 458.

124. Hook, *Towards the Understanding of Karl Marx,* 52, 73.

125. Hegel, *Lectures on the History of Philosophy,* vol. 2, 365.

126. Diogenes Laertius, *Lives of Eminent Philosophers,* vol. 2, 659 (X, 134–35). Quoted as in Marx and Engels, *Collected Works,* vol. 1, 42–43. For the more detailed critique of Democritus' physics for its determinism provided in *On Nature,* see Long and Sedley, eds., *The Hellenistic Philosophers,* 102–4. This section from *On Nature* itself demonstrates how accurate Marx's conception of Epicurus was, despite the paucity of sources available to him at that time.

127. Seneca, *Ad Lucilium Epistulae Morales* (Cambridge, Mass.: Harvard University Press, 1927), vol. 1, 71–73 (Epistle XII); Marx and Engels, *Collected Works,* vol. 1, 41, 43, 82.

128. Epicurus, from *On Nature,* quoted in Sedley, *Lucretius and the Transformation of Greek Wisdom,* 142, 88.

129. Epicurus, in Long and Sedley, eds., *The Hellenistic Philosophers,* vol. 1, 102.

130. Marx and Engels, *Collected Works,* vol. 1, 45.

131. Ibid. pp. 44–45. The influence of Epicurus on the development of science suffices to demonstrate that his philosophy in no way contradicted realism, even while emphasizing abstract possibility.

132. Plutarch, *Moralia,* vol. 14 (Cambridge, Mass.: Harvard University Press, 1967), 137–49. Plutarch's critique of Epicurus is mainly contained in two works in his *Moralia:* "That Epicurus Actually Makes a Pleasant Life Impossible" and "Reply to Colotes," both of which Marx replied to extensively in his Notebooks and in the remaining fragment from the Appendix to his doctoral thesis.

133. Holbach, quoted in Marx and Engels, *Collected Works,* vol. 1, 102.

134. Ibid., 174.

135. Marx and Engels, *Collected Works,* vol. 6, 142.

136. Marx and Engels, *Collected Works,* vol. 1, 478, 473; Lucretius, *On the Nature of the Universe,* 88 (3.861–70).

137. Mehring, *Karl Marx,* 26–27.

138. Marx and Engels, *Collected Works,* vol. 1, 30.

139. Ibid., 446. This rendition by Marx of Epicurus' view is strikingly similar to what Marx was later to call his "favorite maxim": "*Nihil humanum a me alienum puto* [Nothing human is alien to me]." Karl Marx, "Confessions," in Teodor Shanin, ed., *Late Marx and the Russian Road* (New York: Monthly Review Press, 1983), 140.

140. Marx and Engels, *Collected Works,* vol. 1, 30.

141. Aeschylus, quoted in ibid., 31. The ancient materialist critique of religion was developed most fully, Marx believed, in Lucretius and Lucian, but he threw scorn upon the view that such ideas (i.e. the destruction of the ancient mythology) had brought down ancient civilization. "Would the ancient world not have perished," he asked, "if scientific research had kept silent about the errors of religion, if the Roman authorities had been recommended ... to excise the writings of Lucretius and Lucian?" Marx and Engels, *Collected Works*, vol. 1, 190. Marx was of course aware of Lucian's vehement biographical narrative "Alexander the Quack Prophet" in which the Epicureans were depicted as the most courageous opponents of superstition and religious quackery, the latter symbolized above all by Alexander of Abonoteichus (who responded to this opposition by burning Epicurus' *Principal Doctrines* and attempting to stone one of Epicurus' followers to death). See Lucian, *Selected Satires* (New York: W.W. Norton, 1962), 267–300.

142. Marx and Engels, *Collected* Works, vol. 1, 73.

143. Ibid., 70, 471. Hegel in his *Logic* had claimed that the principle of the atom was itself a negation of the finite, a "principle of idealism," that is, of the intellect. See Georg Wilhelm Friedrich Hegel, *Science of Logic* (New York: Humanities Press, 1969), 155.

144. Farrington, *Science and Politics in the Ancient World*, 148.

145. Marx and Engels, *Collected Works*, vol. 1, 468.

146. Marx wrote out an outline of the contents of Hegel's *Philosophy of Nature* at the time that he was working on his doctoral dissertation.

147. Hume too is celebrated in the foreword to Marx's doctoral thesis, because of his anti-theological position; as is Kant in the appendix to the thesis (though more ambiguously) for his disproof in the *Critique of Pure Reason* of the ontological proof of God's existence. Bacon is referred to in connection with the critique of religion by Marx as early as 1842. See Marx and Engels, *Collected Works*, vol. 1, 30, 104, 201.

148. Alexander Herzen, *Selected Philosophical Works* (Moscow: Foreign Languages Publishing House, 1956), 103, 205, 221–23.

149. Marx and Engels, *Collected Works*, vol. 4, 124–26. The German Enlightenment philosopher Gottfried Wilhelm Leibniz (1646–1716) represented, for Marx, a further extension of the seventeenth-century metaphysical tradition of Descartes and Spinoza. Leibniz's metaphysics derived much of its coherence from its adamant rejection of the materialism of Epicurus, Gassendi, Hobbes, and Locke, its defense of "final cause (God)," and its general idealist standpoint. See G.W. Leibniz, *Philosophical Essays* (Indianapolis: Hackett, 1989), 245, 281–82, 292, 318, 329.

150. Marx and Engels, *Collected Works*, vol. 5, 141–42. On the influence of Epicurus (via Lucretius) on Hobbes's notion of social contract, see Mayo, *Epicurus in England*, 121. Marx referred to the political covenant in a passage that he added when revising his doctoral thesis. Marx and Engels, *Collected Works*, vol. 1, 53.

151. Lucretius, *On the Nature of the Universe* (Oxford verse translation), 169.

152. Plutarch, *Moralia*, vol. 14, 313.

153. Marx and Engels, *Collected Works*, vol. 4, 128–29. See also Boris Hessen, "The Social and Economic Roots of Newton's *Principia*," in Nikolai Bukharin et al., *Science at the Cross Roads: Papers Presented at the International Congress*

of the History of Science, and Technology, 1931 (London: Frank Cass, 1971), 181. Hessen argues that in Hobbes materialism was made more acceptable since it was aimed at the educated and the scientific community, while religion would continue to dominate the masses. "The living soul was cut out of materialism and it became hostile to mankind. This abstract, calculating, formally mathematical materialism could not stimulate revolutionary action."

154. Marx and Engels, *Collected Works*, vol. 4, 129–33.
155. Karl Marx, *Early Writings* (New York: Vintage, 1975), 424.
156. Friedrich Engels, *Ludwig Feuerbach and the Outcome of Classical German Philosophy* (New York: International Publishers, 1941), 67.
157. Marx and Engels, *Collected Works*, vol. 1, 201.
158. Alexei Mikhailovich Voden, "Talks with Engels," in Institute of Marxism–Leninism, *Reminiscences from Marx and Engels* (Moscow: Foreign Languages Publishing House, n.d.), 332–33.
159. Ibid., 333.
160. Ibid., 326.

2. The Really Earthly Question

1. Karl Marx and Friedrich Engels, *Collected Works* (New York: International Publishers, 1975), vol. 1, 225.
2. See Karl Marx, "Preface to *A Contribution to a Critique of Political Economy*," in Marx, *Early Writings* (New York: Vintage, 1974), 424.
3. David McLellan, *Karl Marx* (New York: Harper & Row, 1973), 56; Franz Mehring, *Karl Marx* (Ann Arbor: University of Michigan Press, 1962), 41.
4. See Sidney Hook, *Towards the Understanding of Karl Marx* (New York: John Day, 1933), 259–61.
5. Marx and Engels, *Collected Works*, vol. 1, 224–63.
6. Feuerbach, quoted in Mark Wartofsky, *Feuerbach* (New York: Cambridge University Press, 1977), 436. Marx's view of Bacon and Descartes, as shown in *The Holy Family*, was remarkably similar to that of Feuerbach; as was his understanding of the relationship of Bacon to Hobbes.
7. Ibid., 197; Marx and Engels, *Collected Works*, vol. 1, 103.
8. See Mehring, *Karl Marx*, 52–53; Alfred Schmidt, *The Concept of Nature in Marx* (London: New Left Books, 1971), 22.
9. Ludwig Feuerbach, *The Fiery Brook* (Garden City, N.Y.: Doubleday, 1972), 164–65.
10. Ibid., 168, 185,
11. Ibid., 161, 171.
12. Ludwig Feuerbach, *The Essence of Christianity* (Boston: Houghton Mifflin, 1881), 270.
13. Karl Marx, *Writings of the Young Marx on Philosophy and Society* (Garden City, N.Y.: Doubleday, 1967), 95.
14. Feuerbach, *Fiery Brook*, 172, 198.
15. Michel de Montaigne, *An Apology for Raymond Sebond* (Harmondsworth: Penguin Books, 1993), 170–75.
16. Feuerbach, *Fiery Brook*, 243–45.
17. Marx and Engels, *Collected Works*, vol. 1, 400.
18. Marx, *Early Writings*, 328.

19. Ibid., 329, 331.
20. Ibid., 386.
21. Ibid., 343, 318–21.
22. Ibid., 319.
23. Ibid., 239; Thomas Müntzer, *Collected Works* (Edinburgh: T. & T. Clark, 1988), 335. See also Friedrich Engels, *The Peasant War in Germany* (New York: International Publishers, 1926), 68.
24. Marx, *Early Writings*, 239.
25. Ibid., 302.
26. Ibid., 359–60.
27. Ibid., 174; G.W.F. Hegel, *Philosophy of Nature* (New York: Humanities Press, 1970), vol. 1, 212. Hegel added: "The aim of these lectures [on the philosophy of nature] is to convey an image of nature, in order to subdue this Proteus: to find in this externality only a mirror of ourselves, to see in nature a free reflection of spirit: to understand God." Ibid., 213.
28. Hegel, *Philosophy of Nature*, vol. 1, 212. Translation follows Stephen Houlgate, ed., *The Hegel Reader* (Oxford: Blackwell, 1998), 260.
29. Auguste Cornu, *The Origins of Marxian Thought* (Springfield, Ill.: Charles C. Thomas, 1957), 37–44.
30. Marx, *Early Writings*, 390.
31. Ibid., 389–91.
32. Ibid., 398–99.
33. Ibid., 355.
34. Ibid., 381–82, 385, 400.
35. Ibid., 320.
36. Ibid.
37. Ibid., 348–49.
38. Feuerbach, quoted in Wartofsky, *Feuerbach*, 451–52.

3. Parson Naturalists

1. Charles Darwin, *Autobiography* (New York: Harcourt, Brace, 1958), 59.
2. Ibid., 87; Charles Coulston Gillispie, *Genesis and Geology* (Cambridge, Mass.: Harvard University Press, 1996), 219; Atonello La Vergata, "Images of Darwin," in David Kohn, ed., *The Darwinian Heritage* (Princeton, N.J.: Princeton University Press, 1985), 949; Stephen Jay Gould, *Leonardo's Mountain of Clams and the Diet of Worms* (New York: Crown Publishers, 1998), 296.
3. Darwin, *Autobiography*, 56–58.
4. Thomas Malthus, *An Essay on the Principle of Population and A Summary View of the Principle of Population* (Harmondsworth: Penguin, 1970), 205. (All further citations to the *Essay on Population* in this edition will refer to it as the *First Essay*.)
5. Francis Bacon, *Philosophical Works* (Freeport, N.Y.: Books for Libraries Press, 1905), 91, 456, 471–72.
6. Loren Eisely, *Darwin's Century* (New York: Doubleday, 1958), 14–15; John C. Greene, *The Death of Adam* (Ames, Iowa: Iowa State University Press, 1959), 1–3.
7. John Ray, *The Wisdom of God Manifested in the Works of Creation* (London: Benjamin Walford, 1699), 35–39, 41, 49; Greene, *The Death of Adam*, 8–10.

8. Ray, *The Wisdom of God*, 53, 81, 116, 257, 425.

9. Greene, *The Death of Adam*, 5.

10. William Paley, *Natural Theology* (London: R. Faulder, 1803), 9.

11. Ibid., 344. In comparing Paley's use of the metaphor of the "invisible hand" to that of Smith, Stephen Jay Gould has contended that "the two usages are diametrically opposed.... Paley's invisible hand is God's explicit intent (though He works, in this case, indirectly through the bird's instinct, and not by a palpable push). Smith's invisible hand is the *impression* of higher power that doesn't actually exist at all." Gould, *Eight Little Piggies* (New York: W.W. Norton, 1993), 150–51. Nevertheless, it can be argued, in contradistinction to Gould, that these two usages, one for the market, the other for God, were in a sense mutually reinforcing aspects of the dominant, bourgeois view of society. The Smithian perspective, while not outwardly teleological, tended to reify the market and endow it with an almost providential perfection. It is no accident that Malthus, a Protestant parson, came to symbolize both the harsh religious outlook of nineteenth-century English society, and its no less harsh political economy. In his work the two invisible hands—the double teleology of Smith and Paley—were equally present.

12. See D.L. LeMahieu, *The Mind of William Paley* (Lincoln: University of Nebraska Press, 1976), 177–81.

13. William Paley, *The Principles of Moral and Political Philosophy* (New York: Harper & Brothers, 1867), 36–38, 44.

14. Ibid., 99–103, 278.

15. Paley, *Natural Theology*, 539–42.

16. Malthus, *First Essay*, 201–12; Thomas Robert Malthus, *An Essay on the Principle of Population; or A View of its Past and Present Effects on Human Happiness; With an Inquiry into Our Prospects Respecting the Future Removal or Mitigation of the Evils which it Occasions* (Cambridge: Cambridge University Press, 1989), vol. 2, 140–41. (All further citations to this edition will refer to it as the *Second Essay*.)

17. Malthus, *Second Essay*, vol. 2, 101–5; Leslie Stephen, *The English Utilitarians* (London: Duckworth, 1900), vol. 2, 156.

18. Robert Wallace, *Various Prospects of Mankind, Nature and Providence* (London: A. Millar, 1761), 107, 114–17, 125.

19. William Godwin, *Enquiry Concerning Political Justice and its Influence on Morals and Happiness* (Toronto: University of Toronto Press, 1946), vol. 2, 515–18.

20. Ibid., 518.

21. Condorcet, Jean-Antoine-Nicholas Caritat, Marquis de, *Sketch for a Historical Picture of the Progress of the Human Mind* (New York: Noonday Press, 1955), 188.

22. Ibid., 188–89.

23. Malthus, *First Essay*, 71.

24. Ibid., 177; Karl Marx and Friedrich Engels, *Historisch-Kritische Gesamtausgabe* (*MEGA*), part 4, vol. 9 (Berlin: Dietz Verlag, 1991), 229.

25. Malthus was very consistent in avoiding references to the overpopulation of the earth in the modern sense, even correcting those few passages in his work where he had inadvertently left the impression that human population had surpassed the means of subsistence, changing this to "easy means of subsistence." See Edwin Cannan, *A History of Theories of Production and*

Distribution in English Political Economy from 1776 to 1848 (New York: Augustus M. Kelley, 1917), 108.

26. Malthus, *First Essay*, 120, 134.
27. Ibid., 124.
28. Malthus, *Second Essay*, vol. 1, 329.
29. Malthus, *First Essay*, 76.
30. Ibid., 89.
31. Cannan, *A History of Theories*, 112.
32. Malthus, *First Essay*, 106.
33. Ibid., 129; *Second Essay*, vol. 1, 312–13; Eiseley, *Darwin's Century*, 332.
34. Joseph Schumpeter, *History of Economic Analysis* (New York: Oxford University Press, 1954), 581.
35. Malthus, *An Essay on the Principle of Population and a Summary View of the Principle of Population*, 239.
36. Thomas Robert Malthus, *Pamphlets* (New York: Augustus M. Kelley, 1970), 185; David Ricardo, *Principles of Political Economy and Taxation* (Cambridge: Cambridge University Press, 1951), 67; Malthus, *First Essay*, 100.
37. Malthus, *Second Essay*, vol. 2, 212; Piercy Ravenstone, quoted in Kenneth Smith, *The Malthusian Controversy* (London: Routledge & Kegan Paul, 1951), 224.
38. Malthus, *First Essay*, 89, 98.
39. Ibid., 81, 92, 103, 124.
40. Malthus, *Second Essay*, vol. 1, 17–19, 81; vol. 2, 97.
41. Godwin, *Enquiry Concerning Political Justice*, vol. 2, 517; John Avery, *Progress, Poverty and Population: Re-reading Condorcet, Godwin and Malthus* (London: Frank Cass, 1997), 11.
42. Malthus, *First Essay*, 118–19.
43. Ibid., 118, 133.
44. Ibid., 134, 143.
45. Ibid., 94, 97, 102.
46. Ibid., 115.
47. See Alan Macfarlane, *Marriage and Love in England: Modes of Reproduction 1300–1840* (Oxford: Blackwell, 1986).
48. Thomas Robert Malthus, *Occasional Papers* (New York: Burt & Franklin, 1963), 139.
49. Cannan, *History of Theories*, 104, 113.
50. Patricia James, Introduction to the *Second Essay*, vol. 1, ix–xv.
51. Malthus, *Second Essay*, vol. 2, 141.
52. Ibid., vol. 2, 127–28.
53. Ibid., vol. 2, 192.
54. Malthus, *First Essay*, 142.
55. Malthus, *Pamphlets*, 18.
56. Malthus to Ricardo, August 17, 1817, in David Ricardo, *Works and Correspondence* (Cambridge: Cambridge University Press, 1952), vol. 7, 175.
57. Karl Marx, *Early Writings* (New York: Vintage, 1974), 408–9.
58. Cobbett, quoted in Smith, *The Malthusian Controversy*, 120.
59. Malthus, *First Essay*, 183–84.
60. On the wages fund theory, see Maurice Dobb, *Theories of Value and Distribution since Adam Smith* (Cambridge: Cambridge University Press, 1973), 131–34.

61. The fact that reformers like Place advocated trade union organization while also adhering to the Malthusian wages fund theory posed less of a contradiction than might at first appear. Place saw the purpose of trade unions as limited to that of equalizing wages, and while wages could not be increased in general (because of the relation of population to subsistence), particular sections of the working class could benefit enormously. In order for workers in general to improve their condition, according to Place, it was first necessary to promote birth control, which would reduce the pressure of population on subsistence. Needless to say, such Malthusian notions were treated with unmitigated scorn by working-class radicals. See E.P. Thompson, *The Making of the English Working Class* (New York: Vintage, 1963), 769—79; Pedro Schwartz, *The New Political Economy of J.S. Mill* (London: London School of Economics and Political Science, 1968), 28, 74, 245—56.

62. Schumpeter, *History of Economic Analysis*, 580—81.

63. Malthus was, it is well known, immensely proud of the influence that his *Essay* exerted on such important contemporary figures as William Paley, William Pitt, and David Ricardo, but it was Thomas Chalmers who, as his most important disciple, was to embrace the full implications of Malthus's population theory, including the link between natural theology and political economy that it entailed.

64. Robert Young, "The Historiographic and Ideological Contexts of the Nineteenth-Century Debate on Man's Place in Nature," in Mikuláš Teich and Robert Young, eds., *Changing Perspectives in the History of Science: Essays in Honour of Joseph Needham* (London: Heinemann, 1973), 373.

65. Thomas Chalmers, *On the Power, Wisdom and Goodness of God as Manifested in the Adaptation of External Nature to the Moral and Intellectual Constitution of Man* (London: William Pickering, 1834), vol. 1, 17—21.

66. Ibid., vol. 1, 15, 24, 64—65.

67. Ibid., vol. 1, 22, 252; vol. 2, 7, 34—35.

68. Ibid., vol. 2, 45—47.

69. Ibid., vol. 2, 49

70. Thomas Chalmers, *On Political Economy in Connexion with the Moral State and Moral Prospects of Society* (Glasgow: William Collins, 1853), vol. 2, 338. Chalmers, in the Malthusian spirit, sought to replace public relief with a parish-based system of self-help and church relief, which he helped to establish in Glasgow.

71. Chalmers, *On the Power*, 28—29; see also Gillispie, *Genesis and Geology*, 210—16.

4. The Materialist Conception of History

1. Karl Marx, *Capital* (New York: Vintage, 1976), vol. 1, 766—67, 800. Giammaria Ortes (1713—1790) was a political economist, philosopher, poet, and physician. Until age thirty he was a Venetian monk, but left the monastery to study. He was a critic of bourgeois property relations and the money economy, and laid stress on the maldistribution of wealth. Hal Draper, *The Marx—Engels Glossary* (New York: Schocken Books, 1986), 158.

2. Friedrich Engels, "Outlines of a Critique of Political Economy," in Karl

Marx, *The Economic and Philosophical Manuscripts of 1844* (New York: International Publishers, 1964), 221, 212.

3. Ibid., 210.
4. Ibid., 199, 218.
5. Ibid., 197–98, 218–22.
6. Ibid., 222; Robert Owen, *Selected Works* (London: William Pickering, 1993), vol. 2, 361, 367–69.
7. Karl Marx, *Early Writings* (New York: Vintage, 1975), 408–9.
8. Friedrich Engels, *The Condition of the Working Class in England* (Chicago: Academy Chicago, 1984), 308–17.
9. Ibid., 113–17, 309.
10. Ibid., 79–84.
11. Ibid.., 126–238; Howard Waitzkin, *The Second Sickness* (New York: Free Press, 1983), 66–71. This discussion of Engels's treatment of environmental conditions in Manchester has been extracted from John Bellamy Foster, *The Vulnerable Planet: A Short Economic History of the Environment* (New York: Monthly Review Press, 1994), 57–59.
12. Lewis Mumford, *The City in History* (New York: Harcourt, Brace & World, 1961), 472.
13. Marx, *Early Writings*, 302, 359–60.
14. Friedrich Engels, *Ludwig Feuerbach and the Outcome of Classical German Philosophy* (New York: International Publishers, 1941), 17–18.
15. Max Stirner, *The Ego and its Own* (Cambridge: Cambridge University Press, 1995), 5, 7, 324.
16. Karl Marx and Friedrich Engels, *Collected Works* (New York: International Publishers, 1975), vol. 5, 58–59.
17. Ibid., 6–8.
18. Ibid., 139.
19. Ibid., 7.
20. Translation in this sentence follows Karl Marx, "Theses on Feuerbach," in Engels, *Ludwig Feurbach*, 82–84.
21. Marx and Engels, *Collected Works*, vol. 5, 7–8.
22. Karl Marx, *The Poverty of Philosophy* (New York: International Publishers, 1963), 110, 114; Lucretius, *On the Nature of the Universe* (Harmondsworth: Penguin Books, 1994), 88.
23. Marx and Engels, *Collected Works*, vol. 5, 29.
24. Ibid., 31–32.
25. Ibid., 39–41. It is worth noting that Darwin's pathbreaking coral reef theory was published only a few years before Marx and Engels made this statement, recognizing coral reefs as a realm of nature of comparatively recent origin in geological time that remained largely untouched by humanity.
26. Ibid., 41–43.
27. Ibid., 32–34, 64–65, 401.
28. Ibid., 374.
29. Ibid., 476.
30. Y.M. Uranovsky, "Marxism and Natural Science," in Nikolai Bukharin et al., *Marxism and Modern Thought* (New York: Harcourt, Brace, 1935), 139; Alexander Ospovat, "Werner, Abraham Gottlob," *Dictionary of Scientific Biography*, vol. 14, 257–59. On Steininger, see Karl Alfred von Zittel, *History of*

Geology and Paleontology (New York: Charles Scribner's Sons, 1901), 258–59.

31. Abraham Gottlob Werner, *Short Classification and Description of the Various Rocks* (New York: Hafner Publishing Co., 1971), 102; Rachel Laudan, *From Mineralogy to Geology: The Foundations of a Science, 1650–1830* (Chicago: University of Chicago Press, 1987), 88.

32. Laudan, *From Mineralogy to Geology*, 94–95.

33. Werner, quoted in Ospovat, "Werner, Abraham Gottlob," 259–60; Immanuel Kant, *Cosmogony* (New York: Greenwood Publishing, 1968), 132–33; Paolo Rossi, *The Dark Abyss of Time: The History of the Earth and the History of Nations from Hooke to Vico* (Chicago: University of Chicago Press, 1984), 111–12.

34. Laudan, *From Mineralogy to Geology*, 139–40.

35. Martin J.S. Rudwick, ed., *Georges Cuvier, Fossil Bones and Geological Catastrophes: New Translations and Interpretations of the Primary Texts* (Chicago: University of Chicago Press, 1997), 70, 80, 265–66. Marx was familiar with Cuvier's great work *The Revolutions of the Globe* and probably read it at the time of his early geological studies. See Marx and Engels, *Collected Works*, vol. 42, 322. Cuvier's work was also highlighted in Hegel's *Philosophy of Nature*, with which Marx was well acquainted. Marx continued his studies of geological literature throughout his life, later taking copious notes on Charles Lyell's *Principles of Geology*.

36. The tendency to view Werner principally in terms of the subsequent "Neptunist" tradition is central to the argument of Charles Coulston Gillispie, *Genesis and Geology* (Cambridge, Mass: Harvard University Press, 1966). Moreover, a commonplace of the history of geology within the English tradition is that the concept of geological time was developed primarily by James Hutton and Charles Lyell. Although it is true that Hutton and Lyell, within their generally uniformitarian perspectives, placed unprecedented emphasis on the principle of deep, geological time, it would be wrong to assume that the notion of geological time was not emerging—on somewhat different bases—on the Continent too, through the Wernerian tradition, as represented by the work of Werner and many others—including Cuvier.

37. G.W.F. Hegel, *Philosophy of Nature* (New York: Humanities Press, 1970), vol. 3, 15–24, 33–36. The concept of *generatio aequivoca* was common to Aristotle, Lucretius, Bacon, and Hegel. It had both a more specific meaning in which it was assumed that worms could be spontaneously generated by dung, for example, and a more general meaning that suggested that life originally emerged out of inanimate matter without the necessary intervention of God. Lucretius used the concept in both senses but emphasized the latter. In Hegel and Marx only the more general sense is evident, and was heavily influenced by the views of Wernerian geognosy. Hence, Hegel's general treatment of geognosy and *generatio aequivoca* fits well with a thoroughgoing materialist perspective. Nevertheless there intrudes into his analysis as another (and, he thinks, perhaps superior) hypothesis an approach opposed to the notion of human evolution out of animals and of separate creation, more in line with the account of Genesis. There is no doubt that Hegel wanted to defend an anthropocentric (and ultimately religious) view in these areas, and only reluctantly gave way to the discoveries of science. Ibid., 23.

38. Hegel not only referred to *generatio aequivoca* but also insisted that life and

inorganic matter were radically distinct. "Even if the earth was once devoid of living being, and limited to the chemical process, etc., as soon as the flash of living being strikes into matter, a determinate and complete formation is present; and emerges fully armed, like Minerva from the brow of Jupiter. The account of creation given in Genesis is still the best, in so far as it says quite simply that the plants, the animals, and man were brought forth on separate days." Ibid., 22.

39. Marx and Engels, *Collected Works*, vol. 2, 304–5. (Unlike the *Collected Works* edition, the Vintage and International Press editions of Marx's *Early Writings* contain an obvious mistake here: referring to "geogeny" rather than "geognosy.")

40. Lucretius, *On the Nature of the Universe*, 195 (5.780–800). In referring to "generatio aequivoca" Marx (though he raised the question primarily in a geological context—that is, the self-generation of the earth) may have been aware of the work of Pierre Louis Moreau de Maupertuis (1698–1759), who had first brought Newtonian analysis to France. Maupertuis had opposed the deterministic and creationist aspects of Newtonianism and had gone back to Epicurus and Lucretius for inspiration, emphasizing contingency. He was a strong critic of natural theology and the argument from design. Along with other materialists, Maupertuis referred to "spontaneous generation" in explaining the origin of life. This idea took different forms, some more sophisticated than others. In its more sophisticated version, it was developed by Jean Baptiste Pierre Antoine de Monet, Chevalier de Lamarck (1744–1829), in terms of the spontaneous generation of only the simplest organisms out of lifeless matter, which gradually became transformed into more complex organisms, in accordance with the scale of nature. The idea of spontaneous generation was thus associated with the transformation (or evolution) of species. (Maupertuis, in contrast to Lamarck, had advocated a saltation theory of evolution, the most common form of evolutionary theory before Darwin, in which new species emerged not gradually, but by sudden leaps.) For materialists/evolutionists, opposed to creationism, it was essential that life had originated at some point from lifeless matter, though the process by which this had occurred was unclear. See Ernst Mayr, *The Growth of Biological Thought* (Cambridge, Mass.: Harvard University Press, 1982), 328–29, and *One Long Argument: Charles Darwin and the Genesis of Modern Evolutionary Thought* (Cambridge, Mass.: Harvard University Press, 1991), 18.

41. Valentino Gerratana, "Marx and Darwin," *New Left Review*, no. 82 (November–December 1973), 60–82; Friedrich Engels, *Anti-Dühring* (New York: International Publishers, 1939), 82.

42. Richard Levins and Richard Lewontin, *The Dialectical Biologist* (Cambridge, Mass.: Harvard University Press, 1985), 277; Rachel Carson, *Lost Woods* (Boston: Beacon Press, 1998), 230.

43. The original pieces by Oparin and Haldane are to be found in Appendix I of J.D. Bernal's monumental work, *The Origins of Life* (New York: World Publishing Company, 1967).

44. See Georg Wilhelm Friedrich Hegel, *Lectures on the Philosophy of World History: Introduction* (Cambridge: Cambridge University Press, 1975), 173–79, 218; Massimo Quaini, *Geography and Marxism* (Totowa, N.J.: Barnes & Noble Books, 1982), 20–26.

45. Carl Ritter, *Comparative Geography* (New York: Van Antwerp, Bragg & Co., 1881), xxi, 59. On Ritter, see T.W. Freeman, *A Hundred Years of Geography* (London: Gerald Duckworth, 1961), 32–40, 321.

46. George Perkins Marsh, *Man and Nature* (Cambridge, Mass.: Harvard University Press, 1965), ix, 35–36, 42–43; Lewis Mumford, *The Brown Decades* (New York: Dover, 1971), 35.

47. Rudolf Matthäi, quoted in Marx and Engels, *Collected Works*, vol. 5, 471.

48. Ibid., 471–73.

49. Ibid., 475–76, 479, 481.

50. Marx and Engels, *On Religion* (Moscow: Foreign Languages Publishing House, n.d.), 95.

51. Charles Fourier, *Selections* (London: Swan Sonnenschein, 1901), 77, 109, 115–17, 120, and *The Theory of the Four Movements* (Cambridge: Cambridge University Press, 1996), 160–61; Owen, *Selected Works*, vol. 2, 69, 84–85.

52. Marx and Engels, *Collected Works*, vol. 1, 220.

53. Pierre Joseph Proudhon, *What is Property?* (Cambridge: Cambridge University Press, 1994), 82–84.

54. Marx and Engels, *Collected Works*, vol. 4, 32.

55. Karl Marx and Friedrich Engels, *The Communist Manifesto* (New York: Monthly Review Press, 1998), 52–53.

56. Pierre Joseph Proudhon, *System of Economical Contradictions* (New York: Arno Press, 1972), 28, 468–69.

57. Ibid., 96–97.

58. Ibid., 98–101.

59. Ibid., 117–18.

60. Ibid., 126–28.

61. Ibid., 168, 174–75.

62. Proudhon, quoted in Karl Marx, *The Poverty of Philosophy* (New York: International Publishers, 1963), 155–56.

63. Ibid., 99, 115; Karl Marx, *Grundrisse* (New York: Vintage, 1973), 84–85.

64. Marx, *The Poverty of Philosophy*, 119–20. Marx was of course aware that the concept of providence had been employed in antiquity by the Stoics in opposition to Epicurean materialism—as depicted in Cicero's *Nature of the Gods.*

65. Ibid., 98–99, 132–44, 184.

66. Ibid., 109–10; Lucretius, *On the Nature of the Universe*, 88 (3.861–70). It is in this same section that Marx made his well-known, often misinterpreted, epigrammatic statement that "the hand-mill gives you society with the feudal lord; the steam-mill, society with the industrial capitalist." Rather than suggesting some kind of technological determinism, Marx was endeavoring to transcend Proudhon's ahistorical conceptions of technology, society, ideas, and categories by pointing out that all social relations, technologies, and ideas themselves were historical in nature, part of a ceaseless process of change, and that all attempts to argue on the basis of eternal principles were therefore mistaken. The only truly immutable fact, as Epicurus had said, was mortality itself.

67. Marx, *The Poverty of Philosophy*, 61–63.

68. Ibid., 159–60, 162–63.

69. Ibid., 69.

70. Ibid., 126, 114.

71. On the origins of the *Manifesto*, see Rob Beamish, "The Making of the Manifesto," in Leo Panitch and Colin Leys, eds., *The Communist Manifesto Now: Socialist Register 1998* (London: Merlin, 1998), 218–39; and Dirk J. Struik, ed., *The Birth of the Communist Manifesto* (New York: International Publishers, 1971).

72. Ted Benton, "Marxism and Natural Limits," *New Left Review*, no. 178 (November–December 1989), 82; Reiner Grundmann, *Marxism and Ecology* (New York: Oxford University Press, 1991), 52, and "The Ecological Challenge to Marxism," *New Left Review*, no. 187 (May–June 1991), 120; Victor Ferkiss, *Nature, Technology and Society* (New York: New York University Press, 1993), 108; Anthony Giddens, *A Contemporary Critique of Historical Materialism* (Berkeley: University of California Press, 1981), 59–60; John Clark, "Marx's Inorganic Body," *Environmental Ethics*, vol. 11, no. 3 (Fall 1989), 258; Michael Löwy, "For a Critical Marxism," *Against the Current*, vol. 12, no. 5 (November–December 1997), 33–34. Even Bhaskar, despite his normally exemplary scholarship, falls prey to this view, referring to "the technological Prometheanism" of Marx's "middle and later works." Roy Bhaskar, "Materialism," in Tom Bottomore, ed., *A Dictionary of Marxist Thought* (Oxford: Blackwell, 1983), 325. Most influential of all in this regard is Leszek Kolakowski, *Main Currents of Marxism*, vol. 1 (New York: Oxford University Press, 1978), 412–14. This critique of Marx as "Promethean" has recently been subjected to a series of rebuttals by various authors. See John Bellamy Foster, "Marx and the Environment," in Ellen Meiksins Wood and John Bellamy Foster, eds., *In Defense of History* (New York: Monthly Review Press, 1997) 149–62; Paul Burkett, *Marx and Nature: A Red and Green Perspective* (New York: St. Martin's Press, 1999); and Walt Sheasby, "Anti-Prometheus, Post-Marx," *Organization & Environment*, vol. 12, no. 1 (March 1999), 5–44.

73. Wade Sikorski, *Modernity and Technology* (Tuscaloosa: University of Alabama Press, 1993), 138.

74. Jean-Paul Sartre, *The Search for a Method* (New York: Vintage, 1963), 7. On the nature of Marx criticism, which regularly attaches to Marx views that he strenuously attacked, see John Bellamy Foster, "Introduction," in Ernst Fischer, *How to Read Karl Marx* (New York: Monthly Review Press, 1996), 7–30.

75. The relation of Aeschylus' *Prometheus Bound* to debates within antiquity over science and materialism is described in admirable detail by Benjamin Farrington in his *Science and Politics in the Ancient World* (New York: Barnes & Noble, 1965), 67–86.

76. Parts of the following argument on the *Manifesto* were earlier developed in John Bellamy Foster, "The Communist Manifesto and the Environment," in Panitch and Leys, eds., *The Communist Manifesto Now*, 169–89.

77. Marx and Engels, *The Communist Manifesto*, 7–9.

78. Marx and Engels, *Collected Works*, vol. 5, 32–34, 64–65, 401.

79. Marx, *Capital*, vol. 1, 637–38.

80. Marx and Engels, *The Communist Manifesto*, 9–10, 40.

81. See Friedrich Engels, *The Housing Question* (Moscow: Progress Publishers, 1975), 92, and *Anti-Dühring*, 319.

82. Marx and Engels, *The Communist Manifesto*, 10.

83. See, for example, Michael Löwy, "Globalization and Internationalism: How

Up-to-Date is the 'Communist Manifesto'?" *Monthly Review*, vol. 50, no. 6 (November 1998), 20.

84. Francis Bacon, *Novum Organum* (Chicago: Open Court, 1994), 43.
85. Marx and Engels, *The Communist Manifesto*, 11.

5. The Metabolism of Nature and Society

1. The following analysis does not address, except tangentially, the relation of Marx's economic-value analysis in *Capital* to his conception of nature since this has already been accomplished by Paul Burkett in his *magnum opus*, *Marx and Nature: A Red and Green Perspective* (New York: St. Martin's Press, 1999). Rather the concern here is with the more direct ecological analysis in *Capital*, associated with the concepts of metabolic rift and sustainability—and the relation of these to Marx's materialist conceptions of nature and history. For a greater understanding of how the argument here relates to Marx's critique of political economy the reader is therefore encouraged to turn to Burkett's book.
2. Karl Marx, *Capital*, vol. 1 (New York: Vintage, 1976), 283; Karl Marx, *Capital*, vol. 3 (New York: Vintage, 1981), 949–50, 959.
3. Karl Marx, *Grundrisse* (New York: Vintage, 1973), 604–8.
4. Ibid.
5. On Anderson's origination of the classical rent theory, see Joseph A. Schumpeter, *A History of Economic Analysis* (New York: Oxford University Press, 1951), 263–66.
6. James Anderson, *An Enquiry into the Nature of the Corn Laws; with a View to the New Corn Bill Proposed for Scotland* (Edinburgh: Mrs. Mundell, 1777), 45–50, and *Observations on the Means of Exciting a Spirit of National Industry* (Edinburgh: T. Cadell, 1777), 376.
7. David Ricardo, *Principles of Political Economy and Taxation* (Cambridge: Cambridge University Press, 1951), 67.
8. James Anderson, *Essays Relating to Agriculture and Rural Affairs* (London: John Bell, 1796), vol. 3, 97–135. The conflict between tenant farmer and landed proprietor over investment in agricultural improvements, which was to become a central element of Marx's critique of capitalist agriculture in Britain, was already visible in Engels's 1844 "Outlines." See Friedrich Engels, "Outlines of a Critique of Political Economy," in Karl Marx, *Economic and Philosophical Manuscripts of 1844* (New York: International Publishers, 1964), 209–10.
9. James Anderson, *A Calm Investigation of the Circumstances that Have Led to the Present Scarcity of Grain in Great Britain: Suggesting the Means of Alleviating that Evil, and Preventing the Recurrence of such a Calamity in the Future* (London: John Cumming, 1801), 73–75.
10. Ibid., 12, 56–64; Edwin Cannan, *A History of Theories of Production and Distribution in English Political Economy from 1776 to 1848* (New York: Augustus M. Kelley, 1967), 114–15.
11. Karl Marx and Friedrich Engels, *Historisch-Kritische Gesamtausgabe* (*MEGA*), part 4, vol. 9 (Berlin: Dietz Verlag, 1991)
12. Karl Marx, *Theories of Surplus Value*, part 2 (Moscow: Progress Publishers, 1968), 147–48.

13. Anderson, *Essays Relating to Agriculture*, vol. 3, 97–135; Marx, *Capital*, vol. 3, 757; Marx, *Theories of Surplus Value*, part 2, 244.

14. Given the general neglect of Anderson's work, even in the nineteenth century, it is interesting to note that not only Marx but Darwin too drew extensively on Anderson—in Darwin's case Anderson was regarded as a reliable source of information on animal breeding and heredity, and was frequently cited in Darwin's *The Variation of Animals and Plants under Domestication*. See Charles F. Mullett, "A Village Aristotle and the Harmony of Interests: James Anderson (1739–1808) of Monks Hill," *The Journal of British Studies*, vol. 8, no. 1 (1968), 94–118.

15. James Anderson, *Recreations in Agriculture, Natural-History, Arts, and Miscellaneous Literature* (London: T. Bentley, 1801), vol. 4, 376–80.

16. Marx, *Capital*, vol. 3, 915–16. This point was prefigured by Marx (also on the basis of Liebig) in the *Grundrisse*, 754.

17. See the detailed summary and set of extracts from Liebig's long introduction to the seventh (1862) edition of his *Organic Chemistry in its Application to Chemistry and Physiology* in *The Chemical News*, vol. 7, no. 182 (May 30, 1863), 256–58; also vol. 7, no. 183 (June 6, 1863), 268–70; vol. 7, no. 165 (June 20, 1863), 292–94; vol. 7, no. 186 (June 27, 1863), 302–5. Translations of the "Preface" and "Introduction" to the seventh edition of Liebig's great work on agricultural chemistry were not published in English, even though all the rest of the book eventually was, and even though all of Liebig's previous editions had been issued in English only months after their appearance in German. The reason was that this "Introduction" (or "Einleitung") was seen as too critical of English high farming. The English publisher of Liebig's works actually destroyed the copy in his possession. (See William H. Brock, *Justus von Liebig* [Cambridge: Cambridge University Press, 1997], 177). Consequently, the only published translations in English were the lengthy excerpts in *The Chemical News* referred to above. An unpublished translation of the "Einleitung," however, was produced by Lady Gilbert, the wife of one of England's most distinguished agricultural chemists, Henry Gilbert, in January 1863, and has been maintained for many years in the archives of the Rothamsted Experimental Station (now IACR–Rothamsted) in Hertfordshire. This manuscript has been provided to me courtesy of the Institute Librarian, Mrs. S.E. Allsopp. In what follows I occasionally refer to this archival manuscript, cited as Liebig, "Einleitung." For the published version in German, see Justus von Liebig, *Die Chemie in ihrer Anwendung auf Agricultur und Physiologie*, vol. 1 (Brunswick, 1862), 1–156.

18. F.M.L. Thompson, "The Second Agricultural Revolution, 1815–1880," *Economic History Review*, vol. 21, no. 1 (1968), 62–77. Some parts of the subsequent discussion in this section have been developed previously in my article "Marx's Theory of Metabolic Rift: Classical Foundations for Environmental Sociology," *American Journal of Sociology*, vol. 104, no. 2 (September 1999), 373–78.

19. The classic argument for this is Thompson's "Second Agricultural Revolution," see previous note. Thompson stipulates that the second agricultural revolution occurred over the years 1815–1880, that is, beginning with the agricultural crisis that immediately followed the Napoleonic Wars (and which was the setting in which Malthus and Ricardo discussed the issue of differential rent).

I have narrowed this down to 1830–1880 in order to distinguish the crisis that preceded the second agricultural revolution from that revolution proper, for which the turning points were the British Association for the Advancement of Science's commissioning of a work on the application of chemistry to agriculture from Liebig in 1837, the publication of his *Agricultural Chemistry* in 1840, and J.B. Lawes's building of the first factory for the production of synthetic fertilizer a few years later.

20. If the first agricultural revolution was bound up with the origins of capitalism (as Ellen Meiksins Wood has argued), the second agricultural revolution was bound up with the shift to industrial capitalism, and the third agricultural revolution with the rise of monopoly capitalism. See Wood, *The Origin of Capitalism* (New York: Monthly Review Press, 1999); and Fred Magdoff, Fred Buttel, and John Bellamy Foster, eds., *Hungry for Profit* (New York: Monthly Review Press, 1999).

21. Marx and Engels, *Historisch-Kritische Gesamtausgabe* (*MEGA*), part 4, vol. 9, 199–324. Marx's excerpts in his notebooks from Liebig and Johnston on agricultural chemistry and geology during the period 1850–1853 were very extensive. The extracts from Liebig take up around forty pages in *MEGA* (ibid., 172–213), while his extracts from Johnston take up around fifty-five pages (ibid., 276–317, 372–86).

22. Lord Ernle, *English Farming Past and Present* (Chicago: Quadrangle, 1961), 369; Daniel Hillel, *Out of the Earth* (Berkeley: University of California Press, 1991), 131–32. Liebig contended that "the battle-fields of Leipzig, Waterloo and the Crimea" had been raided for bones. Liebig, "Einleitung," 85.

23. This work is sometimes known as *Agricultural Chemistry* to distinguish it from Liebig's *Animal Chemistry* (1842), the title of which also referred to *Organic Chemistry*. In the following discussion *Agricultural Chemistry* (following this convention) is used as the short title for his first work on agriculture—primarily dealing with plants; while the title *Animal Chemistry* is used for his 1842 work on animal physiology and pathology.

24. Brock, *Justus von Liebig*, 149–50.

25. J.M. Skaggs, *The Great Guano Rush* (New York: St. Martin's Press, 1994) 225; Liebig, "Einleitung," 79.

26. Margaret W. Rossiter, *The Emergence of Agricultural Science: Justus Liebig and the Americans, 1840–1880* (New Haven, Conn.: Yale University Press, 1975), 3–9; Karl Marx and Friedrich Engels, *Collected Works* (New York: International Publishers, 1975), vol. 38, 476; James F.W. Johnston, *Notes on North America* (London: William Blackwood & Sons, 1851), vol. 1, 356–65; Marx, *Capital*, vol. 3, 808.

27. George E. Waring, Jr., "The Agricultural Features of the Census of the United States for 1850," *Bulletin of the American Geographical and Statistical Association*, vol. 2 (1857), 189–202 (reprinted in *Organization & Environment*, vol. 12, no. 3 [September 1999], 298–307); Henry Carey, *Letters to the President on the Foreign and Domestic Policy of the Union and its Effects as Exhibited in the Condition of the People and the State* (Philadelphia: M. Polock, 1858), 54–55. For a general assessment of Waring's work, see John Bellamy Foster, "'Robbing the Earth of its Capital Stock,'" *Organization & Environment*, vol. 12, no. 3 (September 1999), 293–97.

28. Henry Carey, *The Past, Present and Future* (New York: Augustus M. Kelley,

1967), 298–99, 304–08; originally published in 1847.

29. Henry Carey, *Principles of Social Science* (Philadelphia: J.B. Lippincott, 1867), vol. 2, 215, and *The Past, Present and Future*, 298–99, 304–8. Marx's relation to Carey was complex. By 1853 Marx had read all of Carey's major works up to that date, including *The Slave Trade Domestic and Foreign*, which Carey himself sent to Marx. Yet, he did not read Carey's *Principles of Social Science*, probably his most important work, until 1869, more than a decade after it was published. Marx was generally highly critical of Carey, whom he viewed as a "harmonizer" and as an indifferent economist. But he found his work useful in certain respects. Both Carey and Marx made similar points about the degradation of the soil and its relation to long distance trade and the urban–rural division; both relied extensively on the work of Liebig; both were highly critical of the Malthusian–Ricardian rent theory. Furthermore, Marx saw Carey as one of the main exponents (along with James Anderson) of the crucial concept of "earth-capital" (capital associated with human "improvements" on nature and thus part of the value calculus—a concept that Marx distinguished from earth-matter). On Marx's views on Carey, see especially Marx and Engels, *Selected Correspondence* (Moscow: Progress Publishers, 1975), 78–79, 212–15 (Marx to Engels, June 14, 1853; Marx to Engels, November 26, 1869); Marx, *Grundrisse*, 883–93. Marx, it is worth adding, had some influence on Carey, since in his work on the slave trade Carey quoted extensively in two places from Marx's writing in the *New York Daily Tribune*. The most detailed discussion of Marx's relationship to Carey is to be found in Michael Perelman, "Political Economy and the Press: Karl Marx and Henry Carey at the *New York Tribune*," Discussion Paper Series, no. 85–9, School of Behavioral and Social Sciences, California State University, Chico, 1985. Perelman demonstrates that Marx's famous articles on British rule in India in the *Tribune*, which have frequently been seen as advocating the thesis that imperialism was playing a progressive role by promoting industrialization in the periphery, were written expressly to counter Carey's entirely negative interpretation of Britain's international role and part of a struggle to gain theoretical hegemony within the *Tribune* itself. For a balanced assessment of Carey, see Schumpeter, *History of Economic Analysis*, 515–19. For a recent detailed treatment, see Michael Perelman, "Henry Carey's Political-Ecological Economics," *Organization & Environment*, vol. 12, no. 3 (September 1999), 280–92.

30. Justus von Liebig, *Letters on Modern Agriculture* (London: Walton & Maberly, 1859), 175–78, 183, 220.

31. Liebig, quoted in K. William Kapp, *The Social Costs of Private Enterprise* (New York: Schocken Books, 1971), 35.

32. Liebig, quoted in Karl Kautsky, *The Agrarian Question* (London: Zwan, 1988), vol. 1, 53; Liebig, "Einleitung," 80.

33. Justus von Liebig, *Familiar Letters on Chemistry*, (Philadelphia: T.B. Peterson, 1852), 44. Published as part of *Complete Works on Chemistry* (comprising a number of separate works bound under a single cover).

34. Edwin Chadwick, *Report on the Sanitary Condition of the Labouring Population of Great Britain* (Edinburgh: Edinburgh University Press, 1965), 121–22; Friedrich Engels, *The Condition of the Working Class in England* (Chicago: Academy Press, 1969).

35. Justus von Liebig, *Letters on the Subject of the Utilization of the Metropolitan Sewage* (London: W.H. Collingridge, 1865); Justus von Liebig, *The Natural Laws of Husbandry* (New York: D. Appleton, 1863), 261.

36. Marx and Engels, *Collected Works*, vol. 42, 227; Marx, *Capital*, vol. 1, 638.

37. Marx's notebooks contain extensive extracts from two works by Liebig, including his *Agricultural Chemistry*, three works from the English soil scientist James F.W. Johnston, and numerous works in geology, including Charles Lyell's *Principles of Geology*. See E. Coleman, "Short Communication on the Unpublished Writings of Karl Marx Dealing with Mathematics, the Natural Sciences and Technology and the History of these Subjects," in Nikolai Bukharin et al., *Science at the Cross Roads: Papers Presented at the International Congress of the History of Science and Technology, 1931* (London: Frank Cass, 1971), 233–34.

38. Marx, *Capital*, vol. 3, 949–50.

39. Marx, *Capital*, vol. 1, 637–38. The need for the "restoration" of the constituents of the soil was a point that Marx took directly from Liebig's "Introduction" to the 1862 edition of his *Agricultural Chemistry*. Liebig, "Einleitung," 97.

40. Marx and Engels, *Collected Works*, vol. 11, 333.

41. Marx, *Capital*, vol. 1, 348.

42. Marx, *Grundrisse*, 527.

43. Marx, *Capital*, vol. 1, 283, 290.

44. Marx and Engels, *Collected Works*, vol. 30, 40.

45. Karl Marx, *Texts on Method* (Oxford: Basil Blackwell, 1975), 209; Marx, *Grundrisse*, 158, 361. Adolph Wagner had employed the concept of *Stoffwechsel* after Marx to argue that "The operation of the economic system leads necessarily to a continuous *exchange*, analogous in fact to the natural material exchange *in the (natural) components* of the mass of goods which are at the disposal of the economic system at a given time." Marx saw this as reflecting his views, which Wagner had quite likely lifted without attribution from his work. Marx, *Texts on Method*, 109.

46. The wider, social understanding of metabolism, drawn from the *Grundrisse*, has been powerfully developed by István Mészáros in *Beyond Capital* (New York: Monthly Review Press, 1995).

47. Karl Marx, *Early Writings* (New York: Vintage, 1974), 328.

48. Marx, *Grundrisse*, 489.

49. Tim Hayward, *Ecological Thought* (Cambridge: Polity, 1994), 116.

50. Marx, *Capital*, vol. 3, 959.

51. Justus von Liebig, *Animal Chemistry or Organic Chemistry in its Application to Physiology and Pathology* (New York: Johnson Reprint, 1964); Franklin C. Bing, "The History of the Word 'Metabolism,'" *Journal of the History of Medicine and Allied Arts*, vol. 26, no. 2 (April 1971), 158–80; Brock, *Justus von Liebig*, 193; Kenneth Caneva, *Robert Mayer and the Conservation of Energy* (Princeton, N.J.: Princeton University Press, 1993), 117.

52. Julius Robert Mayer, "The Motions of Organisms and their Relation to Metabolism," in Robert Bruce Lindsay, ed., *Julius Robert Mayer: Prophet of Energy* (New York: Pergamon, 1973), 75–145; Caneva, *Robert Mayer and the Conservation of Energy*, 262–65; Brock, *Justus von Liebig*, 312–13; Juan Martinez-Alier, *Ecological Economics* (Oxford: Basil Blackwell, 1987), 110. On "vital

materialism," see Timothy Lenoir, *The Strategy of Life: Teleology and Mechanics in Nineteenth Century German Biology* (Boston: D. Reidel Publishing Co., 1982). Thomas Hall gives two reasons for seeing Liebig as a "vital materialist" rather than a vitalist: (1) the contention that behind the "vital force" lay chemical processes (to which the former was not however reducible); (2) the emergence of his "vital force" out of ordinary matter—suggesting an "emergentist" argument. Thomas S. Hall, *Ideas of Life and Matter: Studies in the History of General Physiology 600 B.C. to 1900 A.D.* (Chicago: University of Chicago Press, 1969), vol. 2, 269–71.

53. Y.M. Uranovsky, "Marxism and Natural Science," in Nikolai Bukharin et al., *Marxism and Modern Thought* (New York: Harcourt, Brace, 1935), 140; Lindsay, *Julius Robert Mayer*, 11–12; Hal Draper, *The Marx–Engels Glossary* (New York: Schocken Books, 1986), 189.

54. Marina Fischer-Kowalski, "Society's Metabolism," in Michael Redclift and Graham Woodgate, ed., *International Handbook of Environmental Sociology* (Northampton, Mass.: Edward Elgar, 1997), 120; Eugene Odum, "The Strategy of Ecosystem Development," *Science*, vol. 164 (1969), 262–70.

55. Alfred Schmidt, *The Concept of Nature in Marx* (London: New Left Books, 1971), 86–88.

56. Paul Heyer, *Nature, Human Nature, and Society: Marx, Darwin and the Human Sciences* (Westport, Conn.: Greenwood Press, 1982), 12. Schmidt, it should be noted, acknowledges in a footnote that Liebig had applied the concept of metabolism to the social sphere, in his *Chemische Briefe*, as early as 1851, before Moleschott. Schmidt, *The Concept of Nature in Marx*, 218.

57. Friedrich Engels, *Anti-Dühring* (Moscow: Progress Publishers, 1969), 99; Marx and Engels, *Collected Works*, vol. 25, 578–79, 601. The main context of Engels's discussion here was a critique of Liebig's speculation on the origins of life, which saw life as existing as long as matter.

58. Fischer-Kowalski, "Society's Metabolism," 133; Marx, *Capital*, vol. 3, 195.

59. Fischer-Kowalski, "Society's Metabolism," 119–20.

60. Ibid., 122.

61. Ibid., 121, 131.

62. Karl Marx, *Theories of Surplus Value*, part 3 (Moscow: Progress Publishers, 1971), 301; Marx, *Capital*, vol. 3, 195; Engels, *The Housing Question* (Moscow: Progress Publishers, 1975), 92.

63. Marx, *Capital*, vol. 1, 860; Liebig, "Einleitung," 85.

64. Marx, *Capital*, vol. 3, 754.

65. Ibid., 948–49.

66. Ibid., 911.

67. Marx and Engels, *Collected Works*, vol. 24, 356. See also Teodor Shanin, ed., *Late Marx and the Russian Road* (New York: Monthly Review Press, 1983).

68. Marx, *Capital*, vol. 3, 216; Engels, *Anti-Dühring*, 211–13. Engels did not attribute the destruction of the soil resulting from large estates simply to capitalism but also mentioned its role in the Roman era, citing Pliny.

69. Marx and Engels, *Collected Works*, vol. 46, 411.

70. Marx and Engels, *Collected Works*, vol. 42, 559; Karl Marx, *Capital*, vol. 2 (New York: Vintage, 1978), 322.

71. Marx, *Capital*, vol. 1, 892–93.

72. Marx and Engels, *Selected Correspondence*, 102.

73. Juan Martinez-Alier and J.M. Naredo, "A Marxist Precursor of Energy Economics: Podolinsky," *Journal of Peasant Studies*, vol. 9, no. 2 (1982), 207–24; Juan Martinez-Alier, *Ecological Economics* (Cambridge, Mass.: Basil Blackwell, 1987), 45–63, and "Political Ecology, Distributional Conflicts and Economic Incommeasurability," *New Left Review*, no. 211 (May–June 1995), 71.

74. Marx and Engels, *Collected Works*, vol. 46, 410–13. See also Burkett, *Marx and Nature*, 131–32.

75. Kozo Mayumi, "Temporary Emancipation from the Land," *Ecological Economics*, vol. 4, no. 1 (1991), 35–56.

76. See Jean-Paul Deléage, "Eco-Marxist Critique of Political Economy," in Martin O'Connor, ed., *Is Capitalism Sustainable?* (New York: Guilford, 1994), 48; Ward Churchill, *From a Native Son* (Boston: South End Press, 1996), 467–68; Nicholas Georgescu-Roegen, *The Entropy Law in the Economic Process* (Cambridge, Mass.: Harvard University Press, 1971), 2. For a powerful response to these criticisms closely related to the one that follows, see Burkett, *Marx and Nature*, 79–98.

77. Thomas Malthus, *Pamphlets* (New York: Augustus M. Kelley, 1970), 185; Marx and Engels, *Collected Works*, vol. 34, 151–59.

78. Campbell McConnell, *Economics* (New York: McGraw Hill, 1987), 20, 672; Alfred Marshall, *Principles of Economics* (London: Macmillan, 1920).

79. Marx, *Capital*, vol. 3, 955.

80. Marx, *Capital*, vol. 1, 323; Lucretius, *On the Nature of the Universe* (Harmondsworth: Penguin Books, 1994), 13–14 (1.145–60).

81. Marx, *Grundrisse*, 706, 361. Marx's reference here to labor as "form-giving fire" can also be seen as related to what he frequently referred to in *Capital* as labor's "vital force." In this respect he seems to have adopted Liebig's notion of "vital force" as life-as-action, actively transforming matter and creating new organizational forms. This was consistent with Marx's own "emergentist" approach. See Hall, *Ideas of Life and Matter*, 269–71.

82. Marx, *Capital*, vol. 1, 134; Karl Marx, *Critique of the Gotha Programme* (Moscow: Progress Publishers, 1971), 11.

83. Marx, *Grundrisse*, 325; see also Michael Lebowitz, *Beyond Capital* (New York: St. Martin's Press, 1992), 96–100.

84. Alec Nove, "Socialism," in John Eatwell, Murray Milgate, and Paul Newman, eds., *The New Palgrave Dictionary of Economics*, vol. 4 (New York: Stockton Press, 1987), 399.

85. Ibid.; Marx and Engels, *Selected Correspondence*, 190.

86. Marx, *Capital*, vol. 3, 195–97; Andrew McLaughlin, "Ecology, Capitalism, and Socialism," *Socialism and Democracy*, vol. 10 (1990), 69–102.

87. Karl Marx and Friedrich Engels, *The Communist Manifesto* (New York: Monthly Review Press, 1998), 40; Marx, *Capital*, vol. 1, 637–38, and *Capital*, vol. 3, 959.

88. Marx, *Grundrisse*, 87, 471, 497.

89. Marx, *Capital*, vol. 1, 873–76.

90. Ibid., 877–88.

91. Ibid., 885–90.

92. Ibid., 891–92.

93. Ibid., 895.

94. Ibid., 905–6.

95. Ibid., 915.

96. Ibid., 912, 925.

97. Ibid., 798.

98. Ibid., 769, 929.

99. Ibid., 931–40; Marx, *Grundrisse*, 276. Marx had taken extensive extracts from Wakefield with vertical markings in the margins emphasizing precisely these points in his notebooks of 1850–1853. See Marx and Engels, *MEGA*, part 4, vol. 9, 486–91.

100. Marx, *Capital*, vol. 1, 939.

101. Engels, *Anti-Dühring*, 351–52.

102. Bertell Ollman, *Social and Sexual Revolution* (Boston: South End Press, 1979), 56–57.

103. William Morris, *News from Nowhere and Selected Writings and Designs* (Harmondsworth: Penguin Books, 1962), 244–46, 267; William Morris, "Three Letters on Epping Forest," *Organization & Environment*, vol. 11, no. 1 (March 1998), 93–97.

104. Lucretius, *The Nature of the Universe*, 13–15 (1.145–225).

6. The Basis in Natural History for Our View

1. The term "tormented evolutionist" is taken from Adrian Desmond and James Moore, *Darwin: The Life of a Tormented Evolutionist* (New York: W.W. Norton, 1991). The term "reluctant revolutionary"—also used to describe Darwin—is taken from Michael Rose, *Darwin's Spectre* (Princeton, N.J.: Princeton University Press, 1998).

2. In this respect Alfred Russell Wallace, as a socialist, did not face the same dilemma as Darwin.

3. Desmond and Moore, *Darwin*, 291–98.

4. Ibid., 296.

5. Rose, *Darwin's Spectre*, 49–50; Paul B. Sears, *Charles Darwin: The Naturalist as a Cultural Force* (New York: Charles Scribner's Sons, 1950), 20; Henry Fairfield Osborn, *From the Greeks to Darwin* (New York: Charles Scribner's Sons, 1927), 37–43, 57–63. Similar to Sears, but less far-reaching, Ernst Mayr contends that, "Nothing of any real consequence happened after Lucretius and Galen until the Renaissance." Mayr, *The Growth of Biological Thought* (Cambridge, Mass.: Harvard University Press, 1982), 91.

6. Ernst Mayr, *One Long Argument: Charles Darwin and the Genesis of Modern Evolutionary Thought* (Cambridge, Mass.: Harvard University Press, 1991), 3, 13.

7. Desmond and Moore, *Darwin*, 341, 369.

8. Thomas H. Huxley, *Darwiniana* (New York: D. Appleton and Co., 1897), 13; Desmond and Moore, *Darwin*, 320–23; Loren Eiseley, *Darwin's Century* (New York: Doubleday, 1958), 133; Ruskin, quoted in J.W. Burrow, "Editor's Introduction," in Charles Darwin, *The Origin of Species by Means of Natural Selection* (Harmondsworth: Penguin Books, 1968), 20.

9. Stephen Jay Gould, *Full House: The Spread of Excellence from Plato to Darwin* (New York: Three Rivers Press, 1996), 138.

10. Darwin, *The Origin of Species*, 68.

11. Ibid., 116–17.

12. Ibid., 119, 129; Stephen Jay Gould, *Eight Little Piggies* (New York: W.W. Norton, 1993), 302.

13. Darwin, *The Origin of Species*, 116.

14. Mayr, *One Long Argument*, 79–81, 184; Gould, *Full House*, 41.

15. Marx to Engels, June 18, 1862, in Karl Marx and Friedrich Engels, *Selected Correspondence* (Moscow: Progress Publishers, 1975), 120.

16. Desmond and Moore, *Darwin*, 201.

17. Diane Paul, "Fitness: Historical Perspectives," in Evelyn Fox Keller and Elisabeth A. Lloyd, eds., *Keywords in Evolutionary Biology* (Cambridge, Mass.: Harvard University Press, 1992), 112–14.

18. Burrow, "Editor's Introduction," 33.

19. Sumner, quoted in Richard Hofstadter, *Social Darwinism in American Thought* (Boston: Beacon Press, 1955), 58. See also William Graham Sumner, *Social Darwinism* (Englewood Cliffs, N.J.: Prentice-Hall, 1963). John D. Rockefeller quoted in Alan Chase, *The Legacy of Malthus: The Social Costs of the New Scientific Racism* (New York: Alfred A. Knopf, 1977). On Conrad and the critique of exterminism, see Sven Lindquist, *Exterminate all the Brutes* (New York: New Press, 1996).

20. Stephen Jay Gould, *Ever Since Darwin* (New York: W.W. Norton, 1977), 34–38; Burrow, "Editor's Introduction," 33.

21. Adrian Desmond, *Huxley: From Devil's Disciple to Evolution's High Priest* (Reading, Mass.: Perseus Books, 1997), 276–80; Gould, *Ever Since Darwin*, 33; Hal Hellman, *Great Feuds in Science* (New York: John Wiley & Sons, 1998), 81–85.

22. Mayr, *One Long Argument*, 40–41.

23. Lyell and Mill, quoted in ibid., 41; Huxley, *Darwiniana*, 42, 54.

24. Huxley, *Darwiniana*, 54, 82–85.

25. Ibid., 57, 85–91.

26. Ibid., 6, 12, 20, 77.

27. Burrow, "Editor's Introduction," 46–47; Eiseley, *Darwin's Century*, 211–16, 233–44, 252–53; Hellman, *Great Feuds in Science*, 105–19.

28. Thomas Huxley, *Lay Sermons, Addresses and Reviews* (New York: D. Appleton and Co., 1871), 246

29. Eiseley, *Darwin's Century*, 239–42.

30. James A. Secord, "Introduction" in Charles Lyell, *Principles of Geology* (Harmondsworth: Penguin Books, 1997), xxiv; Huxley, *Darwiniana*, 52; Desmond, *Huxley*, 271–72.

31. Paul Shorey, *Platonism: Ancient and Modern* (Berkeley: University of California Press, 1938), 17; Desmond, *Huxley*, 595; Huxley, *Lay Sermons*, 346. Huxley did criticize Lucretius, along with earlier philosophers and scientists, for adopting the notion of spontaneous generation. For the historical context of Tennyson's great poem *In Memoriam*, written in 1850, in which the line "Nature, red in tooth and claw" appears, see Stephen Jay Gould, *Dinosaur in a Haystack* (New York: Random House, 1995), 63–75. Tennyson also wrote a long poem entitled "Lucretius"—a fanciful account of the death of the great Roman poet that also delved into Lucretius' philosophical concepts. See Alfred Lord Tennyson, *The Poems of Tennyson in Three Volumes* (Berkeley: University of California Press, 1987), vol. 2, 707–21.

32. Ernst Haeckel, *Monism as Connecting Religion and Science: The Confession of*

Faith of a Man of Science (London: Adam & Charles Black, 1895), 4; Anna Bramwell, *Ecology in the 20th Century* (New Haven, Conn.: Yale University Press, 1989), 44.

33. Haeckel, quoted in Frank Benjamin Golley, *A History of the Ecosystem Concept in Ecology* (New Haven, Conn.: Yale University Press, 1993), 207.

34. Haekel, *Monism*, 73–74.

35. Stephen Jay Gould, *Ontogeny and Phylogeny* (Cambridge, Mass.: Harvard University Press, 1977), 77–78.

36. Karl Marx and Friedrich Engels, *Collected Works* (New York: International Publishers, 1975), vol. 40, 551; vol. 41, 232, 246–47. December 19, 1860, letter from Marx to Engels, quoted according to Karl Marx and Friedrich Engels, *Selected Correspondence, 1846–1895* (New York: International Publishers, 1936), 126. Marx's statement is reminiscent of Kant's "Critique of Teleological Judgment." Teleology is denied; but the essential task of providing a *rational* explanation for *real* natural processes is affirmed.

37. William Liebknecht, "Reminiscences of Marx," in Institute of Marxism-Leninism, ed., *Reminiscences of Marx and Engels* (Moscow: Foreign Languages Publishing House, n.d.), 106; Friedrich Lessner, "Before 1848 and After," in ibid., 161.

38. Paul Heyer, *Nature, Human Nature and Society* (Westport, Conn.: Greenwood Press, 1982), 12–13.

39. Marx and Engels, *Collected Works*, vol. 41, 381.

40. Liebknecht, "Reminiscences of Marx," 106; Huxley, *Darwiniana*, 303–475; Marx and Engels, *Collected Works*, vol. 43, 183; Huxley, *Lay Sermons*, 130–39. It is worth noting that Jenny Marx and Marx's daughters also attended Huxley's lectures on occasion and left reports behind on them.

41. Frederick Albert Lange, *The History of Materialism* (New York: Humanities Press, 1950).

42. Hal Draper, *The Marx–Engels Chronicle* (New York: Schocken Books, 1985), 116.

43. Francis C. Haber, *The Age of the World: Moses to Darwin* (Baltimore, Md.: Johns Hopkins University Press, 1959), 285.

44. Marx and Engels, *Collected Works*, vol. 42, 304–5, 320–24, 327. Marx's error in praising Trémaux (although he noted "the geological blunders" and deficiencies "in literary-historical criticism" of the latter) has recently been stressed by Stephen Jay Gould, who observes of Trémaux's book, "I have never read a more absurd or poorly documented thesis." Stephen Jay Gould, "A Darwinian at Marx's Funeral," *Natural History*, vol. 108, no. 7 (Spring 1999), 64.

45. Ralph Colp, Jr., "The Contacts Between Karl Marx and Charles Darwin," *Journal of the History of Ideas*, vol. 35, no. 2 (April–June 1974), 330.

46. Karl Marx, *Capital*, vol. 1 (New York: International Publishers, 1976), 461, 493.

47. Anton Pannekoek, *Marxism and Darwinism* (Chicago: Charles H. Kerr, 1912), 50; K. Timiryazeff, "Darwin and Marx," in David Ryazanoff, *Karl Marx: Man, Thinker and Revolutionist* (New York: International Publishers, 1927), 170–73.

48. Marx and Engels, *Collected Works*, vol. 25, 330.

49. Karl Marx, *Capital*, vol. 1 (New York: Vintage, 1976), 285–86.

50. Institute of Marxism-Leninism, *Ex Libris, Karl Marx und Friedrich Engels*

(Berlin: Dietz Verlag, 1967), 132–33; Charles Lyell, *The Geological Evidences of the Antiquity of Man* (Philadelphia: George W. Childs, 1863), 376–77.

51. Alfred Russell Wallace, "The Origin of Human Races and the Antiquity of Man Deduced from the Theory of 'Natural Selection,'" *Journal of the Anthropological Society of London*, vol. 2 (1864), clxii–clxiii. Wallace's argument on the role of tool making in evolution and its effect in insulating the human body from change was part of a much more dubious attempt to explain the origin of human races, the actual anatomical similarity of which he thought could be explained by the fact that human evolution since the beginning of tool making had taken the form almost exclusively of the development of the "mind," which he argued distinguished the white European with "his" greater intellect from other "degraded races." Although Wallace, as a Darwinian evolutionist, did not adhere to many of the specific racist beliefs common within the educated classes of Europe in his day, he nonetheless argued in this paper that

> *"the preservation of favoured races in the struggle for life"* ... leads to the inevitable extinction of all those low and mentally undeveloped populations with which Europeans come in contact. The red Indian in North America, and in Brazil; the Tasmanian, Australian and New Zealander in the southern hemisphere, die out, not from any one special cause, but from the inevitable effects of an unequal mental and physical struggle. The intellectual and moral, as well as the physical qualities of the European are superior.... [and] enable him when in contact with the savage man, to conquer in the struggle for existence ... just as the weeds of Europe overrun North America and Australia, extinguishing native productions by the inherent vigour of their organization, and by their greater capacity for existence and multiplication.

Ibid., clxv. There is no doubt that such arguments helped to justify an imperialist policy of racial domination (and even extermination) summarized by Joseph Conrad's character Kurtz in *Heart of Darkness*: "Exterminate all the brutes." See Lindqvist, *Exterminate All the Brutes*.

52. Friedrich Engels, *The Dialectics of Nature* (New York: International Publishers, 1940), 281.

53. Stephen Jay Gould, *An Urchin in the Storm* (New York: W.W. Norton, 1987), 111–12. The approach to gene–culture coevolution first developed by Engels and developed later on by anthropologists as a result of new paleontological discoveries remains the best alternative to the positivistic, sociobiological approach made famous in Charles J. Lumsden and Edward O. Wilson, *Promethean Fire: Reflections on the Origin of Mind* (Cambridge, Mass.: Harvard University Press, 1983).

54. Gould, *Ever Since Darwin*, 207–13.

55. Sherwood L. Washburn, "Tools and Human Evolution," *Scientific American*, vol. 203, no. 3 (September 1960), 63.

56. Sherwood Washburn and Ruth Moore, *Ape into Man* (Boston: Little, Brown, 1974), 186. See also Kenneth P. Oakley, *Man the Toolmaker* (London: British Museum, 1972); Rose, *Darwin's Spectre*, 156–58.

57. Friedrich Engels, *Anti-Dühring* (Moscow: Progress Publishers, 1969), 83–93, 220.

58. Daniel P. Todes, *Darwin Without Malthus: The Struggle for Existence in Russian*

Evolutionary Thought (New York: Oxford University Press, 1989), 36–39.

59. Marx and Engels, *Collected Works*, vol. 45, 106–8.

60. Marx and Darwin, quoted in Margaret A. Fay, "Marx and Darwin: A Literary Detective Story," *Monthly Review*, vol. 31, no. 10 (March 1980), 41. This was the only contact between Marx and Darwin. For many years it was believed that Marx had written a letter to Darwin offering to dedicate a volume of *Capital* to the latter, based on an 1880 letter from Darwin found among Marx's papers. Recent scholarship has proven, however, that the letter from Darwin was written not to Marx but to Marx's future son-in-law, Edward Aveling, who, along with Eleanor Marx Aveling, was at one time in charge of Marx's papers (after the death of Engels). Aveling, who had received a doctorate in zoology at the London University and had gone on to be a lecturer in comparative anatomy in London Hospital, met Darwin on a number of occasions, and offered to dedicate his book, *The Student's Marx* (1881), to Darwin, who had earlier given his views on some of the articles from which the book was compiled. Darwin, however, refused, not wishing to be associated with Aveling's radical secularism. Ibid.

61. Tyndall, quoted in Desmond, *Huxley*, 445.

62. A.S. Eve and C.H. Creasey, *Life and Work of John Tyndall* (London: Macmillan, 1945); Roy McLeod, "Tyndall, John," *Dictionary of Scientific Biography* (New York: Charles Scribner's Sons, 1976), vol. 13, 521–24; James R. Friday and Roy M. McLeod, *John Tyndall, Natural Philosopher, 1820–1893: Catalogue of Correspondence, Journals and Collected Papers* (London: Mansell, 1974); Elbert Hubbard, *Tyndall* (East Aurora, N.Y.: Roycrofters, 1905).

63. John Tyndall, *Fragments of Science* (New York: A.L. Burt Co., n.d.), 443–47; Marx and Engels, *Collected Works*, vol. 45, 50.

64. Tyndall, *Fragments of Science*, 450, 458, 478, 484–85.

65. Ibid., 462.

66. Ibid., 475–76, 485–86, 491.

67. Ibid., 500, 641; Hellman, *Great Feuds in Science*, 112–13.

68. Tyndall, *Fragments of Science*, 499; Eve and Creasey, *Life and Work of John Tyndall*, 185–94.

69. Marx and Engels, *Collected Works*, vol. 45, 50–51; Desmond, *Huxley*, 444–46.

70. Engels, *Anti-Dühring*, 393. Engels cited Diogenes Laertius' *Lives of Eminent Philosophers*, the only ancient history of philosophy to survive, which was not only the main biographical source on Epicurus, but was also the source of the three letters by Epicurus that had survived. See Diogenes Laertius, *Lives of Eminent Philosophers* (Cambridge, Mass.: Harvard University Press/ Loeb Classical Library, 1925), vol. 2, 572–75, 590–93 (Diogenes Laertius X, 43–44, 61). The notes for Engels's comments here appear to be those of a fragment included in *The Dialectics of Nature*. Although the editors of Marx and Engels's work were unable to discern the year in which this fragment was written, the fact that it contains precisely those passages from Epicurus (as well as Leucippus and Democritus) cited by Engels suggest that the fragment was connected to the "Old Preface." Significant in this respect is the fact that the notes specifically from the Greek atomists are in Marx's handwriting, suggesting that he gave a direct hand to Engels here. See Marx and Engels, *Collected Works*, vol. 25, 470–71, 672. With regard to A. Kekulé, Engels cited a pamphlet, *Aims and Achievements of Chemistry*, published in

Bonn in 1878.

71. Engels, *Anti-Dühring*, 395–96.

72. Ibid., 444; Alexei Mikhailovich Voden, "Talks with Engels," in Institute of Marxism-Leninism, ed., *Reminiscences of Marx and Engels*, 332–33.

73. Engels, *Dialectics of Nature*, 7, 13.

74. The phrase "the revolution in ethnological time" is taken from Thomas R. Trautmann, *Lewis Henry Morgan and the Invention of Kinship* (Berkeley: University of California Press, 1987), 35, 220. On Brixham cave, see Jacob W. Gruber, "Brixham Cave and the Antiquity of Man," in Melford E. Spiro, ed., *Context and Meaning in Cultural Anthropology* (New York: Free Press, 1965), 373–402; and Donald K. Grayson, *The Establishment of Human Antiquity* (New York: Free Press, 1983), 179–88.

75. Cuvier quoted in Grayson, *The Establishment of Human Antiquity*, 51.

76. Gruber, "Brixham Cave," 382–83, 396; Lyell, *Geological Evidences*.

77. John Lubbock, *Pre-historic Times* (London: Williams & Norgate, 1890), 1.

78. Geikie, quoted in Gruber, "Brixham Cave," 374.

79. Lewis Henry Morgan, *Ancient Society, Or Researches in the Lines of Human Progress from Savagery Through Barbarism to Civilization* (New York: World Publishing Company, 1963), preface.

80. The significance of *Ancient Society* as an attempt to construct a provisional outline of a *general theory* of development that was shared by a humankind which Morgan viewed as one—as opposed to the actual description of this development in all of its details—is strongly emphasized in Emanuel Terray, *Marxism and "Primitive" Societies* (New York: Monthly Review Press, 1972). Morgan's general theory, as Eleanor Leacock has emphasized, was not meant to run roughshod over regional differences and cultural specificities. Indeed, *Ancient Society* shows the closest attention to such differences. But it was meant to provide a unified conception of the ethnological evolution of humankind—one directly opposed to the racial arguments then prevalent. See Eleanor Leacock, "Introduction," in Friedrich Engels, *The Origin of the Family, Private Property and the State* (New York: International Publishers, 1972), 11.

81. Lucretius, *On the Nature of the Universe* (Harmondsworth: Penguin Books, 1994), 154–61 (5.1010–1296); Lubbock, *Pre-historic Times*, 6; Glyn Daniel and Colin Renfrew, *The Idea of Prehistory* (Edinburgh: Edinburgh University Press, 1988), 9; Grayson, *The Establishment of Human Antiquity*, 12.

82. Morgan, *Ancient Society*, 9–10, 20; Lucretius, *On the Nature of the Universe*, 152–53 (5.925–75).

83. Morgan, *Ancient Society*, 5, 42; Lucretius, *On the Nature of the Universe*, 155–56 (5.1031–91).

84. Morgan, *Ancient Society*, 19, 26–27, 44; Lucretius, *On the Nature of the Universe*, 161–62 (5.1280–96).

85. Eleanor Leacock, "Introduction, Part 1," in Morgan, *Ancient Society*, lxi.

86. Morgan, *Ancient Society*, 36. Some analysts have seen this statement as associated with nineteenth-century racist theories. See, for example, Trautmann, *Lewis Henry Morgan*, 30. But since Morgan is here talking about the Paleolithic period, that is, the very earliest human cultures, no such conclusion is logically warranted. The question of the gradual enlargement of the human brain over millions of years had by that time become an important part of

Darwinian evolutionary theory, not least of all in the work of Darwin himself.

87. Trautmann, *Lewis Henry Morgan*, 32, 172–73. Elsewhere Trautmann writes, "Lucretius, whom he [Morgan] would later regard as the first proponent of evolutionism long before Darwin, is among the very first purchases of Latin texts" in the Morgan library. In addition to a copy of *De rerum natura* in Latin, Morgan also possessed English prose and verse translations. Thomas R. Trautmann and Karl Sanford Kabelac, *The Library of Lewis Henry Morgan* (Philadelphia: American Philosophical Society, 1994), 41, 198.

88. Trautmann, *Lewis Henry Morgan*, 173. Trautmann, however, is incorrect in writing in the subsequent page of his book that "There are no specific linkages between Darwin's ideas and Morgan's." One need only point to the linkage between the two in the theory of the evolution of the human brain.

89. Carl Resak, *Lewis Henry Morgan, American Scholar* (Chicago: University of Chicago Press, 1960), 100. Horace (like Virgil) in his younger years was much influenced by Epicurus, admiring Lucretius' poem.

90. Institute of Marxism-Leninism, *Ex Libris, Karl Marx und Friedrich Engels*, 132–33.

91. Karl Marx, *Grundrisse* (New York: Vintage, 1973), 182.

92. Marx, *Capital*, vol. 1, 286.

93. Karl Marx, *Ethnological Notebooks* (Assen, Netherlands: Van Gorcum, 1972); Engels, *The Origin of the Family, Private Property and the State*, 71–73.

94. Teodor Shanin, ed., *Late Marx and the Russian Road* (New York: Monthly Review Press, 1983). Marx took extensive extracts from Lyell's *Principles of Geology* in 1869, followed in the 1870s by extracts from numerous works in geology and chemistry. See E. Coleman, "Short Communication on the Unpublished Writings of Karl Marx Dealing with Mathematics, the Natural Sciences and Technology and the History of these Subjects," in Nikolai Bukharin et al., *Science at the Cross Roads Papers Presented at the International Congress of the History of Science and Technology, 1931* (London: Frank Cass, 1971), 233–35.

95. Marx, *Capital*, vol. 1, 286.

96. Eugene S. Hunn, "The Value of Subsistence for the Future of the World," in Virginia D. Nazarea, ed., *Ethnoecology* (Tuscon: University of Arizona Press, 1999), 23–36.

97. Karl Marx and Friedrich Engels, "Preface to the Second Russian Edition of *The Manifesto of the Communist Party*," in Shanin, ed., *Late Marx and the Russian Road*, 138–39.

98. Joseph Lester (edited, with additional material by Peter J. Bowler), *E. Ray Lankester and the Making of Modern British Biology* (Oxford: British Society for the History of Science, 1995), 10–11, 51–52, 183–92; E. Ray Lankester, *From an Easy Chair* (London: Archibald & Constable, 1909), 117–23.

99. Lester, *E. Ray Lankester*, 89, 173, 179–81; E. Ray Lankester, *The Kingdom of Man* (London: Watts & Co., 1912), 9–13, 34–37, 45. Lankester's materialism also led him to anticipate in some respects the theory of Oparin and Haldane on the origins of life. See Lester, *E. Ray Lankester*, 90–91.

100. E. Ray Lankester, *Science from an Easy Chair* (New York: Henry Holt, 1913), 368–69.

101. Lester, *E. Ray Lankester*, 185–87; Gould, "A Darwinian Gentleman at Marx's Funeral."

102. Desmond and Moore, *Darwin*, 657–58; Edward Aveling, *Charles Darwin and Karl Marx: A Comparison* (London: Twentieth Century Press, n.d.), 12–13; Stephen Jay Gould, *The Rock of Ages* (New York: Ballantine, 1999).

103. Friedrich Engels, "Letter to Friedrich Adolph Sorge," in Philip Foner, ed., *Karl Marx Remembered* (San Francisco: Synthesis Publications, 1983), 28.

Epilogue

1. Karl Marx and Friedrich Engels, excerpt from *The German Ideology*, in Karl Marx, *Writings of the Young Marx on Philosophy and Society* (Indianapolis: Hackett, 1967), 408. This is a crossed-out passage in the manuscript, not included in *The Collected Works* edition.

2. Stephen F. Cohen, "Introduction," in Nikolai Bukharin, *How it All Began* (New York: Columbia University Press, 1998), vii–xxviii.

3. Nikolai Bukharin, *Philosophical Arabesques*, chapter 8, forthcoming Monthly Review Press, quotations from draft of English translation.

4. Nikolai Bukharin, *Historical Materialism: A System of Sociology* (New York: International Publishers, 1925), 108; Stephen F. Cohen, *Bukharin and the Bolshevik Revolution* (New York: Oxford University Press, 1980), 118.

5. Nikolai Bukharin, "Theory and Practice from the Standpoint of Dialectical Materialism," in Bukharin et al., *Science at the Cross Roads: Papers Presented at the International Congress of the History of Science and Technology, 1931* (London: Frank Cass, 1971), 17.

6. Alexei Mikhailovich Voden, "Talks with Engels," in Institute of Marxism-Leninism, *Reminiscences of Marx and Engels* (Moscow: Foreign Languages Publishing House, n.d.), 333. Despite his extremely close and still fascinating reading of the French materialists, Plekhanov shows virtually no knowledge of the most important branch of ancient materialism, that of Epicurus and Lucretius. See Georgi Plekhanov, *Selected Philosophical Works* (Moscow: Progress Publishers, 1974), vol. 1, 482–94.

7. Karl Marx and Friedrich Engels, *Collected Works* (New York: International Publishers, 1975), vol. 25, 532; Friedrich Engels, *Ludwig Feuerbach and the Outcome of Classical German Philosophy* (New York: International Publishers, 1941), 68.

8. E.P. Thompson, *Making History* (New York: New Press, 1994), 98.

9. See the excellent discussion of this in Helena Sheehan, *Marxism and the Philosophy of Science* (Atlantic Highlands, N.J.: Humanities Press, 1985), 53–64.

10. This was a provisional assessment that I recently espoused, but that I now regard as much too simplistic, as a result of the more extensive research undertaken for this book. See John Bellamy Foster, "Marx's Theory of Metabolic Rift: Classical Foundations for Environmental Sociology," *American Journal of Sociology*, vol. 104, no. 2 (September 1999), 399. At the time of writing that article I still adhered to a modified version of the Lukácsian prohibition against any "dialectics of nature," attributing this prohibition to Marx himself. I now view the question of the dialectics of nature once again as an open one.

11. Georg Wilhelm Friedrich Hegel, *The Phenomenology of Mind* (New York: Harper & Row, 1967), 81.

12. Marx and Engels, *Collected Works*, vol. 1, 65; Marx, *Letters to Kugelman* (New York: International Publishers, 1934), 112.

13. Marx and Engels, *Collected Works*, vol. 1, 65; Lucretius, *On the Nature of the Universe* (Harmondsworth: Penguin Books, 1994), 88 (3.861–70); Karl Marx, *The Poverty of Philosophy* (New York: International Publishers, 1963), 110.

14. Marx and Engels, *Collected Works*, vol. 25, 492–93, 582.

15. Ibid., 314; Thomas S. Hall, *Ideas of Life and Matter: Studies in the History of General Physiology 600 B.C. to 1900 A.D.* (Chicago: University of Chicago Press, 1969), vol. 2, 279.

16. Ted Benton, "Engels and the Politics of Nature," in C.J. Arthur, *Engels Today: A Centenary Appreciation* (New York: St. Martin's Press, 1996), 88. In this essay Benton shifts quite radically from his earlier analysis of Engels's ecology (and by implication Marx's ecology). Engels is no longer characterized as a narrow "Promethean" thinker, but rather as dialectical realist, deeply cognizant of ecological limits.

17. Marx and Engels, *Collected Works*, vol. 25, 499–501.

18. Ibid., 583–85.

19. Ibid., 23.

20. Engels, *Ludwig Feuerbach*, 67.

21. Marx and Engels, *Collected Works*, vol. 25, 459–60. Engels's argument deliberately stresses the similarity, even in mental faculties, extending even to the power to reason, between human beings and animals, while focusing on the qualitative change arising from the specifically human social organization of labor (which played the central role in human evolution). This non-anthropocentric perspective which attributed emotions and reason to animals was extremely unpopular in the late nineteenth century—such views were often criticized as anthropomorphizations. Yet, this was the general standpoint adopted by Darwin too. See Charles Darwin, *The Expression of the Emotions in Man and Animals* (New York: Oxford University Press, 1998).

22. Marx and Engels, *Collected Works*, vol. 25, 460–61. In his mature assessment of "Engels and the Politics of Nature," Ted Benton admits that this statement by Engels contradicts the "unqualified Prometheanism sometimes attributed to Marx and Engels." Benton, "Engels and the Politics of Nature," 77–78, 92.

23. For a discussion of Morris's argument on production for use versus production for profit, see John Bellamy Foster, *The Vulnerable Planet: A Short Economic History of the Environment* (New York: Monthly Review Press, 1994), 67–68.

24. William Morris, "Notes on Passing Events," *Commonweal*, vol. 2 (October 23, 1886), 122.

25. William Morris, *Selected Writings* (New York: Random House, 1934), 647.

26. Ibid., 648.

27. August Bebel, *Woman in the Past, Present and Future* (London: Zwan, 1988), 204, 207–8.

28. Karl Kautsky, *The Agrarian Question* (London: Zwan, 1998), vol. 2, 214–15.

29. Ibid., vol. 2, 217.

30. Ibid., 216–17.

31. V.I. Lenin, *Collected Works* (Moscow: Progress Publishers, 1961), vol. 5, 155–56.

32. Rosa Luxemburg, *Letters* (Atlantic Highlands, N.J.: Humanities Press, 1993),

202–3 (Luxemberg to Sonja Liebknecht, May 2, 1917).

33. Bukharin, *Historical Materialism*, 108–12.

34. Ibid., 77, 111–13.

35. Ibid., 104, 111.

36. Ibid., 75, 89.

37. Lynn Margulis et al., "Foreword to the English-Language Edition," in V.I. Vernadsky, *The Biosphere* (New York: Copernicus, 1998), 15; Richard Levins and Richard Lewontin, *The Dialectical Biologist* (Cambridge, Mass.: Harvard University Press, 1985), 47.

38. N.I. Vavilov, "The Problem of the Origin of the World's Agriculture in the Light of the Latest Investigations," in Bukharin et al. *Science at the Cross Roads*, 97–106.

39. Foster, *The Vulnerable Planet*, 94–95.

40. See Nikolai Bukharin et al., *Marxism and Modern Thought* (New York: Harcourt, Brace, 1935), 147, 230–32.

41. Murray Fessback and Arthur Friendly, Jr., *Ecocide in the U.S.S.R.* (New York: Basic Books, 1992); Foster, *The Vulnerable Planet*, 96–101.

42. Lenin, *Collected Works*, vol. 38, 294. In *Materialism and Empirio-Criticism* Lenin had contended that materialism and idealism had been launched, respectively, by Democritus and Plato. Lenin, *Collected Works*, vol. 14, 130.

43. Douglas Weiner, "The Changing Face of Soviet Conservation," in Donald Worster, ed., *The Ends of the Earth* (New York: Cambridge University Press, 1998).

44. For the complex story of Lysenkoism in the Soviet Union, see Levins and Lewontin, *The Dialectical Biologist*, 163–96; Sheehan, *Marxism and the Philosophy of Science*, 220–28.

45. See Foster, *The Vulnerable Planet*, 96–101.

46. Georg Lukács, *Tactics and Ethics* (New York: Harper & Row, 1972), 136–40.

47. Antonio Gramsci, *Further Selections from the Prison Notebooks* (Minneapolis: University of Minnesota Press, 1995), 293.

48. Antonio Gramsci, *Selections from the Prison Notebooks* (New York: International Publishers, 1971), 448.

49. See Max Horkheimer, *The Eclipse of Reason* (New York: Oxford University Press, 1947), 92–127; Max Horkheimer and Theodor W. Adorno, *Dialectic of Enlightenment* (New York: Herder & Herder, 1972).

50. Alfred Schmidt, *The Concept of Nature in Marx* (London: New Left Books, 1971), 59, 166.

51. For a systematic critique of Schmidt's argument, see Paul Burkett, "Nature in Marx Reconsidered: A Silver Anniversary Assessment of Alfred Schmidt's *Concept of Nature in Marx*," *Organization & Environment*, vol. 10, no. 2 (June 1997), 164–83.

52. Christopher Caudwell, *Studies and Further Studies in a Dying Culture* (New York: Monthly Review Press, 1971), xix.

53. Thompson, *Making History*, 95.

54. Christopher Caudwell, *Illusion and Reality* (New York: International Publishers, 1937), 184–85.

55. In the text I refer to *Heredity and Development* as if it were a separate work, though it was in fact a part (even the capstone) of Caudwell's "studies and further studies in a dying culture." But when finally published *Heredity and*

Development was included in Christopher Caudwell, *Scenes and Actions: Unpublished Manuscripts* (New York: Routledge & Kegan Paul, 1986), 163–204.

56. Ibid., 202–3.
57. Ibid., 174–76, 187.
58. Ibid., 170–72.
59. Ibid., 173.
60. Thompson, *Making History*, 98.
61. See the analysis in Sheehan, *Marxism and the Philosophy of Science*, 367.
62. See E.P.Thompson, *William Morris* (New York: Pantheon, 1977), and *Customs in Common* (New York: New Press, 1991); Raymond Williams, *Resources of Hope* (New York:Verso, 1989), 210–26, and *Problems in Materialism and Culture* (New York: Verso, 1980), 67–85.
63. Sweezy's ecological approach to economics is evident throughout his work in his emphasis on the "qualitative value problem" and the distinction between use value and exchange value—both of which were connected to his analysis of wasteful production (wasteful in relation to a system of production for use) under monopoly capitalism. See Paul M. Sweezy, *The Theory of Capitalist Development* (New York: Monthly Review Press, 1972), "Cars and Cities," *Monthly Review*, vol. 24, no. 11 (April 1973), 1–18, "Capitalism and the Environment" (co-authored with Harry Magdoff), *Monthly Review*, vol. 41, no. 2 (June 1989), 1–10, and "Socialism and Ecology," *Monthly Review*, vol. 41, no. 4 (September 1989), 1–8; also Paul A. Baran and Paul M. Sweezy, *Monopoly Capital* (New York: Monthly Review Press, 1966). The significance of the use value/exchange value distinction and its relation to waste under monopoly capitalism is further discussed in John Bellamy Foster and Henryk Szlajfer, eds., *The Faltering Economy* (New York: Monthly Review Press, 1984), and John Bellamy Foster, *The Theory of Monopoly Capitalism* (New York: Monthly Review Press, 1986).
64. J.D. Bernal, *Science in History* (Cambridge, Mass.: MIT Press, 1969), vol. 1, 53–54, 191.
65. Needham, quoted in Sheehan, *Marxism and the Philosophy of Science.*, 333.
66. J.D. Bernal, *The Origins of Life* (New York:World Publishing Co., 1967), 182.
67. J.B.S. Haldane, "Preface," in Friedrich Engels, *The Dialectics of Nature* (New York: International Publishers, 1940), xiv.
68. Levins and Lewontin, *The Dialectical Biologist*, 11, 73, 85–106, 134–35.
69. Yrjö Haila and Richard Levins, *Humanity and Nature: Ecology, Science and Society* (London: Pluto Press, 1992). For an attempt to apply Haila and Levins's concept of "ecological formations" to history, see Foster, *The Vulnerable Planet*, 34.
70. See especially Stephen Jay Gould, *Ever Since Darwin* (New York:W.W. Norton, 1977).
71. Fred Magdoff, Less Lanyon, and Bill Liebhardt, "Nutrient Cycling, Transformations and Flows," *Advances in Agronomy*, vol. 60 (1997), 1–73.
72. Despite the fact that Levins and Lewontin write a regular column in *Capitalism, Nature, Socialism*—a column consistently filled with remarkable insights into ecological thought and research—their own systematic contributions in this area, represented by such works as *The Dialectical Biologist* and *Humanity and Nature*, have thus far had little discernible impact on contributors to that important journal. "Ecological Marxist" analyses of environmental

crisis, insofar as they have a basis in science, tend to be based on energetics, and to ignore evolution.

73. For example, James O'Connor's *Natural Causes* (New York: Guilford, 1998) represents a pathbreaking attempt to bring Marx's "conditions of production," including external nature, into the dialectic of capital, but suffers from an inability to understand how these material conditions of production are related to Marx's materialist conception of nature (as well as history); and to his analysis of the metabolism of nature and society. In Marx's complex dialectical analysis the alienation of nature is more than simply a backdrop to the alienation of labor. In contrast, the more dialectical treatment of Paul Burkett derives from the fact that it takes as its starting point Marx's own dialectical conception of natural–social relations (as these relate primarily to the circuit of capital). See Paul Burkett, *Marx and Nature: A Red and Green Perspective* (New York: St. Martin's Press, 1999).

74. See Meira Hanson and Ariel Salleh, "On Production and Reproduction, Identity and Nonidentity in Ecofeminist Theory," *Organization & Environment*, vol. 12, no. 2 (June 1999), 207–18; Mary Mellor, *Feminism and Ecology* (Cambridge: Polity, 1997).

75. Haila and Levins, *Humanity and Nature*, 11.

76. Georg Wilhem Friedrich Hegel, *Lectures on the History of Philosophy* (Lincoln: University of Nebraska Press, 1995), vol. 2, 280–81; Diogenes Laertius, *Lives of Eminent Philosophers* (Cambridge, Mass.: Harvard University Press/Loeb Classical Library, 1925), vol. 2, 555 (X, 25–27).

77. David Sedley, *Lucretius and the Transformation of Greek Wisdom* (Cambridge: Cambridge University Press, 1998), 133, 190–97; David Sedley, "Epicurean Anti-Reductionism," in Jonathan Barnes and Mario Mignucci, eds., *Matter and Metaphysics: Fourth Symposium Hellenisticum* (Naples: Bibliopolis, 1988), 297–327.

78. A.A. Long and D.N. Sedley, eds., *The Hellenistic Philosophers: Translation of the Principal Sources with Philosophical Commentary* (Cambridge: Cambridge University Press, 1987), 137.

INDEX

Please remember that this is a library book,
and that it belongs only temporarily to each
person who uses it. Be considerate. Do
not write in this, or any, library book.

WITHDRAWN